HYMNS TO THE GODDESS AND HYMNS TO KĀLĪ

The Selected Works of Sir John Woodroffe (Arthur Avalon)

The Dance of Shiva: *Fourteen Indian Essays*

The Garland of Letters: *Essays on Tantra/Mantra Śāstra*

The Great Liberation: *Mahānirvāṇa Tantra*

Hymns to the Goddess and Hymns to Kālī: *Karpūrādi Stotra*

Introduction to Tantra Śāstra

Is India Civilized? : *Essays on Indian Culture*

Kamakalavilasa

Mahamaya: *Cti-Shakti or Power as Consciousness*

Principles of Tantra

The Serpent Power: *Shat-Chakra-Nirūpana and Pādukā-Panchakā*

Shakti and Shakta

The World As Power

SIR JOHN WOODROFFE

(At the Konarak Temple of Sun-god in Orissa)

Courtesy : Mr P. K. DUTTA

HYMNS TO THE GODDESS AND HYMNS TO KĀLĪ

Karpūrādi Stotra

SIR JOHN WOODROFFE
(*Arthur Avalon*)

New Age Books
New Delhi (India)

THE SELECTED WORKS OF SIR JOHN WOODROFFE
(ARTHUR AVALON)

HYMNS TO THE GODDESS AND HYMNS TO KALI

ISBN: 978-81-7822-448-0
First NAB Edition: Delhi, 2014

NAB Cataloging-in-Publication Data
The Selected Works of Sir John Woodroffe
HYMNS TO THE GODDESS AND HYMNS TO KALI
(Arthur Avalon)
ISBN 978-81-7822-448-0

Published by
NEW AGE BOOKS
A-44 Naraina Industrial Area, Phase-I
New Delhi (India)-110 028
E-mail: nab@newagebooksindia.com
Website: www.newagebooksindia.com

Printed and published by
RP Jain for NAB Printing Unit
A-44, Naraina Industrial Area
Phase-I, New Delhi-110 028. India

PREFACE

THE Goddess or Devī (as the Hindus call Her) is God (as the Western worshippers address Him) in Its Mother aspect. The latter not uncommonly deem such attribution of ſeminine quality to be " heathenish " ; but this condemnation (for the criticism has, of course, this intendment) is itself singularly foolish in that it is thereby implied that of two sets of terms (neither of which is in its strict sense applicable to the Deity as the Author of ſorms), one is, in fact, a more correct description than the other. In the Navaratneśvara it is said : " That Devī, who is existence, consciousness, and bliss, should be thought of as a female or as a male, or as pure Brahman. In reality, however, She is neither male nor neuter (that is to say, that She is not bound to any particular form). " No one contends that the Brahma-tattva in the supreme abode beyond appearances is masculine as opposed to feminine, or the latter as contrasted with the former. Like all else in this matter, words are but the babbling endeavour of our plane to express that which is above it. It is not easy, then, to explain the condemnation except upon the assumption that those who pronounce it think their mother's sex to be inferior to their own, and that thus Deity is unworthily described by any other terms than those of masculine excellence. But Hindus, who ever place the name of mother before that of father, and to whom *garbha dhāraṇapoṣābhyām pitur mātā garīyasi*, have no partiality for such mistaken notions. On the other hand, it is possible that they might not understand the Christian expression " Mother of God," nor approve it even after they had learnt the limited and special sense which theology gives to this epithet. The Tāntrika would least of all admit the insufficiency of the conception of God as Mother. For the Devī manifests in his own mother, in his prakṛti (as he calls his wife), and in all women. As the Kubjikā Tantra says: " Whosoever has seen the feet of woman let him worship them as those of his guru " (*Strīnām pādatalam driṣṭvāguruvad-bhāvayet sadā*). Whilst male and female are both Her aspects, yet S'akti is, in a sense, said to be more revealed in the female than in the male form. And so the Muṇḍamāla Tantra says: " Wherever there is a śakti (female), there I am." On account of this greater manifestation, women are called S'akti. From this, however, it must not be supposed that S'akti is less present in such forms as S'iva and Kṛṣṇa and others. If, as the author of the Tantra Tattva says, a sādhaka who is a worshipper of the Kṛṣṇamūrti desires to see Him as as Kālī, Bhagavān, who fulfils the desires of devotees, will assume that form. All forms come into existence upon the manifestation of consciousness in the play of Her whose substance is consciousness.

Though the Sāktānandataranginī says: Devī is worshipped on account of Her soft heart (*komalāntah-karaṇam*), yet the use of the term " Mother " has other grounds than those which are founded upon an appeal to the natural feelings which the sweetness of the word " Mother " evokes. The meaning of the term " Devī " is *prakāsātmikā*, or that which is by its nature Light and Manifestation. And the word is used in the feminine gender because the One, as S'akti and Prakṛti, bears and nourishes all things as their Mother. The Devī is therefore the Brahman revealed in Its Mother aspect (*S'rimātā*) as Creatrix and Nourisher of the worlds.

Worshippers of Devī or S'akti are called S'āktas. But those who have a true knowledge of S'akti-tattva without which, according to S'āstra, Nirvānamokṣa is unattainable, will in thought surpass the sectarianism which the terms " S'ākta ", " Vaiṣṇava " and " S'aiva " ordinarily connote. Whatever forms the Devī assumes in Her aspect with attributes are but Her forms. As the author last cited says, the sādhaka will know Her, whether the appearance be that of Kṛṣṇa, Durgā, or Mahādeva. The Vaiṣṇava may consider Her as Viṣṇu in the form of S'akti, or the S'ākta may look upon Her as S'akti in the form of Viṣṇu. To those who, immersed in the ocean of Her substance, which is citśakti, are forgetful of all differences which appertain to the world of form, Kṛṣṇaśakti, S'ivaśakti, or Kālīśakti, and all other manifestations of śakti, are one and the same. And so Rāmaprasāda, the Bengali poet and Tāntrik, sang : " Thou assumeth five principal forms according to the differences of worship. But, O Mother ! how can you escape the hands of him who has dissolved the five and made them into one ? "

(The hymns to the Devī in this volume (introduced by a *stotra* to Her Spouse the Kālabhairava) are taken from the Tantra, Purāna, Mahābhārata, and S'ankarācārya, who was " the incarnation of devotion " (*bhaktāvatāra*) as well as a great philosopher ; a fact which is sometimes ignored by those who do not wish to be reminded that he, whose speculative genius they extol, was also the protagonist of the so-called " idolatrous Hinduism.") As his great example amongst many others of differing race and creed tell us, it is not, from the view of religion, the mark of discernment (even though it be the mode) to neglect or disparage the ritual practice which all orthodoxies have prescribed for their adherents. *Stava* and *pūjā* are doubtless the *sādhana* appropriate to the first of the several stages of an ascent which gradually leads away from them ; but they are in general as necessary as the higher ones, which more immediately precede the attainment of *brahmabhāva* and *siddhi*.

Apart, however, from this aspect of the matter, and to look at it from the point of view of that modern product, the mere "student of religions," who is not infrequently a believer in none, a knowledge of ritual (to use that term in its widest sense) will help to a greater and more real understanding of the *mahāvākya* of the Āryas than can be gained from those merely theoretical expositions of them which are now more popular. Those, again, whose interests are in what Verlaine called "mere literature" will at least appreciate the mingled tenderness and splendour of these Hymns, even in a translation which cannot reproduce the majesty of the sanskrit *ślokas* of the Tantra and Purāṇa, or the rhyme and sweet lilting rhythms of S'ankara.

Of the Hymns now published, those from the Mahābhārata and Candi have already been translated ; the first, in the English edition of the Mahābhārata, by Protap Chandra Roy and by Professor Muir in his "Original Sanskrit Texts," and the second by Mr. Pargiter, whose rendering of the Mārkandeya Purāṇa (of which it is the most celebrated portion) has been printed by the Asiatic Society of Bengal.

Ādyākālīsvarūpastotra has also been previously published as part of a rendering by myself of the Mahānirvāṇa Tantra. The first two sets of Hymns have been translated afresh. In the translation of such works a Sanskrit dictionary (however excellent) is not either a sufficient or reliable guide. It is necessary to study the Hindu commentators and to seek the oral aid of those who possess the traditional interpretation of the *S'āstra.* Without this and an understanding of what Hindu worship is and means, absurd mistakes are likely to be made. I have thus, in addition to such oral aid, availed myself of the Commentaries of Nīlakaṇṭha on the Mahābhārata, of Gopāla Chakravarti and Nāgogi Bhatta on Candī, and of Nīlakantha on the Devībhāgavata. As regards the Tantra, the great Sādhana S'āstrā, nothing which is of both an understanding and accurate character can be achieved without a study of the original texts undertaken with the assistance of the Tāntrik gurus and pandits, who are the authorized custodians of its traditions.

The other *stotras* are now rendered in English for the first time; at least, I have come across no translation of them.

The text of the Tantrasāra which has been used is that edited by Shrījut Rasik Mohun Chatterjee. It is not free from faults, which have necessitated reference to other Manuscripts. A more correct text of the Tārāshtakam, from the Nīla Tantra, is given in the Brihatstotraratnākara, to which reference has also been made for the hymns of Vālmiki and Indra.

Both Ellen Woodroffe and myself have collaborated in the translation of the hymns by S'ankara. For the rest, as also for the Introduction and Commentary, I am alone responsible. Some of the notes deal with matter familiar enough to the Hindu reader but have been inserted for the use of his English friends. Other portions of the commentary will, I believe, be found to be of use to both.

March 1, 1913 JOHN WOODROFFE

CONTENTS

HYMNS TO THE GODDESS

HYMN TO KĀLĪ

HYMNS TO THE GODDESS

INTRODUCTION

SANĀTANA BRAHMAN is called *sakala* when with *Prakṛti*, as It is *niṣkala* when thought of as without *Prakṛti* (*prakṛteranya*), for *kalā* is *Prakṛti*.[1] To say, however, that S'akti exists in or with, the Brahman is an accommodation to human thought and speech, for the Brahman and S'akti are in fact one. S'akti is eternal (*anādirūpā*), and *Brahmarūpā*, and both *nirguṇā* and *saguṇā*.[2] She, the Goddess (*Devī*), is the *caitanyarūpiṇi devī* who manifests all *bhūta*; the *ānandarūpiṇi devī* by whom the Brahman, who She is, manifests Itself,[3] and who, to use the words of the S'āradātilaka, pervades the universe as does oil the sesamum seed. "*Sa aikṣata,*" of which *S'ruti* speaks, was itself a manifestation of S'akti, the *paramāpūrvanirvāṇaśakti*, or Brahman, as S'akti.

From the *paraśaktimaya* issued *nāda*, and from *nāda*, *bindu*[4]. The state of subtle body known as *kāmakalā* is the *mūla* of *mantra*, and is meant when the Devī is spoken

---

[1] S'āradā Tilakam (chap. i.). See *Introduction to Tantra S'āstra* by Sir John Woodroffe—*sub. voc.* "S'iva and S'akti," of which the above is in part (with added matter) an abbreviation.

[2] *Praṇamya prakṛtim nityām paramātmasvarūpinīm* (chap. i.). S'āktānandatarangini, both Tāntrik works of high authority.

[3] Kubjikā Tantra (First Paṭala).

[4] Sāradā (*loc. cit*).

of as *mūlamantrātmikā*.[1] The *Parambindu* is represented as a circle the centre of which is the *Brahmapada*, wherein are *Prakṛti-puruṣa;* the circumference of which is encircling *māyā*. It is in the crescent of *nirvāṇakalā* the seventeenth, which is again in that of *amākalā* the sixteenth, digit of the moon circle (*candramaṇḍala*), situate above the sun-circle (*sūryamaṇḍala*), the *Guru* and the *Hamsah* in the pericarp of the 1,000 petalled lotus (*sahasrārapadma*). The *bindu* is symbolically described as being like a grain of gram (*canaka*), which under its encircling sheath contains a divided seed—*Prakṛti-Purusa* or S'akti-S'iva.[2]

It is known as the S'abda Brahman.[3] A polarization then takes place in *paraśaktimaya*. The Devī becomes *unmukhi*. Her face is turned to S'iva. There is an unfolding which bursts the encircling shell.[4] The *devatāparaśaktimaya* exists in the threefold aspect of *bindu*, *bija*, and *nāda*, the last being in relation to the two former. An indistinct sound then arises[5] (*avyaktātmāravobhavat*). *Nāda*, as Rāghava Bhatta[6] says, exists in three states, for in it are the three *guṇas*. The S'abda Brahman manifests Itself in the threefold energies, *Jnāna*, *Ichhā*, and *Kriyā S'akti*.[7] For, as the Vāmakeśvara

[1] See Bhāskararāya's Commentary on the Lalitā Sahasranāma (verse 36), and the Pādukāpancaka in *The Serpent Power*.

[2] See Ṣatcakranirūpaṇa of Purnānanda Svāmi in *The Serpent Power*.

[3] S'āradā (*loc. cit*).

[4] *Ibid*.

[5] *Ibid*.

[6] See Commentary on verse 49 of the Ṣatcakranirupaṇa, and generally as to the subject-matter of this Introduction, my "*Introduction to Tantra S'āstra*."

[7] See Goraksha Samhitā, Bhutaśuddhi Tantra, and Yogini Tantra, Part I, p. 10.

Tantra says, the Devī Tripurā is threefold, as Brahmā, Viṣṇu, and Īśa. Paraśiva exists as a septenary under the forms of S'ambhu, S'adāśiva, Īśāna, Rudra, Viṣṇu, and Brahmā. The last five are the *Mahāpreta*, four of whom form the support, and the fifth the seat, of the bed on which the Devī is united with Paramaśiva in the room of *cintāmaṇi* stone on the jewelled island clad with clumps of *kadamba*, and heavenly trees set in the ocean of ambrosia.[1]

S'akti is both *māyā* and *mūlaprakṛti*, whose substance is the three *guṇas*, representing nature as the revelation of spirit (*sattva*); nature as the passage of descent from spirit to matter, or of ascent from matter to spirit (*rajas*), and nature as the dense veil of spirit (*tamas*). The Devī is thus the treasure-house of *guṇas* (*guṇanidhih*).[2] *Mūlaprakṛti* is the womb into which the Brahman casts the seed from which all things are born.[3] The womb thrills to the movement of the essentially active *rajoguṇa*, and the now unstable *guṇas* in varied combinations under the illumination of S'iva (*cit*)) evolve the universe which is ruled by Maheśvara and Maheśvarī. The dual principles of S'iva-S'akti, which are the product of the polarity manifested in *Paraśaktimaya*, pervade the whole universe, and are present in man in the *svayambhulinga* of the *mūlādhāra* and the Devī Kuṇḍalinī, who in serpent form encircles it. The *S'abdabrahman* assumes the form of the Devī Kuṇḍalinī, and as such is in the form of all breathing creatures (*prāṇi*), and in the form of letters appears in prose and verse. She is the luminous vital energy (*jīvaśakti*), which manifests as *prāṇa*. Through the

[1] See Ānandalaharī of S'ankarācārya, verse 8. The *dhyāna* is well known to the Tantrik *sādhaka*.

[2] Lalitā, verse 121.

[3] Bhagavadgītā (chap. xiv., verses 3,4).

various *prakṛta* and *vaikṛta* creations, issued the Devas, men, animals, and the whole universe, which is the work and manifested form of the Dẹvī. For, as the Kubjikā Tantra says, " Not Brahmā, Viṣṇu, and Rudra create, maintain, and destroy, but Brāhmī, Vaiṣṇavī, Rudrāṇī. Their husbands are but as dead bodies. "

The Goddess (*Devī*) is the great S'akti. She is *māyā*, for of Her the *māyā* which produces the *samsāra* is. As Lord of *māyā*, She is Mahāmāyā.[1] Devī is *avidyā* (nescience), because She binds; and *vidyā* (knowledge), because She liberates and destroys the *samsāra*.[2] She is Prakṛti,[3] and, as existing before creation, She is the *ādya* (primordial) śakti. She is the *vācaka-śakti*, the manifestation of *cit* in Prakṛti; and the *vācya śakti* or *cit* itself. The *ātmā* should be contemplated as Devī.[4]

S'akti or Devī is thus the Brahman revealed in its Mother aspect (*srimātā*)[5] as creatrix and nourisher of the worlds. Kālī says of Herself in Yoginī Tantra:[6] "*Saccidānandarupāham Brahmaivāham sphuratprabham.*" So the Devī is described with attributes both of the qualified[7] Brahman, and (since that Brahman is but the manifestation of the Absolute), She is also addressed

---

1 *Mahāmāyā* without *māyā* is *nirguṇā*, and with *māyā*, *saguṇā*. S'āktānandatarangini (chap. i.).

2 S'āktānandatarangini (chap. i.).

3 Brahmavaivarta Purāṇa (chap. i.); Prakṛtikhanda. Br. Nāradiya Pr.

4 See chap. ii. of Devī Bhāgavata.

5 Devī is worshipped on account of her soft heart. S'āktānandatarangini (chap. iii.).

6 Part I., Chapter X.

7 Such as Mukunda, an aspect of Viṣṇu. Lalitāsahasranāma, verse 838.

with epithets which denote the unconditioned Brahman.[1] She is the great Mother (*ambikā*) sprung from the sacrificial hearth of the fire of the Grand Consciousness (*cit*) decked with the Sun and Moon; Lalitā—"She who plays"—whose play is world-play; whose eyes, playing like fish in the beauteous waters of Her Divine face, open and shut with the appearance and disappearance of countless worlds, now illuminated by Her light, now wrapped in her terrible darkness.[2] For Devī, who issues from the great Abyss, is terrible also in Her Kālī, Tārā, Chinnamastā, and other forms. S'āktas hold that a sweet and complete resignation of the self to such forms of the Divine Power denotes a higher stage of spiritual development.[3] Such dualistic worship also speedily bears the fruit of knowledge of the Universal Unity, the realization of which dispels all fear. For the Mother is only terrible to those who, living in the illusion of separateness (which is the cause of all fear), have not yet realized their unity with Her, and known that all Her forms are those of beauty.

The Devī as Parabrahman is beyond all form and *guṇa*. The forms of the Mother of the universe are threefold. There is first the Supreme (*para*) form, of

---

[1] *Ibid*, verse 153, and Commentator's note to Chapter II., where Devī is addressed as Supreme Light (*paramjyotih*), Supreme Abode (*paramdhāma*), Supreme of Supreme (*parātparā*).

[2] See the Lalitā.

[3] See the saying of Rāmaprasāda, the poet-devotee of Kālimā, quoted at p. 714 in Babu Dinesh Chunder Sen's "History of Bengali Literature."

"Though the Mother beat him, the child cries 'Mother! O Mother!' and clings still tighter to her garment. True, I cannot see Thee, yet am I not a lost child. I still cry 'Mother!'"

which, as the Viṣṇu Yāmala[1] says, "none know." There is next Her subtle (*sūkṣma*) form, which consists of *mantra*. But, as the mind cannot easily settle itself upon that which is formless,[2] She appears as the subject of contemplation in Her third or gross (*sthūla*) or physical form, with hands and feet and the like, as celebrated in the *Devīstotra* of the Purāṇas and Tantras. Devi, who as *Prakṛti* is the source of Brahmā, Viṣṇu, and Maheśvara,[3] has both male and female forms.[4] But it is in Her female forms that she is chiefly contemplated. For, though existing in all things, in a peculiar sense female beings are parts of Her.[5] The Great Mother, who exists in the form of all Tantras and all Yantras,[6] is, as the Lalitā says, the "unsullied treasure-house of beauty," the sapphire Devī[7] whose slender

---

[1] *Mātastvatparamamrūpam tanna jānāti kashchana* (see chap. iii. of S'āktānandatarangini)

[2] *Amurtauchitsthironasyāt tatomurtim vichintayet* (*ibid.*, chap. i., as was also explained to Himavat by Devī in the Kurma Purāṇa).

[3] *Ibid.*, and as such is called Tripurā (see Bhāskararāyā's Commentary on Lalitā, verse 125).

[4] *Ibid.*, chap. iii., which also says that there is no eunuch form of God.

[5] So in Candi (Mārkaṇḍeya Purāṇa) it is said :

> " *Vidyāh samastāstava devī bhedāh,*
> *Stryah samastāsakalā jagatsu.* "

The Tāntrika, more than all men, recognizes the divinity of woman, as was observed centuries past by the author of the Dabistan. The Linga Purāṇa also, after describing Arundhati, Anasūyā and Shachi to be each the manifestation of Devī, concludes : " All things indicated by words in the feminine gender are manifestations of Devī." Similary the Brahmavaivarta Purāṇa.

[6] *Sarvatantrarūpā Sarvayantrātmikā* (See Lalitā, verse 53).

[7] Padma Purāṇa says : " Viṣṇu ever worships the sapphire Devi. "

waist,[1] bending beneath the burden of the ripe fruit of her breasts,[2] swells into jewelled hips heavy[3] with the promise of infinite maternities.[4] Her litanies depict Her physical form from head to foot, celebrating Her hair adorned with flowers and crowned with gems; Her brow bright as the eighth-day moon; Her ruby cheeks and coral lips; teeth like to "the buds of the sixteen-syllabled *mantra*," and eyebrows curved as are the arches at the gate of the palace of Kāmarāja; Her nose; Her teeth; Her chin; Her arms; and "Her twin breasts offered in return for that priceless gem which is the love of Kāmeśvara"; Her waist girdled with jewelled bells; Her smooth and faultless limbs rounded beneath the "jewelled disc of the knee like the

---

[1] *Āpivarastanatatimtanuvrittamadhyām* (Bhuvaneśvarīstotra), *tanumadhya* (Lalitā, verse 79). *krishodari* (Ādyakālisvarūpāstotra, Mahānirvāṇa Tantra, 7th Ullāsa).

[2] *Stotra* and *dhyāna* commonly represent Her as having large, full, and erect breasts—*pīnastanādye* (in Karpurādistotra), *pīnonnatapayodharām*) (in Durgā-dhyāna of Devī Purāṇa), *bakshojakumbhāntarī* (in Annapurṇāstava) *āpīvarastanatatim* (in Bhuvaneśvarīstotra)—which weight her limbs—*kuchabharanamitāngīm* (in Sarasvatidhyāna), *annapradānaniratāngstanabhāranamrām* (in Annapūrṇastava). And the Lalitā , verse 15, says: "Her golden girdle supports Her waist, which bends under the burden of Her breasts, thrice folding the skin below Her bosom" (*trivalīvalayopetām*).

[3] So it is said in the tenth *śloka* of the Karpūrākhyastava *samantādāpīnastanajaghanadhrikyauvanavatī*. S'ankarācarya, in his Tripurāsundarīstotra, speaks of Her *nitamba* (buttocks) "as excelling the mountain in greatness" (*nitambajitabhūdharām*). The Javanese also call Her Loro Jongram. "The pure exalted virgin with beautiful hips."

[4] The physical characteristics of the Devi in Her swelling breasts and hips are emblematic of Her great Motherhood, for She is *S'rimātā*.

sapphire-studded quiver of the God of Love" descending in lines of grace to Her bright louts feet,[1] which dispel the darkness of Her worshippers.[2] For moonlight is She, yet sunbeam, soothing all those who are burnt by the triple fires of misery (*tāpatraya*). Her face, Her body from throat to waist, and thence downwards, represent the *vagbhava* and other *kūta*. The colour of the Devī varies according to the form under which She is contemplated. Thus, in conferring liberation, She is white; as controller of women, men, and kings, She is red; and as controller of wealth, saffron. As creatrix of enmity, She becomes tawny; and in the thrill of love, passion (*śṛngāra*), She is of the colour of the rose. In the action of slaying She becomes black. Thus, Devī, the Supreme Light, is to be meditated upon as differently coloured according to Her different activities.[3]

After the description of the form of the Devī in *brahmāṇḍa* follows that of Her subtle form, called Kuṇḍalinī in the body (*piṇḍāṇḍa*). As the Mahādevī[4] She exists in all forms as S'arasvatī, Lakṣmī, Gāyatrī,

[1] See the Lalitāsahasranāma, verse 4 *et seq.* "Her brow (*aṣṭamīcandravibhrājadalika sthala śobhitā*), Her eyebrow (*vadanasamara māngalyagrihatoranacillika*), Her twin breasts (*kāmeśvarapremaratnamani pratiphalastani*), Her waist (*ratnakinkinikārabhyarashanādāma bhūṣitā*), "Her thighs, known only to Kameśa" (*Kāmeśajnātasaubhāgya mardavorudvayānvitā*), Her lower limbs (*indragopa parikṣipta smaratunā bhajandhikā*); Her instep 'arched like the back of a tortoise,' the bright rays from her nails and the soles of Her feet in beauty shaming the lotus."

[2] From the beautiful litany to the Devī in the Lalitāsahasranāma.

[3] Bhāskararāya's Commentary on Lalitā, verse 170.

[4] She whose body is, as the Devī Purāṇa says, immeasurable.

Durgā, Tripurasundarī, Annapurnā, and all the Devī who are *avatāra* of the Brahman.[1]

Devī, as Satī, Umā, Pārvatī, and Gourī, is spouse of S'iva. It was as Satī, prior to Dakṣa's sacrifice (*dakṣayajna*) that the Devī manifested Herself to S'iva[2] in the ten celebrated forms known as the *daśamahāvidyā*—Kālī, Bagala, Chinnamastā, Bhuvaneshvarī, Mātanginī, Shorosī, Dhumāvatī, Tripurasundarī, Tārā, and Bhairavī. When at the *dakṣayajna* She yielded up Her life in shame and sorrow at the treatment accorded by Her father to Her husband, S'iva took away the body, and, ever bearing it with him, remained wholly distraught and spent with grief. To save the world from the forces of evil which arose and grew with the withdrawal of His divine control, Viṣṇu, with his discus (*cakra*), cut the dead body of Satī, which S'iva bore, into fifty-one fragments, which fell to earth at the places thereafter known as the fifty-one[3] *mahāpīthasthānas*, where Devī, with her Bhairava, is worshipped under various names.

Thus the right and left breasts fell at Jalandhara and Ramgiri, where the Devī is worshipped as Tripuramālinī; the *yoni* at the celebrated shrine at Kamrup in Assam, where the Devī is worshipped as Kāmākṣā or Kāmākhyā (see *ibid.*);[4] the throat, shoulders, nose, hands,

---

[1] S'āktānandatarangini (chap. iii.).

[2] In order to display Her power to Her husband who had not granted, at Her request, His permission that She might attend at Dakṣa's sacrifice (see "*Principles of Tantra*" and for an account of the *daśamahāvidyā*, their *yantra* and *mantra*, the Daśamahāvidyā upāsanārahasya of Prasanno Kumar Shastri).

[3] The number is variously given as 50, 51, and 52.

[4] Here at Her shrine the menstruation of the earth which, according to Hindu belief, takes place in the month of Assar, is

arms, eyes, fingers, tongue, buttocks, lips, belly, chin, navel, cheeks, thighs, teeth, feet, ears, thumbs, heels, toes (some at Kālighat), waist, hair, forehead, with skeleton (several of these parts being themselves divided), fell at other *pītha*, at each of which the Devī is worshipped under different names in company with a Bhairava or S'iva, also variously named. Thus, the Devī at Kālighat is Kālikā, and the S'iva Nakuleśvara, and the Devī at Kamrup is Kāmākshā, and Her Bhairava is Ramānanda.

These are but some only of Her endless forms. She is seen as one and as many: as it were, but one moon reflected in countless waters.[1] She exists, too, in all animals and inorganic things, since the universe, with all its beauties, is, as the Devi Purāṇa says, but a part of Her. All this diversity of form is but the infinite manifestations of the flowering beauty of the one Supreme Life—a doctrine which is nowhere else taught with greater wealth of illustration than in the S'ākta S'āstras and Tantras. The great Bharga in the bright sun, and all Devatā, and, indeed, all life and being are worshipful, and are worshipped, but only as Her manifestations.[2] And he who worships them otherwise is, in the words of the great Devībhāgavata,[3] "like unto a man who. with the light of a clear lamp

---

said to manifest itself. For three days during *ambuvāchī* no cooked food is eaten by the women, nor does any cooking take place in the house.

[1] Brahmabindu Up, p. 12.

[2] See chap. iii. of the S'āktānandatarangini, where it is said: "The Parabrahman, Devi, S'iva, and all other Deva and Devī are but one, and he who thinks them different from one another goes to Hell."

[3] Hymn to Jagadambikā in Chapter XIX.

in his hands, yet falls into some waterless and terrible well." It is customary nowadays to decry external worship, but those who do so presume too much. The ladder of ascent can only be scaled by those who have trod all, including its lowest, rungs. The S'akti-rahasya summarises the stages of progress in a short verse, thus: " A mortal who worships by ceremonies, by images, by mind, by identification, by knowing the self, attains *kaivalya*." Before *brahma-bhāva* can be attained the *sādhaka* must have passed from *pūjābhāva* through hymns and prayer to *dhyāna-bhāva*. The highest worship[1] for which the *sādhaka* is qualified (*adhikāri*) only after external worship, and that internal form known as *sādhāra*[2] is described as *nirādhāra*. Therein Pure Intelligence is the Supreme S'akti who is worshipped as the Very Self, the Witness freed of the glamour of the manifold universe. By one's own direct experience of Maheśvari as the Self, She is, with reverence, made the object of that worship which leads to liberation.

J. W.

---

[1] Sūtasamhitā, 1, 5, 3, which divides such worship into Vedic and Tāntrik (see Bhāskararāya's Commentary on Lalitā, verse 43).

[2] In which Devī is worshipped in the form of *mantra* according to the instructions of the Guru.

HYMN TO KĀLABHAIRAVA

BY

S'ANKARĀCĀRYA

KĀLABHAIRAVA
(KĀLABHAIRAVĀṢṬAKA)

1

I WORSHIP Kālabhairava,[1] Lord of the city of Kāśi,[2]
Whose sacred lotus feet are worshipped by the
King of Devas,[3]
The compassionate One,
Whose sacrificial thread is made of serpents,
On whose forehead shines the moon.[4]
The naked one,[5]
Whom Nārada[6] and multitudes of other Yogis adore.
Kāśikāpurādhinātha kālabhairavam bhaje.[7]

2

I worship Kālabhairava, Lord of the city of Kāśi,
Blazing like a million suns,

---

1 S'iva as such.

2 Benares. The Kāśipanchakastotra of S'ankara says that the pure Ganges is the flow of knowledge and Kāśi is S'iva's mind (*Jnānapravāhāvimalādigangā sakāśikāham nijabodharūpah*).

3 Devarāja or Indra.

4 Hence S'iva is called Candraśekhara.

5 *Digambaram*, as are the *Yogis* of whom He is Master. For He is clothed with space itself.

6 The *Ṛṣi* of that name.

7 The refrain is: "I worship Kālabhairava, Lord of the city of Kāsi."

Our great Saviour in our voyage across the ocean of the world.[1]
The blue-throated,[2] three-eyed [3] grantor of all desires,
The lotus-eyed, who is the death of death,[4]
The imperishable One,
Holding the rosary of human bone[5] and the trident.[6]
Kāśikāpurādhinātha Kālabhairavam bhaje.

3

I worship Kālabhairava, Lord of the city of Kāsī,
The primeval cause,[7]
Holding in His hands trident, axe, noose, and staff[8]
—Him of the black body,[9]
The first of all Deva[10], imperishable, incorruptible,
Lord formidable and powerful,

---

[1] A constant simile. The world is a storm-tossed ocean not free of danger, even in moments of calm, for therein many dangers, perils, and terrors lie.

[2] For S'iva swallowed the poison which issued at the churning of the ocean to save the earth from its dangerous presence.

[3] For with the ordinary eyes He bears in the forehead the eye of wisdom.

[4] S'iva is the conqueror of death ("*mrityunjaya*"), for he gives that knowledge which frees man of its terrors.

[5] Even often of the low-caste Candālas and others, for S'iva is the adored and protector of all.

[6] His peculiar weapon.

[7] For all causes potentially lie in His destructive energies, the manifestation of which is the prelude of re-creation.

[8] *S'ūla, tangka, pāśa, danḍa,* His implements.

[9] As Kālabhairava. Usually he is white and smeared with ashes "shining like a mountain of silver."

[10] Hence He is called Mahādeva.

Who loves to dance wonderfully. [1]
Kāśikāpurādhinātha kālabhairavam bhaje.

4

I worship Kālabhairava, Lord of the city of Kāśi,
Of great and beautiful body,
The giver of both enjoyment and liberation, [2]
Who loves and smiles upon all His devotees,
Whose body is the whole world,
Whose waist is adorned with little tinkling bells; [3]
Beautiful are they, and made of gold.
Kāśikāpurādhinātha kālabhairavam bhaje

5

I worship Kālabhairava, Lord of the city of Kāśi,
The protector of the bridge of *dharma*, [4]
Destroyer of the path of *adharma*, [5]
Liberator form the bonds of *karma*, [6]
The all-pervading giver of welfare to all,

---

[1] *Vichitratāṇḍavapriyam.* S'iva is often pictured dancing as Natarāja. The place of the dance is the body of the individual and the world spoken of as *vanam* (the forest), on account of the multitude of its components. He as the inner *ātman* causes all things to dance into and out of life, and again into it. All life and activity comes through Him, "the unseen Lord of the stage."

[2] *Bhuktimuktidāyakam*—that is, He gives both worldly and heavenly enjoyment, and that release from both which is the unending bliss of liberation.

[3] Hung on a girdle.

[4] Righteousness. For *dharma*, religion, law, and duty, are the bridge whereby the dangerous waters of the world are passed.

[5] Unrighteousness.

[6] The cause and fruit of action whereby man is bound to the phenomenal world until by knowledge, *karma* is exhausted and destroyed, and liberation (through S'iva, with whose essential being His worshipper becomes one) is attained.

Whose golden body is adorned with serpent coils.
Kāśikapurādhinātha kālabhairavam bhaje.

6

I worship Kālabhairava, Lord of the city of Kāśi
Whose feet are beautiful with the lustre of the gems thereon—
The stainless, eternal Iṣṭadevatā, [1]
One without a second, [2]
Destroyer of the pride, and liberator from the gaping jaw of the God of Death. [3]
Kāsikāpurādhinātha kālabhairavam bhaje.

7

I worship Kālabhairava, Lord of the city of Kāśi, [4]
Whose loud laughter broke the shell of many an egg of the lotus-born ; [5]
Strong ruler, at whose glance the net of sin is broken ; Giver of the eight powers, [6]
Whose shoulders serpents garland.
Kāśikāpurādhinātha kālabhairavam bhaje.

---

[1] The desired (or patron) Deity of the devotee.

[2] For He is the Supreme Unity.

[3] See *ante*, p. 16, note 4.

[4] Each world (for there are many) is called an egg of Brahmā the creator (*brahmāṇḍa*). S'iva the great Destroyer by His loud laughter shatters them.

[5] Brahmā.

[6] *Siddhi*—namely, *aṇimā, mahimā, garimā, laghimā, prāpti, prākāmya, iṣitva,* and *vaṣitva.* The power to become very small, vast, light, heavy, power of vision and movement, the powers of creation and control over the worlds and their Lords. These *siddhi* are powers of the all-pervading *ātmā,* and to greater or less degree may be acquired by S'ivayogins according as they realize their unity therewith.

8

I worship Kālabhairava, Lord of the city of Kāśī,
The Saviour of all, giver of great fame,
The all-pervading One,
Who purifies of both sin and virtue the people of Kāśī;[1]
The ancient Lord of the world,
Wise in the wisdom of all moralities.[2]
Kāśikāpurādhinātha kālabhairavam bhaje.

[1] *Kāśivāsiloka puṇyapāpaśodhakām*: for to the liberated there is neither sin nor virtue which are qualities of the phenomenal *jīvātma* only. The liberated are above both.

[2] *Nītimargakovidam.*

HYMNS TO THE DEVĪ
FROM TANTRA

BHAIRAVĪ[1]

(BHAIRAVĪSTOTRA)

FROM THE TANTRASĀRA[2]

1

THUS shall I pray to Thee, O Tripurā,[3]
To attain the fruit of my desires,
In this hymn by which men attain that Lakṣmī,[4]
Who is worshipped by the Devas.

2

Origin of the world thou art,
Yet hast Thou Thyself no origin,
Though with hundreds of hymns.
Even Brahmā, Viṣṇu, and Maheśvara[5] cannot
know Thee.[6]
Therefore we worship Thy breasts, Mother of all
S'āstra,[7]
Shining with fresh saffron.

---

1 Fem. of Bhairava, a name of S'iva.

2 P. 596, Ed. Rasik Mohun Chatterjee.

3 See Tripurasundari—*post*.

4 Devī of prosperity.

5 S'iva.

6 In the Viṣṇu Yāmala, Viṣṇu says of the Devī: "Thy supreme form none know" (*mātastvatparamarūpam tannajānāti kashchana*), (*see* chap. iii S'āktānandatarangini).

7 *Vāngmaya.*

3

O Tripurā,[1] we adore Thee,
Whose body shines with the splendour of a thousand risen suns,
Holding with two of thy hands a book[2] and rosary of *rudrākṣa* beads,[3]
And with two others making the gestures
Which grant boons and dispel fear.[4]
With three lotus eyes is Thy lotus face adorned.
Beauteous is Thy Neck with its necklace of large pearls.[5]

4

O Mother, how can the ignorant, whose minds are restless with doubt and dispute,
Know Thy form ravishing with its vermilion,[6]
Stooping with the weight of Thy breasts,[7]
Accessible only by merit,
Acquired in previous birth?

---

[1] See *post.*

[2] *Vidyā.*

[3] Seed of a plant sacred to the worship of S'iva.

[4] That is, She makes the *mudrā vara* and *abhaya.* In the first the hand is held forth in front of the body with the palm upward and horizontal, the fingers together, and the thumb crossing the palm to the fourth finger. In the second the hand is held up with the fingers and thumb in the same positions with the palm towards the spectator.

[5] *Tāra,* the ordinary pearl, is called *muktā.*

[6] *Sindūra,* the Bhairavi's body is painted with vermilion and Her garments also are red.

[7] *Kuchabharaṇamrām* (see Introduction).

5

O Bhavāni,[1] the *munis*[2] describe thee in physical form;[3]
The *S'ruti* speaks of Thee in subtle form ;
Others call Thee presiding Deity of speech ;
Others, again, as the root of the worlds.
But we think of Thee
As the untraversable ocean of mercy, and nothing else.

6

Worshippers contemplate Thee in their heart
As three-eyed, adorned with the crescent moon,
White as the autumnal moon,
Whose substance is the fifty letters,[4]
Holding in Thy hands a book, a rosary, a jar of nectar, and making the *vyakhya mudra.*[5]

---

[1] The Devi is Bhavāni as the spouse and giver of Life to Bhava.

[2] Sages.

[3] There are three forms of the Devi—the gross or physical, with hands, feet, etc. ; the subtle (*sūkṣma*), consisting of *mantra* and the supreme (*parā*), which is the real or own (*svarūpā*). The form of the Devi has both *prakāśa* and *vimarśa* aspects—that is real and secondary or manifested. Thus the Vāmakeśvara Tantra says: "The Devi Tripurā is Her real form. She who is of a red colour is the manifested one."

[4] Of the alphabet or *mātṛkā* (*panchāśadākṣaramayīm*). These letters stand for the *vṛtti* (functions and qualities of being). The Devi is thus *mātṛkāmayī*, or composed of *mātṛkā*.

[5] *Vyakhya.* according to the S'abda Kalpadruma = *vivaraṇam* (description), or *grantha* (book), and also commentary, but here denotes a *mudrā* of that name.

7

O Tripurā, Thou art S'ambhu[1] united with Pārvatī.[2]
Thou art now Viṣṇu embraced by Kamalā,[3]
And now Brahmā born of the lotus.[4]
Thou art again the presiding Devī of speech,
And yet again art the energy of all these.

8

I, having taken refuge with the four—
Bhāvas,[5] *Parā*, and others[6] born of the *vāgbhava* (*bīja*),[7]

---

[1] S'iva, one of the forms of the four *mahāpreta*, whose bīja is "*Hsau.*"

[2] The androgyne form, called *ardhanārīśvara*, half being S'iva and the other half S'akti. According to Hindu belief, the wife is the pure and sacred (*puṇyā*) half of her husband's body, and besides shares the purity and merits of her husband according to the common saying *S'arīrārdham smṛtā jāyā puṇyā puṇyāphale samā.*

[3] Lakṣmī.

[4] That is, the power of destruction, maintenance, and creation.

[5] The four *bhāvas* are states or conditions of Kuṇḍalinī appearing as sound and its subtle elements, and are *Parā*, whose abode (*sthāna*) is the *mūlādhāra*; *Paśyantī* in the *svādhiṣṭhāna*; *Madhyamā* in the *anāhata*; and *Vaikharī* in the *viśuddha* issuing through the the throat (see next note). There appears, however, to be some difference as to the location of the second.

[6] *Parā* is the first condition of Kuṇḍalinī in the form of tāmasik sound in the *Mūlādhāra*; *Paśyantī* is the *bhāva* when Kuṇḍalinī, associated with *manas*, reaches the position variously stated as the *svādiṣṭhāna* or *maṇipūra*; *Madhyamā*, when it reaches the *anāhatacakra*, associated with *buddhi*; and *Vaikharī* is when Kuṇḍalinī issues through the throat in the form of the fifty letters. It is said that though there are thus four kinds of speech, the gross-minded do not understand the first three, and think speech to be *Vaikharī* alone.

[7] That is, *Āim* the *bīja* of Sarasvatī. The Devī is 'three syllabled' (*Tryakṣarī*)—that is, the *bīja* of the three divisions of the

Shall never in my heart forget Thee, the supreme Devatā,
Whose substance is existence and intelligence,[1]
And who expresseth by Thy throat and other organ
The *bhāva* appearing in the form of letters.[2]

9

The blessed, having conquered the six enemies,[3]
And drawing in their breath,[4]
With steady mind fix their gaze on the tip of their nostrils,
And contemplate in their head Thy moon-crested form,[5]
Resplendent as the newly risen sun.

10

The Vedas proclaim that Thou createth the world,
Having assumed the other half of the body of the enemy of Kāma.[6]
Verily is it true, O Daughter of the mountain and the only World-mother,
That had this not been so,
The multitude of worlds would never have been.

Panchadaśi, *Vāgbhava*, *Kāmarāja* and *S'akti*. According to the Vāmakeśvara Tantra, Vāgiśvari is the *jnānā śakti*, which is in the *vāgbhava* division, and confers salvation, the *kāmarāja* and *śakti* divisions being the *kriyā* and *ichchhā sākti* (see the Lalitā, verse 126).

1 *Sacchinmayī*, the Brahman being *sat* and *chit*.

2 That is, they ultimately so appear, though previously existing as subtle elements of sound.

3 The six sins: Lust (*kāma*), anger (*krodha*), greed (*lobha*), delusion (*moha*), pride (*mada*), envy (*mātsaryā*).

4 *Akunchya vayam* by *pūraka* of *prānāyāmā*.

5 As S'akti of S'iva.

6 S'iva. The Androgyne form *ardhanārīśvara*.

11

In company with the wives of the Kinnaras,[1]
The Siddha women,[2] whose eyes are reddened by wine [3]
Having worshipped Thee with the flowers of celestial trees[4]
In Thy *pitha*[5] in the caverns of the golden mountain,[6]
Sing Thy praises.

12

I worship in my heart the Devi whose body is moist with nectar, [7]
Beauteous as the splendour of lightning,
Who, going from Her abode to that[8] of S'iva,[9]
Opens the lotuses on the beautiful way[10]

---

[1] A lower order of Devas (*devayoni*).

[2] Wives of the Siddhas, also celestial spirits (*devayoni*) inhabiting the atmospheric plane (*bhuvah*).

[3] *Asvāditāsavarasāruna ṇetrapadma.*

[4] *Pādapa,* so called because the tree drinks by its roots. As to the celestial trees (see " Wave of Bliss " *post*).

[5] Seat or shrine.

[6] Sumeru.

[7] For She as Kuṇḍalinī goes from the *mūlādhāra* to the *śiva-sthāna* in the *sahasrāra* and returns moist with the nectar of Her union with Him.

[8] *Rajādhani.* Literally capital city of S'iva.

[9] That is from the *mūlādhāra cakra* to the *śivasthāna.*

[10] The *suṣumnā* is the central " nerve " (*nādi*), or, rather, channel of energy in the body in which the lotuses (*ṣatcakra*) are threaded with their heads normally downwards. As Kuṇḍalinī becomes stirred by the yoga process, She ascends from the

of the *suṣumnā.*[1]

13

O Tripurā, I take refuge at Thy lotus feet,
Worshipped by Brahmā, Viṣṇu, and Maheśvara;
The abode of bliss, the source of the Vedas,
The origin of all prosperity;
Thou whose body is Intelligence itself.[2]

14

I shall never forget Her who is the giver of happiness;
She it is, O Mother, who, in the form of the Moon,
Creates the world full of sounds and their meanings,
And again, by Her power in the form of the Sun,
She it is who maintains the world.
And She, again, it is who, in the form of Fire, destroys the whole universe at the end of the ages.[3]

---

mūlādhāra and enters the higher *cakra.* As She does so, the lotuses upturn and expand again, closing on her departure.

[1] The text which has *sausuvartma kamalāni vikāshayantim,* is not, however, intelligible, and the metre is short. Possibly it is a misprint for *saumyang.*

[2] That is, nothing but intelligence *caitanyamātra tanu.*

[3] *Nādā,* as Rāghava Bhatta says, exists in the three states of *nibodhikā* or *bodhinī, nāda,* and in the form of *bindu,* according to the predominance of the *guṇa.* These three and the *śaktis, jnānā, kriyā* and *ichhā,* of which they are special manifestations, are said to be in the form of sun, moon, and fire respectively. The moon (*indu*) is *ichchhā* (will and desire), the eternal precursor of çreation. *Kriyā* is like the sun, which makes all things visible. *Jnānā* is fire, as it burns up all actions (see Ṣatcakranirūpaṇā, verse 49, and Sāradā Tilaka, chap. i.).

15

Men worship Thee under various names—
As Nārāyaṇa [1]; as She who saves from the ocean of Hell;[2]
As Gauri;[3] as the allayer of grief;[4] as Sarasvati,[5]
And as the three-eyed giver of knowledge.[6]

16

O Mother of the world, such as worship Thee with twelve Verses of this hymn attain to Thee, and gain all powers of speech [7] and the supreme abode.

---

1 As Viṣṇu.

2 *Narakārnatārinī.*

3 Spouse of S'iva. The Devī Purāṇa says; "She who was burned by the fire of *yoga* was again born of Himālaya; as She has the colour of the conch, jasmine, and moon, she is called Gaurī." Her colour is golden. S'iva said to Pārvati: "O Daughter of Himālaya, I am white as the moon and thou art dark. I am the sandal-tree, and thou art, as it were, a snake entwined round it." Pārvati, taking umbrage at this remark upon Her dark complexion, went away to the forest, and there, by the performance of austerities, gained for herself a golden complexion beautiful as the sunlit sky.

4 *Khedāshāmine.*

5 S'iva.

6 Devī of speech and learning.

7 *Vāksiddhi* or *siddhi* of words.

BHUVANES'VARI[1]

FROM THE TANTRASĀRA[2]

1

Now I pray for the attainment of all blessings to
Bhuvaneśvari,
The cause and Mother[3] of the world,
She whose form is that of the S'abdabrahman,[4]
And whose substance is bliss.

2

Thou art the primordial One,[5]
Mother of countless creatures,
Creatrix of the bodies[6] of the lotus-born,[7] Viṣṇu
and S'iva.
Who creates, preserves, and destroys the three
worlds.
O Mother! by hymning Thy praise I purify my
speech.

---

[1] The Devi in her aspect as Lord and Ruler of the world.

[2] P. 567.

[3] *Ambikā.*

[4] *Sākṣātśabdabrahmasvarūpiṇi*: the "sound" or manifested Aparabrahman, as opposed to the absolute, the Parabrahman. The Devi and the S'abdabrahman are, in fact, one, though men speak of Her as His S'akti (power).

[5] Ādyā.

[6] *Vapuhpratipādayitri.* The Devas have bodies, subtle though they be, as the S'abdabrahman Himself has.

[7] Brahmā.

3

O Daughter of the Mountain-King,[1]
Thou art the cause of the world-destroying energy of S'iva,[2]
Who manifests in earth, water, fire, ether, the sacrificer, the sun and moon,[3]
And who destroyed the body of Manmatha.[4]

4

O Mother! men only worship the triple-streamed Gangā[5]
Because She shines in the matted hair of S'iva,[6]
Which has been purified
By the dust of Thy lotus feet.

5

As the moon[7] delights the white night lotus[8] and none other,

---

[1] Himavat, whose daughter, as Pārvatī, the Devī was.

[2] For they derive their power from the Devī, the All-Mother, whose children they are, and who also manifests as their Spouse.

[3] These constitute the eight-fold forms (*aṣṭamūrti*) of S'iva, viz, Sarva, Bhava, Rudra, Ugraha, Bhīma, Paśupati, Īśāna, Mahādeva.

[4] The Deva of Love.

[5] *Trisrotah,* for there are three Ganges: the heavenly (Mandākinī), earthly (Alakanandā), and that of the nether world (Bhogavatī).

[6] As to the descent of Gangā into the *jaṭa* of S'iva (see Hymn to Ganga, *post*).

[7] Literally Lord of *Kalā*. *Kalā* is a digit of which there are sixteen in the moon. The *amākalā* is that from which the nectar is distilled.

[8] *Kumudinī,* which blooms and opens at night.

As the sun delights the day lotus [1] and none other,
As one particular thing only delights one other,
Thou, O Mother ! delightest the whole universe by
Thy glances.

6

Although Thou art the primordial cause of the
world,
Yet art Thou ever youthful ;
Although Thou art the Daughter of the Mountain-
King,[2]
Yet art Thou full of tenderness.
Although Thou art the Mother of the Vedas,[3]
Yet they cannot describe Thee.[4]
Although men must meditate upon Thee,
Yet cannot their mind comprehend Thee.[5]

7

O Mother of the worlds !
Those who have reached that birth amongst men
Which if so difficult to attain,
And in that birth their full faculties,
Yet nathless do not worship Thee,

---

1 *Kamalinī.*

2 Mountain (*S'aila*), which is that which is made of masses of stone (*S'ilā*)—a rhetorical comparison between the hardness of stone and Her tenderness.

3 *Trayā.* The whole Veda is so called because it consists of song, prose, and verse ; or because the Rik, Yajus, and Sāma are alone referred to as Veda.

4 *Cf.* verse 2 of Mahimnastava of Puṣpadanta.

5 Literally, "Though thou art to be meditated upon, thou dost not stay in the path of mind" (*cf.* Mahimnastava, *loc. cit,* and S'ruti, which says, "*Yato vāco nivarttante aprāpya manasā saha.*")

Such, though having ascended to the top of the
stairs,
Nevertheless fall down again.[1]

8

O Bhavānī!
Such as worship Thee with fragrant flowers and
sandal paste,
Ground with cool water[2] and powdered camphor,
Gain the sovereignty of the whole world.

9

O Mother! like the sleeping King of serpents,[3]
Residing in the centre of the first lotus,[4]
Thou didst create the universe.
Thou dost ascend like a streak of lightning,[5]
And attainest the ethereal region.[6]

---

[1] That is, as the subsequent fall makes the ascent useless, so human incarnation is without avail for those who, without excuse in such incarnation, do not worship the Devī.

[2] Kālidāsa in the Ritusamhāra says that in the hot weather women should wear fine cloth, powder their hair with fragrant scent, and smear their breasts with sandal, ground with cool water.

[3] She as Kuṇḍalinī resembles a sleeping serpent with three and a half coils abiding in the *mūlādhāra*.

[4] The *Mūlādhāra cakra* (see last note).

[5] *Vidyullatā balaya vibhramamudvahanti*. This is the sense of the passage which may literally mean that the Devī carries the beauty (*vibrahma*) of wristlets, like a streak of lightning, or "the Devī is sporting like a streak of lightning."

[6] *Khamasnuvānā*. Kham is here S'iva in the *Sahasrāra*, whither the Devī repairs when Her passion is aroused by the lightning of the *Kāmāgni* around Her fanned by the leftward revolution of the red *Kandarpavayu*.

10

Thy body, having been moistened with the nectar
flowing from That,[1]
Thou dost again reach Thy abode[2] by that way.[3]
O Mother and Spouse of Maheśvara!
They in whose heart Thou glitterest are never
reborn.

11

O Gaurī! with all my heart
I contemplate Thy form,
Beauteous of face,
With its weight of hanging hair,
With full breasts[4] and rounded slender waist,[5]
Holding in three hands a rosary,[6] a pitcher,[7] and
a book,
And with Thy fourth hand making the *jnānamudrā*.[8]

12

O Bhuvaneśvarī
Yogis who have restrained their senses
And have conquered the six enemies,[9]
In *yoga* with calm minds behold Thee
Holding noose and a goad,

---

[1] That is the *Sahasrārapadma*.

[2] *Mūlādhāra*.

[3] *Margenātena*—that is, the *nādi suṣumnā*.

[4] *Apīvarastanatatim*.

[5] *Tanuvrittamadhyām*.

[6] *Japamāla*, with which *japa* or recitation of *mantra* is done.

[7] *Kalaśa*.

[8] Literally, holding *cintā*, which is a name for the *jñāna mudrā*, or manual gesture so called.

[9] The six sins (see p. 27, n. 3).

And making the *vara* and *abhaya mudrās*.[1]

13

Thou art Lakṣmī,
Rivalling the lustre of molten gold,
Holding two lotuses in two of Thy hands,
And with the other two making the gestures which
grant boons and dispel fear.[2]
Four elephants holding jars (in their trunks),
Sprinkle Thy head with nectar.[3]

14

O Bhavānī ! Thou art Durgā,[4] seated on a lion,
Of the colour of *durvā* grass,[5]

---

[1] That is, the gestures (*Mudrā*) which grant boons and dispel fear. In the first the hand is held horizontally, the palm open, the fingers close to each other, and the thumb across the palm and touching the root of the third finger. The second is the same, but the hand is held upwards vertically, the palm being shown to the spectator.

[2] That is, the *vara* and *abhayamudrās*, *ante*.

[3] In this form the Devī is respresented as being surrounded by four elephants, which pour nectar over her from jars held in their trunks.

[4] One of the names of Bhuvaneśvarī (see p. 171 of Prosanna Kumar Shastri's "Daśamahāvidyā").

[5] Of a dark green. It is not clear why this colour is here mentioned, as the colour of Durgā is a golden yellow. It is, however, the colour of other forms, which are those of the one and the same Devī. Thus the colour of Kālī is that of *anjana* (black, collyrium), Tārā is *nīlā* (dark blue), Mātanginī is *asitā* (black) or *shyāmāngī* (dark green). The hue of Shodashī (S'rī) is that of the rising sun (*bālārkākanti*), at it is that of Bhuvaneśvarī (*uddaddinakaradyuti*). The colour of Bhairavī is said to be that of a thousand rising suns; of Chinnamastā that of a million suns;

Holding in Thy eight hands various kinds of dreadful weapons,
And destroying the enemies of the immortals.[1]

15

I remember again and again the dark[2] primeval Devi[3] swayed with passion,[4]
Her beauteous face heated and moist with the sweat (of amorous play),[5]
Bearing a necklace of *Ganjā* berries,[6] and clad with leaves.

16

O Spouse of S'rikaṇṭha,[7]
I place on my head Thy blue lotus feet,
Which are followed by[8] the Vedas,

Dhūmāvatī is of an ashen colour (*vivarnā*); Bagalāmukhī is all yellow (*pītavarṇā*), and Kamalā is said to be like lightning (*saudāminisannibhā*)—see Prosanna Kumar Shastri's "Daśamahāvidyā".

[1] The Daityas. enemies of the Devas, whose Protectress the Devī is.

[2] *Asitakānti.* It is difficult to arrive at English translations for some Sanskrit words of colour. Mātanginī here referred to is also spoken of as *shyāmāngī* or dark green; and dark green and dark-blue seem also to be used interchangeably.

[3] Mātanginī, one of the *Daśamahāvidyā.*

[4] *Anangatantrām*—influenced or swayed by Ananga ("the bodiless one"), a name of the Hindu God of Love, Kāma.

[5] *Avirnidāsha jalashikharashobhivaktrām.* The cause is shown in the preceding line—play and union with her Lord.

[6] Red and black berries used as goldsmiths' weights.

[7] S'iva, the "beautiful throated," also called Shitikaṇṭha ("peacock-throated"), from the colouring caused by His drinking the venom which arose at the churning of the ocean.

[8] *Anugamyamānau*—that is, the Vedas worship and adore Her.

As swans are lured by the tinkling sound of an
anklet.

17

O Bhavānī! I worship thy body from ankle to
knee,[1]
Upon which the bull-bannered one[2] gazes with
great love,
And who, as if not satiated by looking thereon with
two eyes,
Has yet made for himself a third.[3]

18

I call to mind thy two thighs,[4]
Which humble the pride of the trunk of an elephant,
And surpass the plantain-tree in thickness and
tenderness.[5]
O Mother! youth[6] fashioned those thighs
That they may support as two pillars the weight of
thy (great) hips,[7]

---

[1] *Janghā. cf.* Lalitāsahasranāma, verse 18, where the Devī's calves are compared to "the sapphire-studded quiver of the God of Love, with rounded ankles and instep arched like the back of a tortoise."

[2] S'iva, also called *Vriṣaddhvaja.*

[3] S'iva is always represented with three eyes, the third being the eye of wisdom, which in man opens on the realization of divinity.

[4] *Uru* (*cf.* Lalitāsahasranāma, verse 17. "The symmetry and smoothness of Her thighs are known only to Kāmeśa (S'iva). Her knees shine like jewelled discs."

[5] *Cf.* First Canto of Kālidāsa's Kumāra Sambhavam.

[6] *Madhyamenabayasā.*

[7] *Shroni.*

19

Looking at thy waist,[1] it would seem as if it had
been absorbed
And become the great bulk of thy breasts and
hips.[2]
By the youth[3] which clothes the body with hair,[4]
May it ever be resplendent in my heart!

20

O Devi! may I never forget thy navel,[5]
As it were a secure inviolate pool,[6]
Given to Thee by Thy blooming youth,
Filled with the liquid beauty[7] of the beloved of
Smara,[8]

---

[1] *Murtirmadhyastava.*

[2] *Shronyaustanauchayugapat prathayishyatochchairbālyāt parena bayasā parihristasārah*—that is, the waist is so slender and the breasts and hips so heavy that it would seem that the greater part of the body, which goes to the making of the waist, had been taken away and put into the breasts and hips, and formed their bulk.

[3] *Bālyātparenabayasā.* Literally the age which follows childhood, which is the cause of these changes in woman's body.

[4] *Romāvalivilāsitena,* which appears with puberty (*cf.* verse 15 of the Lalitā).

[5] *Nābhi,* which also means any navel-like cavity.

[6] *Pallalamapradhriṡyam*—from all but S'iva: a similar idea to that of verse 17 of the Lalitā, where it is said that the beauty of the Devi's thighs are known only to Her Lord Kāmeśa (S'iva).

[7] *Lāvanyavāribharitāng.*

[8] That is, Rati, Spouse of Kāma or Smara, the God of Love, son of Kṛṣṇa and Rukmini. The son of Kāma is Aniruddha, and his companion is Vasanta, the spring. He is armed with a bow-and-arrows, the bow string being a line of bees, and the arrows flowers of different plants.

He who was fearful of the fire from the eyes of
Hara.[1]

21

Thy two lotus-like breasts, smeared with sandal,
Which bear ashes telling of S'iva's embrace,[2]
Call to mind the vermilion-painted temples moist
with ichor[3]
Of some (impassioned) elephant
Rising from his bath in waters,
Flicked with foam.[4]

22

O Mother! Thy two arms, beauteous with the water
Dripping from Thy body bathed from neck to throat,
Seem to have been formed by the crocodile-bannered One,[5]
As long nooses wherewith to hold the throat of his
enemy[6] (S'iva).

---

[1] When the Devas desired a commander for their forces in their war with Tāraka, they sought the aid of Kāma in drawing S'iva towards Pārvati, whose issue alone could destroy the demon. Kāma undertook the mission, and shot his arrows of love at S'iva, when the latter was doing *tapas*. S'iva, however, who was offended at this disturbance of his devotions, burnt Kāma down with a flash from the fire of His third eye. Subsequently Kāma was reborn in the form of Pradyumna at the request of Rati.

[2] For S'iva's body is covered with ashes.

[3] *Samadasyakumbhau*, the ichor which exudes from the temples of elephants in rut.

[4] The ashes are thus compared to foam, and the sandal paste to the vermilion with which the temples and foreheads of fine elephants are painted.

[5] That is, Kāma, the God of Love.

[6] For S'iva burnt him (see *ante* n. 5). The Devī's arms embrace the neck of S'iva.

May I never forget them!

23

O Daughter of the Mountain-King,
Again and again have I looked upon Thy shapely neck,
Which has stolen the beauty of a well-formed shell,
And is adorning with pleasing necklace and many another ornament;
Yet am I never satiated.

24

O Mother! he has not been born in vain [1]
Who oft calls to his mind
Thy face, with its large round eyes and noble brow,
Its radiant cheeks and smile,
The high, straight nose,
And lips red as the *bimba* fruit. [2]

25

Whoever, O Devī! contemplates upon Thy wealth of hair,
Lit by the crescent moon, [3]
Resembling a swarm of bees hovering over fragrant flowers,
Is freed of the ancient fetters which bind him to the world. [4]

[5] *Sa eva jātah.* Literally, "He is indeed born." His birth is fruitful.

[1] The fruit of the tree called *tyālākucho* in Bengali, which, when ripe, is very red, and to which the lips of young women are often compared (*cf.* Meghadūta, verse 2, "*Pakvabimbādharoṣṭhī*").

[2] The Devī bears the crescent moon on her head as does S'iva.

[3] *Tasya svayam galati Devī purāṇapāshā*—that is, he is freed of rebirth, the fruit of *Karma*. Here commences the *phala* (fruit or result portion) of the *stotra*.

26

The mortal who in this world
Devoutly from his heart reads this hymn,
Sweet to the ears of the wise,
Attains for ever all wealth in the form of that Lakṣmi
Who attends the crowned kings who are prostrate at Her feet.

ĀDYAKĀLI

(ĀDYAKĀLĪSVARŪPASTOTRA)[1]

FROM THE MAHĀNIRVĀṆA TANTRA

1. *HRĪM*,[2] O destroyer of time ![3]
2. *S'RĪM*,[4] O terrific one ![5]
3. *KRĪM*,[6] Thou who art beneficent,[7]

---

[1] From the Mahānirvāṇa Tantra, Seventh Ullāsa, verses 12 *et seq*. This hymn to the primordial Kāli contains a hundred of her names all beginning with " K. " Thus Kālī, Karāli, Kalyāni, Kalāvatī, Kamalā, Kalidarpaghni, Kaparddiśakripanvitā, etc. *Kādi* is that which has " Ka " in the beginning. In the Tantrarāja, Devī says to S'iva : " The syllable ' Ka ' is in Thy form, and that Ṣ'akti confers all *siddhis* " (see Lalitā Sahasranāma, where a number of the following names occur).

[2] The *Māyābīja* (see Fifth Ullāsa, verse 10).

[3] Kāli (see Fourth Ullasa, verses 30 *et seq*.). She is thus called *Kālakarshinī*.

[4] *Bīja* of Lakṣmi, Devī of prosperity or beauty.

[5] Karālī.

[6] The Bījābhidāna says *Ka* = Kālī, *Ra* = Brahmā, *Ī* = Mahāmāyā. The half circle of *candrabindu* is the universal Mother, and the point is the destroyer of misery.

[7] Kalyāṇī, or She who bestows peace and happiness (see the Lalitā, verse 73). According to the Padmapurāṇa, Devī is worshipped as Kalyāṇī in the Malaya mountains.

4. Possessor of all the arts,[1]
5. Thou art Kamalā,[2]
6. Destroyer of the pride of the Kali Age.[3]
7. Who art kind to him of the matted hair,[4]
8. Devourer of Him who devours,[5]
9. Mother of Time[6]
10. Thou art brilliant as the fires of the final dissolution.[7]
11. Spouse of Him of the matted hair.[8]
12. O Thou of formidable countenance,[9]
13. Ocean of the nectar of compassion,[10]

---

[1] Kalāvati (see the Lalitā, verse 74). The *Kalā*, or arts, are sixty-four in number. The S'akti should always be *Kalāvatī*. Devī is also called *Kalāmālā*, or garland of the arts. Kalāvatī may also mean possessed of all arts complete.

[2] A name of Lakṣmī-Devī is Kamalā, for She is all S'aktis. In verse 73 of the Lalitā, Devī is called Kāmakalārūpā, on which Bhāskararāya says that there are three *bindus* and the *hārdakala*. The first *bindu* is called Kāma, and the last Kalā ; but according to the rule *pratyāhāra*, Kamalā includes all four. Kālikā Purāṇa says, Devī, is alone indicated by Kāma.

[3] Kalidarpaghni.

[4] Kapardīśakripanvitā. *Kapardīśa* is a title of S'iva derived from his matted hair.

[5] Kālikā, because She devours S'iva as Mahākāla (see Mahānirvāṇa Tantra, Fourth Ullāsa, verse 31).

[6] Kālamātā.

[7] Kālānalasamadyuti.

[8] Kapardinī. Spouse of S'iva, called *Kapardi* from his matted hair (see Lalitā, verse 151). The Viśva says that *Kaparda* means the matted hair of S'iva and the cowdung cakes. When S'iva incarnated, as Mailāra, his spouse was decked with a garland of cowdung-cakes.

[9] Karālāsyā.

[10] Karunāmritasāgarā (see Lalitā, verse 73).

14. Merciful,[1]
15. Vessel of mercy,[2]
16. Whose mercy is without limit,[3]
17. Who art attainable alone by Thy mercy,[4]
18. Who art fire,[5]
19. Tawny,[6]
20. Black of hue,[7]
21. Thou who increaseth the joy of the Lord of creation,[8]
22. Night of darkness,[9]
23. In the form of desire,[10]
24. Yet liberator from the bonds of desire,[11]
25. Thou who art dark as a bank of cloud,[12]

---

[1] Kripāmayi.

[2] Kripādhārā.

[3] Kripāpārā.

[4] Kripāgamā.

[5] Kṛṣānu. *Kṛṣānuretas* is an epithet of S'iva whose male seed is fire.

[6] Kapilā.

[7] Kṛṣṇā.

[8] Kṛṣṇānandavivardhinī. Kṛṣṇa is here the supreme Lord.

[9] Kālaratrī. The Lalitā, verse 101, speaks of the Devī as attended by hosts of S'aktis, Kālarātrī, and others—that is the twelve S'aktis from Kālarātri to Tankārī, one in each petal of the *anahāta padma*. The Varāha Purāṇa says that Raudrī, who was born form darkness and went to the Blue Mountain to perform penance (the S'akti causing destruction) is called Kālarātrī.

[10] Kāmarupā (*ibid.*, verse 73), Kalika Purāna-says that Devi is called Kāma because She came to the secret place in the Blue peak of the great mountain (Kāilāsa) along with S'iva, for the sake of desire, and because She fulfils desires and destroys and restores the body of Kāma.

[11] Kāmapāśavimocinī.

[12] Kādambinī. In the heat of India the rain-cloud is welcome, and in some of Her forms She is dark.

26. And bearest the crescent moon,[1]
27. Destructress of sin in the Kali Age,[2]
28. Thou who art pleased by the worship of virgins,[3]
29. Thou who art the refuge of the worshippers of virgins,[4]
30. Who art pleased by the feasting of virgins,[5]
31. And who art in the form of the virgin,[6]
32. Thou who wanderest in the Kadamba forest,[7]
33. Who art pleased with the flowers of the Kadamba forest,[8]

---

[1] Kalādhārā.

[2] Kalikalmaṣanāśinī (see Lalitā, verse 113), Kūrma Purāṇa says that the repetition of the names of Devī destroys the multitude of sins in the Kali Age.

[3] Kumārīpūjanapritā. The *Kumārī pūjā*, or worship of virgins, is a *pūjā* common in Bengal. The worship is by men, whereas the *sadhavapūjā*, or worship of married women, is done by women. Or Kumārī may directly refer to the Devī Herself. She is known as the unmarried Kumārī. A *sūtra* of the S'iva Sūtras runs *Iccāśaktih Umā kumārī*. The energy of desire is Umā, the unmarried. Bhāskararāya (Commentary, Lalitā, verses 25, 40) says: "As play She creates the universe, hence She is Kumārī, or She destroys (*mārayate*) the ground (*ku*) of the great illusion. Hence She is Kumārī; Kumārī is the enjoyer and not to be enjoyed, as She is one with the *Yogi*, the enjoyer.

[4] Kumārī pūjakālayā, or "who art the refuge of such worshippers."

[5] Kumārībhojanānanda. The *Kumārīs* are feasted at the *Kumārī pūjā*.

[6] Kumārīrūpadhārinī. So a very young marriageable girl is called Gauri.

[7] Kadambavanasanchārā (see Hymn to Tripurasundari, *post*).

[8] Kadambapuṣpasantoṣā (see Lalitā, verse 73).

34. Who hast Thy abode in the Kadamba forest,[1]
35. Who wearest a garland of Kadamba flowers,[2]
36. Thou who art youthful,[3]
37. Who hath a soft low voice,[4]
38. Whose voice is sweet as the crv of a *Cakravāka* bird,[5]
39. Who drinkest *Kādambari* wine,[6]
40. And art pleased with the *Kādambari* wine,[7]

---

[1] Kadambavanavāsini (see the Lalitā, verse 23). The palace of *Cintāmani* is surrounded by a gallery of gems (*maṇimaṇḍapa*). Around this is the grove of Kadamba trees, which in the Purāṇās are said to be seven yojanas in height in the space between the walls of gold and silver. The Bhairavayāmala says the abode of Bindu is the ocean of nectar. The five *yonis*—that is, the five *śakti* angles in the *śricakra* — are the divine trees. There is the grove of *Nīpa* trees. Within that is the gallery of gems. Within that is the palace of *Cintāmaṇi*.

[2] Kadambapuṣpamālini. The Lalitā, verse 8, speaks of Devī as decked above her ears with clusters of Kadamba flowers.

[3] Kishorī.

[4] Kālakaṇṭhā. Devi is also called Kālakaṇṭhī, or wife of Kālakaṇṭha, a name of S'iva whose throat was coloured by the poison he swallowed at the churning of the ocean. According to Devī purāṇa, Kālakaṇṭha was worshipped at Kālanjara.

[5] Kalanādaninādini. Water-birds which sing to one another at night—the male to the female and the latter to the male—sitting on opposite banks of the river. Their passionate devotion is often alluded to by the poets.

[6] Kādambarīpānaratā.

[7] Kādambarīpriyā. *Kādambari* is mead. Bhāskararāya (Commentary, Lalitā), dealing with the Tripura Upanishad, which prescribes that mead, fish, flesh, and cooked cereals should be offered to the Devatā, says that it enjoins those who are allowed to take wine, flesh, etc., that they should do so after first dedicating them to the Brahman, and minimize the habit by gradation (see the same idea expressed in Manu v., 56, Bhāg. Pr. XI., 5-11).

41. And whose cup is a skull,[1]
42. Who wearest a garland of bones,[2]
43. Who art pleased with the lotus,[3]
44. And who art seated on the lotus,[4]
45. Who abidest in the centre of the lotus,[5]
46. Whom the fragrance of the lotus pleases,[6]
47. Who movest with the swaying gait of a *hamsa*,[7]
48. Destroyer of fear,[8]
49. Who assumeth all forms at will,[9]
50. Whose abode is at Kāmarūpa,[10]
51. Who ever dallies at the Kāmapitha,[11]
52. O Beautiful One,[12]
53. O creeper which givest every desire,[13]

---

[1] Kapālapātraniratā.

[2] Kamkālamālyadhārini.

[3] Kamalāsanasantuṣṭā.

[4] Kamalāsanavāsini.

[5] Kamalālayamadhyasthā.

[6] Kamalāmodamodini.

[7] Kalahamsagati. *Hamsa* is variously translated goose, swan, flamingo. A swaying waddle like that of a duck is admired. As the swans live in the celestial lake called Mānasa, so She lives in the minds (*mānasa*) of Her devotees.

[8] Klaibyanāśini.

[9] Kāmarūpini (see also *post*).

[10] Kāmarūpakritavāsā (see next note).

[11] Kāmapīthavilāsinī. Kāmarūpa, the great Tantrika centre in Assam, one of the *Mahāpīthas*, where the genital organ of the Devī fell on the severance of Her dead body by Viṣṇu after the *Dakṣa Yajna*. Kāmarupa is also one of the *Ādibhuta*, which are in the *Mūlādhāra* and other tattvik centres (see the Lalitā, verse 82).

[12] Kamanīyā.

[13] Kalpalatā. The *Kalpa* tree is one of the celestial trees in the heaven of India, which yielded whatever one desired. Woman is likened to a creeper (*Latā*) embracing and depending on her

54. Whose beauty is Thy ornament,[1]
55. Adorable as the image of all tenderness,[2]
56. Thou with a tender body,[3]
57. And who art slender of waist,[4]
58. Who art pleased with the nectar of purified wine,[5]
59. Giver of success to them whom purified wine rejoices,[6]
60. The own Deity of those who worship Thee when joyed with wine,[7]
61. Who art gladdened by the worship of Thyself with purified wine,[8]
62. Who art immersed in the ocean of purified wine,[9]
63. Who art the protectress of those who accomplish *vrata* with wine,[10],

husband (see also the Lalitā, where the Devī is called *Bhaktimatkalpalatikā*, the *kalpa* creeper of the devotee).

1 Kamanīyavibhūṣanā, or "who art the possessor of beautiful ornaments."

2 Kamanīyagunārādhyā ; or it may mean that the Devī is to be worshipped by the worshipper with all best and tender feeling.

3 Komalāngī.

4 Krishodarī. Literally, small of belly (see Bhuvaneśvarī *stotra*, *apivarastanatating tanuvrittamadhyām*, and the Lalitā, verse 79, *tanumadhyā*).

5 Kāranāmritasantoshā. *Kārana* is one of the technical terms given to the purified wine consumed as an element of the Tāntrika pancatattva.

6 Kāranānandasiddhidā.

7 Kāranānandajapeshtā.

8 Kāranārchchanaharshitā.

9 Kāranārnavasangmagnā.

10 Kāranavratapālinī. *Vratas* are ritual acts and devotional exercises which do not belong to the obligatory (*nitya*) *karma*.

64. Whom the fragrance of musk gladdens,[1]
65. And who art luminous with a *tilaka* mark of musk,[2]
66. Who art attached to those who worship Thee with musk,[3]
67. Who lovest those who worship Thee with musk,[4]
68. Who art a mother to those who burn musk as incense,[5]
69. Who art fond of the musk-deer,[6]
70. And who art pleased to eat its musk,[7]
71. Whom the scent of camphor gladdens,[8]
72. Who art adorned with garlands of camphor,[9]
73. And whose body is besmeared with. camphor and sandal paste,[10]
74. Who art pleased with purified wine flavoured with camphor,[11]
75. Who drinkest purified wine flavoured with camphor,[12]

---

[1] Kastūrīsaurabhāmodā. Musk is used in worship to scent *candan*, etc.

[2] Kastūrītilakojjvalā. The *tilak* is the mark worn by sectarian Hindus on the forehead.

[3] Kastūrīpūjanaratā.

[4] Kastūrīpūjakapriyā.

[5] Kastūrīdāhajananī.

[6] Kastūrīmrigatoshinī.

[7] Kastūrībhojanapritā.

[8] Karpūrāmodamoditā. Camphor is burnt in worship during *ārati*, and is used to scent the *pādya*, betel leaf, etc., offered to the Devī.

[9] Karpūramālābharanā. Balls of camphor are strung together in a garland.

[10] Karpūracandanākshitā.

[11] Karpūrakāranāhladā.

[12] Karpūrāmritapāyinī.

76. Who art bathed in the ocean of camphor,[1]
77. Whose abode is in the ocean of camphor,[2]
78. Who art pleased when worshipped with the *bīja* "*Hūm*,"[3]
79. Who threatenest with the *bīja* "*Hūm*,"[4]
80. Embodiment of *Kulācāra*,[5]
81. Adored by Kaulikas,[6]
82. Benefactress of the Kaulikas,[7]
83. Observant of *Kulācāra*,[8]
84. Joyous one,[9]
85. Revealer of the path of the Kaulikas,[10]
86. Queen of Kāśi,[11]
87. Allayer of sufferings,[12]

---

[1] Karpūrasāgarasnatā.

[2] Karpūrasāgarālayā.

[3] Kūrchchabījajapapritā. *Hūm* is the *Kūrchhabīja*.

[4] Kūrchchajapaparāyayanā—that is, She who mutters "*Hūm*" when conquering the demons. The Devī then constantly uttered the *hūmkāra* with its threatening, roaring sound.

[5] Kulīna. *Kula*, according to the Tantra, means S'akti. *Akula* = S'iva. The union of *Kula* with *Akula* is called Kaula, the essence common to both S'iva and S'akti. Hence Devī is *Kaulinī* (see Lalitā, verse 37). Both *Kula* and *Akula* are in the *Sahasrāra*. *Kulācāra* is the way of the *Kaula* division of Tantrik worshippers.

[6] Kaulikārādhyā. The *Kaulikas* are followers of *Kulācāra* (see last note). So also in the Lalitā, verse 17, the Devī is addressed as "adored by *Dakṣinas* and *Adakṣinas*."

[7] Kaulikapriyakārinī.

[8] Kulacārā, *v. ante*.

[9] Kantukinī.

[10] Kulamārgapradarshinī.

[11] Kaśīśvarī. Kāśi is Benares, the sacred city of S'iva.

[12] Kartahartrī; and thus the Lalitā speaks of the Devī as the moon-light which soothes those burned by the triple fires of misery.

88. Giver of blessings to the Lord of Kāśi,[1]
89. Giver of pleasure to the Lord of Kāśi,[2]
90. Beloved of the Lord of Kāśi,[3]
91. Thou whose toe-ring bells make sweet melody as Thou moveth,[4]
92. Whose girdle bells sweetly tinkle,[5]
83. Who abidest in the mountain of gold,[6]
94. Who art like a moonbeam on the mountain of gold,[7]
95. Who art gladdened by the recitation of the *mantra* " *Klīm,*"[8]
96. Who art the *Kāma Bīja,*[9]

---

[1] Kāśīśavaradayinī (" Lord " is S'iva).

[2] Kāśīśvarakritāmodā.

[3] Kāśīśvaramanoramā.

[4] Kalamanjīracaranā.

[5] Kvanatkāncīvibhūṣanā.

[6] Kāncanādrikritāgarā (the mountain Kāncana or Sumeru). Durvāsa says in his Lalitāstavaratna (verses 2-4) : " Let the gold mountain be victorious whose body is the universe resounding with the music of celestial women living in the golden bowers of creepers of the mountain peak. We salute the three peaks which are the seats of Brahmā, Viṣṇu, and S'iva, extending to the four quarters of the earth. In their midst is another peak 400 yojanas (a yojana is eight or nine miles) in height, making the place beauteous with the golden rays of its flowers, and I worship it." The Lalitā Sahasranāma (verse 22) also addresses Devī as dwelling on the middle peak of Mount Sumeru.

[7] Kāncanācalakaumudi.

[8] Kāmabījajapānanda. The *Kāma bīja* is "*klīm.*" When the "*Ka*" and "*La*" are eliminated, the remaining "*īm*" is called *kāmakalā*, which is in the *turīya* state. In the Lalitā, verse 225, Devī is called creatrix of the *mantra klīm* ("*klīmkarī*"). *Klīmkāra* is *S'ivakāma,* and She is His wife.

[9] Kāmabījasvarūpinī—that is, She is "*klīm*" itself.

97. Destructress of all evil inclinations,[1]
98. And of the afflictions of the *Kaulikas*—[2]
99. Lady of the Kaulas,[3]
100. O Thou who by the three *bijās*, "KRĪM" "HRĪM" "S'RĪM" art the Destructress of the fear of death[4]—
(To Thee I make obeisance.)

---

[1] Kumatighnī. Devī is also (Lalitā, verse 78) *Sadācāra pravarttakā*, because She makes men move to right action.

[2] Kulīnārtināśinī.

[3] Kulakāminī.

[4] *Krīm, Hrīm, S'rīm mantravarṇena kālakanṭakaghātinī.*

LAKṢMĪ[1]

(LAKSMĪSTOTRAM)

FROM THE TANTRASĀRA[2]

O DEVĪ KAMALĀ,[3] beloved of Viṣṇu,
Adored by the three worlds,
As Thou art constant to Viṣṇu, be Thou constant to me.
Whoever worshipping Lakṣmī, reads these twelve names of Her—
Iśvarī, Kamala,[4] Lakṣmī, Calā,[5]
Bhūti,[6] Haripriyā,[7] Padmā,[8] Padmālayā,[9] Sampat,[10]

---

[1] Lakśmī, commonly called S'rī, Devi of prosperity and beauty: the S'akti, or Spouse of Viṣṇu, who rose resplendent from the sea at the churning of the ocean by the Devas and Asuras, and then reclining on the breast of Hari, gazed upon the enraptured Devas. As her Lord assumes various forms, so does She.

[2] P. 577.

[3] Because She appeared from the lotus.

[4] Feminine of Īśvara, or Lord, or Ruler.

[5] Or Cancalā, the fickle one, for nothing is so fickle as wealth and prosperity—" here to-day and gone to-morrow."

[6] Prosperity.

[7] Beloved of Hari (Viṣṇu).

[8] Lotus.

[9] Who dwells in the lotus.

[10] Wealth.

Uchaih,[1] S'ri[2] Padmadhārini,[3]
With such an one, his wife and children,
Laksmi ever abides.

[1] The exalted One, for prosperity exalts.
[2] Beauty and prosperity.
[3] Holding the lotus in her hands.

TĀRĀ[1]

(TĀRĀṢṬAKAM)[2]

From the NĪLA TANTRA

1

O Mother, Devī Nīlasarasvatī[3] Tārā,

[1] The Matsyasūkta, Tārārṇava, and Nīla Tantras deal with particulars or Tārā or Tāriṇī, one of the Mahāvidyā, whose *bīja* is *Hrīm Strīm, Hūm* (*Kurccha*), *Phaṭ* (see verse 4). She is called Nīlasarasvatī, because She playfully gives the power of speech. She is called Tārā on account of her being deliverer or saviour (*tārakatvāt*). She gives both pleasure (*sukha*) and liberation (*mokṣa*). She is called also *Ugratārā*, because She saves from formidable and horrible calamities. Ṛṣi Vaśiṣṭha is said to have cursed this *vidyā*, and then raised the curse so that *siddhi* might be gained from Her by *japa* of the *bīja Hrīm, Strīm, Hūm, Phaṭ,* after which She again became glorious. Her Mantra is also given as *S'rīm, Hrīm, Strīm, Hūm, Phaṭ* (giver of wealth and beauty); another is *Hrīm, Hrīm, Strīm, Hūm, Phaṭ* (giver of all desires); another is *Aim, Hrīm, Strīm, Hūm, Phaṭ* (giver of speech), and *Hrīm, Strīm, Hūm, Phaṭ* (giver of liberation). Her Yantra is an eight-petalled lotus surrounded by a circle, with inverted triangle in the centre with *Hūm*. On the petals are *Hrīm, Strīm, S'rīm, Hūm*. There is also a *Yantra* (*Tārāṣatkoṇa*) of two superimposed triangles, making a star.

[2] From the Nīla Tantra (see also Tantrasāra, p. 610, R. M. Chatterjee's edition, and the Brihatstotraratnākara, p. 283, where a more correct text is given).

[3] The blue Sarasvatī, Devī of speech (see note 1,*ante*). Nīla Tantra says She is in the form of all language (*sarvabhāṣā ayī*). The Nilasarasvatī Yantra is figured at p. 93 of the Dashamahāvidyā.

Refuge with Thee I crave.
Giver of prosperity and wealth art Thou
To those who worship Thee. Standing on S'iva,
Thy right foot upon His breast and left upon His thigh.
Ever art Thou, with smiling lotus-like face.
Thy three eyes are, as it were, full-blown lotuses.
In Thy hands Thou holdest a knife,[1] a skull, a lotus, and a sword.

2

Thou art the presiding Devi of speech.
Thou art the creeper which grants all desires.[2]
Thou art the giver of all *siddhi*,[3]
And the power to write both verse and prose.
Three are Thine eyes, as it were blue lotuses.
Ocean of kindness and compassion art Thou.
I pray Thee of Thy mercy shower upon me the nectar of prosperity.

3

O Sharbhā,[4] I pray Thee remove my fears.
Proud Lady, brilliant are Thy garments,
Bright with coiling serpents.
Thou art clad in tiger skin.
Thy waist is adorned with tiny tinkling bells.
Thou holdest the heads of two demons
Dripping with blood, just severed by the sword.
Thy waist is girdled with heads of demons,

---

[1] *Karttri* (for *dhyāna* see p. 94 Daśamahāvidyā).
[2] As did the celestial *Kalpa* tree in Indra's heaven.
[3] Material success, psychical powers, spiritual attainment.
[4] Spouse of S'iva (Sharbha).

As it were with a garland.
Thus art Thou beautiful, O formidable One.[1]

4

O Devī Tārā, attained with difficulty,
I take refuge with Thee.
Thou art beautiful with form both amorous and charmful.[2]
Thou art *Bindu* and the half-moon,[3]
Whose substance is *Hrim* and *Phat*.[4]
Thou art *mantra*[5] and the shelter of all.
Thy forms are threefold—
Gross, Subtle, and Supreme.
Thou art beyond the reach of Veda.[6]

---

[1] Her *dhyāna* is given as follows: The Devī is in the midst of four blazing funeral pyres; Her feet as described in verse 1; formidable, with garland of severed heads; short of stature; big-bellied; tiger skin round the waist; youthful; four-armed; protruding tongue; giving *vara*; holding the articles mentioned in verse 1 (the skull and lotus in left hands); a *ṛṣi* Akshobhya in the form of a serpent on her head; her body lustrous as that of the moonbeams; formidable teeth; smiling face; three eyes blazing like the morning sun.

[2] *Māyānanga vikārarūpalalane.*

[3] *Ardhacandrātmike* —that is, the crescent sign below the bindu in *candra bindu.* She is both bindu and Nāda (see Introduction). It is also said that there are eight *varṇa* above the *bindu* of *Hrīm,* commencing with *ardhacandra,* and ending with *unmani*, of which the third is *Nāda.* Here, as the Mahāsvachchanda Tantra states, the Devī should be contemplated.

[4] Two tantrik *bīja mantras*: as to *Hūm* (see p 56, note 1, *ante*). *Phat* is the *astra* or weapon *mantra* (see note 1, p. 50, *ante*).

[5] *Mantrātmike* (see p. 2, *ante*).

[6] *Vedanāngnahigocharā*, as to her three forms (*vide ante*).

5

By the service of Thy lotus feet,
Men of good deed attain *sāyujya*[1] liberation.
O Parameśvari, Thou art the Spouse of Him[2]
Who is Brahmā, Visnu, and the three-eyed One.
O Mother! he who neglects to serve Thy lotus feet,
But serves instead the Devas, Indra, and others,
Who are themselves plunged in the ocean of *samsāra*,[3]
Is indeed and most truly ignorant.

6

O Mother! those Devas who receive on their crowns
The pollen which comes from Thy lotus-like feet,[4]

---

[1] Literally, "becoming one with the Deity." Identification of the self and the Deity with attributes; one of the four forms of qualified liberation—*Sālokya*, *Sārūpya*, *Sāmīpya*, *Sāyujya*. Those who know the Brahman and such worship to be imperfect reject them, and attain the unconditioned bliss (*kaivalya*) which transcends all other states. But these others must be passed before the end is reached, which the S'aktirahasya summarizes by a short verse: "A mortal who worships by ceremonies, by images, by mind, by identification, by knowing the self attains *kaivalya*."

[2] That is Parameśvara, in whom the threefold energies which manifest in the *trimūrti* are contained *tasyastri parameśvari trinayanabrahmādi samnyātmanah.*

[3] The Deva, in this like man, is a *samsārin* or inhabitant of of the *samsāra*, which comprises earth, the *antarikṣa*, and heaven (*svarga*), the abode of the Deva. The latter has wife and children, is engaged in conflict with demons, and so forth. When the merit which gains the Deva heaven is exhausted, he descends to earth again.

[4] That is, the Deva bow their heads at the feet of the Devi, receiving on their heads the dust of Her feet.

Are able to keep their promise of conquest,
And to gain victory over their enemies in battle—
Such, without a doubt, are sheltered in Thy lap.
But their enemies who send forth the defiant challenge,
"I am a Deva, and none is equal to me in the whole world,"
Perish and meet such death as befits them.

7

Bhūta, Preta, Piśācha, Rākṣasa,
Daitya, foremost of Dānava, Yakṣa, Lords of Naga,[1]
Wrathful Dākinī, great birds,[3] tigers, and other dreadful creatures
Forthwith take flight at but the remembrance of Thy name,
And are powerless to do aught of evil.

8

Who serves Thy lotus feet, to him *siddhi*[4] is given.
He surpasses the Lord of speech,[5]
And obtains the beauty of Kāma.[6]
He can charm and paralyze[7] multitudes of elephants upon the field of battle,

---

[1] Various spirits and inferior divinities of more or less evil and malignant character.

[2] A form of S'akti attendant on the Devī in Her terrible forms.

[3] *Khacara* (vultures, eagles, etc.).

[4] *Vide ante*, p. 57. note 3,

[5] Brihaspati.

[6] Deva of Love.

[7] He has the powers of *mohanam* and *stambhanam*, the latter being one of the *Tāntrika Ṣatkarma*.

And has power to stay the flow of water.[1]
The Siddha[2] and prosperity are under his control.

PHALAŚLOKA.[3]

Whoever, being pure and self-controlled,
Reads this eight-versed hymn to Tārā,
At morn, at noon, at evening,
To him is given
The power to write beautifully in prose or verse,[4]
Knowledge in all *S'āstra*,
Imperishable fortune,
The enjoyment of whatsoever he may desire,
Fame, beauty, and wealth,
The love of all men,
And at the end liberation.

[1] A particular form of *Stambhanam* called *jalastambha*.

[2] Devayoni of that name inhabiting the *antarikṣa*.

[3] Fruit or result of the stotra.

[4] *Labhate devyām kavitvām.*

MAHIṢĀMARDINĪ[1]

(MAHIṢĀMARDINĪSTOTRA)

FROM THE TANTRASĀRA[2]

1

O CANDĪ ![3] wander in my heart,
By whom the act of formidable Asura[4] was shattered,
Destroy the calamities which deeply pierce me,
Arising from the mass of malice and fears (which assail me),
So that, free from danger,
And protected by the lotus cluster of Thy feet,
My swan-like[5] mind may swim and rejoice in the ocean of bliss.

---

1 A title of Durgā, S'akti of S'iva as the powerful victrix of demons. She is Mahiṣamardinī, as the slayer of Mahiṣa. The Daitya S'umbha attacked Her in the form of a buffalo (*Mahiṣa*; see Candi).

2 P. 574.

3 A form of the Devī assumed for the destruction of the Daitya Canda, and who assisted in the destruction of the demon Raktabīja (see Mārkandeya Purāṇa).

4 Mahiṣa.

5 *Manohamsa*, the *hamsa*, is variously described as a swan, goose, and flamingo.

2

What fear of his enemies has he who worships Thee?
The Devas who worship Thy feet stamping on beast and noose,[1]
Having abandoned the form of Narasimha,[2]
Whose towering mane reached the summit of Mount Sumeru,
And whose fingers are outstretched to tear (the breast of) Hiraṇyakaśipu,[3]
Now worship the lion,[4] the enemy of the elephant.[5]

3

O Caṇḍī! when the syllables, the letters of which speak of Thee,
Reach the ear, then Brahmā and other Devas
Sing the truth, touching Puruṣa and Prakṛti.[6]

---

[1] The Devī is standing on Her lion (*v. post*) with the noose (*pāśa*) beneath Her feet.

[2] The Man-lion (*Avatāra*) of Viṣṇu, in which He destroyed the Daitya Hiraṇyakaśipu, father of His devotee Prahlāda.

[3] See last note. The *avatāra* is generally represented with the King of the Daityas across his knees, tearing asunder with his hands and claws the latter's belly.

[4] Which accompanies the Devī as Durgā. After the destruction of Hiraṇyakaśipu, Viṣṇu's wrath was not appeased. The world trembled, fearing what he might do. The Devas asked the help of S'iva, who assumed the Sharabha form—that of a lion with wings and eight feet—who tossed up Viṣṇu into the air and held him there until he had become powerless. The lion then went to the feet of Durgā, whom he accompanies.

[5] *Gaja*, the elephant form subsequently assumed by the Asura, Mahiṣa.

[6] S'iva and S'akti, the "Male" and "Female" elements, from whose union springs the universe (see *Introduction to Tantra S'āstra* and *Principles of Tantra.*)

O Devī ! be to-day gracious to me,
Devoted as I am to the kissing of Thy beautiful lotus feet,
The one and only glittering abode of the essence of the nectar of all Devatās.

4

If, because of my following your way of Kula,[1]
I suffer reproach better is it that I shall thus be without fame.
Let me not have that which comes of the worship of Keśava[2] and Kauśika ;[3]
Rather, O Mother ! let my heart rest in meditation on Thy lotus feet,
Worshipped by Brahmā, Hari, the enemy of Smara[4] and the enemy of the Daityas.[5]

5

O Mother ! if I be engaged in the rightful[6] contemplation of Thy lotus feet,

---

1 That is, *Kulācāra,* one, and the highest, of the divisions of Tāntrik worshippers often misunderstood, and therefore subject of reproach ; and which is contrasted in the next line but one with the more popular and conventional worshipper of Keśava and Kauśika.

2 Viṣṇu.

3 An epithet both of S'iva and Indra, probably here the former.

4 Smara, the God of Love ; S'iva, who slew him, is his "enemy."

5 *Daityāri* : usually an epithet of S'rī Kṛṣṇa, but as Hari has already been mentioned, possibly the reference may be to Indra.

6 *i. e.,* orderly, according to the direction and sequence of the dhyāna or stotra.

7 Literally, "If I be deprived of."

What matters it if I know not [7] other sacred places ?[1]
May Thy lotus feet be ever present to my mind—
Thy feet which are the wealth of our wounds ! [2]
O propitious Mother ! do Thou forgive me.

6

Verily and without doubt, even the Lord of Bhūtas[3] would have perished,[4]
Maddened as He was with the joy of the embrace of (Thee who art) His own self,[5]
Had He not enjoyed the lotus fragrance of Thy feet,
Full of honey from which drop liquid sandal,
And the nectar, there haply fallen from the moon.[6]

---

[1] *Siddhāspada,* where the perfect (*siddha*) are, or where *Siddhi* (power and perfection) may be gained.

[2] That is, they are the healers of our pain.

[3] S'iva Bhūteśvara or Bhūtanātha. *Bhūta,* which in a general sense means "beings," specifically refers to the spirits and ghosts by whom S'iva is surrounded and of whom He is Master.

[4] It is by the Devī's aid that S'iva is Parameśvara, for without S'akti He is nothing, and without Her life-giving energy and support cannot exist. As the Kubjikā Tantra says : "Without their S'aktis the husbands are but *preta* " (inert corpses). So also the Jnānārnava : " O beloved, pure Sadāśiva without S'akti is without motion like a corpse, for without S'akti He can do nothing. "

[5] *Svātmānam parirabhya.* Literally, having embraced Himself. The Devī is, however, in a dualistic sense, His sacred half, and in reality one with Him and His own self (see Mahānirvāṇa Tantra, chap. i.).

[6] *Daivādvichyuta candra candanarasaprāgalbhya garbashravat*— " Haply " in the poetical sense, as the nectar should be in the moon, but it happens to be dropping from the sacred feet of the Devī. Moreover, the Parambindu, which is S'ivaśakti, is in the crescent of Nirvāṇakalā,which is by Amākalā the sixteenth digit

7

O Mother ! let the stream of heavy showers of holy devotion torwards Thee
Be ever shed upon me,
Struggling and drowning, alas! as I am in the endless ocean of illusion,[1]
Without taste of the springing water of the Bliss of Brahman,[2]
Which dispels the weight of mental afflictions from numbers of Devas.

8

May (Thy) glory,[3] dark as collyrium cloud,
Be ever in my heart.
From its glittering lustre were born the three Devatās,
Who create, maintain, and destroy the world,
Whose substance is pure intelligence and bliss,[4]
Dispelling the darkness which overspreads the heart
By the (glory of the unnumbered) millions of their rays !

9

May[5] Devi Mahiṣāmardinī, who hath power to destroy

---

of the moon-circle (*Candramaṇḍala*), whence flows the nectar which, as Ichchhā, is the eternal precursor of creation (see Commentary, verse 49, of the Ṣatcakranirūpaṇa in *The Serpent Power*).

[1] *Viddhā*, not as the original has it, *Siddha*.

[2] *Brahmānandasarābhiṣeka* in the original should be *Brahmānandarāsābhiṣeka*.

[3] *Mahas*, not *maham*, as in the text.

[4] *Nirmalacidānandatrayamdaivatam*.

[5] Verses 9 to 12 are a free rendering of a text which in parts is so corrupt as to be untranslateable with accuracy.

The proud enemies of the Devas,
And is the slayer of many another demon,
Ever conquer!
She it was who, having severed the head of the Asura Mahiṣa,
Seized upon him who assumed the form of a buffalo by his magic art
Upon the field of battle,
Now bellowing, now running, now lowering his head downward,
Falling upon the battlefield, and then vanishing from it for a while.

10

She kills the Asuras upon the battlefield.
Terrible it was, with the dancing of the weapons and streamers [1] of the enemy.
With a cloud of thrown discus and other missiles.
There the copper-coloured weapon [2] dashed and flashed from the enemy's arrows—
Enemies so stout, strong, and tall, proud of wealth and power,
The field of battle thus seemed to have been swept by a tempest,
Most hideous it was, thickly spread with limbs and dead bodies of Asuras,
In whose blood and flesh birds slaked their thirst and appeased their hunger.

11

Let the Sādhaka meditate upon Devī Mahiṣāmardinī.

[1] Chowrie.

[2] That is, fire.

Rushing now here, now there on the field of battle
for the slaughter of the enemies,
Attended by eight companion Mātrikas,[1]
Ear-ringed with eight-petalled lotuses,
Within each petal of which are writ the eight
syllables
Mahiṣāmardinyai namah.[2]
Formidable was that field with the tossing of the
huge curved horns of Mahiṣa,
Deeply black, maddened, wandering to and fro,
horribly roaring
Whose instant death was desired of the Devas.

12

Let the Sādhaka meditate
Upon the auspicious black *Bhagavatī*[3] Mahiṣā-
mardinī,
Holding in Her hands discus, lance, axe, shield,
arrow, bow, and trident,
Making the gesture[4] which dispels fear ;
Her long, matted hair is like a bank of cloud,
Covering Her face most formidable,
Loudly screaming, now with peals of terrible
laughter,
And then with Her threats greatly frightening the
Daitya heroes.

13

O Devi ! such as in this manner
Meditate upon Thy faultless form,

---

[1] The Devīs so called.

[2] Salutation to the Devī slayer of Mahiṣa.

[3] For She has all powers.

[4] Tho *abhaya mudrā* (see p. 36, note 1).

Worshipped by Indra and other Devas,
To them it is given to attack the cities of their enemies,
And, conquering their enemies, to gain a kingdom;
They, too, acquire nectar of the knowledge of poesy,
And power to arrest, banish and slay.[1]

14

O Mother ! salutation to Thee !
May Thou conquer !
Whosoever, meditating upon Thy lotus feet,
Utters this Thy hymn,
In the palms of the hands of all such
Are forthwith wealth, fulfilment of desire, and liberation.

---

[1] *Stambhanam, uchchātanam,* and *māraṇam,* three of the Tāntrik *Ṣaṭkarma.*

ANNAPŪRṆA[1]

(ANNAPŪRṆĀSTOTRA)

FROM THE TANTRASĀRA[2]

1

SALUTATION to thee, O Devi !
Dispenser of blessings, beloved of S'ankara,[3]
Dear to devotees,
Annapūrṇe.

2

Thou hast assumed form by *māyā*[4]
Beloved of S'ankara.
Salutation to Maheśvari,[5]
O Annapūrṇé ! obeisance to Thee.[6]

---

[1] A name of the Devī as She who bestows food, whose sincere devotee will never want rice. In one hand She holds a rice-bowl, and in another a spoon for stirring the boiled rice.

[2] P. 570.

[3] S'ivé.

[4] All forms of the Devī, as also the forms of all *Devatā*, whether in the strict sense *avatāra* or not, are māyik, but to the worshipper none the less real.

[5] Feminine of Maheśvara, a title of S'iva as great Lord and Ruler of the worlds.

[6] *Annapūrṇé namostute*—the refrain.

3

O Mahāmāyā ! [1] beloved Spouse [2] of Hara,[3]
Giver of the fruit of desire,
Queen of *Suras*.[4]
O Annapūrṇé ! obeisance to Thee.

4

O Mahādevī with the lustre of a thousand rising suns,
Three eyed,
Crested with the crescent moon.[5]

5

O Devī ! clad in fine garment,
Ever giving rice, [6] Sinless One,
Who delights in the dance of S'iva.
Crested with the crescent moon.[5]
O Annapūrṇé ! obeisance to Thee.

6

O Devī ! fulfiller of the desires of devotees,[7]
Destructress of worldly pain,
Bending under the weight of Thy breasts.[8]

---

1 The Devī as She who yields and is yet Herself unaffected by *māyā*.

2 *Dharmaputi*—that is, a wife married with religious rites. There are other forms of marriage.

3 S'iva.

4 *Devas*.

5 As is S'iva.

6 *Annadānaratā*, or food generally.

7 *Sādhakas*, those who practise *sādhanam* (see *Introduction To Tantra S'āstra*)

8 *Kucabhārānate* (see Introduction).

O Annapūrṇé ! obeisance to Thee.

7

Thou residest in the centre of the six-petalled lotus,[1]
And art in the form of the six-fold *śakti*,[2]
Thou art Brahmāni and all others,[3]
O Annapūrṇé ! obeisance to Thee.

8

O Devī ! adorned with crescent moon,
All empires[4] are Thy gifts,
Giver of delight to Sarva[5],
O Annapūrṇé ! obeisance to Thee.

9

Thy lotus feet are worshipped by Indra and other *Devās* ;
Thou assumest the form of Rudra and other *Devas*,
Giver of wealth.
O Annapūrṇé ! obeisance to Thee.

---

[1] That is, the *svādhishṭhāna padma.*

[2] *Sharangayuvatimaye,* which equals *sharangaśaktisvarūpe.* The sixfold *śaktis* are : *Hṛdayānga śakti, śirongga śakti, śikhānga śakti, netrānga śakti, avachānga śakti,* and *astrānga śakti* which refer to the *Tāntrika nyāsa,* done on the heart, head, crownlock, eyes, the body, and the concluding gesture with the palms of the hands, accompanied by the *astra bīja* or "*phat.*"

[3] That is, Indrāṅi, Kaumāri, and other *Mātrikas.*

[4] *Sāmrājya.*

[5] *Sarvānandakare.* Sarva is one of the eight forms (*aṣṭamūrti*) of S'iva ; or it may literally mean "giver of delight to all."

10

Whoever[1] at time of worship
Devoutly reads this hymn,
In his house Lakṣmī[2] ever abides;
True is this and without doubt.

11

Whoever having recited[3] the *mantra* daily,
Reads this hymn at dawn of day,
Obtains wealth of rice
And prosperity.

12

Not to all and any should this hymn be revealed,
For be it made known to one who is unworthy,
Then ills fall upon him,
Therefore should it be carefully concealed.

---

[1] This is the *phala* (fruit or result) portion of the *stotra.* All devotional works contain a *phala* chapter or verse, which states the result or reward (*phala*) to be obtained by their perusal, recitation, or hearing. If any worshipper invokes Devī by any particular name, such as Annadā, he obtains the corresponding fruit. So the Sūta Samhitā (iv, 33, 29, 30) says: "All names are attributed by His own *māyā* to Brahman, yet some apply specially by the wish of S'iva Himself. O sages! by the repetition of such names one becomes the supreme Lord Himself and before His lotus face Sadāśiva dances with His Spouse" (see Bhāskararāya Commentary, Introduction to second Chapter of the Lalitā-sahasranāma).

[2] Devī of prosperity and wealth.

[3] Literally, "made *japa* of"

SARASVATĪ[1]

(SARASVATĪSTOTRA)

From the TANTRASĀRA[2]

1

HRĪM, HRĪM[3] is Thy most pleasing *bīja*,[4]
O Thou whose moon-like[5] beauty is heightened

[1] Devi of speech, eloquence, knowledge, and learning, and S'akti of Brahmā ; but formerly, according to the Purāṇic account, the Spouse of Viṣṇu, represented as a fair woman with either four or two arms, and often as seated on a lotus holding a *vīnā*. The Bhāradvaja Smr. says : "Sarasvatī is She who ever resides in the tongue of all beings and who causes speech." According to the Vasiṣṭha Rāmā, cited in the Lalitā, verse 137, She is called Sarasvatī as the possessor (*vati*) of the *saras* (flow of nectar from the *brahmarandhra*). The Brahma Purāṇa says the Devī created Sarasvatī from Her tongue, and from Her shoulders the science of love.

[2] P. 579.

[3] The *bīja*, or "seed" mantra of the Devi whose other *bīja* is the *vāgbhava bīja* or "*aim.*"

[4] See last note.

[5] The colour of Sarasvatī is white. Thus She is elsewhere represented as "white, holding the *vīnā*" (*Svetavīnādharā*), "adorned with white flowers" (*svetābharaṇabhūṣitā*), "holding a white rosary" (*svetākṣasūtrahastāca*), "besmeared with white sandal paste" (*svetacandanacarcitā*), "clad in white raiment" (*svetāmbaradharā*), and the like. Here Her whiteness is compared to the moon.

By the lotuses (which surround Thee).[1]
O auspicious and favourable Devī!
Forest fire[2] of the forest of evil thoughts,
Whose lotus feet are worshipped by the universe.
O lotus seated upon a lotus,
Joy dost thou cause to those who salute Thee,
Destroyer of Ignorance,
Spouse of Hari,[3]
Substance of the world.[4]

2

AIM, AIM[5] is Thy favourite *mantra*,
Thou who art both form and formlessness,[6]
Who art the wealth of the lotus face of the lotus-born,[7]
Embodiment of all *guṇas*,[8] yet devoid of attributes,[9]
Changeless, and neither gross nor subtle.[10]

---

[1] She is seated on and represented as surrounded by lotuses.

[2] *Dāvāgni*. She destroys such thoughts.

[3] Viṣṇu

[4] *Samsārasāre*. The *samsāra* is the illusory world of birth and rebirth, which is said to be *asara* (unreal, unsubstantial, fleeting). The reality behind this phenomenal illusion is the Devi, who plays, and whose play is world-play.

[5] The *vāgbhavabīja*.

[6] *Rūpārūpaprakāśe*.

[7] Brahmā, whose Spouse She is.

[8] The "qualities," or conditions, which are the substance of *Prakṛti* or *sattva, rajas,* and *tamas*.

[9] She is *nirguṇā*, for She and the *Parabrahman* are in Their essence one.

[10] The forms of the Devī are threefold: *parā* (supreme), *sūkṣmā* (subtle), which consists of *mantra* and *sthūla* (gross or physical), with hands and feet. But She is neither of these in the sense that the only true form (*svarūpa*) is above and beyond them both.

None know Thy nature, nor is Thy inner reality
known.[1]
Thou art the whole universe;
And Thou it is who existeth within it.
Thou art saluted by the foremost of Devas.
Without part Thou existeth in Thy fulness everywhere.[2]
Ever[3] pure art Thou.

3

Greatly art Thou pleased with the recitation[4] of the *mantra HRĪM.*[5]
Thy crown is white as snow.[6]
Thy hands play with the *vīnā.*[7]
O Mother! Mother! salutation to Thee.
Burn, burn my sloth and grant me great intelligence.[8]
Thou art Knowledge itself.
The *Vedānta* ever sings of Thee.

---

[1] *Nāpivijnātatattve*; another reading being ***nāpivijnānatattve.*** The reference is to Her supreme (***para***) form, of which the Viṣṇu Yāmala says "none know" (***Mātastvatparamam rūpam tannajānāti kashcana*** (see chap. iii. of the S'āktānandatarangini).

[2] She as the Brahman is ***akhaṇḍa*** "everywhere" and yet in the limited sense "nowhere," in the sense that She is at some particular place and not elsewhere, or partly here and partly there.

[3] In past, present, and future.

[4] ***Japa,*** which includes that which would not be understood as recitation in the English sense—viz., ***manasa*** or mental, and the inaudible ***japa.***

[5] The bīja of the Devī.

[6] Her colour is white

[7] A stringed musical instrument.

[8] *Dehibuddhimprashastām*; the great prayer to Her.

S'ruti[1] speaks of Thee.
O giver of liberation ! O way to liberation !
Whose power is beyond all understanding.
O giver of happiness,[2] adorned with a white necklace,[3]
Grant to me Thy favours.

4

Thou art intelligence, intelligence, intelligence,[4]
Thy names are memory, resolution, mind, and hymn of praise.[5]
Eternal and fleeting,[6]
Great cause, saluted by *Munis*,[7]
New and old ;[8] sacred current of virtue,[9]
Saluted by Hari and Hara.[10]
Ever pure, beauteous of colour,
The subtlest element[11] of things—

---

[1] Revelation; generally applied to the Vedas in which Sarasvatī is spoken of (see Muir, O.S.T., verse 339). She is also called Mother of Vedas.

[2] *S'āradā.*

[3] See note 5, p. 74, *ante*.

[4] *Dhī.*

[5] *Dhāranā, dhriti* (or constancy), *mati*. She is the "hymn of praise," for it is composed of words, and She is the Devī thereof, and word and speech itself.

[6] She eternally exists as the reality behind all appearance, and is the cause of the fleeting appearance itself.

[7] Sages.

[8] See note 6 *ante*. She ever appears in new forms, and yet Herself in Her aspect as *Atmā*, persists as the one and same.

[9] *Punya.*

[10] Viṣṇu and S'iva.

[11] *Mātra*—the atomic part of things.

Yea, even the very half thereof.[1]
Thou art the giver of intelligence, intelligence, intelligence.
Who art the giver of joy to Mādhava.[2]

5

In the form of *HRĪM*, *KṢĪM*, *DHĪM*, *HRĪM*,[3]
Thou holdest a book,
Thou art joyful, of smiling face, and of good fortune.
Innocence, current of charm,[4]
With all powers of arrest[5].
Burn, burn my sin,
And dispel the darkness of my evil thoughts.
O praiseworthy of all!
Thou art *Gih*, *Gauh*, *Vāk*, and *Bhāratī*.[6]
It is Thou who grantest success to the tongue of the greatest of poets,

---

[1] *Mātrārdhatattve*. She is so very subtle : or alternatively the Mātrārdha below the *Sāhasrāra*.

[2] The husband of Mā or Lakṣmi—that is, Viṣṇu, whose Spouse She was. She as Prakṛti gives joy to the *paramātmā*, who is the enjoyer (*bhoktā*).

[3] The mantra, as currently recited is *Om Om Kshīm*, *Kshīm*, *svarupe*. "*Kshīm*," for She is the destructress of sin.

[4] *Mohemugdhapravāhe*. *Mugdhā* is generally used in connection with *nāyikā*—that is, a simple, artless innocent maiden, as yet unacquainted with love. The general and correct reading is *mugdhemohapravāhe*.

[5] *Stambhanam* ; one of the six "magical" powers known as the *ṣatkarma*, whereby a person may be paralyzed in action or speech. So a disputant might seek the power of *stambhanam* to close the mouth of, or confuse his adversary.

[6] Various words which all mean "word" or "speech."

As also in the attainment of all (forms of) knowledge.[1]

6

I pray to Thee, I pray to Thee, I bow to Thee,
Come to my tongue and never leave me.
May my intelligence[2] never go astray,
May my sins be taken away,
May I be free from sorrow.
In time of peril may I never be bewildered.
May my mind work freely without impediment[3]
In *Śāstra* disputation and verse.

7

He who chastely[4] lives, observing silence[5] and religious devotions,[6]
Abstaining from flesh and fish[7] on the thirteenth day of the month,[8]
And bowed with devotion, early each morning
Praises Thee with the most excellent verse.
Will, skilful in speech, surpass even Vācaspati.[9]
The uncleanliness of his sins will be swept away.
Such an one gains the fruit of his desires,

---

[1] Literally, the giver of *siddhi* (success) in all knowledge of which She is the presiding Devī.

[2] Both *buddhi* and *manas*.

[3] *Prasaratu* ("flow freely").

[4] He who is *brahmachārin*. Here commences the *phala* portion of the *stotra*.

[5] *Maunin*.

[6] *Vratin*. The *vrata* are voluntary religious practices and devotions as distinguished from the obligatory daily ritual.

[7] *Nirāmishah*.

[8] The *trayodaśi*; the *Sarasvati vrata* day.

[9] Or Brihaspati, the Lord of Speech.

The Devī protects him as though he were Her
own child.
Poetry flows from his mouth,
Prosperity attends his house,
And every obstacle to success will disappear.

8

Whoever reads without interruption the whole of
this hymn
Twenty-one times on the thirteenth day of the
month,[1]
Both on the dark and the light side of the month,[2]
And meditates on Sarasvatī garmented in white,
Adorned with white ornaments,
Such an one attains in this world the fruit of his
desires.
This auspicious hymn has been made by Brahmā
himself;
Whoever daily reads it with care acquires
immortality.[3]

---

[1] *Trayodaśi*

[2] The month is divided into two halves (*pakṣa*), according as the moon is waxing or waning.

[3] *Amṛtatvam*—that is, liberation (*mukti*).

DURGĀ[1]

(DURGĀS'ATANĀMA STOTRA)[2]

From the VIS'VASĀRA TANTRA

1

Saith Īśvara :[3]
I shall tell thee the hundred names of Durgā.
By the grace of this hymn the chaste[4] Durgā is satisfied.
Listen, then, thereto.

2-13

OM.
Chaste one.[5]

---

[1] Manifestation of the S'akti of S'iva in warrior form as the Destructress of demonic beings, enemies to *Devas* and men. According to one account, She is so called as having slain the Asura Durgā, son of Ruru (Skanda Purāṇa). Another account of the origin of Durgā is given in Candī (Mārkandeyapurāṇa), where the combined *tejas*, like a mountain of all the Devas, manifested as the Devi Durgā for the destruction of the *Asura* Mahiṣa.

[2] P. 573, Tantrasāra from the Viśvasāra Tantra.

[3] The Lord S'iva.

[4] *Satī*.

[5] *Satī*, or faithful. The name of the daughter of Dakṣa. Brahma Pr. says: " The faithful Spouse Satī became Umā, who ever dwells with S'iva."

Virtuous one.[1]
Beloved of Bhava.[2]
Spouse of Bhava.[3]
The Manifested Brahman.[4]
Liberatrix from the world of births and deaths.
Destructress of distress.[6]
Victorious one.[7]
Primordial one.[8]
Three-eyed,[9]
Holder of the spear.[10]

---

1 *Sādhvi*, or chaste. She is of unequalled virtue as being attached to none but Her Lord (see Lalitā, verse 43, where Bhāskararāya cites the Ācārya (Saundaryalahari), which says: "How many poets share the wife of Brahmā? Cannot everyone by means of wealth become the Lord of S'rī (Viṣṇu)? But, O virtuous one, first among faithful women, your breasts are untouched save by Mahādeva, not even by the paste of Kuravaka." (a kind of paste made of the leaves of the red amaranth used to redden the cheeks, breasts, palms, and soles of Hindu women). Devī Bhāg. Pr. also says: "Thou art praised as Sādhvi on account of Thy unequalled fidelity to Thy Lord."

2 *Bhavaprita*. Bhava is S'iva

3 *Bhavāni*.

4 *Aryā*, which literally means noble, but which here means, as the commentator Nilakaṇṭha says in reference to the hymn to Durgā in the Mahābhārata (see *post*) *prāpyabrahmasvarūpa*, the own form of the accessible Brahman as distinguished from the *Nirguṇa* Brahman beyond thought and speech. The very nature of the Devi is manifestation, and She is near to us in the world.

5 *Bhavamochinī*—that is, from the *samsāra* or phenomenal world.

6 Durgā—that is, *Sa ya durgatim harati*.

7 *Jayā*

8 *Ādyā*.

9 *Trinetrā*.

10 *S'ūladhārinī*. The *śūla* is a weapon of the Devī.

Spouse of Him who holds the *pināka* Bow.[1]
Wonderful one.[2]
Whose bell sounds fearfully.[3]
Of great austerities.[4]
Manas.[5]
Buddhi.[6]
Ahamkāra.[7]
In the form of *citta.*[8]
Funeral pyre.[9]
Knowledge.[10]
Whose substance is all *mantras.*[11]
Reality.[12]

---

[1] *Pinākadhārini*—that is, Spouse of S'iva, who wields the *Pināka* bow broken by Rāma ; hence he is called *Pinākin.*

[2] *Citrā.*

[3] *Candaghantā,* the first of the nine Durgās in the *Durgā Kavaca.*

[4] *Mahātapāh.* For the Devī as Umā Aparṇā did great austerities to gain S'iva as Her husband.

[5] See p. 87, note 5 *post.*

[6] *Ibīd.*

[7] *Ibīd.*

[8] *Cittarupā.* *Citta* is mental substance.

[9] *Citā,* which in Tantra has a twofold meaning (*smaśānam dvividham Devī citā yonīmāheśvari*) for, whereas on the first the body is burnt, so in the second is the fire which consumes passion (Niruttara Tantra, chap. i.).

[10] *Citih = jnānā.*

[11] *Sarvamantramayī.*

[12] *Satyā,* that which persists through the threefold time—past, present, and future—of which the opposite is *asatyā.* That which is real and not fictitious (*yathārthasvarūpa*). The epithet *Satyā,* which occurs thrice in this *stotra,* has also, besides "real," three other meanings: (1) Eternal, (2) the best (*uttamā*), and (3) *sthitiśila,* whose nature it is to exist.

Whose nature is the true bliss.[1]
Endless one.[2]
In whom are the three dispositions.[3]
Accessible by devotion.[4]
Auspicious.[5]
Pervading all things.[6]
Spouse of S'ambu.[7]
Mother of *Devas*.[8]
Contemplation.[9]
Fond of gems.[10]
All knowledge.[11]
Daughter of Dakṣa.[12]

---

1 *Satyānandasvarūpinī.*

2 *Anantā.*

3 *Bhāvini.* In the ordinary sense *bhāvini*, as sentimental, emotional, is a term which, according to the Amarakośa, is commonly applied to women, as are the terms *pramadā* (pleasing), *kāntā* and *lalanā* (beautiful), and *nitambinī* (possessing beautiful *nitamba* or buttocks). But here the word refers to the *bhāvas, paśu, vīra,* and *divya,* which are each manifestations of Her.

4 *Bhāvagamyā.*

5 *Bhāvyā.*

6 *Sadāgatih.*

7 *S'āmbhavī,* Spouse of S'iva (S'ambhu).

8 *Devamātā.*

9 *Cintā.*

10 *Ratnapriyā.*

11 *Sarvavidyā*; and so also the Lalitā, verse 137, speaks of Her as being all the *S'āstras* (*śāstramayī*). The Brahma Pr. says that from Her breath came the Vedas; from the tip of Her throat the sixty-four sciences; from the rest of Her limbs all other Tantras; and from Her shoulders the science of love.

12 *Dakṣakanyā.* Dakṣa was one of the Prajāpatis and father-in-law of S'iva, who was married to his daughter Satī, a manifestation of the Devī.

Destroyer of Dakṣa's sacrifice.[1]
Who eat not even a leaf during Thy austerities.[2]
Of various colour.[3]
Red.[4]
Having a red colour.[5]
Clad in silken garment.[6]
Pleased with sweet-sounding anklets.[7]
Of unbounded power.[8]
Terrifying.[9]
Beautiful.[10]
House lady.[11]
Forest Durgā.[12]
Daughter of Matanga.[13]

---

[1] *Dakṣayajnavināśinī.* Because on Her account S'iva, Her husband, destroyed the *dakṣayajna.*

[2] *Aparṇā* (see Hymn entitled " May the Devi Grant Me Pardon ", *post*).

[3] *Anekavarṇā.*

[4] *Pātalā* : a reddish-pink, the colour of the Bhairavimurti.

[5] *Pātalāvatī.*

[6] *Pattāmbara paridhānā.*

[7] *Kalamanjīraranjinī.*

[8] *Amiyavikramā.*

[9] *Krūrā.* Literally, " cruel "—that is, to the demonic beings which She destroyed, though even not truly so, for as Candī says, She destroyed them not only for the happiness of the world, but for their own happiness, so that being slain by Her hand they might go to heaven.

[10] *Sundarī.*

[11] *Purasundarī.*

[12] *Vanadurgā* : the Devī of the forests. The foresters, before entering the forests, offer *pūjā* to Vanadurgā as protectress against their dangers and terrors.

[13] *Mātangī* ; that is, of the *Ṛṣi* Matanga.

Worshipped by the sage Matanga.[1]
Spouse of Brahmā.[2]
Great Ruler.[3]
Aindrī.[4]
Kaumārī.[5]
Vaiṣṇavī.[6]
Cāmundā.[7]
Varāhi.[8]
Lakṣmi.[9]
In the form of the Puruṣa.[10]
Pure one.[11]

---

1 *Matangamunipūjitā.*

2 *Brāhmī.*

3 *Maheśvarī* (feminine of Maheśvara), an appellation of S'iva.

4 Spouse of Indra, one of the eight Mātṛkās.

5 Spouse of Kārtikeya or Skanda, the leader of the celestial hosts. The Devī is also Mother both of Kumāra and Gananātha (Gaṇeśa), and is so called in the Lalitā, verse 94 (*Kumāragananāthāmbā*), where it is said that the Devatā of egoism (*ahamkāra*) is Kumāra. The Varāha Pr. says : "Viṣṇu is the Puruṣa, or S'iva is so called, Avyaktā is Umā or Laksmī, the lotus-eyed. From the interaction of these two arises *ahamkāra*. This *ahamkāra* is the *guha* (*skanda*), the leader of the army."

6 The *vaiṣṇavī śakti*.

7 See Hymn entitled " May the Devi Grant Me Pardon ", *post*.

8 S'akti of Varāha, the boar incarnation, one of the eight *Mātṛkas*.

9 Devī of wealth, prosperity, and beauty.

10 *Puruṣākritih.* Puruṣa is man, male, or person; the primeval man ; the spirit of the universe, manifesting as Brahmā, Viṣṇu, S'iva, etc. ; the passive spectator of the acts of Prakṛti. But in their ground both are one. Therefore Devī is in such sense Puruṣa also. So Kṛṣṇa, to screen his action from Rādhikā, manifested as Kālī.

11 *Vimalā.*

Essence of all.[1]
Knowledge.[2]
Action.[3]
The Supreme One.[4]
Giver of *buddhi*.[5]
Who art all.[6]
Whose love is unbounded.[7]
Mounted on a bull.[8]
Destructress of S'umbha and Niśumbha.[9]
Slayer of the Asura Mahiṣa.[10]
Slayer of Madhu and Kaitaba.[11]
Destructress of Caṇḍa and Muṇḍa.[12]
And of all Asuras.[13]

---

[1] *Utkarṣinī,*.

[2] *Jnānā*, for the Devī is *jnānā, kriyā*, and *ichchhā śakti*.

[3] *Kriyā*.

[4] *Satyā* (see *ante*, p. 83, note 12).

[5] *Buddhidā*. *Buddhi* (intellect), the function of which is determination (*niścayakārinī*), is part of the fourfold *antahkaraṇa*: constituted by *Buddhi* and *Manas* (aspects of mind), *Ahamkāra* (egoity) and *cintā* (contemplation).

[6] *Bahula-bhumā*.

[7] *Bahulapremā*.

[8] *Sarvavāhanavāhanā*. Literally whose vehicle (*vāhana*) is the *vāhana* of Sarva (S'iva), or a bull.

[9] *Niśumbhaśumbhahananī*. These were two *Daityas*, or enemies of the Devas, slain by the Devī (see Candī). The Daityas were sons of Diti and the Devas children of Aditi, hence they are called *Āditeya*.

[10] *Mahiṣāsuramardinī* (*vide ibid.*).

[11] *Madhukaitabahantrī*. Two *Daityas* (*ibid*).

[12] *Caṇḍamuṇḍavināśinī* : two generals of S'umbha and Niśumbha (*ibid.*)

[13] *Sarvāsuravinarśa*.

And of all Dānavas.[1]
Whose substance is all *S'āstra.*[2]
Existence.[3]
Holder of all weapons.[4]
In whose hands are various weapons.[5]
Holder of many weapons.[6]
Virgin.[7]
Maiden.[8]
Kaiṣorī.[9]
Youthful.[10]
Ascetic one.[11]
Apraudhā.[12]

---

1 *Sarvadānavaghātinī.* The Dānavas were enemies of the Devas, children of Danu, a daughter of Dakṣa and Kāśyapa.

2 *Sarvaśāstramayī.*

3 *Satyā.*

4 *Sarvāstradhāriṇī. Astra* is a weapon which is thrown—a projectile ; and *śastra,* in the next verse, is a weapon which is held.

5 *Anekaśastrahastā* (see last note).

6 *Anekāstrasyadhāriṇī.*

7 *Kumārī.*

8 *Kanyā.*

9 A girl up to fifteen years of age is so called (*Kaiṣoram āpancadaśāt*). It is said that up to sixteen years one is known as *bālā.* At thirty one is *Taruṇī,* at fifty-five *praudhā,* and above that *vriddhā.* As the verse runs :

Aṣōdaśād bhaved bālā,
Trinśatā tarunī matā,
Panca pancāśatā praudhā,
Bhaved vriddhā tatah param.

10 *Yuvatī.*

11 *Yati* : one who controls the passions is an ascetic. The Devī practised great austerities to gain S'iva as Her husband.

12 That is, below fifty-five years old, an adult woman who is no longer bashful or timid in the presence of her lord.

Praudhā.[1]
Old mother.[2]
Giver of strength.[3]

14

For him who daily reads[4] these 108[5] names of Durgā
There is nothing impossible in the three worlds.
He obtains wealth, crops, sons, wife, horses, and elephants ;
He accomplishes the *caturvarga*,[6]
And gains lasting liberation.

15

Having worshipped the Devī Kumārī,[7]
And meditated upon Sureśvarī,[8]
The devotee should worship, [9]
And then read with devotion the 108 names of Durgā.
O Devi ! such an one gains the fruition[10] which *Devas* have ;

[1] Over fifty-five years old.

[2] *Vriddhamātā.*

[3] *Balapradā.* The litany in the Tantrasāra here ends at the 87th name, short of the prescribed number of names.

[4] Here commences the *phala* portion.

[5] *Sic* ; *vide ante.* Wherever 100 or 1,000 is mentioned (the former in the title of the present hymn) 108 or 1,008 is to be understood, for zero is an inauspicious number.

[6] *Dharma, artha, kāma,* and *mokṣa*—piety, wealth, desire, and liberation—(see *Introduction to Tantra S'āstra*).

[7] See " Hymn to Annapurṇā " *post.*

[8] Mistress of Suras (Devas).

[9] *i.e.,* make *pūja.*

[10] *Siddhi* (see *Introduction to Tantra S'āstra*).

Kings become his servants,
And he obtains a kingdom and all prosperity.

16

He who, versed in the *śāstric* injunctions
In accordance therewith, writes this *mantra*
With saffron mixed with cows' pigment,[1] red lac,[2]
camphor, and the three sweets,[3]
And then wears it, becomes himself Purāri.[4]

17

Whoever writes and then reads this hymn
On a Tuesday in *Amāvāsya*,[5]
At night, when the moon is in *S'atabhiṣā*,[6]
Attains all wealth and prosperity.

---

[1] *Gorocanā*.

[2] *Alakta*.

[3] *Madhutraya*—that is, ghee, honey, and sugar.

[4] S'iva.

[5] The fifteenth day of the dark half of the lunar month; a very dark day on which *S'avāsana* and similar rites are also accomplished.

[6] There are twenty-seven lunar mansions, of which *S'atabhiṣā* is the twentyfourth, containing a hundred stars.

TRIPUṬĀ[1]

(TRIPUṬĀSTOTRAM)

FROM THE TANTRASĀRA[2]

1

I CONTEMPLATE the good Guru who is Light itself,[3]
Sitting with his *S'akti*[4]
In the lotus of the head,[5]
Two-armed, gracious, very gracious,
Whose moon-like face is full of grace,
Making with his hands the gestures which grant
boons and dispel fear.[6]

2

Such as recite[7] thy primordial golden *bija*

---

[1] Tripuṭā and Tripurā are separate Devis, but the former is *antargatā* of Tripurā—that is, forms part, is included in, and a particular manifestation of Tripurā. In the same way the Devis Ekajaṭa, Nilasarasvati, Ugratārā, Mahogrā, are each *antargatā* of Tārā.

[2] Tantrasāra, p. 571.

[3] *Prakāśasvarūpa*. *Prakāśa* is light and manifestation.

[4] Spouse.

[5] That is, the *Sahasrārapadma*.

[6] That is, he is making the two *mudrās* called *vara* and *abhaya* respectively.

[7] Literally, " make *japa* ".

S'RĪM,[1]
Attain all prosperity and fortune.

3

O Mother!
He who contemplates Thy second *bīja*,
Adorned by numbers of Devas,
"*HRĪM,*"[2]
Gains all prosperity.

4

The chiefs of men who meditate upon Thy *bīja*,
Lustrous as the sun,

---

[1] As is frequently the case in Tāntrik works, the *mantra* is not given in the text, but must be spelt out. Thus the Sanskrit is *vakamvahnisamstham trimurtyā prajuṣṭam śaśānkenayuktam*—that is, "*vakam* with *vahni* attended by *trimurti*, combined with *śaśāngka.*" *Vakam* = "S'" (*tālavya*). *Vahni* is the "fire." ="r," *trimūrti* = the long vowel ī, and *śaśāngka,* the moon in "whose lap is the hare," or "man in the moon" = "m" (*anusvāra*). S'+r+ī+m = *śrīm* the *Lakshmībīja* (see the Ādyakālīstotra of Mahānirvāṇa Tantra).

[2] Literally, *Nabhovahni* (not *vāyu,* as the text has it, for the *vāyu bīja* is *yam*); *miśram* (not *mitram* as Prasanna Kumāra Shāstrī's edition has it); *tatovāmanetram sudhā dhāmavimbam niyojyaikāvaktram*—that is, *nabhas* combined with *vahni,* and then *vāmanetra* and the receptacle of nectar (the moon) applicable in the case of Ekavaktra. *Nabhas*= "*ha*" or "*bha*" (here the former), *vahni* = "*ra,*" *vāmanetra* = long ī, and the moon is *anusvāra* ("m"), H+r+ī+m = *Hrīm,* known as the *māyā bīja.* Then the *śloka* more clearly points to the *bīja* meant by saying it is that applicable to Ekavaktra. The latter is the Bhairava of Bagalāmukhī, whose *bīja* is also *Hrīm.*

" *KLĪM*,"[1]
Charm the three worlds,
And by recitation thereof become like unto Īśvara.

5

O beloved of the enemy of Smara ! [2]
Those who contemplate Thy body[3] thrice[4] and recite these three *bījas*[5]
Render their enemies speechless,
Lakṣmī shines in their house,
And they become the God of Love[6] to women.

6

The presiding Devatā of Speech
Blesses their mouth with poetry and prose.
Harmful animals cause them no harm,
Even the Suras[7] salute them.

---

[1] Literally, *Virinchim kṣitistham tatovāmanetram vidhum nādayuktam*—that is, *virinchi*, *kṣiti* and *vāmanetra*, together with moon combined with *nāda*. *Virinchi* = " *ka* ", *kṣiti* = "*La*," *vāmanetra* = long ī, the moon = " m " (*anusvāra*). K + l + ī + m = *Klīm*. The three elements of the mantra are given—viz., *S'rīm, Hrīm, Klīm*—but the actual *bīja* of Tripuṭā is *S'rīm, Hrīm, Klīm, Hrīm, S'rīm, Klīm, Klīm, S'rīm, Hrīm*.

[2] The Deva of love (Kāma), of whom S'iva is described as the enemy, for he burnt him with the fire of his eye (see p. 40, note 1).

[3] *Anga*.

[4] Literally, make *japa*. "Thrice," as follows *S'rīm, Hrīm, Klīm, Hrīm, S'rīm, Klīm, Klīm, S'rīm, Hrīm*."

[5] See last note.

[6] The beautiful youth Kāma. *Cf.* Verse 5 of Karpūrādistotra.

[7] The Devas.

Their feet are the head ornaments of kings,[1]
The *siddhis*[2] are in their hands,
Malignant stars relinquish them.

7

Let the *Sādhaka* meditate upon an eight-petalled lotus[3]
Set upon a throne studded with various gems,
Placed upon an altar
Standing on the floor of a jewelled house
Amidst a forest of *Pārijāta* trees.[4]

8

Let him then meditate upon two angles[5] in the lotus,
And the Devī Herself in the lotus as follows:
Her lustre is that of molten gold,
With earrings[6] on her ears,
Three-eyed, of beauteous throat,
Her face like the moon,
And bending from the weight of Her breasts.[7]

9

She holds in many arms, decked with diamonds and other gems,

---

1 That is, he sets his feet on the heads of kings.

2 The great powers, *aṇimā*, *laghimā*, etc. (see p. 18, note 6).

3 The heart lotus (not *anāhata*) in which the *Iṣṭadevata* is worshipped.

4 One of the celestial trees (see HYMN "Wave of Bliss", *post*).

5 *Yoni*. There are five *yonis* or *śakti* angles in the *S'rīcakra*.

6 *Kuṇḍala*.

7 *Subakṣojanamrām*.

Two lotuses, a noose,[1] bow, golden goad,[2] and
flowery arrows.[3]
Her body is adorned with great jewels,
Slender is She of waist[4] and beautifully girdled.

10

Her lotus feet glitter with beautiful anklets,[6]
Crowned, adorned, and gracious,
Holding two white fly-whisks,[7] a mirror, jewel-
case,[8] and a box filled with camphor.[9]

11

Creatrix of the three worlds,
Destructress of the pain of the world,
Destructress and ruler of the world,
Ever full of Bliss,

---

[1] *Pāśakam.*

[2] *Angkuśa.*

[3] *Puṣpavānām* (see Comm. Lalitā, verse 2) According to the Yoginīhṛdaya, the noose is *Ichchā*; the goad, *jnāna*; and the bow and arrows the *kṛyā śaktis* respectively.

[4] *Sumadhyām.*

[5] She wears a *candrahāra,* so called because it has a moonlike ornament in its centre.

[6] *Tulākota.*

[7] *Cāmara* or chowrie, the bushy tail of the Cāmara (the yak; *bos grunniens*), used as a fly-whisk or fan, an insignia of royalty, and also used as a streamer on the heads of horses.

[8] *Karanda—alangkāra pātra.*

[9] *Samudgam,* translated in the Bengali as a *pān*-box with camphor, which is put into *pān* (betel).

Half of the letter *Hā* ;[1] of the nature of the threefold *Bindu*,[2]
The threefold *S'akti*,[3]
It is Her I worship.

12

The *Sādhaka* who, having thus for a long time contemplated Her
On a *yantra*[4] set before him,
And welcomed[5] her with great deuotion,
Worshipping Her with *Svayambhu* flower[6]
Attains, even though he be of the lowest[7] *siddhi*[8] in the *caturvarga*.[9]

---

[1] *Hakārārddhavarṇām*—that is, She is *Kāmakalā-svarūpā* (see Ādyākālīstotram, p. 43, and the *Kāmakalāvilāsa*, cited in the Lalitā sahasranāma, verse 73.) Another name for *Kāmakalāsvarūpā* is *Kāmapurasvarūpā*. The half *Ha* resembles a *bindu*, of which there are three—viz., the *bindu* at the base of the triangle from which the *A-ka-tha trikoṇa* emanated and the *visargah* above. See Kālīcarana's commentary on the Pādukāpancakam, in *The Serpent Power*.

[2] *Tribindusvarūpā*—there are three such in *Kāmakalā*.

[3] *Jnāna, ichchhā,* and *kryā śaktis* of the Devī.

[4] Diagram used in Tantrik worship (see *Introduction to Tantra S'āstra*.)

[5] With the *āvāhana mantra*—viz., *iha āgacha iha āgacha, iha tishtha, iha tishtha atra adishthānam kuru mama pujām, grihāna.* ("Come here, come here ! Stay here, stay here ! accept my worship ").

[6] See Mātṛkābheda Tantra. The word *puṣpa* (flower) has here a technical sense. *Puṣpaśabdena atra riturucyate. Mātṛkābhedatantra pramānānusārena anurāyāh kanyāyāh prathama eva riturātrā uccyate. Tantrāntaretu vivāhitāyāh eva bālāyāh rituratra vivakṣitah.*

[7] *Pāmara*, one who is low or vile, a very contumelious term.

[8] Success, perfection. fruition.

[9] That is, *Dharma* (religion, piety), *artha* (wealth), *Kāma* (desire and its fulfilment), and *Mokṣa* (liberation). (See *Introduction to Tantra S'āstra*).

13

Whoever after having done worship[1]
Of S'ri,[2] S'ripati,[3] Pārvati,[4] Īśvara,[5] Rati,[6] and
Kāmadeva,[7]
Together with the *Ṣadānga* Devatā[1] of the Devi,
Recites[2] the *mantra* on Thy *yantra*,[10]
Becomes a King among men.

14

Having worshipped the two *nidhis*,[11] S'ankha and
Padma,
On the two sides of the lotus,

---

1 *Pūjā.*

2 *Lakṣmī.*

3 *Viṣṇu.*

4 Devī as daughter of Himavat.

5 S'iva.

6 Spouse of Kāma, the God of Love.

7 The God of Love.

8 That is, the six *āvarana* or attendant Devatās on the Devī.

9 Makes *japa* of.

10 See *Introduction to Tantra S'āstra.*

11 There are eight gems or treasures (*nidhi*) of Kubera—viz., *padma, mahāpadma, makara, kachchapa, mukunda, nīla, nanda, śankha.* The Mārkaṇḍeya Purāṇa gives the meaning of *nidhi* in the followng *śloka* (" Lakṣmī is the presiding *Devatā* of the *vidyā,* called *Padminī.* The *nidhis* are Her supporters. Listen while I speak of them ") :

Padminīnāma yā vidyā,
Lakṣmī stadadhi devatā,
Tadādhārāsca nidhaya,
Stan me nivadatah śrinu.

And the Mahiṣis,[1] regents of the quarters,[2] and
their weapons,
Attains, even though he be of the most vile,[3] the
eight *siddhis*[4] of S'iva.

15

Thou art the earth, *Vidhātrī*,[5] creatrix of the world;[6]
Thou art water, and in the form of Viṣnu preserveth the world;
Thou art fire, and in the form of Rudra destroyeth
the world;
Thou existeth in the form of *Aiśvarya*;[7]
Thou art the air of the world.

16

Thou art the primeval[5] and auspicious one,[8]
Spouse of S'ambhu,[9] refuge (of Thy worshippers).

---

1 That is, the S'aktis Brāhmī, etc.

2 The *lokapālas* or guardians of the points of the compass (N., N. W., W., S. W., N.E, E., S.E., and S. Indra, Yama, Varuna, Kubera, Vivasvat, Soma, Agni and Vāyu).

3 *Pāmara.*

4 *Aṇimā*, *Laghima*, etc.

5 *Vidhātrī* = Creatrix; but both the terms *Vidhātrī* and Creatrix of the world are used in the text.

6 The six *aiśvarya* are *S'rī* (beauty and auspiciousness), *Vīrya* (power), *jñāna* (Wisdom), *Vairāgya* (dispassion), *Kīrti* (glory) and *Māhātmya* (greatness). Bhagavan is He who is possessed of these six *aiśvarya*. All these are in the Devī who is hence called Bhagavatī (see Devī Bhāg. Pr., Saktirahasya; Bhāskararāya, *op. cit.*, verse 65), and as here, *Aiśvarya rūpā.*

7 *Ādyā.*

8 *S'ivé*, voc. of *S'ivé*, feminine of *S'iva.*

9 S'iva.

Who ever moves in the *Brahmarandhra*[1] of the world
The supporter of all, yet Thyself without support.
The only pure One in the form of ether.[2]
O Bhavānī ! be gracious to me.

17

Thou hast humbled the pride even of the *Ṛṣis*
By plunging them into the ocean of the world.
Thou art intelligence and bliss and light itself.[3]
How, then, can I know thee ?
O Bhavānī ! be gracious to me.

18

O Bhavānī ! even an ignorant man[4]
Who, meditating on Thy form, recites[5] Thy *mantra* a *lakh* of times
Acquires all poetic power,
And those things in the three worlds which are most difficult of attainment.
O Bhavānī ! be gracious to me.

19

Thou art that which supports[6] and that which is supported.[7]
Thou pervadeth the world,

---

1 The opening in the top of the head, whence in the case of *yogis* the soul on death issues.

2 *Ākāśakalpā*.

3 *Prakāśasvarūpā*.

4 *Mandaceta*.

5 Makes *japa*.

6 *Ādhāraśakti*.

7 *Tvāmādheyarūpā*.

And art in the form of the world which is pervaded
by Thee.[1]
Thou art both negation[2] and existence.[3]
O Bhavānī ! be gracious to me.

20

Thou art the atom[4] and ever-pervading.[5]
Thou art the whole universe.
No praise of Thee is sufficient.
Yet Thy qualities prompt me to sing Thy praise.
O Bhavānī ! be gracious to me.

21

To him who reads and recites [6] at morn, noon, and
evening
This most secret hymn,
There is nothing impossible in the three worlds,
Such an one attains Thy nature.[7]
O Bhavānī ! be gracious to me.

---

1 *Jagatvyāpyarūpā.*

2 *Abhāva,* the last of the seven categories of Kanāda's system (Vaiśeṣika Sūtra). Thus darkness is the *abhāva* of light.

3 *Bhāva.*

4 *Aṇu.*

5 *Vibhu.*

6 Makes *japa.*

7 *Svarūpam labhante*—that is, he attains that form of liberation which is known as *svārūpya mukti* (receiving the same form as that of the Devatā worshipped).

HYMNS TO THE DEVĪ
FROM PURĀṆA

MOTHER OF THE WHOLE UNIVERSE

(SARVAVIS'VAJANANĪ)

FROM THE DEVĪBHĀGAVATA[1]

1

I call to mind the Mother of the whole universe,
Who has created this world, both real and unreal,[2]
And who, by Her own power with its three *guṇas*,[3]
Protects it, and having destroyed it, She then
plays,[4]

---

[1] First Skandha, (chap. ii.).

[2] *Sadāsatsvarūpam*, on which Nīlakaṇṭha says: *Vyavahāra drishtyā sat, paramārthadarshanena asat*; that is the world is real (*sat*) from the point of view of practical life and reason; to all those, in short, who have not experimentally realized the *Advaita Tattva*; but to those who have, and from the transcendental standpoint, it is, in fact, unreal (*asat*).

[3] *Sattva, rajas*, and *tamas*, the substance of S'akti, as *Prakṛti* (see Introduction).

[4] *Ramate*—that is, "in her own self" (*svasminnevakrīrate*) (*N*) She shines. Hence She is also called Lalitā. "She who plays;" Padma pr. says, "having passed beyond the worlds, She plays; hence She is called Lalitā." Beyond S'akti and S'iva there exist various manifestations of Parāśakti and Sadāśiva, each in its own sphere. But Mahāśakti, who is Paramaśiva, crossing all worlds in the supreme sphere of *Mahākailāsa*. She it is who is known as Lalitā and Kāmeśvarī.

2

Commonly is it said that Brahmā creates the universe,
Yet the learned in Veda and Purāṇā
Speak of His birth from the navel lotus of Murāri,[1]
Although it is said He creates, yet He is Himself dependent therein.[2]

3

Even Murāri in the blossom of whose navel lotus, Brahmā was born—
Deeply sleeps upon his serpent bed[3] at the time of dissolution.
Therefore Ananta with his thousand hoods is His support.
How can He who is Himself supported
Be called a leader[4] in the creation of the world?

4

Even the water of Ocean[5] which is a liquid substance
Cannot exist without a container; therefore[6]
I take refuge with Her, the Mother of all beings,

---

[1] Viṣṇu as Enemy of the Daitya Mura.

[2] Because He is born, He creates dependent on Bhagavati. In the next verse the argument is: "Let Brahmā be not the creator; why not, then, Viṣṇu?" To which the answer is given of His dependence on Ananta.

[3] Viṣṇu reposes on the 1,000-headed Serpent Ananta.

[4] *Netra.*

[5] Which is again the support of Ananta.

[6] And that container requires a support. Therefore the *ādhāraśakti* is the Mother of all. For this reason, in commencing any *pūja*, the Ādhāraśakti is worshipped on account of Her being the supporter of all, and that S'akti is none but the Mother of all.

Who exists in all things in the form of Power.[1]

5

Brahmā in the lotus,
Seeing that the eyes of Visnu were closed in deep slumber,[2]
Prayed to that Devi with whom I take shelter.[3]

---

[1] *S'aktirūpā.*

[2] *Yoganidra*, the sleep of *pralaya*.

[3] That He might be roused from his sleep and take part in the cosmic process. Sūta continues ; "Having meditated upon Her who is *Māyā* and *Saguṇā*, and giver of liberation and *Nirguṇā*, I will tell you, O *munis*, the whole Purāṇa, which is the best and the most sacred S'rīmadbhāgavata of 18,000 Sanskrit S'lokas."

AMBIKĀ[1]

(ELEVENTH MĀHĀTMYA OF CAṆḌĪ)[2]

1

DEVĪ, Thou who removeth the pain of Thy suppliants,[3]
Be gracious, Be gracious, O Mother of the world!
Be gracious, O Queen of the universe!
Protect the universe.
Thou art, O Devī! the Iśvarī of all moving and unmoving things.[4]

2

Thou art the only support of the world,
Because Thou wert in the form of earth.
By Thee who existed in the form of water
Is the whole universe pervaded.
Thou art She whose powers are unsurpassed.

3

Thou art the Vaiṣṇavī S'akti[5] of eternal power;

---

[1] Mother.

[2] When the great Lord of the Asuras was slain by the Devī, Indra and other Devas (Agni at their head), with shining faces, offered praise to Kātyāyanī, because of the fulfilment of their desire.

[3] Literally, "Those who come to take shelter with Her."

[4] That is, the organic and inorganic world.

[5] The energy of Viṣṇu, the sustaining power of the Universe.

Thou art the seed of the universe,
And the supreme *Māyā*.
All this universe has been bewitched by Thee.
Thou, when pleased, art the cause of salvation to men.

4

All sciences are parts of Thee,
As also all women without exception[1] throughout the world.[2]
By Thee alone, O Mother! is the universe filled.
How can we praise Thee?
Art thou not beyond all Praise of highest speech?

5

When,[3] O Devi![4] being in the form of the universe,
And bestowing heaven[5] and liberation,[6]
Thou art worshipped,
What words, howsoever sublime, suffice for Thy praise?

---

[1] *Sakalā*. Nagoji Bhatta is not happy in his Commentary when he says that *sakalā* here means "endowed with the sixty-four arts" (*kalā*), such as dancing, music, painting, literature, acting, etc., and who are devoted to their husbands, modest, etc. The Devi is not, according to this noble line, in these only but in all women, however ignorant of the "arts" or low born they may be.

[2] *Vidyāh samastāstavadevi bhedāh.*
Striyah samastāh sakalā jagatsu.

The Devībhāṣyam of Panchānana Tarkaratna translates the verse as, "All sciences, all things (*bhedāh*), and all women are of Thee."

[3] The verse here changes from *upendra vajrā* to *anustup* metre.

[4] That is, She who is, as Nagoji says, of a shining nature (*dyotanaśilā*).

[5] *Svarga*.

[6] *Mukti*.

6

O Thou who existeth in the form of *buddhi*[1]
In the heart of all beings,
Who art Giver of heaven and liberation—
O Devi Nārāyaṇi ![2] salutation to Thee.

7

In the form of moments, minutes, and other fractions of time,
Thou art the cause of (worldly) change.
At the time of the dissolution of the universe
Thou art all-powerful.[3]
Nārāyaṇi all reverence to Thee.

8

O Auspicious One ! auspicious with all auspiciousness,
Accomplisher of all successful things,
Giver of refuge, Three-eyed one ;[4]
O Gaurī ![5] O Nārāyaṇi ! all reverence to Thee.

9

O Eternal One ! who art the energy[6]
Of creation, maintenance, and destruction ;

---

[1] That is, *nischayātmakam jnānam*.

[2] For she is the support of all beings ; *fem.* of Nārāyana, a name of Viṣṇu.

[3] For She is in the form of time.

[4] As is Her Spouse S'iva with his third eye of wisdom.

[5] Either as Nagoji says "white Devī," or the Devī of that name, who issued from the body of Mahādevī.

[6] The commentator says "that She is the possessor of it" (*śakti*) ; but there is in reality no difference between *śakti* and the possessor of *śakti*, though human understanding and speech may make such difference.

Who art the abode of the qualities,[1]
And are yet beyond them—[2]
O Nārāyanī ! all reverence to Thee.

10

O Thou who ever savest those in poverty and pain,
Who take shelter with Thee !
O Remover of the pains of all !
Nārāyaṇī, all reverence to Thee.

11

Rider in an aerial car yoked with swans,[3]
Who assumed the form of Brāhmanī,[4]
Who sprinklest water in which *kuśa* grass [5] is steeped [6]—
Nārāyaṇī, all reverence to Thee.

12

Who holdeth trident, moon, and serpent,[7]
Riding on a great bull [8]
In the form of Maheśvarī [9]—
Nārāyaṇī, all reverence to Thee.

---

[1] The *guṇas*—the three *sattva, rajas,* and *tamas,* and their derivatives, the *Tattwas.*

[2] Nagoji says that *guṇāśraye gunamaye=guṇāśraye agunamaye.* Though the *gunas* inhere in Her, She is not as is the *jīva,* affected by them.

[3] See next note.

[4] S'akti, or energy of Brahmā whose vehicle (*vāhana*) is a swan (*hamsa*), or flamingo, as it is variously rendered.

[5] Grass used in *pitṛ kṛyā and agni kṛyā.*

[6] As Brahmā does with the holy water (*śāntijalam*) from his pot called *kamaṇḍalu.*

[7] Associated with S'iva.

[8] The *vāhana* of S'iva.

[9] S'akti, or energy of Maheśvara or S'iva.

13

Who art attended by fowl and peacock.[1]
O faultless One!
Who holdeth a great *śakti*-weapon,[2]
And existeth in the form of Kaumārī,[3]—
Nārāyaṇī, all reverence to Thee.

14

Who holdeth Thy great implements,
Which are the conch, discus, mace, and bow;
Who art in the form of Vaiṣṇavī,[4]
Be gracious,
Nārāyaṇī, all reverence to Thee.

15

Who holdeth the formidable discus,
And hast uplifted the earth with Thy tusks[5]—
O auspicious One! in the form of a boar[6]—
Nārāyaṇī, all reverence to Thee.

16

O Thou who in the fierce man-lion form[7]
Didst put forth effort to slay the Daityas,

---

[1] Both the cock and peacock are said in the Mahābhārata to be the *vāhana* of Kārtikeya. Gopal Chakravarti renders it, however, as "the best of peacocks."

[2] A kind of missile, dart spear, lance, or pike.

[3] The S'akti of Kumāra, or Kārtikeya, son of S'iva and Pārvatī and Commander of the celestial hosts.

[4] The S'akti of Viṣṇu, who holds the conch, discus (cakra), etc.

[5] See next note.

[6] Viṣṇu, in His boar-incarnation, uplifted on His tusks the world which had been submerged in the waters.

[7] As S'akti of Viṣṇu in the *narasimha* incarnation, in which He slew the Daitya Hiranyakaśipu.

And who hast delivered the three worlds—
Nārāyaṇi, all reverence to Thee.

17

Who weareth a diadem and beareth a great thunder-bolt,
Who dazzles with Thy thousand eyes,[1]
Destructress of the life of Vritra,[2]
Who art Aindri,[3]
Nārāyani, all reverence to Thee.

18

Who art in the form of S'ivadūti,[4]
Destructress of the great host of the Daityas,
Of terrible form and loud and terrible voice—
Nārāyaṇi, all reverence to Thee.

19

Whose visage is formidable with its teeth,
Adorned with a garland of severed heads—
O Camuṇḍā ![5] destructress of Muṇḍa[6]—
Nārāyaṇi, all reverence to Thee.

---

[1] The Devi is here invoked as Aindri, the śakti of Indra, who is crowned, and whose weapon, like that of Jupiter, is the thunder-bolt and who has a thousand eyes.

[2] An Asura slain by Indra.

[3] See note 1, *ante.*

[4] The Devi is known as S'ivadūtī, because S'iva was engaged by Her as messenger to S'umbha and Niśumbha.

yatoniyukto dautyena tayā devyā śivah svayam
śivadūtiti lokesmingstatah sā khyutim āgatā.

Caṇḍi, eighth Māhātmya.

[5] Devi is so called because She slew the Asuras Caṇḍa and Muṇḍa (see verse 25, chap. vii. Candi).

[6] *Muṇḍamathane*; not as one translation of the Caṇḍi has it, " who grindest shaven heads. "

20

Lakṣmī, modesty, great knowledge,[1]
Faith (in *śāstras*), nourishment, *svadhā*;[2]
Truth, permanent and unchangeable;
Great night of dissolution, great nescience[3]—
Nārāyaṇī, all reverence to Thee.

21

Understanding,[4] Sarasvatī, the Best of all.
All Powers,[5] Spouse of Babhru,[6] Dark One,[7]
Primeval S'akti.[8] Be gracious, O Lady!
Nārāyāṇī, all reverence to Thee.

22

Who art in the form of all things,

---

1 That is, as Nagoji says, the knowledge pertaining to the *Ātman* (*adhyātmavidyā*) contained in the Upaniṣads; not "wide knowledge," as last mentioned translator renders it.

2 *Mantra* of *Pitṛs*.

3 For Devī is both *vidyā* (knowledge) and *avidyā* (nescience), or *Prakṛti*.

4 *Medhā*, which Nagoji says = *dhāraṇāvatī buddhi*, or firm, steady, concentrated *buddhi*.

5 *Bhūti*, which ordinarily means wealth = here, according to Gopal Chakravarti *aiśvaryarūpinī*—that is, the eighth *siddhi*; or, according to Nagoji, it is *sattvapradhāna* ("greatly excelling in *sattva guna*").

6 A name of S'iva, Viṣṇu, or Fire. According to Nagoji the *rajoguna śakti* is here indicated.

7 *Tāmasī*—that is, *tamogunayuktā*.

8 *Niyate*, which ordinarily means fate (*adriṣṭa*); but here denotes, according to Nagoji, the *Mūlaśakti*, the root or primeval S'akti. It does not mean, an stated in the last-mentioned translation, "O self-controlled Queen!". In the case of the Devī there is no self to be controlled. She controls others, not Herself.

Controller of all ; who hast all power ;
From the cause of all fear protect us, O Devi !
O Devī Durgā ! reverence to Thee.

23

Beautiful is Thy face adorned with three eyes.
Guard us from all (formidable) beings.
O Kātyāyani ! [1]
Reverence to Thee.

24

May Thy trident most formidable with flame,
Slayer of countless Asuras,
Protect us from fear,
O Bhadrakālī ! [2]
Reverence to Thee.

25

May Thy bell which destroys the power of Daityas,
Filling the world with its sound,
Guard us from sin,
As a mother [3] protects her children !

26

May Thy sword glittering in Thy hands,
Besmeared with the blood and fat of Asuras as with mire,
Be for our welfare !
O Candikā ; to Thee we bow.

---

[1] According to Gopal, the Devī is so called because She was born in the hermitage of the *Muni* Kātyāyana, but the Vedantists say that *Kātya* is he who is devoted to the Brahman (*brahmaniṣṭa*), and She who is attained by them is Kātyāyanī.

[2] Auspicious Kālī.

[3] *Anah.*

27

Thou, when gratified, dost destroy all forms of
disease;
But if displeased, Thou dost destroy all longed-for
desires.
Such as take shelter with Thee need fear no danger,
Since they become verily a refuge to themselves.[1]

28

O Mother, who hast shown Thyself in many forms,
Who else than Thee is able to achieve
That destruction of the great Asuras,
Enemies of righteousness,[2]
Which Thou hast wrought to-day.

29

In the sciences,[3] in all scriptures,[4] and in the great
sayings'[5]
Which are the lamp of knowledge,[6]
Who else is there but Thee
Who makes this universe again and again[7] revolve

---

1 As Gopal says, even Rajahs, not to mention others, become the slaves of such an one.

2 *Dharma.*

3 There are fourteen kinds of *vidya*—viz., four Veda, six Anga, Mimāmsa, Nyāya, Dharmaśāstra, Purāṇā. Gopal says *vidyā* and *upavidyā*, such as Indrajāla, Gārudakadyāh, Dhanurvidyā, etc.

4 *S'āstra*—that is, *tarka* (logic), *nīti.* etc.

5 Literally; the "first sayings"—that is Veda or the Karmakāṇḍa.

6 *Viveka*=*jnāna* (Gopal).

7 *Ativa.*

In the pit[1] of delusion[2] steeped in darkness.

30

Where there are Rākṣasas[3] and greatly poisonous serpents;
Where there are (armed) enemies;
Where there are highway robbers;
Where there is the forest and ocean[4] fire,
There abiding,[5] Thou dost guard the universe.

31

Queen of the universe art Thou and its guardian;
In the form of the universe Thou art its maintainer.
By the Lords[6] of the universe art Thou worshipped.
They, its supporters, have great devotion to Thee.[7]

32

O Devī! be gracious;
Ever protect us from the fear of enemies
As Thou hast just now saved us by the slaughter of the Asuras.

---

[1] The reference is to the *saṃsāra*. It is a "pit," for men fall into it; and it is "dark," for it obstructs knowledge.

[2] *Mamatvam*, which Gopal defines as *asvakīye svakīyatvābhimānah*—the sense of ownness in respect of a thing not one's own —*e.g.*, to take the body to be the self; to think I am white, I am tall, etc

[3] Demonic beings.

[4] That is, the submarine fire.

[5] Because She pervades all things.

[6] Indra, Brahmā, etc.

[7] Gopāla Chakravartī renders it: "Those who are devoted to Thee are themselves worshipped—even by Indra, Brahmā, etc., the Lords of the Universe—therefore Thou art the supporter of the universe."

Make cease at once the sins of the whole world
And the great dangers which come of all portents.[1]

33

O Devī! who takest away the afflictions of the universe.
Be gracious to us who make obeisance to Thee.
O Thou who art worthy of all praise,
Grant boons to the dwellers in the three[2] worlds.[3]

---

[1] Unusual phenomena, such as earthquakes, comets, hurricanes, etc.

[2] *Bhuh, bhuvah, svah* (see *Introduction to Tantra S'āstra*).

[3] Then Devī said: " Now I bestow a boon, O Devas " (Caṇḍī).

CAṆḌIKĀ

From the FOURTH OR SHAKRĀDI [1] MAHĀTMYA OF CAṆḌĪ (MĀRKAṆḌEYA PURĀṆA)

1

May that Devī by whose power this world was
spread,
The perfect form of the powers of countless Devas,[2]
The Mother [3] worshipped by Devas and Maharṣis,[4]
Do good to us.

2

May that Caṇḍikā whose peerless majesty and
power
Neither Bhagavān Ananta,[5] Brahmā, nor Hara[6]
can declare,
Turn Herself towards us for the destruction of the
fear of evil,
And the protection of the whole world.

---

[1] When the enemies of the Devas were vanquished by the Goddess, Shakra and the other Devas, bowing down before Her, their hair "erect with exultation," thus sang Her praises.

[2] Her form was that of their combined powers.

[3] *Ambika.*

[4] Great *Ṛṣis* or Seers.

[5] Viṣṇu.

[6] S'iva, for they, too, adore Her.

3

We bow to Her who is good fortune itself in the dwellings of the virtuous,
Ill-fortune in those of the sinful,
Reason[1] in the hearts of the intelligent, faith in those of the good,
Modesty in that of the high born.
Protect, O Devi ! this universe.

4

How can we describe Thy thought-transcending form,
Or, Thy greatly abounding strength which destroyed the Asuras,[2]
Or, O Devi ! those great deeds of Thine
Done in battle midst hosts of Devas, Asuras, and others ?

5

Thou art the cause of all the worlds,
Though Thy substance is the three *guṇas*,[3]
Yet is no fault known in thee.[4]
Incomprehensible art Thou even to Hari, Hara,[5] and other Devas,[6]

---

1 *Buddhi.*

2 Enemies of the Devas.

3 *Sattva, Tamas, Rajas.* Nature as spirit, as the veil of spirit, and of descent and ascent from spirit to matter and matter to spirit (see *Introduction to Tantra Sāstra*).

4 Ordinarily, the world which consists of the *gunas* is imperfect, but She who is it and yet transcends it, is perfect.

5 Viṣṇu and S'iva.

6 As the Viṣṇu Yāmala cited in the S'āktānandatarangiṇī, says (*Mātastvatparamam rūpam tanna jānāti kashchana*, chap. iii.) " Her supreme form is that which none know."

Thou art the refuge of all.
The whole world is but a part of Thee,[1]
Unmanifested,[2] primeval, supreme Prakṛti.[3]

6

O Devi! Thou art *Svāhā*,[4]
By the utterance whereof all Devas in all sacrifices are satisfied.
Thou art also declared by men to be *Svadhā*,[4]
Which satisfies the *pitṛs*[5].

7

Thou, O Devi! whose great *vrata*[6] surpasses all thought,
Art the supreme knowledge full of power
Which is the cause of liberation
Ever sought to be gained by those *Munis*[7] desirous thereof,
Who have strictly controlled their senses and are free of all faults.[8]

---

1 Not as it has been rendered, "Thou art the entire world which is composed of parts"—the world is but a part of Her. Hindu belief is not pantheistic in the ordinary European sense of the word.

2 *Avyākrita*, of which Nagoji Bhatta says: *Ṣadvidha vikāra-rahitatvāt*, on account of its being void of the six forms of change.

3 Of whom the S'āktānandatarangini says: "*Pranamya prakritim nityām paramātma.svarūpinīm*" (chap. i.).

4 The *Mantra* of that name.

5 The lunar ancestors of the human race and the earthly ancestors of the seventh degree, to whom offering is made in *pitṛkriyā*.

6 Vow or voluntary rite(see *Introduction to Tantra S'āstra*).

7 Sages.

8 This passage has been rendered: "Thou studiest with Thy organs, which are the essence of strength well restrained." But the Devi does not study, nor has She organs restrained or otherwise.

8

Thou art in the form of sound.
The repository of spotless [1] Ṛg [2] and Yajus [2] hymns,
And of the Sāman [2] hymns wherein are the verses of the charmful *Udgitha*, [3]
Devī, Thou art the threefold Veda [4] and Bhagavatī;[5]
For the maintenance of the world Thou art the science of *Vartta* ; [6]
Thou art the supreme destroyer of its pains. [7]

9

O Devī ! Thou art the power of understanding [8]
By Which the essence of all *S'āstras* is known ;
Thou art Durgā, [9] the vessel wherein we cross the dangerous ocean of the world.
Devoid of attachment art Thou. [10]
S'rī [11] also, who hast made Thy abode in the heart of the enemy [12] of Kaiṭabha, [13]

---

[1] Because they were breathed out by Iśvara.

[2] Of the Vedas so named.

[3] Part of the Sāmaveda, the office of the Udgātri.

[4] See p. 33, note 3.

[5] For She has all powers.

[6] *i.e.*, agriculture, cattle-rearing, and trading.

[7] As the Lalitā Sahasranāma says, "She soothes like moonlight all those who are burnt by the triple fires of misery" (*tāpatraya*) of phenomenal existence.

[8] *Medhā*, which Gopal Chakravarti says = *Dhāranāvatī buddhi*.

[9] Nagojī says : "*Duhkhaprāpyatvena durgāsi iti uchyate*" (to be attained to with great difficulty).

[10] *Asangā-nirlepā* (G. C.) *cidānandamayitvāt* (on account of Her being *cit* and *ānanda*).

[11] Lakṣmī.

[12] Viṣṇu,

[13] The *Daitya* brother of Madhu.

Thou art indeed Gaurī,[1] who hast fixed Thy dwelling in the moon-crested Deva.[2]

10

Smiling spotless like unto the full moon,
Resplendent as the finest gold
And lovely was thy face.
Yet wonderful it was that swayed by wrath
The Asura Mahiṣa suddenly smote Thy face when he saw it.

11

Greatly marvellous indeed it was that when he had seen Thy face,
Wrathful, terribly frowning, beauteous as the rising moon,
Mahiṣa did not forthwith yield up his life,
For who can live after beholding the wrathful king of Death ? [3]

12

O Devī, our supreme Lady
Be gracious for the sake of the world.
For when wrathful Thou dost suddenly destroy the generations of the enemies.[4]
It is but now made known to us
That the mighty army of the Asura Mahiṣa has met its end.

13

Those to whom Thou, O bestower of prosperity ! art gracious,

---

[1] Daughter of guru, the Lord of the Mountains.

[2] S'iva, who bears on His head the crescent moon.

[3] Yama.

[4] That is, the *Daityas*.

Are esteemed in all lands,
Their wealth and fame increases,
And their *dharma, artha, kāma, mokṣa*[1] know no lessening.
Praiseworthy are they maintaining sons, servants, and wives.

14

By thy grace, O Devī! the virtuous man, ever honoured,
Does ever daily all religious acts,
And thereafter gains heaven by Thy grace;[2]
Therefore art Thou of a surety the giver of fruit in the three worlds.

15

O Durgā; the remembrance of Thee destroyest the fear of all creatures,
When called to recollection by those in health Thou dost bestow a truly good mind.
O remover of poverty, pain, and fear,
Who but Thee art ever compassionate for the good of all.

16

By the slaying of these foes the world gains happiness.
O Devi! Thou hast slain them with the desire
That they should not always sin so as to merit hell,[3]
But that by death in battle they may go to Heaven.

---

[1] The four aims of being.

[2] Nagoji Bhatta says *tatah* here means that after that (*svarga*), and in order of time they gain *mokṣa* (liberation).

[3] Not "Let these practise sin so as to descend to Hell for long." as it has been rendered. The Devi's desire is to save even Her foes. The translation of the alternative reading given by the translation referred to is nearer the sense of the text.

17

Seeing them, why dost Thou not (by Thy look) turn them to ashes?
Thou throwest Thy weapon among the enemies, the Asuras,
In order that, being purified by it,
Even these enemies may go to heaven.
Such is Thy merciful intention even towards them.

18

If by the glittering, formidable flashes of Thy sword,
And by the lustre of Thy spear-point,
The eyes of the Asuras were not destroyed,
It was because they gazed on Thy countenance,
Like unto the radiant moon.

19

O Devi! Thy nature it is to subdue the evil works of the wicked.
Thy form, destructive of the strength of those who destroy the Devas,
Surpasses all thought, and is comparable with none.
By this Thou hast manifested Thy kindness even to enemies.

20

Devi! with whom may this Thy valour be compared,
Or Thy most charming form striking fear among foes?
In Thee only, bestower of boons, even upon three worlds,

Are seen both kindness of heart and relentlessness
in battle.

21

By the destruction of their foes the three worlds
have been saved by Thee,
Thou hast led even these to heaven.
Having slain them in the front of battle.
And hast dispelled the fear besetting us from the
maddened enemies of the Devas.
Salutation to Thee, O Devi!

22

With Thy spear protect us, O Devī ![1]
O Mother ! protect us with Thy sword.
By the sound of Thy bell guard us,
And by the twanging of Thy bow-string
Protect us in the East and in the West,
Guard us, O Caṇḍikā ! in the South,
And in the North by the brandishing of Thy
spear.

23

Whatever gentle forms of Thine,
And whatever of Thy terrible forms
Wander in the three worlds,
By these forms protect us and the earth.

24

O Mother ! by Thy sword, spear, and club,

[1] Here follows the *prārthanā* (prayer).

And other weapons, in Thy soft and supple hands,[1]
Guard us on every side.[2]

---

[1] Literally, leaflike (*pallava*), soft, and supple.

[2] The *Ṛṣi* in Caṇḍī continued : Thus was the upholder of the world hymned by the Devas who did worship Her with celestial flowers, perfumes, unguents, and incense upon which the Devi, highly honoured with this hymn, said to the Devas : " Choose what ye desire of me ". On which the latter prayed that whenever they called upon Her She might come to their assistance, and that whatever mortal should praise Her with this hymn should prosper. Bhadrakāli said, " Be it so, " and vanished from their sight.

MAHĀDEVĪ [1]

(From the FIFTH MAHĀTMYA OF CAṆḌĪ) [2]

1

Reverence to the Devī, [3] to the Devī of the Great, [4]
To Her who is auspicious, [5] for ever reverence.
Reverence to Prakṛti [6] who maintains. [7]
Setting our minds wholly upon Her, we make
obeisance to Her.

---

[1] Here not the "Great Goddess," but as Commentator Nagoji Bhatta (cited *post* as N.B.) says, "The Goddess" (Devi) "of the great"—viz., Brahmā, Viṣṇu, and S'iva, for it is by Her power that they enjoy their abode, and it is She whom even they worship—the Mother of all.

[2] The Asuras S'umbha and Niśumbha bereft the Devas of their dominion whereupon the latter prayed to the Goddess for help as follows.

[3] Nagoji says that *Devī* = *prakāśātmika,* that which is by its nature light and manifestation.

[4] *Mahādevī* (see note 1, *ante*).

[5] Because She is the cause of all auspicious things.

[6] *S'ṛṣṭiśakti,* or *śakti* (power) of creation (N. B).

[7] *Bhadrāyai.* Literally, good = *rakṣanaśakti,* the *Vaiṣṇavaśakti,* which maintains (N. B.).

2

Reverence to Her who is eternal,[1] Raudrā,[2]
To Gaurī,[3] and Dhātrī,[4] reverence and again
reverence,
To Her who is moonlight and in the form of the
moon,[5]
To Her who is supreme bliss,[6] reverence for ever.

3

Bending low, we make obeisance to the auspicious
One
Who is prosperity in the form of wealth,
To Siddhi,[7] Nairiti,[8] and to the good fortune of
Kings.[9]
To Sarvānī[10] reverence, and again reverence.

---

[1] *Nityāyai* ; or She is the S'akti Nitya (N. B.).

[2] That is, She is *samhāraśakti* or *śakti* of dissolution, the *tāmasika śakti* (according the Commentator Gopal Chakravarti), as contrasted with Dhātrī, the *rājasika śakti*, and *indorūpā* (moon form), the *sāttvika śakti* (*vide post*).

[3] Daughter of Guru, the Lord of the Mountains.

[4] Creator and upholder.

[5] The moon here stands for all luminous things : or it may mean *indorūpā* in the technical sense of *yoga śāstra*.

[6] *Sukhā* = *paramānandarūpā*.

[7] That is, *aṇimādirūpa* (G. C.), the eight *siddhis*—*aṇimā*, *laghima*, etc.

[8] Gopal Chakravarti says this means *Rākṣasaśakti* (demonic power) ; also *alakṣmī* (misfortune). At the time of worship of of Lakṣmī (Devī of Prosperity) on the fifth day after *vijayadaśamī*, the Devī Alakṣmī is worshipped in the house in the form of a misshapen figure, and then thrown away.

[9] *Bhubritām*, which, according to G. C, means mountains, for wealth in the form of gems, etc., are found therein.

[10] Maheśvarī or S'ivaśakti.

4

To Durgā,[1] to Her who enables men to cross the ocean[2] of the world,
Who is the life and strength [3] and cause of all.
Knower of the distinction between Puruṣa and Prakṛti,[4]
And who is both black [5] and grey, [6] reverence for ever.

5

We prostrate ourselves before Thee, who art at once most gentle[7] and formidable,[8]
Reverence to Her, and again reverence ;

---

[1] Which means, according to Nagoji : " She who is known with difficulty (*duhkhajneyā*).

[2] As N. B. says : *Durgātsamsārātpārāngkaroti*, etc. G. C. says it means She whose abode is not known in either time or space.

[3] For She is not only *antaryāminī*, but remains even at the time of dissolution. She is feminine because She supports all things as their mother.

[4] *Khyātihprakritipuruṣayor bhedajnānām* (N. B.). *Viveka khyātih* is a term in Sānkhya denoting the cause of liberation, the recognition of the self (Puruṣa) by the self ; not as one published rendering runs, " to fame ;"

[5] As *tāmasika śakti*.

[6] *Dhūmra* ; that which is with smoke ; the sacrificial rite ; here the knowledge of the rites.

[7] *Atisaubhāgyā*. As such She is (N. B.) *vidyārūpinī*, as putting an end to the *samsāra*. For this reason She, as G. C. says, greatly delights all.

[8] *Atiraudrāyā*, because, as N. B. says, She, as *avidyā*, is the cause of the *samsāra* with all its terrors.

Reverence to Her who is the material cause of the world,[1].
To the Devi,[2] who is in the form of action, reverence, and again reverence.

6

To the Devī who in all things is called Viṣṇumāyā,[3]
Reverence to Her, reverence to Her,
Reverence to Her, reverence, reverence.[4]

7

To the Devī who is known as intelligence[5] in all beings,
Reverence to Her, reverence to Her,
Reverence to Her, reverence, reverence.

8

To the Devī who dwells in the form of *buddhi*[6] in all beings,
Reverence to Her, reverence to Her,
Reverence to Her, reverence, reverence.

---

[1] *Jagatpratishtāyai* = (as N. B. says) *jagadupādānakāraṇam*; or, as, G. C. has it, She is *sarvāntaryāminī*, who dwells in the inmost being of all things.

[2] Which = (G. C.) *dyotanaśīla*, whose nature it is to lighten, or (N.) *devaśakti*.

[3] Or *mulāvidyā* (Nagoji).

[4] *Namastasyai, namastasyai, namastasyai namo namah.* The refrain throughout the succeeding verses.

[5] *Cetana* = (Nagoji says) *chitśakti*, or mind. She Herself is *nirvikalpacitśakti*, but manifests as *savikalpacitśakti* in all worldly beings.

[6] The mind, as the aspect so named of the *antahkaraṇa*.

9

To the Devī who in the form of sleep abides[1] in all beings,
Reverence to Her, reverence to Her,
Reverence to Her, reverence, reverence.

10

To the Devī who exists in all beings in the form of hunger,
Reverence to Her, reverence to Her,
Reverence to Her, reverence, reverence.

11

To the Devī who exists in all beings in the form of *cāyā*,[2]
Reverence to Her, reverence to Her,
Reverence to Her, reverence, reverence.

12

To the Devī who exists as energy[3] in all beings,
Reverence to Her, reverence to Her,
Reverence to Her, reverence, reverence,

---

[1] *Nidrārūpena.* According to Nagoji, *nidrā = suṣupti,* the state of dreamless sleep where all sense functions are at an end. According to G. C., *svapna* or dreaming sleep also.

[2] Nagoji says this word = *samsāratāpābhāvah,* or lack of worldly pain. The *samsāra* is like a burning flame. In its shadow there is coolness and peace. According to Gopal Chakravarti, however, it = *ātapābhāvah. Ātapāh = prakāśarūpatvātvidyā,* or knowledge on account of its giving light, and therefore as the lack of it She is *avidyā.*

[3] *S'akti* : power, action.

13

To the Devī who exists in the form of thirst [1] in all beings,
Reverence to Her, reverence to Her,
Reverence to Her, reverence, reverence.

14

To the Devī who in the form of forgiveness [2] exists in all beings,
Reverence to Her, reverence to Her,
Reverence to Her, reverence, reverence.

15

To the Devī who exists in the form of race and species in all beings,[3]
Reverence to Her, reverence to Her,
Reverence to Her, reverence, reverence.

16

To the Devī in the form of modesty in all beings,
Reverence to Her, reverence to Her,
Reverence to Her, reverence, reverence.

17

To the Devī existing in the form of peace [4] in all beings,

[1] Which, as Nagoji says, is the desire for that which is not one's own (*anātmīyā*) ; thirst for enjoyment, possession, individual life, etc.

[2] Which is the desire not to return evil to those who have done us wrong, notwithstanding our power to do so (N. B.).

[3] *Jātirūpeṇa* : that which classifies and differentiates one body of beings from another.

[4] Which Nagoji says means the control of the senses and renunciation of all worldly things.

Reverence to Her, reverence to Her,
Reverence to Her, reverence, reverence.

18

To the Devī who exists in all beings in the form of faith,[1]
Reverence to Her, reverence to Her,
Reverence to Her, reverence, reverence.

19

To the Devī existing in the form of beauty in all beings,
Reverence to Her, reverence to Her,
Reverence to Her, reverence, reverence.

20

To the Devī who exists in all beings in the form of prosperity,[2]
Reverence to Her, reverence to Her,
Reverence to Her, reverence, reverence.

21

To the Devī who in all beings exists in the form of their respective callings,[3]
Reverence to Her, reverence to Her,
Reverence to Her, reverence, reverence.

---

[1] That is, Nagoji says, *āstikatvam* (belief in God's existence); or, according to Gopal Chakravarti, also a firm and strong faith in *Veda*.

[2] Wealth, etc.

[3] That is, *jīvikā*, the callings of husbandmen, merchant, cattle-rearing, etc.

22

To the Devī who in the form of memory exists in all beings,
Reverence to Her, reverence to Her,
Reverence to Her, reverence, reverence.

23

To the Devī who in all beings exists in the form of mercy,[1]
Reverence to Her, reverence to Her,
Reverence to Her, reverence, reverence.

24

To the Devī who in the form of contentment[2] exists in all beings,
Reverence to Her, reverence to Her,
Reverence to Her, reverence, reverence.

25

To the Devī who exists in all beings as (their) Mother,[3]
Reverence to Her, reverence to Her,
Reverence to Her, reverence, reverence.

26

To the Devī who in the form of error[4] exists in all beings,

---

[1] Which Nagoji says is the desire of removing the pain of others.

[2] Which Nagoji defines as satisfaction with that which one possesses as distinguished from longing for what one has not got.

[3] She is *janani*, and, as Nagoji says, *pālayitri* (protectress).

[4] *Bhrānti*. A thoroughly Indian conception, though some modern Hindus have lost the sense of it. Gopal Chakravarti gives as an example the classical instance of the *jīva* taking mother-of-pearl to be silver, etc.

Reverence to Her, reverence to Her,
Reverence to Her, reverence, reverence.

27

Reverence to the Devī
Who is the Presiding Deity over the senses of all beings,
Who is ever in all beings,
And who pervades all things.

28

To the Devī who in the form of consciousness,[1]
Having pervaded all the world, exists therein,
Reverence to Her, reverence to Her,
Reverence to Her, reverence, reverence.

29

Praised aforetime by the Devas,
By reason of their obtaining that which they desired;
Worshipped by Surendra[2] on days of victory.
May the Īśvarī,[3] who is the cause of all good.
Do good and auspicious things for us,
And may She ward off all calamities.

30

And may She who is now saluted by us as our Queen,
As also by the Suras,[4] tormented by arrogant Asuras,[5]
Whom we call to mind
As we bow our bodies in devotion to Her,
Destroy at this very moment all our calamities.

---

[1] *Cit* = *citśakti* (N. B.), and according to Gopal Chakravarti, who says the *jīva* is here meant, *caitanya*.

[2] Indra.

[3] Queen and Ruler of the worlds.

[4] The Good Devas.

[5] Their evil enemies.

JAGADAMBIKĀ[1]

FROM THE DEVĪBHĀGAVATA PURĀṆA[2]

1

IT is by Thy power only
That Brahmā creates, Viṣṇu maintains,
And at the end of things S'iva destroys the universe.
Powerless are they for this but by Thy help.
Therefore it is that Thou alone art the Creatrix,
Maintainer, and Destructress of the world.[3]

2

Thou art fame, mind, remembrance,
And our refuge, the mountain-born,[4]
Companion, kindness, faith, and patience,
Earth, Kamalā,[5] health,[6] the arts, and victory,

---

[1] Mother of the world.

[2] Chap. xix., Skandha v., p. 27, of the Bombay Edition (Venkateshvara Press), edited by Khemarāja ; 1823, Shaka (1902), with Commentary by Nīlakantha, hereafter referred to by the letter N.

[3] The Devī, who is the *mahākāraṇasvarūpā,* is also the *kārya-svarūpā.* As cause She is in the effect and is the *śaktirūpa* by which all things are done (N).

[4] Here is meant the S'akti of Rudra (N).

[5] Lakṣmī, Devī of Prosperity and Beauty.

[6] *Puṣṭi* : nourishment.

Contentment, ever victorious,[1] Umā,[2] Ramā,[3]
True knowledge, and the highest *buddhi*.[4]

3

Science, forgiveness, beauty, retentiveness art Thou,[5]
Who art Known in the three worlds as all in all.
Who is there that unaided by Thee can do ought?
Thou art the abode wherein all men dwell.[6]

4

Thou art the upholder.
Were Thou not so, how could the tortoise and serpent uphold the Earth?[7]
Thou art the Earth itself.
Were this not so, how could this weighty world rest on Ether?[8]

5

Those who through Thy *māyā* pray to Devas,
Such as[9] the four-headed One[10], Viṣṇu, Rudra,[11] Fire,

---

1 *Vijayā*. The Devī Pr. says: "After conquering this very powerful King of the Daityas, named Padma, She is known in the three worlds as Vijayā and unconquerable (*aparājitā*)."

2 See Hymn to Annapurṇa, *post*. Here the Īśvara S'akti (N.).

3 A name of Lakṣmī.

4 See p. 87, note 5.

5 *Medhā*, which means, in particular, the retentive faculty or memory, and in general, intelligence.

6 For in Her all men have their being. She is as *Ādhāraśakti*,, their support (N.).

7 As the Purāṇas represent them as doing. The verse deals with the attributes of the *ādhāraśakti*.

8 *Gaganam*.

9 Literally, "headed by," or instances of principal Devas.

10 Brahmā.

11 S'iva.

The White-rayed one'[1] Yama,[2] Vāyu,[3] and Ganeśa
Are indeed ignorant,[5]
For can these do anything without Thy power?[6]

6

O Mother! those who do *homa*, with ghee on fire,
With great ceremony in the name of the Devas,
Are of but small intelligence.[8]
If Thou art not *svāhā*,[8] then how can they make sacrifice?
Do they not worship Thee?
If not they are ignorant.[10]

7

In this world Thou art the giver of enjoyment
To things which move and are still.[11]
Thou givest life to all things being as they are parts of Thee.

---

[1] *Subrāmshu*, or the moon.

[2] Lord of Death.

[3] Lord of the Air.

[4] The elephant-headed Deva, son of the Devī as Pārvatī and S'iva.

[5] *Vimūdha* (see also Umāsanghitā of S'iva Purāṇā).

[6] *Ye vā stuvanti manujā amarān vimudhā,*
Māyā gunaistava caturmukha viṣṇurudrān,
Subrāmshuvahniyamavāyuganeśamukhyān,
Kim tvāmrite janani te prabhavanti kārye.

[7] The sacrifice done with ghee poured into fire.

[8] *Alpadhiyah.*

[9] The mantra used in *homa.*

[10] *Svāhā nacet tamasi te kathamāpuraddhā,*
Tvām eva kim nahi ya janti tato hi mudhah.

[11] Here apparently trees and the like, as contrasted with the animal world. She allots the *karma* (N).

O Mother ! as Thou nourisheth all Thy Suras,[1]
So also dost Thou nourish others.

8

O Mother ! as men who are of good heart,
Never for the mere pleasure thereof
Cut down leafless and bitter (fruited) trees
Which have sprung up in the forest.
Therefore Thou dost even greatly protect the Daityas. [2]

9

Though Thou slayest in the battlefield with Thy arrows the enemies,
Knowing their desire for amorous play with celestial women, [3]
Yet such is Thy nature that even then Thou showest kindness to them.
For Thou so slayest them
That in another body [4] they may obtain fulfilment of their desires.

---

[1] The Devas, Her children.

[2] That is, the Devī does not slay even the Daityas for the mere savage pleasure of killing, and even those whom She slays are slain by Her for the good of the world and their own good, that being slain by Her hand they may go to heaven (see next verse). The Kumārasambhavam says that a man cannot cut down even a poisonous tree if planted by his own hand.

[3] *Devānganāsuratakelimating viditvā.*

[4] That is, a celestial body. For, as Daityas do not perform sacrificial rites, etc., so they cannot gain heaven. But when killed by the hand of the Devī, thither they go to their enjoyment, and Devas are protected.

10

Most wonderful it is that Thou hast assumed body
For the destruction of the Dānavas,[1] famed for
their power,
When Thou mightest have slain them by Thy
mere will.
The cause of this is Thy play[2] and nothing else,[3]

11

Alas! of a verity unhappy are they
Who when the Kali age, the worst of ages, has
come,
Do not worship Thee.
Men cunning and skilled in the Purāṇas
Have made the people devoted to the worship of
Hari and S'ankara,[4]
Who are but Thy creatures.[5]

12

Those who worship with devotion Devas,
Though they know that they are distressed,
harassed by Asuras, and subject to Thy control,
Are of a surety like unto a man

---

[1] Sons of Danu. Enemies of the Devas.

[1] *Krīḍarasa* that is, *līlā*.

[2] *Krīḍārasastava nachānyatarotraheluh* (*cf*. the Vedantic *sutra okavattulīlā kaivalyam*).

[3] Viṣṇu and S'iva.

[4] *Dhūrttaih purāṇa caturairhari śankarāṇām,*
Sevāparāshcha vihitāstava nirmitānām.

Men, the verse says, thus worship the creature instead of the Creatrix.

Who with, the light of a clear lamp in his hands,
Yet falls into some waterless and terrible well.[1]

13

O Mother! Thou art the remover of the pains
which arise from birth,
And art known by those desirous of liberation
As the giver of happiness when Thou art *vidyā*,[2]
And of unhappiness when Thou art *avidyā*,[2]
Surely it is only the ignorant who do not worship
Thee,
Such as are attached to enjoyment without wisdom.[3]

14

Even Brahmā, Hara, and Hari, as all other Suras,[4]
Ever worship Thy lotus feet, which are our refuge.
But those who are of small intelligence and beset
with error
Do not worship Thee.
And so ever repeatedly fall into the ocean of the
world.[5]

---

1 *Jnātvā surāmstava vashān asurārddhitāngshcha,*
Yevai bhajanti bhuvi bhāvayuta vimagnāu,
Dhritvā kare suvimalang khalū dīpakangte,
Kupe patanti manujā vijaletighore.

(See also Umāsanghitā.)

2 Knowledge and nescience, the source of *nivritti* and *pravritti*, with the latter's attendant miseries.

3 *Kilamandadhībirnārāditā janani bhogaparaistathājnaih.*

4 Devas.

5 *Tadvai nayelpa matayo manasā bhajanti,*
Bhrāntāh patanti satatam bhavasāgarete.

15

O Caṇḍī ! [1] it is most surely by the favour of the dust on Thy lotus feet
That Brahmā in the beginning of things creates,
Shauri [2] protects, and Hara [3] destroys the whole world.
He is indeed unfortunate
Who in this world does not worship Thee.

16

O Devī ! Thou art the *Devatā* of speech of both Suras and Asuras.
Without power of speech are even the foremost of Devas
When Thou abidest not in them.
If men do speak, it is because they are not deprived of Thee.[4]

17

Hari,[5] when cursed by the greatly angered Bhrigu,[6]

---

1 Nilakantha derives the word from *chadi* ("the wrathful one fearful to the whole world"). *S'ruti* says of the Brahman: *Mahadbhayam vajramudhyatam* ("great fear and a ready thunderbolt")

2 Viṣṇu.

3 S'iva.

4 Sarasvatī is She who causes speech. Sound springing from the Mūlādhāra wherein is *Devī* Kuṇḍalinī proceeds from the stage of mere sound (parā), the potentiality of growth in the seed to that of *Paśyantī*, when the latter begins to sprout; then to *Madhyamā*, when the first two small leaves appear but inseparate, and lastly, as *Vaikharī*, when they separate, remaining united only at their base.

5 Viṣṇu.

6 The Ṛṣi of that name.

Became Fish, Tortoise, Boar, and Man-lion,[1] and
Dwarf.[2]
How can those who worship Him
Escape the fire of death?

18

As is well-known, the *linga* of S'ambhu[3] in the forest
Fell on earth in like manner by the curse of Bhrigu.
How can those, O Mother! who on earth worship
Him[4] who holds a skull
Attain to happiness either in this world or the next?

19

They who worship the elephant-faced Lord of
Ganas,[5]
Who was born of Maheśa,
With Him in vain take shelter.
They know Thee not, O Devī! Mother of the
Universe,
Who art easy of worship[6] and the giver of the
fruit of all desires.

---

[4] The Matsya, Kūrma, Varāha, and Nrisingha avatāra of Viṣṇu.

[5] *Chalakrit,* which Nīlakantha says = Vāmana Avatāra of Viṣṇu. *Chalakrit,* because Balirāja was deceived by him.

[3] S'iva, who retired into the forest after the death of Satī, and who was powerless to protect even his own *linga*.

[4] S'iva.

[5] Ganeśa, son of S'iva, so powerless.

[6] Devī is (as the Lalitā, verse 133, also says), "easily worshipped" (*sukhā-rādhyā*), without bodily pain by fasting etc., without restrictions on the mode of meditation. In the Kūrma Pr. the Lord describes to Himavat an easy mode of worship if he be unable to meditate on the Supreme Form. The Devī is also "easily pleased" (Lalitā, verse 162, *kṣipraprasādinī*)—that is, even by a little worship as the Saura and S'iva Purāṇas say of the Lord of Umā, with whom the Devī is one.

20

Wonderful it is that through Thy compassion
Even the multitude of enemies slain by Thy sharpened arrows
Have thus been made to reach Heaven.
For had they not been so slain
Calamities and the most painful of painful states would they have suffered
In that hell which is the result of their (evil) *karma*.

21

Even Brahmā, Hara, and Hari
From pride[1] know not Thy power.
How, then, are others able to know it,
Bewildered as they are by Thy (three) *guṇas* of incomparable power?[2]

22

Even *Munis*[3] suffer, who, being ignorant (of Thee).
Do not adore Thy thought-transcending lotus feet,
And are set upon the worship of sun and fire.[4]
By them, even though they read hundreds of *S'ruti*,[5]

---

[1] *Garvabhāvāt*.

[2] Devī is "all-bewildering" (*Sarvamohinī*). In Kūrma Pr., S'iva says: "This *Māyā* is dear to me by which the world is bewildered. I bewilder the whole universe with the Devas, Daityas, and men." The operation of the *tāmasika guṇa* veils from them the truth.

[3] The Mārkaṇḍeya Purāṇa says: "That Divine Devī Mahāmāyā forcibly draws away the minds of even the sages (*Munis*), and leads them into confusion."

[4] Because they are *pratyakṣadevatā*—that is, visible, and She, the supreme ground of them, is beyond vision, mind, and speech.

[5] The reading of much *śruti* (revelation) teaches them nothing, for their ignorance conceals from them its true meaning.

The Supreme object of desire[1] is not known,
which is the essence of all Vedas.

23

Methinks it is Thy (three) *guṇas*,
The power of which is so famed on earth,
Which makes men turn away from devotion (to Thee),
And attaches them to Viṣṇu, Īśa,[2] Bhāskara,[3] Ganeśa,
By (the teaching of) various *Āgamas*[4] of their own devising.[5]

24

O Ambikā! (so great is Thy mercy)
That Thou art not angry with,
But showest kindness to, and maketh greatly prosperous
Even those who, skilful in the *mantra* of delusion,[6]

---

[1] *Paramārthatattva.* S'ankhya says that there are two different kinds of *artha* or object. One is *bhoga* (enjoyment), the second, which is the supreme object (*paramārtha*) is *mokṣa* (liberation). The one exists in the current issuing from Devī (*Avidyā*), the other returns on the other current, which draws to the Devī (*Vidyā*).

[2] S'iva.

[3] The Sun (*Sūrya*).

[4] Here used generally for *S'āstra,* though also used in a special sense as denoting Veda and Tantra, to the latter of which, Nilakantha perhaps refers. *Nānātantraihmohakaih* ("many deluding Tantras"). The reference is here to the dualistic scriptures.

[5] *Svabuddhirachitairvividhāgamaishcha* ("composed by themselves").

[6] *Mohamantranipunām*

Make the best of men[1] turn away from Thy feet
By Āgamas made by themselves,[2]
Teaching of devotion to Hari and Hara.[3]

25

In the Satya age[4] the *sattva guṇa*[5] was very powerful,
Therefore there were no Asadāgamas.[6]
But in the Kali age learned folk conceal Thee (from the people).
And adore those Devas imagined by them (to be objects of worship).[7]

---

[1] According to Nilakantha, Brāhmanas.

[2] Literally, "said by themselves" (*svoktāgamaih*)—that is as Nilakantha says, *puruṣapranītāgamaih* (or Āgamas composed by men and not revealed by S'iva).

[3] Viṣṇu and S'iva who are themselves only the children of the Mother, and as much creatures, though of the highest kind, as others are.

[4] The first and best of the four ages: Satya, Tretā, Dvāpara, and Kalī, the commonly supposed present age. In the second, virtue (*dharma*) decreased by a quarter, in the third by a half, and in the present or Kalī age only a quarter of *dharma* remains.

[5] The *guṇa,* which manifests on the moral plane as goodness.

[6] Literally, "bad Āgama," a name applied by some to the Tantra of the "downward current" (*arddharetas*), but here has a general significance to all *S'āstra,* whether Tantra or otherwise, of a dualistic character (*asachchhāstrāni*).

[7] *Tūrye yuge bhavati chātibalang guṇasya,*
Turyasyatena māthitānyasadāgamāni tvam,
Gopayanti nipunāh kavayah kalauvai
Tatkalpitān suraganā napi sangstuvanti.

"Imagined by them" (*tatkalpitān*). This does not mean that the Devas do not exist. Hari, Hara, Īśa, Ganeśa, Bhāskara, and others have been mentioned in previous verses. The verse is *stutivāda,* in which that which is its direct object, is dealt with to

26

Munis,[1] in whom the *sattva guṇa*[2] is very pure,
Meditate upon Thee,
Who art the giver on earth of the fruit of liberation,
Who art perfect in *yoga*[3] and the supreme knowledge.
Such never again suffer pain in the womb of a mother.[4]
They are only praiseworthy who are absorbed in Thee.

27

Citśakti[5] is in *Paramātmā*,
Therefore also it is manifested[6] in the world,
Wherein it is known as the cause of its creation, maintenance, and destruction.[7]

---

the exclusion of all others. What is meant is that She alone is to be worshipped and not any other. *Kalpanā* is to mistake one thing for another. Thus the world is taken (*kalpitā*) to be real when the Brahman alone is so. And so, too, mother-of-pearl is mistaken for silver (*shuktirajatakalpanā*), or a rope for a snake (*rajjusarpakalpanā*); so people take the Devas to be the ultimate object of worship when it is only the Devī whose manifestations they are, who is such.

[1] Sages.

[2] See Introduction.

[3] *Yogasiddhām*. The manifested Devī as Umā was a great *yoginī*.

[4] Are never reborn. According to Hindu ideas the child suffers great pain and misery in the womb of its mother, the remembrance of which is lost on its birth into the world.

[5] That is, *caitanya* (Nīlakantha). See the Saṃkṣepaśāriraka.

[6] In name and form (*nāmarūpātmaka.*).

[7] *Bhavakrityakartā*. Literally, "performer of worldly action"—that is, those stated. For, according to Vedānta and Nyāya, it works therein by its S'akti, though in S'ankhya the Puruṣa is merely an enjoyer, spectator, and witness (*bhoktā, draṣṭā, sākṣī*).

Who else in this world without Thee and of his own power
Is able to create, move and destroy ?[1]

28

O Mother of the world !
Can the *Tattvas*,[2] deprived of *Cit*,[3] create the world ?
They are lifeless things.[4]
O Devi ! can the *indriyas*[5] with their objects and functions,[6]
Bear fruit without Thee ?

29

O Mother ! had you not as *Svāhā*[7] been the cause thereof,
Even the Devas could not have obtained their enjoined own portion,
Offered in sacrificial rites by *Munis*[8].

---

[1] *Cf.* Dakṣinamūrtisamhitā.

[2] The twenty-four beginning with *Mahat*.

[3] *Vide ante*.

[4] *Jarāni*; mere matter but for the informing life of the Goddess.

[5] The so-called "senses" of knowledge (*Jnānendriya*), viz.: *Cakṣu* (eye), *S'rotra* (ear), *ghrāṇa* (smell), *rasanā* (tongue), *tvak* (skin) and of action (*karmendriya*); viz., *Vak* (speech), *pāni* (hand), *pāda* (feet), *pāyu* (anus), *upastha* (genitals).

[6] *Indriyāni guṇakarmayutāni*. Thus, form (*rūpa*) is the *guṇa* or object (*viṣaya*) of the eye, and *darśana* (or seeing), its function (*karma*).

[7] The *Mantra* used in *Agnikriyā* and wife of Agni.

[8] If the Mantra Svāhā, which is the Devī, be not said, then the Devas get nothing from the *homa*. Their S'astric portion they obtain by virtue only of the Devī as *Svāhā*, the cause thereof.

Therefore Thou maintainest the whole world.[1]

30

By Thee all this universe was in the beginning of things created;
Thou protecteth the Regents of the Quarters among whom Hari and Hara are foremost.
At the dissolution of things Thou devourest the whole universe.
That which has been done by Thee from the creation
Even Devas[2] know not.
What, then, shall we say of unfortunate men?

31

O Mother! Thou hast by slaying the greatly formidable Asura,
Who assumed the form of a buffalo,[3]
Protected the Devas.
Even the Vedas know Thee not as Thou really art.[4]
Small of intellect as we are how can we praise Thee?

32

O Mother! Thou hast accomplished a great work
In destroying this wicked foe of ours,
A thorn painful beyond all thought
(In the side of) the whole world.

---

[1] The Devī protects the Devas, and if the Devas are maintained, then the whole world is maintained, as the Devas are Her agents in the maintenance thereof.

[2] *Manujā*, which here, according to Nīlakantha, includes Devas.

[3] The Demon Mahiṣa.

[4] *Gatingtava yathārthatayā na jagmuh.*

Thy fame will spread throughout the whole
universe.
Do Thou, whose power is known to be incomparable,
By Thy mercy protect us. [1]

[1] The hymn concluding, Devībhāgavata continues, Vyāsa said : " Devī, thus praised, said in soft, sweet voice, 'Oh, best of Devas, tell Me what other thing most difficult and hard to accomplish you would have Me do ?' "

DURGA

(MAHĀBHĀRATA VIRĀṬA PARVAN)[1]

SALUTATION to Thee, O giver of blessings,
Dark[2] Virgin,[3] observant of the vow of chastity,[4]
Whose form is beauteous as that of the rising sun,
And Thy face as that of the full moon ;
Four-armed and faced art Thou.
Wide-hipped, full-breasted,[5]
Wearing emerald sapphire bangles and armlets;
Thou art resplendent as Padmā, Spouse of
    Nārāyaṇa,[7]
And rangest the ethereal regions.
Thy form and chastity[8] are of the purest.
Dark art Thou like the blue-black cloud,
Whose face is beauteous as that of Saṁkarṣaṇa.[9]
Long are Thy two arms, as it were bannered poles
    in honour of Indra.[10]

---

[1] Chap. VI., sung by Yudhiṣthira, when on the way to the City of Virāṭa.

[2] *Kṛṣṇā.*

[3] *Kumāri* (see p. 46, note 3.)

[4] For She observed *brahmacarya.*

[5] *Pinashronipayodhare.*

[6] Lakṣmi.

[7] Viṣṇu.

[8] *Brahmacarya.*

[9] S'iva.

[10] In ancient times a long bamboo surmounted with a flag was set up on the lst of Assar, in honour of Indra to secure rain.

Thou bearest in Thy six other arms
A vessel, lotus, bell, noose, bow, a great discus,[1]
and other weapons.
Purest woman art Thou on earth.[2]
Thy well-formed ears are decked with beautiful
earrings.
Thy face challenges the moon in beauty.
Wonderful is Thy crown, and beautiful is the
braid (of Thy hair).
Thy body is like that of a serpent [3]
Thou glitterest with brilliant girdle round Thy hips,
And shinest like Mount Mandāra encircled by the
snake.[4]
With standing peacock feathers on Thy head,
Thou art resplendent.
By Thy vow of virginity Thou hast maintained
heaven.[5]
It is for this, O slayer of the Asura Mahiṣa,[6]
That Thou art praised and worshipped by the
Devas for the protection of the three worlds.[7]
Foremost of Devas, be gracious to me;

---

1 *Cakra.*

2 *Striviśuddhāchayābhuvī.*

3 *Bhujangā bhogavasena,* which Nilakanṭha says is *Sarpaśarirākārena.*

4 Thus used for the churning of the ocean.

5 *Tridivam* or *svarga* ; for there " the Three " shine.

6 The son of Jambāsura, whom the Devī fought for many years before he was slain by Her (see Mārkaṇḍeya Purāṇa). During the great Durgā festival in autumn, the Devī is represented as slaying this formidable Asura, so called as having assumed the form of a buffalo.

7 *Bhuh, Bhuvah, Svah,* the earthly, atmospheric, and celestial spheres.

Show me Thy mercy, and be auspicious.[1]
Both Jayā and Vijayā [2] art Thou.
Thou givest victory in battle;
Give me, too, victory, O Devi!
Give me now a boon.
Thy constant abode is on the Vindhya, the foremost of mountains.
O Kāli! O Kāli! O Mahākāli! [3]
Thou delightest in wine, meat, and animal sacrifice,[4]
Bestowing boons, going whithersoever Thou wilt.
Thou art ever followed by Brahmā [5] and other Devas,
By those who call upon Thee to lighten their burdens.
As by those who salute Thee at dawn of day.
Nothing is unattainable either by way of wealth or children
Thou art called Durgā by all because Thou savest men from difficulty.[6]
Whether in dangerous lands or sinking in the great ocean,
Thou art the sole refuge of men.
When assailed by robbers, when crossing streams and seas,
As also in wildernesses and great forests,

---

[1] *S'ivābhava.* S'iva is so called because he is auspicious.

[2] Two Companion Devatās of Durgā.

[3] Spouse of Mahākāla, an aspect of S'iva.

[4] *Siddhumāmsapaśupriye. Siddhu* is a spirit distilled from molasses.

[5] *Bhutaih,* which Nīlakaṇṭha says here denotes the oldest beings, Brahmā and other Devas.

[6] Literally, one who rescues from difficulty.

Those who remember Thee, O Mahādevī! are never lost.
Thou art fame, prosperity, constancy, success, and modesty,
Intelligence, knowledge, and man's offspring.
Thou art the two twilights,[1]
Night, the light of sun and moon,
Sleep, beauty, forgiveness, and mercy.
Thou, when worshipped by Thy devotees, destroyest
Ignorance, man's fetters, loss of children and wealth, disease and fear of death.
I who have lost my kingdom seek Thy protection.
I bow to Thee, Sureśvarī, with bended head:
Grant mc protection,
Thou whose eyes are like the leaf of the lotus.
O Thou who art truth itself, be true to us.
O Durgā! give me shelter,
Who art merciful to Thy devotees, protect me.[2]

---

[1] *Sandhya*, early dawn when the stars are vanishing, and evening as they are about to appear.

[2] Thus praised by the son of Pāndu, the Goddess showed Herself to him.

ĀRYĀ[1]

Form the HARIVAMS'Ā

Thou art liberation,[2] prosperity, life,[3]
Fame, modesty, and learning, reverence and intelligence,
Twilight,[4] night, lustrous day,
Sleep and the night of death,[5]
Āryā, Kātyāyanī, Kauśikī,[6]
Observant of *brahmacarya*,[7]
Mother of the leader of the celestial hosts,[8]
Formidable one,[9]
She who undergoes great austerities[10]

---

[1] The sacred hymn as sung in ancient times by *Ṛṣis*, related in chap. lviii of the Harivamśa, a sequel of the Mahābhārata.

[2] *Siddhi* (success,) which here means the supreme *siddhi* or *mukti* (liberation).

[3] That is according to the commentator *jivanam*.

[4] *Sandhyā* or junction-time, morning and evening.

[5] *Kālarātri* which is *pralayarātri*, or the night of the dissolution of all things.

[6] Born in the race of the sage Kuśika.

[7] The virgin state, or the first of the *āśramas*.

[8] Skanda, or Kārtikeya, son of S'iva and the Devī.

[9] *Ugrachārī*, which should be *ugrachārinī*, but this is *Arsha* (composed by *Ṛṣis*), to whom the rules of grammar do not apply.

[10] The Devī practised great austerities to gain S'iva as Her husband.

Jayā and Vijayā, [1]
Contentment, nourishment, forgiveness, mercy, eldest sister of Yama,[2] clad in blue silken raiment,
Of various form,[3] without form, having many forms.[4] With red, half-opened eyes.[5]
Large-eyed protectress of Thy votaries.
O Goddess ! Thou resideth on the peaks of fearful mountains, by rivers, and in caves, forests, and groves.
Greatly worshipped by the S'avara, Varvara, and Pulinda tribesmen,[6]
Thou traverseth in all directions of the world
With peacock-feathered flags.
Thou livest on the Vindhya mountain,
Surrounded by fowls, goats, sheep, lions, and tigers,
Amidst the constant ringing of bells.[7]
Thou holdest the trident and spear.[8]

---

[1] Companion Devatās of Durgā.

[2] Mrityu, the God of Death.

[3] *Bahurūpā* (see the Lalitā, verse 155). The Devi Bhāg. Pr. says, " She is formless because She is supreme, She has many forms because of Her activity " (see also Devi and Vāmana Purāṇas) : " She is also the *S'akti* of the countless Rudras. " The term is much commented upon in the Purāṇas, Upapurāṇas, and Tantras.

[4] *Anekavidharūpinī*.

[5] *Virūpākṣī*. S'iva is also called *Virūpākṣa*. His eyes are, either owing to his state of *samādhi*, or consumption of *bhang*, pictured as in a vague, dreamy, half-open state.

[6] *S'avarair varvaraischaiva pulindaischa supūjitā*—a line worthy of remark, for these were savage and non-aryan tribes.

[7] During worship of the image the worshipper rings a bell. There was a constant ringing of bells.

[8] *Pattisha*, a kind of spear with a sharp edge.

Sun and moon are Thy banners.
Thou art the ninth day of the dark half of the month,
And the eleventh day of the light half thereof.[1]
Baladeva's [2] sister art Thou, glorious one,[3]
Fond of warring [4] (with demons),
Abode of all creatures.
Thou art death,[5] and the supreme end [6] of men,
Daughter of the cowherd Nanda,[7]
Unconquered,
Wearing bark and good cloth;
Raudrī,[8] twilight,[9]
With dishevelled hair,[10]
And who art death,
Fond art Thou of offerings of wine and flesh.[11]
Thou art Lakṣmī,[12]
And assumest the form of Alakṣmī [13] for the destruction of Dānavas,[14]

---

[1] Auspicious days. On the ninth (*Navamī*) there is *Caṇḍīpātha* (reading of Caṇḍī), and on the eleventh (*Ekādaśī*) fasting.

[2] Kṛṣṇa's eldest brother.

[3] *Rajanīya* in text is said to be a wrong reading for *mahanīya*.

[4] *Kalahapriyā*. Literally, quarrelsome.

[5] *Niṣṭha*, which according to the commentator, here means *maraṇam*.

[6] That is, *mukti* (Liberation).

[7] Foster-father of Kṛṣṇa.

[8] The dark (*tāmasika*) energy, called Raudrī, is said to be Cāmuṇḍā· There are said to be nine crores of different Cāmuṇḍās. (see Bhāskararāya Comm., Lalitā, verse 155).

[9] *Sandhyā*.

[10] Kāli and Tāra are always so represented (see Karpūrādistotra).

[11] *Surāmāmsabalipriyā*.

[12] Devī of wealth and prosperity.

[13] Devī of misfortune and poverty.

[14] Sons of Danu, enemies of the Devas.

Thou art Sāvitri [1] of the Vedas,
Mother of Mantras.[2]
Thou art the *Dakṣinā* [3] of the *ṛtvik*,[4] and art in the altars of sacrificial rites,
And the religious sense [5] of *Ṛṣis*.
Thou art Aditi of Devas.[6]
Plough of cultivators, earth of all creatures,
The success of merchants who fare in big ships,[7]
The coast of ocean,
And foremost Yakṣi of the Yakṣas,[8]
Surasā of Nāgās,[9]
Virginity [10] of maidens and good fortune of women,
Knower of the knowledge of Brahman,[11]
Initiation and supreme beauty,
Lustre of light, Rohini [12] of planets.
Lakshmi, most successful art Thou in courts and fortresses,
In the confluence of rivers and in the full moon.
Thou art called Krittivāsa.[13]

---

1 The Gāyatri *mantra*.

2 *Mantraganasya*, or, according to another reading, *bhūtaganasya*.

3 The present offered to the officiating Brāhmaṇa.

4 Priest.

5 *Dharmabuddhi*, a term difficult to translate. A man is said to have *dharmabuddhi* who has great respect for religion and duty.

6 The Devas were children of Aditi, as the Daityas were of Diti.

7 *Sāngyātrikānām* = *potavanijām*.

8 That is, She is the Mother of Kubera, the King of the Yakṣas, a class of *Devayoni*.

9 Mother of the serpent divinities (Nāgās).

10 *Brahmacarya*.

11 *Brahmavādini*.

12 The name of an asterism.

13 The name of S'iva as clad in tiger-skin.

Thou art Sarasvati in the works of Vālmiki,[1]
Memory in those of Dvaipāyana,[2]
Religious sense of *Ṛṣis*[3] and (perfect) mind of
Devas.[4]
Thou art the Goddess of wine,[5]
Adored art Thou by Thy creatures for Thy deeds.
Thou art the charming look of Indra,
And art the thousand-eyed[6],
Devi of ascetics,
Ārani[7] of Agnihotra Brāhmaṇas,[8]
Hunger of all creatures,
Who satisfieth those in heaven.
Thou art *Svāhā*,[9]
Contentment, patience,
Receptacle of the Vasus,[10] hope of men,
Contentment which comes of work fully done;

---

1 Author of the Rāmāyana. Tradition says that he obtained a boon from the Goddess of learning and composed that work.

2 Kṛṣṇa Dvaipāyana, one of the Vyasas, arranger of the Purāṇas, etc., who is said to have had all such *śāstra* by heart.

3 *Vide ante* (see p. 157, note 5).

4 *Mānasi*, which the Commentator says = " *Satyasangkalpātmikā chetovritti* " that is, whose will and thought fully realizes itself.

5 *Surādevi*.

6 Indra.

7 *Ārani* are the two sticks of *samid* wood used to kindle sacrificial fire.

8 Brāhmaṇas who cherish fire in the house and perform *homa* thrice daily.

9 Wife of Agni, the *mantra* used when making *homa*..

10 Of whom there are eight: Apa, Dhruva, Soma, Dhara, Anila, Anala, Pratyusha, Prabhāsa (see Vishnupurāṇa, Book I., chap. xv.)

All the quarters and their opposites,[1]
Flame of fire, lustrous Sakunī,[2]
Pūtanā,[3] the terrible Revatī,[4]
Overpowering sleep of all beings,
Warrior.[5]
Of learning Thou art, *Brahmavidyā*,[6]
Om and *Vaṣat.*[7]
The *Ṛṣis* know Thee as Pārvati amongst women.
As Prajāpati[8] has said, Thou art Arundhatī[9]
amongst women, with but one husband.[10]
The difference of disputants.[11]
Famous also art Thou as Indrāṇī[12]
This universe, mobile and immobile, is permeated
by Thee.
Without a doubt Thou art saviour in all battles.
Amidst fires and on the banks of rivers,
Amidst robbers, in forests and caverns,
When in prison or when assailed by enemies,
And in all times and places where life is in peril.

---

[1] *e g.*, north and south, east and west, etc.

[2] A terrible spirit of that name.

[3] A female demon who attempted to destroy, but who was destroyed by the infant Kṛṣṇa.

[4] Name of the twenty-seventh constellation, containing thirty-two stars.

[5] *Kṣatriyā.*

[6] The science of Brahman.

[7] The *Mahāmantra* "*om*". *Vaṣat* is a *mantra.* As *Svāhā* is used with *homa*, so *srauṣat*, *vauṣat*, *vaṣat*, and *svadhā* are used in *pitṛkriyā.*

[8] Brahmā.

[9] Wife of the sage Vaśiṣṭha, famous for her constancy and devotion.

[10] *Ekabhartrinām.*

[11] *Bhedovivādashīlānām.*

[12] Spouse of Indra.

My heart, my reason, and mind are devoted to Thee.
Deliver me from all sins. Be gracious to me.
Whoever rising at dawn reads[1] for the space of three months
This sacred hymn to Devī compiled by Vyāsa,
Being himself pure and of controlled mind.
Obtains the desired fruit.
Whoever reads it for six months, to him also
The desired fruit is given. Such as read it for nine months obtain celestial vision, and he who reads it for one year gains all such success[2] as man may desire.
O Devī ! as was said by Dvaipāyana, Thou art the supreme divine Brahman.
Thou destroyest the bonds and the fearful destruction of men,
The loss of children and wealth, fear of death and disease.
Thou art in the form of desire, and dost grant the objects thereof.
Having deluded Kaṃsa, Thou enjoyest the whole world,
And I also shall live as a cowherd among kine ;
To accomplish my work I shall become a cowherd of Kaṃsa.[3]

---

1 Here follows the *phala* portion. (see p. 73,note 1).

2 *Siddhi*

3 The tyrant who sought to slay Kṛṣṇa. The Chapter concludes : "Having thus addressed the Devi, the Lord disappeared, and She, too, saluting Him, expressed Her consent by saying, 'So be it'."

DURGĀ[1]

From the MAHĀBHĀRATA[2]

1

I SALUTE Thee, leader of Yogis,[3] one with the Brahman,[4]
Dweller in the Mandāra forest.
Virgin,[5] Kāli,[6] Spouse of Kāpāla,[7] of tawny hue.[8]
Salutation to Thee, Bhadrakāli.[9]
Reverence to Thee, Mahākāli,[10]

---

[1] See p. 120, note 9; p 128, note 1 : p. 81, note 1.

[2] Bhīshma Parvan, s. 43 (see Muir, O. S. T. iv, 432).

[3] *Siddhasenānī*. The *siddhas* are here *yogis* and sages. Nīlakaṇṭha (cited *post* as N.), in his Commentary, says the term means : She who, as leader (literally, commander of an army), gives success in *yoga* and attainment of the supreme abode.

[4] *Āryye*. Literally, noble, but here means, as Nīlakaṇṭha says, *prapya-brahmasvarūpa*—the own form of the accessible Brahman, as distinguished from the *nirguṇa Brahman* beyond thought and speech.

[5] Kumārī. It also means (N.) that She is very young.

[6] See p. 152, note 3.

[7] Kāpālī, one of Her forms. Kāpāla is Rudrā, as leader of Kāpālas (Kāpālikas).

[8] *Kapilākṛṣṇapingalā*

[9] Auspicious Kālī, who gives prosperity to Her devotees.

[10] See p. 152, note 3. The great Kālī, Destructress in the form of death.

Caṇḍi,[1] Fearless one.[2] Salutation to Thee,
Saviour[3] imbued with all good fortune.[4]

2

Of the race of Kata[5] greatly worshipful,
Dreadful one,[6] Giver of victory,[7] Victrix,[8]
Who holdeth a peacock's tail for Thy banner,
And art adorned with various jewels,
Bearing formidable spear, sword, and shield (made of skin).
Younger Sister of the chief of cowherds,[9]
Eldest one,[10] born in the family of the cowherd Nanda,[11]
Delighting in the blood of Mahiṣa,[12]

---

[1] Spouse of Caṇḍa, or Kālāntaka, or Yama.

[2] *Caṇdā*—bold, daring, brave, courageous.

[3] *Tārinī*, for She delivers from calamity.

[4] *Varavarninī* (N.), not "beautiful coloured," as it has been translated.

[5] Kātyāyanī.

[6] *Karāli = krure* or cruel (to demons and other ill-doers). *Karālavadanā* (wide-opened mouth) is an epithet of Kāli. "Gaping-mouthed, terrible, four-armed, with dishevelled hair" — *Karālavadanām ghorām, chatur-bhujām*, as the Kālī *dhyāna* runs.

[7] *Vijaya*—that is, particular (*viśiṣṭa*) victory (N.).

[8] *Jayā*. *Jayā* and *Vijayā* are also the names of two female attendants (*Sakhī*) of Durgā.

[9] Gopendra or Kṛṣṇa. In the Harivamśa and Caṇḍī it is said that with the view of defeating the designs of Kamsa in regard to the destruction of Devakī's offspring, Devī will be born as the ninth child of Yaśodā in the same night as Kṛṣṇa was born as the eight child of Devakī, when Kṛṣṇa would be carried to Yaśodā and She to Devakī.

[10] *Jyeṣtha = śreṣthā*—superior to or best of all.

[11] In whose house Kṛṣṇa was reared.

[12] The Asura of that name (see Caṇḍī).

Kauśikī,[1] wearing yellow garments.

3

With auspicious smile,
Whose mouth devoured all demons,[2]
Salutation to Thee, delighter in battle.
Umā,[3] giver of *shāka*,[4]
In the form of Maheśvara,[5] and in that of Vāsudeva,[6]
Destructress of Kaitabha,[7]
Golden-eyed, with half-opened eyes[8], grey-eyed,[9]
Veda and *S'ruti*,[10] and most sacred.
Propitious to Brāhmaṇas engaged in the sacrificial rites,
Thou art Jātaveda,[11]
And art ever present in the sacred shrines[12] in the chief cities of Jambudvīpa.[13]

---

1 A name of the Devī, as born in the race of the sage Kuśika.

2 *Kokamukhe*—when in battle with Raktabīja.

3 See Hymn to Annapūrṇa, *post*.

4 *Shākambarī*. *Shāka* is a vegetable food given by Devī at the time of famine (Caṇḍī).

5 *Svetā* (N.), not white, as it has been translated.

6 *Kṛṣṇā* (N.), not black, as it has been translated.

7 A Daitya brother of Madhu (Caṇḍī).

8 *Virūpākṣī* (see p. 155, note 5).

9 *Dhūmrākṣī* (N.) says grey and green, like those of a cat.

10 Here Upaniṣads.

11 *Jātavedasī*. Jataveda is a name of Agni (Fire).

12 *Chaityeshu*. Ordinarily this term is applied to the Buddhist shrine, of which it is commonly said: "One should not enter a Jaina's temple or Buddhist *chaitya*, even if pursued by an elephant" (*Hastinā tādyamānopi na gachchet jaina-mandiram* also *dhaitya mandiram*.) Here the term means *devatālaya*.

13 A Purāṇic island by that name, not as it has been translated; "Who dwellest continually near to mountain precipices and sepulchres."

4

Of Sciences Thou art the knowledge of Brahman,
Thou art the liberation of embodied beings,[1]
Mother of Skanda.[2]
O Bhagavatī[3] Durgā ![4] Thou liveth in inaccessible
regions—
Svāhā,[5] *Svadhā,*[6] *Kalā,* and *Kāṣṭhā,*[7]
Sarasvatī,[8] Sāvitrī.[9]
Mother of Vedas and Vedānta [10] art Thou called.
I praise Thee from the pure depth of my heart.
By Thy favour let us be victorious in battle.
Ever dost Thou abide in inaccessible regions,
In places full of fear and difficulty ;
In the houses of Thy devotees, and in Pātāla.[11]
In battle Thou conquereth the Dānavas.[12]

---

1 " The great sleep of embodied beings," according to the last translator : But *Mahānidrā* (great sleep) is here *mukti* (liberation), which is the result of the *Brahmavidyā,* spoken of in the preceding line.

2 Kārtikeya. By this it is meant that She is *sarvadevatārūpā,* in the form of all Devas, of whom Skanda is selected as a type(N.).

3 See p. 120, note 5 ; p. 98, note 5.

4 *Kāntāravāsinī* (N.).

5 Mantra used with *homa,* but here it means that all ritual acts are her embodiment (*Sarvakarmarūpā*).

6 *Mantra* used in *pitṛkriyā* (see last note).

7 *Kalā* is a division of time—one minute forty-eight seconds, and *kāṣṭha* is one-thirtieth of that.

8 Devī of speech and learning.

9 She is *sarvavāng-maya-rūpa*(N.).

10 End of the Vedas or Upaniṣad.

11 The nether world.

12 See p. 156, note 14.

Thou art drowsiness[1] and slumber.[2]

5

Thou hast power to show wonderfully the world,[3]
Modesty,[4] and beauty.[5]
Cause of creation and destruction,[6]
Creatrix,[7] Mother,[8] contentment, nourishment,
constancy,
Light, Supportress of the sun and moon,
Power[9] of Him who possesses power,[10]
In ecstasy[11] Thou art perceived by Siddhas and
Cāranas.[12]

---

[1] *Jambhane = tandrā* (N.), not "destroyer" as it has been translated.

[2] *Mohinī = Nidrā* (N.).

[3] *Māyā = adbhutapradarśanām* (N.).

[4] *Hrī = lajjā* representative of, and including all other actions of mind (N.).

[5] *S'rī*, or prosperity, and other attributes of Lakṣmī.

[6] *Sandhyā*. the intervening period when night is going and morn coming. and *vice versa*, applied here to similar junction times in the creation and dissolution of the world (N.).

[7] *Sāvitrī*. She who, by the lustre of Sūrya, reveals (N.).

[8] Because, as a mother, She supports the world and all beings therein.

[9] *Aiśvarya*. The supreme faculties of omnipresence, omnipotence, etc.

[10] *Maheśvara*. She is the greatest wealth of Brahman.

[11] *Sankya* or *Samādhi*, where light appears and the *ātman* is known (N).

[12] Siddhas here mean those who are liberated whilst yet living (*jīvanmukta*), and Cāranas those who are *siddhas* from their birth.

HYMNS TO THE DEVĪ

From S'aṅkarācārya

TRIPURASUNDARĪ

(TRIPURASUNDARĪSTOTRA)

1

I SEEK refuge with Tripurasundarī,[1]
Who wanders in the Kadamba forest ;[2]
The spouse of the Three-eyed One,[3]
Bank of cloud (in the sky of the heart) of numbers
of sages,[4]

---

[1] The Devī is so called as the Spouse of S'iva, destroyer of the *tripura*, or cities of the three Asuras—Kamalākṣa, Tarakākṣa, and Vidyun-māli. According to the Kālikā Purāṇa, Paraśiva is Tripura, because he has three *pura* in Him, His body becoming triple upon the manifestation therein of Brahmā, Viṣṇu, and S'iva. The Devī is then the S'akti of Paramaśiva.

[2] The Kadamba (*Nauclea cadamba*) is a tree with orange fragrant blossom whereunder Kṛṣṇa played (see *Ādyākālisvarūpaśtotra* in Mahānirvāṇa Tantra). *Kadamba* also denotes number (multitude), and in this sense the *Kadamba* forest is the universe which the Devī permeates.

[3] S'iva with the central eye of wisdom. S'iva is also *Tryambaka*, because He is the father of the three Devas, Brahmā, Viṣṇu, and Rudra (Tarkālangkāra Commentary, Mahānirvāṇa Tantra). The Ṛgvidhāna uses it as equivalent of Mahādeva.

[4] *Muni*. As the bank of cloud gives water, so She quenches the spiritual thirst of *munis*.

Whose hips defeat the mountain by their greatness.[1]
Who is served by celestial women,
Whose eyes are like the newly blown lotus,
And who is dark as the colour of a freshly formed
rain-cloud.[2]

2

I seek refuge with Tripurasundari,
The Spouse of the Three-eyed One,
Who dwells in the Kadamba forest,
And who is ever wandering ;
The Large-eyed One who holds a golden *vinā*,[3]
Wearing a necklace of priceless gems,
Whose face is glowing with wine,[4]
And who of Her mercy grants prosperity to Her
devotees.

3

Ever are we protected by Her whose abode is the
Kadamba forest,
The weight of whose breasts are garlanded with
glittering gems,
Whose breasts are rising,[5]

---

[1] *Nitambajitabhudaram. Nitamba* literally means buttocks, which, however, here reads rather absurdly in English, the side or hips being *pārśa, kakṣa*, or *shroni* (*cf.* tenth śloka of the *Karpurākhyastava* " *Samantādāpinastana-jaghanadhrikyauvanavatī* ") .

[2] That is, of the dark blue colour seen when the blue of the sky appears through a freshly-formed black rain-cloud.

[3] A stringed musical instrument of that name.

[4] *Mukhasamullasattvārunim. Vāruni* is wine made from rice. Here and in following verses the divine ambrosia (*amṛta*) is referred to.

[5] " Rising " (*cf. Durgādhyāna* in " Devī Purāṇa ") *pīnonnata payodharām.* As to weight and greatness, see *Annapūrṇādhyāna*, *Bhuvaneśvaristotra*, " *āpīvarastanatating tanuvrittamadhyām*, " and Introduction.

And excel the mountain in greatness;
Whose cheeks are flushed with wine,[1]
Ever singing sweet songs; the playful one,[2] dark
as a cloud,
Ever compassionate to all.

4

I seek refuge with Tripurasundarī,
The Spouse of the Three-eyed One,
Who stays in the Kadamba forest,
Who is seated in the golden circle and dwells in
the six lotuses,[3]
Ever revealing like lightning the great power (of
devotees),[4]
Whose beauty is like that of the *Jaba* flower,[5]
And whose brow is adorned with the full moon.

5

I take refuge with Her, the sweet speaker,
Daughter of the sage Matanga,[6]

---

[1] *Madārunakapolaya* (see n. 4, p. 170).

[2] *Līlayā.* Play (*līlā*) is the mark of a Deva, and the Devī's substance is play (*līlāmayī*). The Devī is Lalitā ("She who plays"): Padma Purāṇa says: "Having passed beyond the world She plays, hence She is called Lalitā." But the Creation is also Her play.

[3] *Ṣaḍāmbhu*—that is, the six *cakra* or centres in the human body: the *mulādhāra, svādihṣṭhāna, manipūra, anāhata, viśuddha,* and *ājnāpadmas* (see the translation of the Ṣatcakra Nirūpaṇa from the Sanskrit, *The Serpent Power*). The Devī exists as Kuṇḍalinī in these *cakra.*

[4] *Satatasiddhisaudaminim. Siddhi* (power so called), which lies latent, is instantly brought to light by Her.

[5] Scarlet hibiscus, the Tāntrik flower sacred to the Devī.

[6] *Ṛṣi.*

Whose breast is adorned with the *vinā*.[1]
And whose head is beauteous with locks of curling hair;
Who dwells in the lotus;[2]
The destroyer of the wicked,
Whose eyes are reddened with wine;[3]
The charmer of the enemy of the God of Love.[4]

6

I take refuge with Tripurasundarī,
The Spouse of the Three-eyed One,
Who should be meditated upon as in the first flush of Her nubile youth,[5]
Her blue garment stained with drops of blood.[6]
Holding the wine-cup,[7]
Her eyes rolling with wine;[8]

---

[1] The musical instrument which She holds and which rests on Her breast.

[2] For she is also Kamalā or Lakṣmī.

[3] *Madārunāvilochanam* (see p. 170. note 4).

[4] That is, charmer of S'iva who destroyed Kāmadeva with the fire from His eyes when the latter sought to distract him by thought of passion from the *yoga* in which he was engaged.

[5] *Smaretprathama puṣpinīm,* literally "as having the first 'flower'" which is used in the same symbolical sense as in English. The *puṣpotsava* is the religious festival held on its first appearance at puberty.

[6] *Rudhiravīndunīlambaram*—that is, stained with the *puspa* ("flower"). As this first shows itself when woman is ready to bear, so in the blue sky, which is the Devi's garment, signs are seen which herald Her creation.

[7] *Grihītamadhupānikām.*

[8] *Madhuvighurnanetranchalam* (see p. 170, n. 4).

With heavy, high, and close-set breasts,[1]
Dark of colour, and with dishevelled hair.[2]

9

At time of recitation I remember the Mother,
Lustrous as the scarlet hibiscus,[3]
Her body pasted with saffron and sandal,
Her hair kissed by musk ;[4]
The Mother with smiling eyes,[5]
With red garland, ornaments, and raiment,
Who holds the arrow, bow, noose, and goad ;[6]
The charmer[7] of countless men.

---

[1] *Ghanastana bharonnatām* :" heavy " (*cf. Annapūrṇadhyāna Annapradāna-niratām stanabhāranamrām* "); " high " (*cf. Durgādhyana, ante* Introduction); " close," so that, as it is said in the Kumarāsambhavam (chap. i.) of Kalidāsa : " Even the filament of a lotus could not be passed between them " (" *mrinālasūtrāntaramapyalabhyam* ").

[2] *Galitachikurām.* The Devi in this and other forms, as Kāli, Tārā and Chinnamastā is so represented. The epithet is a common one in Tantra (*cf. Karpūrādistotra*, verse 3).

[3] *Jaba*, v. *ante*. So also the Lalitā (verse 147), " whose body is like the China rose."

[4] See the *Ādyākālisvarūpa Stotra* in the Mahānirvāṇa Tantra.

[5] The Devī is, according to the Lalitā Sahasranāma (verse 59) *chāruhāsa* (with beautiful smile), indicating a certain state of consciousness (*prabodha*) of highest bliss.

[6] These are Her weapons. The Tantrarāja (Vāsana chap.) says : " Mind is the bow of sugar-cane, desire the noose, anger the goad, and the five subtle sources of the elements (*tanmātra*) the five arrows of flowers." But the Yoginīhridaya says : " The noose is *Iccāśakti*, and goad *Jnānāśakti*, and the bow and arrows *Kriyāśakti*."

[7] She deludes men with her *māyā* ; hence the Lalitā (verse 137) calls Her " all-bewildering " (*sarvamohinī*). The Kurma Purāṇā says : " This *māyā* is dear to me by which the world is bewildered. I bewilder the whole universe with the Devas, Daityas, and men."

8

I worship the World-Mother
Who is served by celestial women,
The Spouse of Indra,
    Skilful in plaiting hair ;[1]
    The devoted Spouse of Brahmā,
    Anointed with sandal paste ;
    The Spouse of Viṣṇu,
    Adorned with pleasing ornaments.

---

[1] *Cikurabandhasairiṇdhrikām* : for Her hair, which is in some of Her aspects dishevelled, is in others beautifully arranged.

GANGĀ

(GANGĀṢṬAKAM)

1

O BHAGAVATĪ GANGĀ ! [1]
Thou art the playful garland on the head of Hara ;[2]
Such as but touch a drop of the spray of Thy waters
Recline on the lap of the fan-holding women of the
city of the immortals, [3]
Freed of the fear arising from the sinful Kali age. [4]

2

(O Devī Gangā !) may you purify us,
Thou who separateth the earth from Heaven, [5]
Gladdening the creeper-like matted hair on the
head of Hara, [6]
Descending from the region of heaven,
Oozing from out the cave of the golden mountain, [7]
Falling upon the surface of the earth,

---

[1] The River Ganges, in whom the Devī manifests.

[2] S'iva. The Ganges in its descent from heaven at the call of Bhagiratha was caught in the matted hair of S'iva.

[3] *Amarāvati*. The city of Indra.

[4] Kaliyuga. The fourth, and, according to orthodox views, the present age, marked by the prevalence of sin.

[5] By the celestial Ganges called Mandākini.

[6] See note 2 *ante*.

[7] Sumeru.

Purifier (as the River Mandākinī) of the city of the
Devas,
Who art the powerful Destructress of the multitude
of men's sins.

3

The trunks of elephants and their young make play
with Thy waters,
Fragrant with ichor-maddened swarms of bees,
Trickling from the temples of elephants bathing
therein.
Thy stream is browned with the sandal paste
Dropping from the breasts of Siddha women [1] who
bathe therein.
And nigh the river bank Thy water is strewn with
Kuśa [2] grass and flowers,
There thrown by sages [3] at morn and even. [4]
May the water of the Ganges protect us!

4

This divine sin-destroying Bhāgīrathī [5] now on earth
Was in the beginning water in the vessel [6] of the
Primeval Grandfather. [7]
Then it was pure water from the feet of the Lord
(Viṣṇu),

---

1 Siddhas are celestial spirit (*devayoni*) of great purity.

2 A species of grass used in worship.

3 *Munis*.

4 The flower and grass is thrown by them when they worship the Ganges in the morning and evening.

5 Gangā is called Bhagīrathī, because She was brought down from heaven by the prayer of Bhagīratha, son of the solar race, in order to secure heavenly bliss for his kinsmen.

6 *Kamaṇḍalu,* a gourd-shaped vessel used by ascetics.

7 *Pitāmaha.* Brahma is so called.

Who sleeps on the serpent.[1]
Again it was the gem adorning the matted hair of
S'iva,[2]
And, lastly, the daughter of the great sage Jahnu.[3]

5

May the entrancing[4] Gangā falling on the matted
hair[5] of Hara,[6]
Descending from the Lord of Mountains,
Moving sinuously like a serpent to the ocean,
Flowing by the city of Kāśi,[7]
Dispeller of countless worldly fears,[8]
Saviour of those who bathe in Her waters,
Be ever victorious.

6

How can he who has seen Thy wave be bound by
illusion ?

---

[1] The thousand-headed serpent Ananta Deva (see Viṣṇu Purāṇā).

[2] *Ante* p. 175, n. 2.

[3] Hence the river is called Jāhnavi. The verse speaks of the stages of the descent of the heavenly stream. *Ṛṣi* Jāhnu swallowed the Ganges, and then, at the prayer of Bhagīratha, he let it issue from his thigh. The Ganges is called his daughter as She issued from him.

[4] *Manohārinī* (" mind stealer ").

[5] S'iva, like the ascetics, wears a coil of matted hair (*Jaṭa*)

[6] S'iva.

[7] Benares, through which the Ganges flows.

[8] Fearlessness is the special gift of the Devi. The Mārkandeya Purāṇā says: " When You are remembered in times of difficulty, You take away all fear of all beings." She is *Bhayāpahā* (remover of fear); for S'ruti says ("Tai Up." ii. 9, 1): "By knowing the bliss of that Brahman none fear anything."

To him who has drunk of Thy water thou givest a
dwelling in the city of the yellow-clad Deva.[1]
O Gangā! what time the bodies of those who
assume body[2] fall on Thy lap,[3]
For such, O Mother,[4] even Shatakrīta's[5] grandeur[6]
is but a small thing.

7

O Bhagavatī![7] on Thy bank I drink Thy water
only.
I worship Kṛṣṇa, all thirst for worldly enjoyment
having gone.
Destroyer of all sin, Whose companionship is the
stairway to Heaven,[8]
O Devī! Gangā of lightsome, tremulous wave,
Be gracious to me.

8

O Mother! O Spouse of S'ambhu![9]
Who art ever associated with S'ambhu
At death, upon Thy banks, with my hands folded
upon my head,

---

[1] That is, Viṣṇu, who is clad in yellow, and whose city is His heaven (*Vaikuṇṭha*).

[2] Men.

[3] That is, when on death, they are thrown into the Ganges.

[4] The Devī is the Holy Mother (*S'rīmātā*), the first of Her names.

[5] Indra, King of the celestials.

[6] *Pada* or portion.

[7] Feminine of Bhagavan, a term applied to God, and which means He who possesses *Bhaga*.

[8] *Svarga*.

[9] S'iva.

Remembering Thy name and the feet of Nārāyaṇa,[1]
May my devotion to Hara and Hari[2] ever endure
At the time of the festival of life's departure![3]
He who of pure mind reads this sacred eight-versed hymn to Gangā
Will be wholly released of all sin
And will go the region of Viṣṇu.[4]

---

[1] Viṣṇu.

[2] Viṣṇu and S'iva.

[3] Death (*prāṇaprayāṇotsava*), for it is the entrance to heavenly bliss.

[4] *Vaikuṇṭha* (see p. 178. n. 1).

WAVES OF BLISS

(ĀNANDALAHARĪ)

1

O Bhavānī,[1] the four-headed Lord of creatures,[2] is not able to worship Thee,
Nor even the five-headed destroyer of the Tripura,[3]
Nor the six-headed commander of the celestial hosts,[4]
Nor even the thousand-headed Lord of serpents.[5]
If, then, they cannot, tell me who else is able so to do?

2

O Devī! how can we speak of Thy qualities,
Which are not to be described by any *Nigama*,[6]
As the sweetness of ghee,[7] milk, the grape, and honey

---

[1] Bhava is S'iva, and is His name in the watery form of the *aṣṭamūrti* (eight forms). The Vāyu Purāṇa says that He is called Bhava because all things come from Him and subsist in water. The Devī is Bhavānī as the Spouse and giver of life to Bhava.

[2] Brahmā.

[3] S'iva.

[4] Kārtikeya, son of S'iva.

[5] Ananta on whom Viṣṇu reposes.

[6] Generally S'āstra and in special technical sense Tantra in which the Devī is the Guru.

[7] Clarified butter.

Cannot be distinguished and described by words,
But may be perceived by the tongue only;
In like manner Thy beauty can be seen only by
the eyes of Parameśvara.[1]

3

We ever pray to Thee, O Gaurī![2]
Youthful daughter of the Lord of mountains.
Beautiful is the betel[3] in Thy mouth
And the collyrium on Thy eyes;
Beautiful, too, are the saffron on Thy forehead,
The necklet of pearls on Thy throat,
Thy silken garment and the glittering gold waist-
ornament on Thy large hips.[4]

4

May Bhagavatī,[5] Satī,[6] whose lotus eyes sparkle,[7]
Spouse of S'ambhu,[8] on the slope of whose breasts
Rests a beautiful garland of the flowers of the
Mandāra tree,[9]
Whose earring is the pleasing sound from the *vinā*,[10]

---

1 The supreme Lord.

2 See p. 30, note 3.

3 *Tāmbūla*, or pan, which is chewed.

4 *Prithukatitate.*

5 Feminine of Bhagavan.

6 Devī as daughter of Dakṣa (see Introduction).

7 *Ambhoruhacatulacakṣu.* Literally, the lotus eye is ever moving, now glancing here, now there. Motionless eyes in women are not considered beautiful.

8 S'iva.

9 One of the five heavenly trees in the garden and city (*Amarāvati*) of Indra—viz., Mandāra, Pārijāta, Santāna, Kalpavrikṣa, Harichandana.

10 The stringed instrument of that name borne by the Devī as Sarasvatī.

Who stoops (from the weight of her breasts),[1]
Whose beautiful swaying gait is that of the female
elephant [2]—
May that Bhagavatī be ever victorious !

5

O beauteous Aparṇā ![3]
Bestow the fulness of happiness on me,
Thou whose limbs art covered
With ornaments of gold and gems glittering like
the newly risen sun,
Whose eyes are beautiful as those of a doe,
Of whom S'iva is a part,[4]
Who is of the golden colour of lightning,
Beauteous in yellow garments and tinkling anklets.

6

Shines forth does the Devī born in the snowy
mountains. [5]

---

[1] *Nātangī.* So also the Annapūrṇā *dhyāna* represents the Devī as giver of food "stooping from the weight of Her great breasts" (*annapradāna niratāmstanabhāranamrām*, and see verse 6 *post*).

[2] *Mātangīruciragati bhangī bhagavatī.*

[3] Name of the Devi. According to the Kālikā, and Brahma Purāṇas the Devī, as the daughter of Himavat, renounced even leaves as food (*a-parṇā* = without leaf) ; hence she is called by Devas Aparṇā. According to another derivation, the name comes from *apa* (removing), *rina* (debt). So Bhāskararāya, who gives it, says in his *Devīstava* ; "When you have not discharged your debt to me, though I respect your name, O S'ivé why are you not ashamed to bear the name of Aparṇā ? " (discharger of debt) ? According to the Nirukta, *parna* = falling. *Aparṇa* = free from falling.

[4] That is, it is by Her favour that S'iva forms part of Her.

[5] *Himādrehsambhūtā*—that is, the Himālaya, hence She is also called *Girijā* (mountain-born).

Her beautiful hands are like a red leaf.[1]
She is adorned with beautiful flowers and pearls.
Her head, by its weight of hair, seems covered by
a swarm of bees.[2]
It is She with whom S'iva seeks shelter,
Who stoops from the weight of Her breasts,[3]
Whose words are sweet,
The Destructress of ills,[4]
Ever and in all places pervading,[5]
Tender creeper [6] of Intelligence and Bliss.[7]

7

Others worship with reverence the plant with
leaves and particular qualities,
But I know that Aparṇā alone in this world should
be worshipped.[8]
Then the old S'iva garmented with space

---

[1] Either from their natural colour or because dyed with lac.

[2] The bee goes to the lotus; the bees (her hair) settle upon her (lotus) face.

[3] *Kucābharanatā* (see note 1, p. 182).

[4] Disease (*rujānghantrī*).

[5] Literally, one who goes (*gantrī*).

[6] *Latikā*. Dim. of *latā* creeper to which woman is compared, for she clings to her husband as the creeper to the tree. Hence worship with woman in the Tāntrik *Pancatattva* is called *latāsādhana*.

[7] *Cidānanda* which, with *sat* (being), constitutes the nature of the Supreme Being (Parabrahman).

[8] That is, some worship a particular Devatā to gain a particular result—*e.g.*, Sarasvatī for learning, Lakṣmī for wealth etc.; but S'ankarācārya worships the supreme Aparṇā, whom the Devas worship, who is without qualities, and does so only to give Her honour.

Surely grants to Thy worshipper the fruit of full
liberation.[1]

8

Thou art the Mother of all Vedas,
The regulator of all *dharmas* [2]
And the root of all wealth—
Thou whose lotus feet are worshipped even by the
wealth-giver.[3]
O Mother! Thou art the primal cause of all
desires.
Victrix of Kandarpa,[4] Thou art the seed of libera-
tion for the good.[5]
Thou art the Spouse of the Parabrahman.[6]

9

Although my mind be fickle and wanting in great
devotion to Thee,
Yet by Thy mercy Thou should look auspiciously
upon me.
The cloud gives sweet water to the mouth of the
Cātaka[7] bird.

---

[1] Full *kaivalya mokṣa*, liberation above the various *pāda*, *sālokya*, etc. (see p. 59, note 1), for *muktī* is of various kinds.

[2] Law of religion, duty, etc.

[3] That is Kubera, Deva of wealth.

[4] A name of Kāma, God of Love (see p. 40, note 1).

[5] *Satām.* She gives liberation to them.

[6] The Supreme Being, for it preceded S'aktī, as *S'ruti* says, "*Sa aikshata,*" etc. As the S'āradā Tilaka (chap. i.) says: "*Saccidānanda vibhavāt sakalat parameshvarāt, āsīchchaktistītonādonād-bindusadmudbhavah.*

[7] A bird (cuculus melanolcucus) which is said to live on raindrops.

I know not by what (good) fate my mind is
directed.[1]

10

O virtuous One, from the corner of Thine eyes
Cast now a glance of kindness upon me;
Neglect so to do is not proper on Thy part,
Seeing that I have reached the refuge of Thy
initiation.
Alas! the creeper of desire,[2] whose very name
shows that it gives desire,
Yet cannot give that which is desired,
What difference is there between it and any other
common creeper?

11

I, though I have sought refuge with other Devatās,
Have yet placed full trust in Thy lotus feet.
If, nevertheless, your heart is not timely set on me,
Then with whom shall I in my helplessness seek
shelter,
O Mother of the big-bellied one![3]

12

As iron touched by the touchstone becomes at once
gold,

[1] That is, just as the *cātaka* is given something, though it does not and cannot pray for it, so what the writer of the hymn receives must, since his devotion (*bhakti*) is so small and lacking in the force of prayer, be due to some undisclosed merit acquired as the result of past *karma*.

[2] *Kalpalatikā*—that is, a creeper which, like the *kalpa* tree, grants all desires that may be asked of it.

[3] Ganeśa.

As the water of the roadway mixed with that of the Ganges becomes pure,
In like maner will not my heart,
Greatly soiled though it be by my great sins [1]
Become pure if attached with devotion to Thee ?

13

O Īśāni,[2] as the old Lotus-Born [3] and others have said,
The rule is that if others than Thyself art worshipped,
Only the particular fruit desired is gained ;
But Thou giveth more even than is asked for.
Make me, then, ever attached to Thee by day and night.

14

O Spouse of the great Lord of the three worlds ![4]
Most pleasant is Thy abode,
The walls whereof glitter with various gems and crystals,
Whereon Thy image is reflected.
On the summit of Thy abode the quivering light waves of the moon (are shed).
Therein dwell Mukunda,[5] Brahmā, and other Devas.
It is ever victorious.

---

[1] *Tattatpāpaih.* Literally, " those particular sins "—the sins of the hymnist who knows what they are.

[2] Feminine of Īśa (Lord).

[3] Brahmā.

[4] See p. 151, note 7.

[5] Giver of liberation—that is, Viṣṇu.

15

Thy dwelling is in Mount Kailāsa.[1]
Thy worshippers are Brahmā, Indra, and other Devas.
All are subservient to Thee in the three regions.[2]
The number of *siddhis*[3] join their palms (in adoration before Thee.).
S'iva is Thy lover ;
Therefore, O Daughter of the Lord of mountains[4]
Nothing is equal to Thy fortune.

16

The old bull is (S'iva's) carrier.
Poison is his food ;[5] space is his dwelling ;
The cremation ground is his playground ;[6]
Serpents are his ornaments.

---

[1] See *Introduction to Tantra S'āstra.*

[2] See p. 151, note 7.

[3] Great powers, such as *aṇimā*, *laghimā*, etc., the power of becoming extremely light or heavy, of entering into things, etc., which, in their fulness, constitute the *aiśvarya* of the Lord (Īśvara), and in a lesser degree of those who approach His nature.

[4] Himālaya, for Devi was the daughter of the Mountain-King Himavat.

[5] See p. 16, note 2.

[6] Dakṣa, in the Bhāgavata Purāṇa, reproaching S'iva, says: " He roams about in dreadful cemeteries, attended by hosts of ghosts and spirits, like a madman, naked, with dishevelled hair, wearing a garland of dead men's skulls and ornaments of human bone, pretending to be S'iva (auspicious), but in reality Aśiva (inauspicious), insane, beloved by the insane, the Lord of Bhūtas (ghosts and spirits), beings whose nature is essentially darkness " (Muir, O.S.T., iv. 738). The cremation ground is His abode, for there the passions are burnt away.

All things in the world are known to the enemy of Smara ;[1]
But the wealth of all this is due to the greatness of Thy fortune,
O Mother !

17

The Lord of *Paśus*,[2] besmeared with ashes, sits in the cremation ground.
From his nature arises the force which destroys the world.
Out of compassion for the whole world, He held the poison in his throat.[3]
O Kalyāṇi ![4] in all this I see the fruit of his companionship with Thee.

18

O Daughter of the mountain,[5]
When Gangā had seen Thy great beauty,
She was afraid,[6] and turned to water ;
Then S'iva, seeing her sad, lotus-like face,
In his mercy made a dwelling for Her on his own head.[7]

---

[1] God of Love, whom S'iva consumed.

[2] *Paśupati :* a name of S'iva : as to *Paśu* (see *Introduction to Tantra S'āstra*). Here the equivalent of Lord of men.

[3] See p. 16, note 2.

[4] Beneficent one. According to the Padma Purāṇa Devī is worshipped as Kalyāṇi in the Malaya mountain, to which reference is made in verse 20.

[5] See p. 187, note 4.

[6] *Bhītaivāsīt*, or may be abashed.

[7] Jāhnavī, whence Gangā is called Jāhnavī. When Gangā fell from Heaven, S'iva first held Her in the locks of his hair, until Her anger at being called down by Bhagīratha had abated. She

19

O Bhagavati,[1] the Creator having with his own
hands taken Thy bathing water
Mingled with liquid sandal, musk, saffron, and
flowers,
And the dust of Thy moving feet,
Created therewith the lotus-eyed women of the
city of the Devas.[2]

20

If one but contemplates Thee, in play with Thy
maidens,
In pleasing springtide with its flowers and creepers
Upon the lake, beautiful with many a blossoming
lotus and flocks of geese,
The waters of which are rippled by the breeze
from the Malaya mountain,[3]
From such an one all fevered ills[4] pass away.

---

then fell into the Bindu lake, whence issue the seven sacred streams. One branch followed Bhagiratha wherever he went, and on the way flooded the sacrificial flame of the *muni* Jāhnu. In his anger he drank up its waters. Bhagīratha's work seemed to be fruitless. But after intercession, the *muni* allowed the waters to flow from him, and as so, issuing from him, the Ganges is called his daughter Jāhnavī.

[1] See p. 178, note 7.

[2] *Amarāvatī*, the city of Indra.

[3] See note to verse 17.

[4] Literally, fever-produced disease (*jvarajanitapīdāpasarati*).

YAMUNA[1]

(YAMUNĀṢṬAKAM)

1

May the daughter of Kalinda[2] ever cleanse my mind of its impurity,
She whose waters, beauteous as the black body of the enemy[3] of Mura,[4]
Cleanse the overgrowth of plants[5] and shrubs which line its pleasant banks.
Indra's heaven compared with Thy waters is but a thing of straw.
Destructress of the sorrow of the three worlds—
Dhunotu me manomalam Kalindanandinī sadā.[6]

2

May the daughter of Kalinda ever cleanse my mind of its impurity,
She whose stream is highly adorned with overflowing water
Destructress of sin, dark as night, like unto nectar,

[1] The river sacred in particular for its memories of S'rī Kṛṣṇa, who on its banks sported with the cowherd women (*Gopīs*).

[2] Yamunā.

[3] S'rī Kṛṣṇa.

[4] A Daitya slain by S'rī Kṛṣṇa.

[5] *Kunjapunja.*

[6] The refrain is translated in the first line.

Greatly powerful for the destruction of all great sins,
Beneficent One who is black of colour,
Through company with the body of the good son of Nanda[1]
Dhunotu me manomalam Kalindanandinī sadā.

3

May the daughter of Kalinda ever cleanse my mind of its impurity,
The touch of whose shining waves washes away the sins of multitudes of beings.
Devoted to Thee is the *Cātaka* bird,[2] receptacle that Thou art of freshness and sweetness.[3]
Giver of desire,
On the borders of whose banks swans ever dwell,
Dhunotu me manomalam Kalindanandinī sadā.

4

May the daughter of Kalinda ever cleanse my mind of its impurity.
The gentle breeze on Her banks dispels the lassitude
Of those who have rambled and played[4] thereon.
The beauty of Her waters is beyond the power of words;
It is, indeed, the consortment with Her current,

[1] The cowherd who brought up S'rikṛṣṇa, when his life was threatened by Kamsa.

[2] As to which see p. 184, note 7.

[3] Literally, "who are slaves to Her by reason of their inhabitancy of Her banks"

[4] After the *rāsalilā* S'rikṛṣṇa and the *Gopis* are tired by their dance and play, and are refreshed by repose upon Her banks where gentle breezes blow.

Which purifies all rivers, male and
female,[1] on the earth.
Dhunotu me manomalam Kalindanandinī sadā,

5

May the daughter of Kalinda ever cleanse my
mind of its impurity,
Destroyed by (the whiteness of) Her sandy banks
laved by Her waters;
She who is ever white,[2]
Adorned with blossoms beauteous as the rays of
the autumn moon.[3]
May She then purify me by Her waters,
Most excellent that they are for the worship of
Bhava,[4]
(By her white splendour),[5] Destructress of the
darkness of night[6]—
Dhunotu me manomalam Kalindanandinī sadā.

6

May the daughter of Kalinda ever cleanse my mind
of its impurity.
The paste and unguents of the beauteous Rādhikā[7]
Colours Her waters in which Rādhikā plays.

---

[1] Rivers are either male (*nada*) or female (*nadī*). Of the former class are the Sone, Sindu, etc., and of the latter Gangā. Narmadā, Gandakī, etc.

[2] Her sandy banks are so.

[3] Of a soft and silvery white.

[4] For use in the ritual worship of S'iva.

[5] *Malam* (*manomalam*). Impurity is a thing which is dark. The river by the white splendour of its white banks and blossoms is therewith contrasted.

[6] For luminously white is She like the moon.

[7] The beloved of S'rikṛṣṇa.

Possessor is She of the body of the husband[1] of
Rādhikā,
Which by none other may be possessed.
Skilled is She in making Her way through the
seven sleeping oceans,
And in filling them with waters[2]—
Dhunotu me manomalam Kalindanandini sadā.

7

May the daughter of Kalinda ever cleanse my
mind of its impurity!
Her stream is beauteous with the women of the
cowherds,[3]
Made passionate[4] by the scent of the paste and
unguent,
Dropped therein from off the body of Acyuta,[5]
Garlanded is She with clusters of Champak flowers,

---

[1] S'rikṛṣṇa; for He too bathes in her stream, which possesses also His dark colour.

[2] Alluding to the destruction of the Asuras, called Kālakeya. These excluded the Devas from *svarga*. On their chiefs being slain by Indra, they betook themselves to the depths of the ocean, whence they issued at night to destroy the *Ṛṣis*. The latter asked the aid of Viṣṇu, who told them to go to Agastya. He at one sip swallowed all the oceans, which thus disappeared (therefore "sleeping oceans" of text) until the River Ganges was brought down by Bhagiratha when they were again filled with Her waters. This incident is attributed to the Yamunā, both rivers being manifestations of the same Devi.

[3] Literally, *Ali*, which, according to the Amarakośa = *Sakhi*; female friend, referring to the *Gopis* who loved Krishna.

[4] *Lampata*; Whose senses were roused by the scent of the pastes which had fallen from the scented body of Kṛṣṇa.

[5] Kṛṣṇa ("imperishable one").

Set in the flowing [1] hair of Rādhikā.
Of all such as come to bathe in Her waters
Neither is one the servant nor the other master.[2]
Dhunotu me manomalam Kalindanandinī sadā.

8

May the daughter of Kalinda ever cleanse my mind of its impurity!
Pleasant always is She with groves,
Where Nandanandi [3] ever played.[4]
Bright is She with the ripened blossom
Of the *kadamba* [5] and *mallika* [6] flowers upon Her banks.
It is She who safely carries across the ocean of the world [7]
All such men as bathe in Her stream.
Dhunotu me manomalam Kalindanandinī sadā.

---

[1] *Vilola.* Her hair is dishevelled and moving in the movements of breeze and play.

[2] Literally, " In the case of those who come down to bathe in Her waters She ever destroys all righteousness of master and servant "—that is, all are equal in Her waters which purify all without distinction.

[3] The text has *Nandinandana*, but this has no meaning. *Nandanandi* is He who pleases Nanda or Kṛṣṇa, whose foster-father Nanda the cowherd was.

[4] With the *Gopī* women.

[5] A beautiful flowering tree with yellow blooms under, and on which (as when he stole the garments of the bathing *Gopīs*) Kṛṣṇa played (See p. 169, note 2).

[6] A kind of Jasmine.

[7] See p. 16, note 1.

"MAY THE DEVI GRANT ME PARDON"

(DEVI APARĀDA KṢAMĀPANA STOTRA)

1

ALAS! I know not either Thy *mantra*[1] or *yantra*,[2]
Nor how to welcome Thee,[3]
Or how to meditate upon, nor words of prayer to
    Thee,
Nor do I know Thy *mudrā*,[4]

---

[1] *S'abda* is Brahman, and *mantra* the manifestation thereof. From *manana* arises realization of the monistic truth. *Man* of *mantra* comes from the first syllable of *manana*, and *tra* from *trāna*, or liberation from the bondage of the *samsāra*. That is called *mantra* which calls forth (*āmantrana*) the *caturvarga*, and which is the *svarūpa* of Devatā. (See *Introduction to Tantra S'āstra* and the Chapter on Mantra Tattva in *Principles of Tantra*.

[2] *Ibid.*, The Tāntrik diagram which is worshipped in lieu of the image (*pratimā*). The Gāyatrī *Yantra* is figured on the cover of this work. *Mantra* is *Devatā*, and *yantra* is mantra, in that it is the body of the *Devatā*, who is *mantra*.

Yantram mantramayam proktam mantrātmā devataivahi
Dehātmanoryathā bhedo yantradevatayostathā (Kaulavalīya Tantra).

"The substance of *yantra* is *mantra*. *Devatā* is *mantra*. As there is a distinction between body and *ātmā*, so there is between *yantra* and *Devatā*."

[3] By the *āvāhana mantra*, always said in worship of the *pratimā*.

[4] Ritual gesture, it being said; *Devānām modadā mudrā tasmāttām yatnātścaret* (see *Introduction to Tantra S'āstra*)"—" *Mudrā* is giver of pleasure to Devas, therefore it should be done with care."

Or how to lay before Thee my griefs;
But this I know, O Mother!
That to follow Thee is to remove all my pain.

2

By my ignorance of Thy commands.
By my poverty [1] and sloth,
I had not the power to do that which I should have done,
Hence my omission to worship Thy feet.
But, O Mother! auspicious Deliverer of all.
All this should be forgiven ,
For a bad son may sometimes be born, but a bad mother never. [2]

3

O Mother! Thou hast many worthy sons on earth,
But I, your son, am of no worth;
Yet it is not meet that Thou should'st abandon me,
For a bad son may sometimes be born, but a bad mother never.

4

O Mother of the world, O Mother!
I have not worshipped Thy feet,
Nor have I given abundant wealth to Thee;
Yet the affection which Thou bestoweth on me is without compare,
For a bad son may sometimes be born, but a bad mother never.

5

I have abandoned the worship of other Devas

[1] Want of means to perform the proper worship.

[2] A celebrated line; *Kuputtro jāyetā kvacidapi kumātā nabhavati.*

Because of the variety and confusion of the
injunctions relating to their worship.
I am no more than eighty-five years of age, [1]
If Thou will not bestow Thy kindness on me,
What shelter have I without Thy support,
O Mother of the big-bellied Deva ! [2]

6

Prayer, sweet as the sweet melon
Makes even a dog-eater [3] perfect ;
Even a beggar walks without fear
With crores [4] of gold pieces.
O Aparṇā ! [5] this is the fruit of Thy *mantra* entering
their ears.
Who can say, O Mother !
The fruit which is born of the recitation [6] of Thy
mantra ?

7

He who is besmeared with the ashes of the funeral
pyre,[7]
He who swallowed poison,[8]

---

[1] How is this stated if the hymn be the work of S'ankarācārya, to whom it is attributed, for he is said to have died at the early age of thirty-two ?

[2] *Lambodarajanani*. The Deva is the elephant-headed Ganeśa.

[3] That is, a low caste such as the *Caṇḍāla*, who eats any filth.

[4] A crore is 100 lakhs ; a lakh is 100,000.

[5] See p. 182, note 3.

[6] That is, *japa*, which is only recitation (in English) in its lowest form, the highest form being mental (*mānasa*) only. *Japa*, which is defined as *vidhānenā mantroccāraṇam*, is either *vācaka*, *upāmshu*, or *mānasā* (see Tantrasāra, 75 *et seq.*).

[7] S'iva, to whom the rest of the attributes in this verse refer.

[8] See p. 16, note 2.

Who is clothed with space,[1]
With matted hair, garlanded with the Lord of Serpents,
The Lord of men,[2]
The Lord of Ghosts [3] holding a skull in His hands.
Owes his great states as Lord of the World
To his acceptance of Thee as His Spouse, O Bhavānī![4]

8

No desire have I for liberation,
Nor have I desire for wealth,
Nor wish for knowledge,
O Moon-faced One! neither have I wish for happiness!
But this only I beg of Thee,
That my life may pass in the recitation of these words:
Mridānī,[5] Rudrānī,[6] S'ivā, S'ivé, Bhavānī.[4]

9

I have not according to the injunctions laid down therefor

---

[1] S'iva is represented naked, as the Yogins, of whom He is the Master, ever are.

[2] *Paśupati*. *Paśu* literally means animal, but men are also *paśu*.

[3] *Bhūteśa*., S'iva is surrounded by hosts of spirits.

[4] See p. 180, note 1.

[5] Mrida is a title of the *sāttvika* S'iva. She is His Spouse.

[6] Devī is the Spouse of the countless S'ivas called Rudras, in whom the *tamoguna* prevails. The dark (*tamas*) energy, called Raudrī, is said to be Cāmuṇḍā.

Worshipped Thee with the various articles [1] of
worship.
What is there which I have not wrongly done or
omitted in my meditations on the Brahman?
O Dark One! [2] it will be but fitting on Thy part
If Thou bestoweth not kindness on me, helpless
though I am.

10

O Durgā, [3] our Lady! O Ocean of mercy!
When overwhelmed by danger [4] I remember Thee.
Think not, however, this to be deceit on my part,
For children afflicted by hunger and thirst ever
remember their mother.

11

O Mother of the world! [5]

---

[1] *Upacāra.* There are sixteen such, called the *shoḍaśa pūjā upacāra*—viz., (1) *āsanam* (seat); (2) *svāgatam* (welcome); (3) *pādyam* (water for feet) (4) *Argyam* (offering of water, *durva* grass, rice, etc.); (5) and (6) *ācamanīyam*; (water for sipping; twice); (7) *madhuparka* (honey, ghee, milk); (8) *snānam* (bathing); (9) *vasanam* (cloth); (10) *ābharanam* (jewels); (11) *gandha* (scent, sandal paste, etc.); (12) *puṣpa* (flowers); (13) *dūpa* (incense), (14) *dīpa* (lights); (15) *naivedyam* (food); (16) *vandanam* or *namaskāra* (prayer).

[2] *S'yāmā.*

[3] A great name of the Devī. The Devī Purāṇa says that She is so called because the Devas were delivered from fear in difficulty and battle; hence She is deliverer (Durgā). The Mārkaṇḍeya Purāṇa and the Lakṣmī Tantra in the Pancarātra says: "In this place I shall kill a great Daitya (Titan) named Durgama. Hence my name shall be Durgā."

[4] The Mārkaṇḍeya Purāṇa says: When Thou art remembered in times of difficulty, Thou takest away all fear of all things."

[5] *Jagadambā.*

It is nothing wonderful if Thou art full of
compassion for me;
A mother does not abandon her son
Even if he have an hundred faults.

12

There is no such great sinner like me,
There is no such destroyer of sin as Thou.
Now, Mahadevi, you have heard what I have to say,
It remains for Thee to do what may seem fitting
to Thee.

MAṆIKARṆIKĀ

(MAṆIKARṆIKĀSTOTRA)

1

It was on Thy bank, O Maṇikarṇikā ! [1]
That Hari and Hara, givers of *sāyujya mukti*, [2]
Disputed together at the departure festival [3] of a certain one.
Hari [4] said, "Let Him be like unto me ;"
Whereon forthwith from within the body
Came forth S'iva mounted on Garuda, [5]

---

[1] Is the name of a celebrated *ghat* at Benares, where the bodies of the dead are burnt, and at which the gem of the ear ornament of the Devī fell. The Kāśīpancakastotra of S'ankara says that where there is *nivṛtti* of *manas*, there is the great peace. That peace is the foremost of *tīrthas* (here rivers) and Maṇikarṇikā (*Manonivṛtti paramopaśāntih sā tīrthavaryā maṇikarṇikāca*).

[2] One of the forms of qualified *mukti* (liberation); the four muktis are *Sālokya* (remaining in the same region with the Deva), *Sāmīpya* (remaining near the Deva), *Sārupya* (receiving the same form as the Deva), and S*ayujya* (becoming one with the Deva).

[3] *Prayāṇotsava*—that is, death.

[4] Viṣṇu

[5] The Bird King, who is the vehicle (*vāhana*) of Viṣṇu, son of Kaśyapa by his wife Vinetā, elder brother of Aruṇa.

In yellow garment,[1] with the mark of Bhrigu's foot
on His breast.[2]

2

Indra and the Thirty,[3] at the close of their period
of enjoyment,[4]
Descend to earth again,[5]
And are reborn as men, or even as beast, bird, or
worm;
But those, O Mother Maṇikarṇikā! who plunge
into thy waters,
Are freed from sins, and indeed in *Sāyujya*[6] man
becomes
Nārāyaṇa[7] himself, with crown and *Kaustubha gem*.[8]

---

[1] The colour of Viṣṇu's robes. The verse is intended to show the unity of both Viṣṇu and S'iva.

[2] *The Ṛṣis* once disputed amongst themselves as to the relative merits of Brahmā, Viṣṇu, and S'iva, and the *Ṛṣi* Bhrigu was sent to test them. The first and last on being purposely slighted by Bhrigu showed the weakness of resentment. Finding Viṣṇu lying down with Lakṣmi in the daytime he upbraided him for this and planted with force his foot on his chest. Viṣṇu not only took all this in good part, but rubbing the foot of Bhrigu expressed the hope that the latter had not hurt it by his action. On this exhibition of divine quality the palm was adjudged to Viṣṇu, who thereafter bore the mark of Bhrigu's foot on his breast.

[3] *Tridaśah*, a collective name for the other Devas. The thirty-three (three being understood) *gaṇas* of Devas, of which the Devi is Tridaśeśvarī.

[4] In heaven (*Svarga*).

[5] For the enjoyment in *Svarga*, which is part of the worlds of birth and rebirth, is not eternal, but on fruition the *jivātmā* again descends to earth to work out its unexhausted *karma*.

[6] *Sāyujyepi*. As to *sāyujya*, see *ante*, p. 201, note 2.

[7] Viṣṇu.

[8] A great and brilliant gem worn by Viṣṇu.

3

Kāśi[1] is of all cities the most praiseworthy,
For it is the city of *vimukti*[2] adorned with Gangā.
There Maṇikarṇikā is the giver of happiness,
And *Mukti* itself is Her servant.[3]
When Brahmā weighed Heaven with its Devas against Kāśi,
Kāśi, as the heavier, remained on earth,
But Heaven, the lighter, rose to the skies.

4

Nought is better than any part of the banks of Gangā,
But there, where Kāśi is, is the best,
And Maṇikarṇikā, where Īśvara gives *mukti*, is the best of all.
This place, inaccessible even to Devas,
Destroys a mass of sins.
Through many virtues acquired in previous births
Alone may it be attained, and by the pure only.

5

The multitude of being is immersed in the ocean of pain,
How may they gain release?
It was with this knowledge that Brahmā constructed the city of Vārāṇaśi,[4] which gives all bliss.

---

[1] Benares.

[2] *Nirvāṇāmokṣa*, the highest form of *Mukti* (liberation). As the saying goes: "Ayodhyā, Mathurā, Gayā, Kāśi, Kānci, Avantikā, Purī, these seven *tirthas* (places of pilgrimage) give *mukti*, but Kāśi (Benares) gives *nirvāṇa mukti*."

[3] As the servant awaits the orders of his mistress, so *mukti* (liberation) awaits the command of Maṇikarṇikā.

[4] Benares.

Men seek the happiness of Heaven.
But in so doing they but show small desire,
Since from Heaven they must fall again to earth
At the close of their appointed time of happiness.[1]
But Kāśī is the city of liberation,[2]
Ever beneficent, giving *dharma*, *artha*, *kāma*, and *mokṣa*.[3]

6

He who holds the bamboo flute,[4] upholder of the mountain,[5]
Who bears on his breast the *S'rīvatsa*[6] mark,
And S'iva, with venom in His throat,[7]
Who bears Gangā upon his head,[8]
And the husband of Lakṣmī,[9]
Are one and the same.[10]
Many of such, O Mother Maṇikarṇikā!
As bathe in Thy waters become Rudras and Haris.[11]

---

[1] See p. 202, note 5.

[2] *Mukti* (see p. 203, note 2).

[3] Piety, wealth, fulfilment of desire, and liberation.

[4] Kṛṣṇa, who is often so figured.

[5] Mount Govardhana, which Kṛṣṇa, by his might, upheld.

[6] Curls of hair on the breast of Viṣṇu.

[7] At the churning of the ocean, poison issued which, to save the world, S'iva swallowed. It coloured His throat blue; hence he is called Nīlakaṇṭha.

[8] The River Ganges (see p. 188, note 7).

[9] Viṣṇu.

[10] They with Brahmā; for as the Rudrayāmala says: "Though three they are one" (*Ekam murtistrayo deva*). All the Devas and Devīs are but manifestations, with the apparent limitations incident thereto, of the Supreme Unity—the Brahman.

[11] S'iva and Viṣṇu.

How, then, can there be any difference between
them ?[1]

7

Death upon Thy Banks, which is the giver of
happiness,
Is praised even by the Devas.
On him who thus dies S'akra[2] ever looks with His
thousand eyes.
Sāvitrī[3] of a thousand rays welcomes Him as He
ascends (to the heavens).
Such a pure one, mounted on a Bull or on Garuda,[4]
May go to whatsoever abode he will.

8

Even the four-headed Deva,[5]
The *Guru* who initiates into the meaning of the Veda,
Is unable even in an hundred of his[6] years
To describe the purity which arises upon bathing
at midday in Maṇikarṇikā.
But the Deva who bears the moon upon his
forehead,[7]
By the power of his *yoga* knows Thy purity.
S'iva makes that man who dies on Thy Bank
Either Himself or Nārāyaṇa.

---

[1] That is, they cease to differ from one another, having become Hari and Hara, who are themselves one.

[2] Indra, king of the celestials.

[3] The sun (Sūrya).

[4] The first is the vehicle (*Vāhana*) of S'iva. The second, the carrier of Viṣṇu.

[5] Brahmā.

[6] Not human years.

[7] S'iva.

9

All such sin-destroying fruit as is earned by millions of troublesome horse-sacrifices [1]
Exists in the purity which comes from bathing in Maṇikarṇikā.
He, who having bathed therein,
Reads this hymn, goes to the abode of the light of Brahman,
Having crossed the great ocean of this world
As if it were but some little pool.

[1] The Vaidika Aśvamedha.

GANGĀ[1]

(GANGĀSTOTRA)

1

O Devi Sureśvari ! [2] O Bhagavati Gangā !
Saviour of the three worlds of restless waves,
Clear is Thy water circling upon the head of S'iva [3],
May my mind ever repose at Thy lotus feet.

2

Mother Bhāgirathi ![4] giver of happiness,
Renowned in Nigama[5] is the greatness of Thy water ;
Thy greatness is more than I can know,
Protect me, O merciful one, ignorant that I am.

---

1 This hymn to the Devi Ganges, which is in the sweet *pajjhatika* metre, is also rhymed thus :

Devī Sureśvari Bhagavatī Gange,
Tribhuvanatārini taralatarange,
S'ankaramaulī vihārinī vimale,
Mamamatirāstām tavapada kamale.

2 Īśvari (feminine of Īśvara or Lord) of the Suras or Devas.

3 See p. 188, note 7.

4 So called because called down from Heaven by Bhagiratha of the solar race.

5 Tantra.

3

O Gangā ! sprung from the feet of Viṣṇu,[1]
Whose waves are white as snow as moon and pearl,
Remove from me my weight of sin ;
Help me to cross the ocean of the world.

4

They say that him, O Gangā ! who is devoted to Thee
Yama[2] can never behold.
He who has drunk of Thy clear water
Attains of a surety the supreme Abode.

5

O Jāhnavi ! O Gangā ! deliverer of the fallen,[3]
Whose waves are beautiful,
Claving the foremost of mountains,[4]
Mother of Bhiṣma,[5] daughter of the foremost of *munis*.[6]
Protectress of the fallen; praised in the three worlds.[7]

6

O Gangā ! who goeth to the ocean,
Ever free of sadness is he who salutes Thee.

---

[1] Gangā was born at the feet of Viṣṇu. So it is said in the *mantra* used when bathing in the Ganges: " *Viṣṇupādābja sambhūte Gange bhuvanatārini dharma dravīti* " (the Ganges is *dharma* in liquid form) " *vikhyāte pāpam me hara Jāhnavi.*"

[2] Deva of Death.

[3] Into sin.

[4] The Himālaya.

[5] Son of Santanu by Gangā.

[6] See p. 188, note 7.

[7] See p. 151, note 7.

Giver of fruit like unto the *kalpa* tree,[1]
By thy favour the woman who looked coldly
Now casts her loving glances.[2]

7

He who bathes in Thy current, O Mother!
Is never again reborn in woman's womb
O Protectress from hell! O Jāhnavī! O Gangā!
O Destructress of sins! lofty art Thou by Thy greatness.

8

O Thou who art eternal! O wave of purity!
May Thou, bestower of bliss, refuge of Thy worshippers!
From whose eyes come glances of compassion.
Whose feet the lustre of gems on Indra's crown adorn,
Be ever victorious!

9

O Bhāgīrathī![3] dispel my illness, melancholy, and pain,
As also my sins and all my many follies;
Essence of the three regions, necklace (on the breast) of Earth,[4]
Of a surety Thou art my refuge in the world.

---

1 The tree in the paradise of Indra which granted all desires.

2 *Vimukhavanitākritataralāpānge.*

3 So called after Bhagīratha, who called her down to earth (see p. 188, note 7).

4 *Vasudhāhārā*—that is, as a necklace adorns a woman, so the Devī by the flowing lines of Her stream, adorns the Earth.

10

O Alakanandā ![1] O supreme Bliss ![2]
O worshipful by those who despair !
Be Thou merciful.
He whose abode is by Thy Banks
Of a verity dwells in *Vaikuṇṭha*.[3]

11

Better were it to be a fish or tortoise in thy waters,
Or a feeble lizard upon Thy banks, or a poor dog-eater[4]
Within two *kos*[5] of Thy stream,
Than to be a noble king and yet far away from Thee.

12

O Bhuvaneśvarī ![6] pure one, praised of all,
Devī in liquid form,[7] daughter of the foremost of *Munis*,[8]
He who daily reads this hymn to Gangā
Is of a surety ever victorious.

13

They who with devotion in their heart to Gangā (Recite) this hymn
Composed in the sweet, pleasant, charming *pajjhatika* metre,

---

[1] A river flowing from the Himālaya into the Ganges.

[2] *Paramānaṇdā*, as is the Supreme, whose manifestation She is.

[3] The heaven of Viṣṇu

[4] That is, a *caṇḍāla*, one of the lowest and most unclean castes.

[5] A *kos* is two miles.

[6] *Īśvarī*, of the world.

[7] For the Ganges is the manifestation of the Supreme in the form of the sacred river.

[8] Jahnu (see p. 188, note 7).

Which gives the highest happiness,
Gain the eternal bliss of liberation.

14

A worldly [1] man shall read [2] this hymn to Gangā
Which [3] is the essence of the world, the giver of
desired fruit,
The essence of all pure things enjoined.[4]
Composed by S'ankara,[5] the worshipper of S'ankara.[6]
This hymn is ended.

---

[1] *Viṣaya,* which also in a bad sense means a sensua list o materialist.

[2] *Paṭhati*. Literally, "reads," but used for the *vidhiling* tense *paṭhet*. Thus in Caṇḍi it is said : *Paṭhet stotram samāhitah,*' and in the Vatukastotra, "*Paṭhetvāpāṭhayetvāpi*" ("should read or have read to him").

[3] That is, the hymn.

[4] *i.e.,* forms of worship (*pūjā*), sacrifice (*yajna*), etc.

[5] That is, S'ankarācārya.

[6] S'iva.

NARMADA

(NARMADĀSṬAKASTOTRAM)

1

O DEVĪ NARMADĀ ![1] I salute thy lotus-like feet,
Beauteous with the breakers of the heaving waves of ocean,
With which the drops of Thy waters mingle.[2]
O giver of prosperity ! I salute Thy feet bathed in water,
Which destroys rebirth, the cause of which is sin,[3]
As also all fear at the coming of the messenger of death.[1]
Tvadīya pāda pankajam namāmi devi narmadé.

2

O Devī Narmadā ! I salute Thy lotus feet
Giver of celestial (blessing) to the lowly fish in Thy waters,
Foremost of all sacred rivers.[6]

---

[1] One of the sacred rivers of India, and a form of the Devī.

[2] The ocean is the husband of all rivers.

[3] Rebirth is caused by *karma.*

[4] When a man is about to die, a messenger is sent by Yama to take his life.

[5] The refrain is translated in the first line.

[6] The is *stuti* (praise). In all sanskrit works the particular Devatā who is the subject of hymn, meditation or prayer is spoken

Destructress of the heavy weight of sin of the
Kaliyuga,[1]
Giver of welfare to multitude of fine fish, tortoise,
alligators, and ruddy geese.[2]
Tvadīya pāda pankajam namāmi devi narmadé.

3

O Devi Narmadā! I salute Thy lotus-like feet.
The overflow from Thy depths washes away the
sins of the world.
Thou destroyest all great sins and the mountain [3]
of calamities.
O giver of happiness to the son of Mṛkaṇḍu,[4]
At the fearful moment of the world's dissolution.
Tvadīya pāda pankajam namāmi devi narmadé.

4

O Devi Narmadā! I salute Thy lotus-like feet,
And Thy waters worshipped by the son of
Mṛkaṇḍu, S'aunaka, and other enemies of
the Asuras.

---

of as the greatest of all. *Tīrtha* is not only a place of pilgrimage such as a shrine and the like, but also, according to the Amarakośa, a sacred river.

[1] The present or fourth age, marked by the predominance of sin, each of the preceding eras (Dvāpara, Tretā, Satya) being more virtuous than the other. In the Kaliyuga era time works evilly.

[2] The *cakravāka* bird (by some said to be the Brahmini duck) celebrated in sanskrit poetry for its devotion to its mate. During the night-time the male and female birds call to each other from opposite banks of the stream, as I have heard them do on the reaches of the lonely Malia River in Northern Orissa.

[3] *Dāritāpadacalam.*

[4] The *Mahāmuni* Mārkaṇḍeya.

Destructress of rebirth in the ocean of the world,[1]
Portectress from all worldly pains,[2]
Tvadiya pāda pankajam namāmi devi narmadé.

5

O Devi Narmadā ! I salute thy lotus-like feet,
Worshipped by countless lakhs[3] of immortals,[4]
Asuras,[5] Kinnaras,[6] and others,
Whose banks resound with the fearless song of
many lakhs of birds.[7]
Giver of happiness to Vaśiṣṭa, Pipala, Karddama,[8]
and other sages,[9]
Tvadiya pāda pankajam namāmi devi narmadé.

6

O Devi Narmadā ! I salute Thy lotus-like feet,
Held in the minds of the bees,[10] Sanatkumāra,
Naciketa,[11] Kaśyapa,

---

1 The edition used has *punarbhavābdhi janmajam*, but this seems meaningless, and it is read as *janmaghnam*.

2 *Bhavābdhi dukhha barmadé.* Literally, "armour given to the pain of the world."

3 A lakh is 100,000.

4 *Amara—i.e.*, Devas.

5 Demonic spirits, opponents of the Devas or Suras.

6 A class of spirits (*Devayoni*).

7 *Dhīra*—that is because they are undisturbed by men who have become enemies to their brother creation.

8 *Ṛṣis* and *munis* of that name.

9 *S'iṣṭa,* which means a gentle and learned man who governs himself by his own wisdom, and is not governed by external restraints.

10 The bee hovers on the lotus seeking honey. The sages gather round the feet of the Devi seeking the wisdom of which She is the embodiment.

11 *Munis* and *ṛṣis.*

And by the bees, Atri, Nārada and other sages.
Thou who blesseth the work of sun, moon, Rantideva, and Devarāja,[1]
Tvadīya pādapankajam namāmi devi narmadé.

7

O Devī Narmadā; I salute Thy lotus-like feet,
Weapon against lakhs of sins known and unknown,
The Giver of enjoyment and liberation to all beings and animals,[2]
And of happiness to the abode of Virinci,[3] Viṣṇu, and S'iva,
Tvadīya pāda pankajam namāmī devi narmadé.

8

O Devī, Narmadā, ! I salute Thy lotus feet.
How sweet is the sound heard on the banks of Her who has sprung from the hair of S'iva [4].
Destroyer of pain and sin of hunter, and singer [5] of the learned and the fool,
And of the heat of the submarine fire,[6]

---

[1] Indra.

[2] Both enjoyment and liberation is given to men : to animals enjoyment (*bhukti*), though they, too, by merit acquired in present birth may attain future birth in human form.

[3] Brahmā.

[4] *Maheśakeśajātate.* As to Gangā, see p. 188, note 7. It is the same and only Devī who manifests both as Gangā and Narmadā, and all other rivers and things.

[5] Hunting is sinful. The singers are a mixed caste.

[6] *Kirātasūtavādaveṣu pandita śathe.* When the *Dakṣayajna* was destroyed by S'iva, it changed into a mare (*Vadavā*). S'iva followed, and it plunged into ocean. Fire is produced by it. The *S'loka* says that Her water is so great aud pure that it is unaffected by this fire. As regards the rest of this somewhat obscure verse, it means that the Devī is the remover of the sin of all whoever they may be.

Giver of happiness to all being.
Tvadiya pāda pankajam namāmi devi narmadé.

9

Who ever reads but thrice daily this hymn to
Narmadā
Will never fall into misfortune,
He will never see Raurava, [1]
He will never be reborn,
But will reach the glorious abode of S'iva,
So difficult to attain, by this body so easily gained.[2]

---

[1] One of the great hells.

[2] *Sulabhya dehadurlabham.* Not that it is easy to attain human birth. On the contrary, it is said: "*Naratvam durlabham loke* and *vidyātatra sudurlabhā,*" etc. ("The state of a man is difficult to attain, and still more so that of a wise one," cited in Sahitya Darpaṇam, chap. i, by Viśvanātha Kavirāja). What is apparently meant is that, compared with the difficulty of attaining to S'iva, the state of humanity is easily attainable.

ANNAPŪRṆĀ

(ANNAPŪRṆASTOTRA)

1

O Mother Annapūrṇā ![1]
Īśvarī,[2] who ever bestoweth happiness,
Granting gifts and dispelling fear.
O mine of gems of beauty,
Who washeth away all sin,
Who giveth purity to Thy devotees,
Who purifieth the mountain range,[3]
Which is undestroyed even at the time of dissolution,[4]
Presiding Deity of Kāśī,[5]
Maheśvarī[6] in every truth,
O vessel of mercy ! grant me aid.

2

O Thou who hast clothed Thyself in cloth of gold,

---

[1] The name of the Devī, the "bountiful Lady" who gives food and presides over Kāśī, the Holy City of Benares.

[2] Feminine of Īśvara or Lord.

[3] The Himālaya purified by the presence of the Devī, who there incarnated as Pārvatī, daughter of Himavat, the Mountain-King.

[4] *Pralaya*, the destruction of the world.

[5] Benares (see note 1.)

[6] Great Īśvarī (see note 2).

Decked with ornaments made of many and varied
gems,
Whose breasts rounded like a water-jar,
Are resplendent with their necklace of pearls,
Whose beauty is enhanced by the fragrance of the
Kashmir aloe.
O Devi! who presidest over the city of Kāśi,[1]
O Mother Annapūrṇā Īśvari,[2]
O vessel of mercy, grant me aid!

3

O giver of the bliss of *Yoga*,[3]
Destructress of enemies,[4]
Inspirer of devotion to *dharma* and *artha*,[5]
Who art lustrous as the light waves of sun, moon,
and fire,
Protectress of the three worlds[6]
Giver of all dominion[7] and all desires,
Presiding Devi over the city of Kāśi,
O vessel of mercy, grant me aid!

---

1 Benares.

2 Feminine of Īśvara or Lord.

3 Union of the human (*jivātmā*) with the supreme (*paramātmā*) soul effected through the practice of *Yoga*.

4 That is, sin.

5 Two of the fourfold aims (*Caturvarga*) of sentient being—viz., *dharma* (religion, duty, etc.), *artha* (wealth, wherewith life is sustained and religious sacrifices are effected), *Kāma* (desire which prompts great achievements and fulfilment), and *mokṣa* or liberation.

6 That is, *Bhuh*, *Bhuvah*, *Svah*, the terrestrial atmospheric and the heavenly spheres.

7 *Aiśvarya* (lordship).

4

Thou who maketh Thy dwelling in the cave of
Mount Kailāsa,[1]
Who art Gaurī,[2] Umā,[3] and S'ankarī,[4] Kaumārī,[5]
Who giveth us power to understand the meaning
of *Nigama*,[6]

---

[1] The sacred mount and paradise of S'iva; esoterically the Sahasrāra whereto as Kuṇḍalinī She repairs.

[2] The daughter of Guru, the King of mountains (see p. 187, note 4). Gauri also means "fair".

[3] A name of the Devī. When of the age of sixteen she practised great austerities that She might be the Spouse of S'iva, upon which Her mother, endeavouring to persuade Her, said, U ("Oh"), Mā ("not"). As it is said by Kālidāsa in the first Canto of the Kumārasambhavam; "*Umeti matrā tapaso niṣiddhā paschā dumākhyāng sumukhījagāma.*" ("By the words U, Mā, She was thus forbidden by Her mother to practise austerity, thereafter the pure Umā obtained Her name.") Umā is Kumārī, who has renounced all attachment, and is devoted to Her Lord. A *sūtra* runs, "*Icchāśaktih Umā kumārī*" (The energy of will is Umā the unmarried). The Commentary on this *sūtra*, cited by Bhāskararāya, says: "The eternal state is his whose mind has ascended the degrees of *yoga* called *vismaya*, and who realizes the supreme Bhairavata (an aspect of S'iva). That *Yogi* obtains at length the *Icchāśakti* called the Supreme Queen (*Parābhattārika*) known also as Kumārī."

[4] Name of the Devī as Spouse of S'ankara, the benefactor.

[5] Name of the Devī as one of the *aṣtanāyikā* and Spouse of Deva Kārtikeya.

[6] This term, applied to the Veda generally, means particularly the Tantra in the form in which the Devī is *guru* and S'iva, *śiṣya*. As it is said:

Nirgato girijā vaktrāt,
Gatāscha girija śrutim,
Matascha vāsudevasya,
Nigamā parikathyate.

In the Lalitā the Devī is addressed *as nijājnarūpā nigamā* (the *nigama* are the expressions of Thy commands).

Thou art the letters of the *bija*[1] Om[2],
Opener of the panels of the door of liberation,[3]
Presiding Devi over the City of Kāśi,
O vessel of mercy, grant me aid!

5

Thou supporteth all beings visible and invisible,
Whose belly is the vessel which contains the universe.[4]
Thou discloseth the subject of the drama of Thy own play,
And art the fount of the light of wisdom,
Pleasing the mind of the Lord of the universe,
Presiding Devī over the City of Kāśi,
O vessel of mercy, grant me aid!

6

Īśvarī of all men on earth,
The waves of Thy blue-black hair look (beautiful) like plaits.
Īśvarī who ever giveth food,
Bestower of happiness to all, who advanceth all people,

---

[1] The Tāntrik ("seed") *mantras,* such as *Hrīm, Hūm, Klīm,* etc. *Mantras* are classified according to the syllables they contain.

[2] The Mahāmantra *Om,* composed of A + u + m, coalesced by *sandhi* into Om. The three *varṇas* signify the three members of the *Trimurti,* Brahmā, Viṣṇu, and S'iva, who, as the Rudrayāmala says, are born of the Praṇava (Om), and though in appearance three, are yet one (*ekamūrtistrayo devāh*). From the *Praṇava* all Devas, Vedas, sun, moon, and all being comes by the power of Devī, the supreme S'akti.

[3] *Mokṣā,* or unity with the supreme, and therefore liberation from rebirth in the phenomenal world.

[4] *Brahmāṇḍabhāṇḍodarī.* The *Brahmāṇḍa* (universe) is the "mundane egg" of Brahmā.

Presiding Devī over the City of Kāśī,
O vessel of mercy, grant me aid!

7

Thou givest all instruction onwards from the time of initiation,[1]
And art the cause of the threefold manifestation of S'ambhu.[2]
Scented with the Kashmir aloe, Thou art the Īśvarī of the three regions.[3]
Thou art triple waved,[4]
And the night of dissolution.
Thou art the cause of all lastings things,
And fulfiller of the desires of those who desire.
It is Thou who maketh the greatness of peoples.
Presiding Devī over the City of Kāśī,
O vessel of mercy, grant me aid!

8

Thou, Devī, art adorned with all various kinds of gems,
Daughter of Dakṣa,[5]

---

[1] *Dīkṣā*, through which each Hindu passes, by reception of his *mantra*. It is said sometimes that initiation is the third birth, the first being that from the mother, the second is *upanayana* (investiture with sacred thread), and the third is initiation. The Tantras speak of thirty-two *Dīkṣās*, from *Sudhavidyā* to *Anuttara*.

[2] That is, as creator, maintainer, and destroyer.

[3] Bhuh, Bhuvah, Svah (see p. 151, note 7)

[4] For She flows in the form of the three sacred rivers: Gangā, Yamunā, and Sarasvatī.

[5] The father of Satī, a manifestation of Devī, who, dying at the *Dakṣayajna* reappeared as Pārvatī.

Beautiful, pleasing the world
With the sweet milk of Thy left breast.[1]
Thou art Maheśvarī, for Thou givest prosperity to all,
For Thou givest welfare,
And fulfillest the desires of your devotees.
Presiding Devī over the City of Benares,
O vessel of mercy, grant me aid!

9

Thou art She who shinest with the brilliance of millions of suns, moons, and fires.
Whose earrings are brilliant as the sun, moon, and fire,
Who art the cause of the colour of both sun and moon,
Who holdeth a rosary,[2] a book,[3] a noose, and a goad.[4]
Presiding Devī over the City of Benares,
O vessel of mercy, grant me aid!

10

Protectress of Kṣatriyas,[5]
Great dispeller of all fear,
Mother, who art an ocean of mercy,
In very truth the ever auspicious giver of salvation,
The cause of the beauty of Viśveśvara,[6]

---

[1] Because Ganeśa and Kārtikeya, Her children, suck Her right breast.

[2] *Mālā.*

[3] *Pustaka,* which is also known as the *Vidyāmudrā.*

[4] See p. 173, note 6.

[5] The warrior caste.

[6] Lord of the universe.

It was Thou who made Dakṣa to weep.[1]
Remover of all ills,
Presiding Devī over the City of Benares,
O vessel of mercy, grant me aid !

11

O Annapūrṇā ! who art ever full (of bounty),
Who art dear to the life of S'ankara,[2]
O Pārvatī, give me aid !

12

My mother is Devī Pārvatī,
My father is Deva Maheśvara,[3]
My friends and relatives are those who are devoted to S'iva,
And the three regions [4] are my fatherland.

---

[1] When his *yajna* was destroyed by Her husband S'iva. There are two Dakṣas—Prajāpati, and a human king, an incarnation of the former. Though S'iva destroyed the sacrifice, Devī was the instrument. The Lalitā, verse 120, addresses the Devī both as *Dākṣāyanī* (daughter of Dakṣa) and *Dakṣayajna vināśinī* (destroyer of the sacrifice of Dakṣa).

[2] S'iva.

[3] *Ibid.*

[4] See p. 151, note 7.

GANGA

(GANGĀSTOTRA)

BY VĀLMĪKI [1]

1

O MOTHER GANGĀ ! co-wife [2] with the daughter of Himālaya,
Thou art the necklace on the dress of the Earth,[3]
And the banner staff whereby one ascends to Heaven.
O Bhāgīrathi ! [4] I pray to Thee.
May my body perish after it has lived on Thy banks,
After it has drunk Thy pure water
And swung on Thy waves.
And has remembered Thy name and cast looks on Thee.

2

O Mother Gangā ! O deliverer from Hell !

---

[1] From the Brihatstotraratnākara, edited by Jagannātha Mehta (Benares).

[2] *Sapatnī*. Pārvatī, the daughter of Himālaya, is one wife and Gangā the other.

[3] The stream is compared to a necklace of pearls on the dress of a man or woman.

[4] So named as having been called down by Bhagīratha. *Vide ante*, p. 188, note 7.

Even a bird living in the hollow of a tree growing on Thy bank,
Even a fish or a tortoise living in Thy waters
Are greater than a King worshipped by his enemies' wives,
Made afraid by the sound of the bells on the necks of his maddened elephants.[1]

3

Not even a bull or a bird or a horse,
Nor a serpent nor an elephant,
Suffer the pains of rebirth and redeath
If they live at Kāśi[2] on Thy holy banks.
Better off are they than even a Rājā living elsewhere,
Fanned though he be with the *couris*[3] of courtezans,[4]
Whose ever moving golden wristlets sweetly tinkle.

4

O our Supreme Lady Bhāgirathī![5]
O wanderer in the three regions![6]
When shall it be that I shall be fanned
By the hands of heavenly women[7] with their beautiful *couris*?
When, too, shall I be happy enough to see my body
Pecked by crows, devoured by dogs, drawn along the earth by jackals.

---

1 When the bells are rubbed against the necks of tbe elephants. The picture is one of victory, pomp, and beauty.

2 Benares.

3 Whisks made of yak tails.

4 *Vārastrī*.

5 See p. 188, note 7.

6 See p. 151, note 7.

7 *Divyastrī*.

Carried by Thy currents, tossed upon Thy banks,
And borne by Thy waters to and fro!

5

May the daughter of Jahnu [1] be ever victorious and protect us,
She who is like the fresh fibrous stem of the lotus-like feet of Viṣṇu,[2]
Like a garland of jasmine [3] flowers on the head of S'iva,
Like the banner of victory of Lakṣmi presiding over liberation,
She [4] who cleanses us of the stain of sin arising from the Kaliyuga.[5]

6

May Thy sacred water be pure for my daily bathing,
Thy water covered with leaves of palm and *tamāla*,[6]
Of *Sāla* [7] and pine, with all their creepers
On which play no rays of the Sun.[7]
White and brilliant, like the conch, the Moon, and the water-lily,
Stirred by the rising breasts of the wives of the Gandharvas,

---

[1] See p. 188, note 7.

[2] Gangā was born from the feet of Viṣṇu.

[3] *Mālati*. Gangā, on Her fall from Heaven, touched the head of S'iva. There Her white encircling stream is compared to a wreath.

[4] That is, Gangā.

[5] The fourth and worst of the ages.

[6] Names of trees. The reference to pine and palm show the descent of the stream from the Himālaya to the plains of Bengal.

[7] In the caverns of the Himālaya.

Devas, Siddhas, and Kinnaras,[1]
What time they bathe therein.

7

May the water of Gangā, who ever charms, sanctify us;
She who has fallen from the feet of the enemy of Mura,[2]
Who wanders upon the head of the enemy of Tripura,[3]
The Destructress of sins.

8

May the auspicious water of Gangā ever purify us;
The Destructress of sins, the great enemy of sins,
Adorned with waves, wandering in the mountains,
Piercing through the caverns of the Lord of mountains [4]
With roaring sounds.
Stealer of the dust from the feet of Lord Hari.[5]

9

Whosoever at early dawn,
Having cleansed his body
And purified his mind

---

[1] Classes of minor divinities or *Devayoni*.

[2] That is, S'rīkṛṣṇa (Viṣṇu), who slew the Daitya Mura.

[3] That is, S'iva, who conquered the three cities made of gold, silver, and iron of the three Asuras Kamalākṣa, Tārakakṣa, and Vidyunmāli respectively.

[4] Himālaya.

[5] Viṣṇu, from whose feet She was born.

Of all uncleanliness arising from the sinful
Kaliyuga,[1]
Reads this hymn to Gangā composed of eight verses,
Shall never fall into the ocean of the world again,
But shall attain liberation.

[1] *Vide ante*, p. 163, note 6,

MAHĀLAKṢMĪ

(MAHĀLAKSMĪSTOTRA)

By Indra[1]

Indra said:

1

O Mahālakṣmi ! I salute Thee,
Thou art *Mahāmāyā*[2] and *S'rīpitha*.[3]
Worshipped art Thou by Devas,
Holder of conch, disc, and mace.[4]
O Mahālakṣmi ! I salute Thee.

2

O Mahālakṣmi ! I salute Thee.
Mounted art Thou on the back of Garuda.[5]
Thou art a terror most formidable to Asura Kola.
Thou removeth all sins.
O Devi Mahālakṣmi ! obeisance to Thee.
O Mahālakṣmi !
Thou knowest all.

---

[1] From the Brihatstotraratnākara, edited by Jagannātha Mehtā (Benares).

[2] She who is both the Authoress and Victrix of *Māyā* (delusion), the supreme S'akti.

[3] Abode of wealth and beauty.

[4] The implements held by Viṣṇu, Her Spouse.

[5] The bird-king carrier (*vāhana*) of Viṣṇu.

3

Giver of boons art Thou to all ;
Formidable terror to the wicked ;
Remover of all pain and sorrow.
O Devi ! salutation to Thee.

4

O Devi Mahālakṣmi !
Thou art the giver of intelligence and success,
And of both worldly enjoyment and liberation.
Thou art the self of *Mantra*. [1]
O Mahālakṣmi ! obeisance to Thee.

5

Thou art without beginning or end.
O Supreme Devi Mahālakṣmi !
Thou art the primeval power,
And art born of *yoga*.
O Mahālakṣmi ! salutation to Thee.

6

Thou art both gross and subtle,[2]
Thou art terrible and a great power,
Great-bellied art Thou.[3]
Thou removeth all great sins.
O Mahālakṣmi ! obeisance to Thee.

---

[1] *Mantrātmikā* (see Introduction).

[2] See Introduction.

[3] *Mahodari*, for all things are in Her.

7

O Devī Mahālakṣmī !
Thou art the supreme Brahman,
The ever-pervading *Ātman.*
Thou art the great Lord [1]
And Mother of the world.
O Mahālakṣmī ! Salutation to Thee.

8

O Devī clad in white raiment,[2]
Adorned with varied gems.
Mother and upholder of the world art Thou.
O Mahālakṣmī ! obeisance to Thee.

9

The *Sādhaka* [3] who ever reads [4] this hymn to Mahālaksmī.
Composed of eight verses,
Attains a kingdom and all success.

10

Whosoever reads this hymn once a day
Is freed from sin,
He who reads it twice a day
Has ever abundance of paddy [5] and wealth.

---

[1] Maheśvarī.

[2] Lakṣmī is generally clad in red and Sarasvatī in white, but the Supreme S'akti has all the attributes and qualities of the rest.

[3] Worshipper. See *Introduction to Tantra S'āstra.*

[4] Here follows the *phala* portion of the *stotra.*

[5] When *pūjā* is done to Lakṣmī, the *Mūrti* (*Lakṣmīrkānta*) is placed on paddy, which is kept in the Thakurghar for a whole year, and then thrown into the Ganges.

11

Whosoever reads this hymn thrice a day,
All his great enemies perish ;
Mahālakṣmī ever bestows Her grace on him,
Grants him all boons,
And does him all good.

———

HYMN TO KĀLĪ

(KARPŪRĀDI-STOTRA)

PREFACE

THIS celebrated Kaula *Stotra*, which is now translated from the Sanskrit for the first time, is attributed to Mahākāla Himself. The Text used is that of the edition published at Calcutta in 1899 by the Sanskrit Press Depository, with a commentary in Sanskrit by the late Mahāmahopādhyāya Kṛṣṇanātha Nyāya-Pañcānana, who was both very learned in Tantra-S'āstra and faithful to his Dharma. He thus refused the offer of a good Government post made to him personally by a former Lieutenant-Governor on the ground that he would not accept money for imparting knowledge.

Some variants in reading are supplied by this commentator. I am indebted to him for the Notes, or substance of the notes, marked K. B. To these I have added others, both in English and Sanskrit explaining matters and allusions familiar doubtless to those for whom the original was designed, but not so to the English or even ordinary Indian reader. I have also referred to the edition of the *Stotra* published by the Gaṇeśa-Candra-Ghoṣa at Calcutta in 1891, with a translation in Bengali by Gurunātha Vidyānidhi, and a commentary by Durgārāma-Siddhāntavāgiśa Bhattācārya. I publish for the first time Vimalānanda-Svāmī's Commentary to which I again refer later. When in this Introduction or in the Commentary I have not mentioned these two works my authorities are the

Tantras or Tāntrik works which I cite, or the information I have gathered from those whom I have consulted.

One of the chief features of this *Stotra* is that it gives the *mantroddhāra* of the Dakṣiṇā-Kālikā. It not only gives us the *Dhyāna*, *Yantra*, *Sādhana* and *Svarūpa-varṇanā* of the Mahādevī, but it also contains the chief Mantras of Dakṣiṇākālikā. The adjective "*Tava manu-samuddharaṇajanu*" qualifying "*idam stotram*" in S'loka 21 expressly states this fact.

Among the various Mantras of Dakṣiṇā Kālikā the greatest is the "*Vidyā-rājñī*" consisting of 22 syllables (*Dvāviṁsākṣarī*). The mantra gives the fullest and the truest symbol of the Svarūpa of Her. This *mantra* is contained in the first five S'lokas.

The first S'loka	contains	*Krīṁ, Krīṁ, Krīṁ*	(3 *akṣaras*)
2nd ,,	,,	*Hūṁ, Hūṁ*	(2 ,,)
3rd ,,	,,	*Hrīṁ, Hrīṁ*	(2 ,,)
4th ,,	,,	*Dakṣiṇe Kālike*	(6 ,,)
5th ,,	,,	*Krīṁ, Krīṁ, Krīṁ, Hūṁ, Hūṁ, Hrīṁ, Hrīṁ, Svāhā*	(9 *akṣaras*)

So the first five S'lokas give us altogether 22 *akṣaras* *i.e.* the full *Vidyārājñī*.

In Vimalānanda-Svāmī's *Tīkā* of the 5th S'loka in the revised Sanskrit text he has proved by quotations from the 9th paṭala of S'āktānanda-taranginī that this 22-syllabled *mantra* is the full and true representation of the Svarūpa of the Mahādevi. See the quotation which begins with

"*Krīm-kāro mastakaṁ devi Krīm-kāraśca lalātakaṁ*"

and ends with

"*S'vā-śabdena pada-dvandvam hā-kāreṇa nakhaṁ tathā*"

The words "*Svarūpaṁ*" (5th sl.) and "*Sakalaṁ*" (6th sl.) point to this *Vidyārājñī*. After the full *Vidyārājñī* has been given in the first five S'lokas, the 6th S'loka gives the various other Mantras of less importance and significance—ranging from one syllabled to nine-syllabled, 15-syllabled, 21-syllabled and so forth.

This Mantroddhāra has been made following the authority of Kālikā-śruti, Niruttara-Tantra and other Tantras. Many commentators, however, have apparently in the view of Vimalānanda failed to consult the above authorities and have thus fallen into errors and have given a different *Mantroddhāra*. Some take the 1st S'loka to give a one-syllabled *mantra*, the 2nd sloka as also the 3rd, two two-syllabled *mantras*, the 5th a nine-syllabled one and so on : a view which it is contended is opposite to such passages as "*atha hainaṁ brahmarandhre brahma-svarūpinim āpnoti........bṛhad-bhānu-jāyāṁ uccaret*" in the 1st Sūkta of Kālikopaniṣad ; or passages in Niruttara-Tantra (Ch. II) beginning with "*Atha vaksye Kuleśāni Dakṣiṇā-kālikā-manuṁ*" and ending with "*Sarva-mantra-mayī vidyā sṛṣti-sthityanta-kāriṇī.*" The Svāmī further refers me to the end of the Kālikopaniṣad where dealing with the various Mantras of the Dakṣiṇā-Kālikā it is said "*Atha sarvām vidyām prathamaṁ ekaṁ dvayaṁ vā trayaṁ vā nāmatrayaputitaṁ vā kṛtvā japet.*" The great Tāntrik Pūrṇānanda Giri explaining the passage says "*Sarvām vidyām-iti pūrvoktadvāvimśatyakṣaryāh prathama bījaṁ vā bījadvayaṁ vā* etc. (*vide* S'yāmā-rahasyaṁ, Rasikamohan's edition, p. 36.)

From the above consideration, it is clear that at the very beginning in the first 5 S'lokas the 22-syllabled *Mantra* is given and then the others. It may be added here that the fact of Mahākāla's composing the Hymn in 22 S'lokas not more nor less—is also an indication of the correctness of the Svāmī's view, who, in further support of it cites 5 S'lokas dealing with the *Mantroddhāra* from the *Krama-stava* of the Dakṣiṇā-Kālikā under the first 5 Slokas of the Karpūrādi, which will be found in the printed text.

In course of revising his *Vyākhyā* Vimalānanda-Svāmī has in the first six S'lokas given good grounds to prove that the *Stotra* not only contains the *Mantroddhāra* and the *Sādhana* of S'rī-S'rī-Dakṣiṇā-Kālikā but also in it are given the *Mantras* and *Rahasyapūja* of S'rī-S'rī-Tāra and S'rī-S'rī-Tripura-sundarī.

In addition to the Mantroddhāra the following matters are contained in the *Stotra.*

	No. of Slokas
Dhyāna	1, 2, 3, 4, 5, 6, 7, 8, 11
Yantra	18
Sādhana	10, 11, 15, 16, 17, 18, 19, 20
Madya	13
Māṁsa	19
Maithuna	10
Phala-śruti	21, 22

The Slokas 9, 12, 14 contain *stuti* only.

S'lokas 10, 15-18, 20 refer to the Tāntrik *vīrācāra-sādhana. Vīrācāra* is for the class of *sādhaka* who are *vīra-bhāva* and *abhiṣikta.* To those who follow *paśvācāra* this ritual is strictly forbidden. The nature of the *rahasya-pūjā* is indicated in the text, to which I have added an explanatory commentary in English.

To the *Paśu, sādhana* by night is prohibited, for it connotes in S'ākta-sādhana, worship with the *Pañcatattva.* The *Paśu* is still bound by the *pāśa* (bonds) of desire, etc., and he is, therefore, not *adhikārī,* for that which, if undertaken by the unfit, will only make these bonds stronger. For him, on the contrary, there are severe restrictions in this matter, for, as the S'āktakrama cited by the commentator says *Maithunaṁ tatkathālāpaṁ tadgoṣṭhiṁ parivarjayet.*" (The *Paśu* should avoid *maithuna*, conversation on the subject, and the like.) The *Paśu* should avoid the eight forms of *maithuna* known as *aṣṭāṅga maithuna*— viz., *smaraṇaṁ* (thinking upon it), *kirtanam* (talking of it), *kelih* (play with women), *prekṣaṇam* (looking upon women), *guhyabhāṣaṇaṁ* (talk in private with women), *saṁkalpa* (wish or resolve for *maithuna*), *adhyavasāyah* (determination towards it), as well as *kriyāniṣpattih* (actual accomplishment). The Nityā Tantra, which the commentator cites, says: " *Rātrau naiva yajed deviṁ sandhyāyāṁ vā'parāhnake*"—" He (the *Paśu*) should never worship the Devi during the latter part of the day or in the evening or at night." To this, from amongst many other authorities, I may add the Svatantra, which says that the Paśubhāva Sādhaka should do one lakh of *japa* in day time and that a *Vira* devoted to his own Ācāra should do one lakh of *japa* at night:

Paśubhāvarato mantri divā lakṣa-japaṁ caret.
Svācāranirato viro rātrau lakṣa-japaṁ caret.

In connection with this verse I must observe that in the notes to verse 20 it is said that the first half of the 20th S'loka is meant for " *Paśusādhakas* " and that the 2nd half refers to the " *pūrṇābhiṣiktavirasādhaka,*" as also that the word " *paraṁ* " (afterwards) means and refers to the time when the ' *Paśu* ' having received *abhiṣeka* enters *virācāra* and is *adhikāri* for the midnight *puraścaraṇa.* Vimalānanda tells me that this is wrong and that the whole S'loka has reference to the *vira* or *divya-sādhaka* and that no portion of it refers to the *Paśu-sādhaka.*

The quotation just made from the Svatantra-Tantra no doubt seems to lend support to the view that the first part of the S'loka refers to the Paśu, but he informs me and I fully accept the correction that he and other followers of the Sāstra knew the passage to bear a meaning which is consonant with his view, that is, it means this :—*Mantrī* means the *virasādhaka*; the *mantrī* should perform *lakṣa-japa* in the day time following the *ācāra* of the *paśu* (*paśu-bhāvaratah*). The *vira-sādhaka* should perform *lakṣa-japa* in the night following his own *ācāra* (*svācāra-niratah*). The word "*svācāra*" (own *ācāra*) points to his interpretation being correct.

In support of his view the Svāmi cites the following Verses which all say the same thing namely that the initiate should be Brahmacārī during day and at night worship according to Kulācācāra. Kaulāvalī says:

Naktaṁ-bhojī hāviṣyānnaṁ japed vidyām divā śucih.
Dvivāsāh sarvathā vīro brahmacārī bhavet sadā.
Rātrau saṁpūjāyed devīṁ kulācāra-krameṇa tu
Dvijanmanāṁ tu sarveṣām dvidhā vidhi-rihocyate.

Again, Kālikopaniṣad says:

S'āṁbhava-dīksāsu ratah śākteṣu vā divā brahmacārī rātrau nagnah sadā maithunāsaktamānasah Japa-pūjādiniya-maṁ kuryād iti.

Kaulāvalī again says:

Unmukhyāh Kālikāyāśca viśeṣah kathyate' dhunā
Divase brahmacaryeṇa svīyasaṁkhyājapaṁ caret.
Rātrau māṁsāsavairmatsyairmudrābhir maithunodbhavaih.

The reason of the *virasādhaka* being instructed to adopt the *ācāra* of *brahmacāri* in the day-time is the necessity for the concealment of the *virācāra* from the public which Tantra so often insists upon. S'iva says that *virācāra* cannot be understood aright by the common people and therefore must be concealed, as closely as a man should conceal his own mother's sin "*gopayet mātṛ-jāra-vat.*"

Moreover, the worship of Kāli in "*paśvācāra*" is totally forbidden by S'iva. The *Paśu* is precluded by Tantra from the worship of Kāli. For example, the Niruttara-Tantra says:

Divya-bhāvaṁ vīra-bhāvaṁ vinā Kālīṁ prapūjayet.
Pūjane narakaṁ yāti tasya duhkhaṁ pade pade.
Paṣubhāva-rato devi yadi Kālīṁ prapūjayet.
Rauravaṁ narakaṁ yāti yāvad ābhūta-saṁplavaṁ.

(By the worship of Kāli without *Divyabhāva* and *Virabhāva* the worshipper suffers pain at every step and goes to hell. If a man who is of the *Paśubhāva* worships Kāli then he goes to the *Raurava* Hell until the time of final dissolution).

Vimalānanda-S'vāmi says: The worship of Kāli without the use of wine, though seen in many places, is Paurāṇik and not Tāntrik (*i.e.* sanctioned by the Tantra.)

Verses 1-8, 11, the first part of verse 20, and 21 (except at midnight) deal with *japa* of the *mantra* of, and *dhyāna* upon, the Devi, which, of course, may be done by the *Paśu*. Verses 9, 12, 13 and 14 are *stuti*, and 22 is the usual *phalaśloka*, which states the reward to be gained by the reading of the *Stotra*.

Verses 10, 15-18, and the second portion of verse 20 deal with *Latāsādhana*. The *śakti* of this *sādhana* is ordinarily the own wife of the *sādhaka*, married according to the Vaidik injunctions; the *svaśakti* or *ādyāśakti*, as she is technically called in Tantra. One's own wife is *Ādyā*-S'akti and *Sādhana* should be done with her aid (*Adyā-śaktīh svadārāh syāt tāmevāśṛtya sādhayet*). With her is practised that *śaktisādhana*, the aim of which is the acquirement of self-control, which, checking the outward-going current, places the *sādhaka* upon the path of *nivṛtti*. Indeed, the Kaulikārcanadīpikā says, "Without *ādyā śakti* worship is but evil magic". (*Ādyāśaktiṁ vinā pūjā abhicārāya kalpate*). It is only the *siddha*, which term is here used in the special sense of one who has obtained complete control over his passions, to whom is permitted another *śakti* (*paraśakti*). So the Prāṇatoṣinī quotes, "a man shall obtain *siddhi* with his own *śakti*, and afterwards (that is, when he is *siddha*) he should make *japa* with *paraśakti*" (*Svaśaktau siddhim āpnuyāt paraśaktau tadā japet*). And similarly Niruttara Tantra says, that the *sādhaka* who is *siddha* in Kulācārā may worship "another" woman. (*Siddha-mantrī kulācāre parayoṣām prapūjayet*). In both these cases *paraśakti* has a double meaning *viz.*, "another" woman that is corporeal woman, or "Supreme" that is the Supreme Woman who in the body is Kuṇḍalinī-S'akti. This latter appears to be the sense in the quotation which speaks of the *siddhamantrī*. It has been said also, as in the Mahānirvāṇa Tantra, that *paraśakti* must (if unmarried) be married either by Vaidika or S'aiva rites, or (if married and the husband is dead) according to the latter rite. Further, that which determines the moral character of an act is the intention with which it is done. As the Kaulāvalīya says, when a man's intention is bad then his act is so, otherwise there is no fault:

Ata eva yadā yasya vāsanā kutsitā bhavet.
Tadā doṣāya bhavati nānyathā dūṣaṇaṁ kvacit.

As an example of the same act and varying intention, it is aptly said: "A wife is kissed with one feeling and a daughter's face with another". (*Bhāvena cumbitā kāntā bhāvena duhitrānanam*). A *Mantrin* who is given over to lust, for the subjugation of which the *sādhana* is prescribed, goes, as is said in the Tantrasāra, to the Hell called Raurava. (*Lingayonirato mantrī raurakam narakam brajet*). In the words of the Āhārabheda-Tantra—*Vāmācāro bhavet tatra vāmā bhūtvā yajet parām.* "One may be a *Vāmācārī* if one can worship *Vāmā* being oneself a woman." This is on the principle that a worshipper should always be like the object of his worship. Woman is *Devatā*, and the embodiment of the Supreme S'akti, and is as such honoured and worshipped, and is, when *pūjyā śakti* never the subject of enjoyment.

Verses 15 and 16, as sufficiently appears from their context, refer to the *sādhana* of those who are not *siddha*.

Verses 10, 17 and 18 apply to both *sādhaka* and *siddha*; as to verse 20, see pp. 238, 239 *ante*.

By such *sādhana* the last vestiges of the most powerful of such bonds is sought to be destroyed, and with such destruction the seed of *karma* and rebirth. He, like S'iva, becomes destroyer of Smara, and S'iva Himself. Verses 4, 18 and 20 refer directly to this fruit of *sādhana*. Others indicate the material and intellectual greatness on earth of the *sādhaka*, who devoutly worships the Devī. To him is given mastery over all persons and things of the world, which on death, if *siddha*, he leaves for the dwelling by the Supreme Feet (verse 17), or Nirvāṇa. As S'iva says in the Kālīvilāsa-Tantra "I have told you, my beloved, all about the five Tattvas, Sādhana in the cremation ground and with the funeral pyre ; now listen to the doctrine of the Siddha-vīra."

Madyaṁ matsyaṁ tathā māṁsaṁ mudrāṁ maithunam eva ca
S'maśānasādhanaṁ bhadre citāsādhanam eva ca.
Etat te kathitaṁ sarvaṁ siddhavīramataṁ śṛṇu.

It is the *sādhana* of the cremation-ground on which all passion is burnt away. There are two kinds of cremation-ground, of which the one is the funeral pyre (*citā*), and the other *yonirūpā mahākālī*. As the first Chapter of the Niruttara-Tantra says there are two cremation grounds namely that which is the funeral pyre and *yoni* which, in its *sūkṣma* sense, is the Devī, the *śmaśāna* being in the same sense dissolution or *pralaya*. (*S'maśānaṁ dvividhaṁ devi citā yoni prakīrtitā*). In even the *sthūla* sense the *sādhaka* must be *susādhaka*, for union without right disposition—*japa*, *dhyāna* etc.—is the animal *maithuna* of a *paśu*.

Sloka 19 refers to animal and human sacrifice to Kālī. Reference to this sacrifice is also made in the Kālikā-Purāṇa, and the Tantrasāra speaks of a substitute in the figure of a man made of the paste of cereals. The latter work also says that by the sacrifice of a man one acquires great prosperity, and the eight *siddhis*. (*Naradatte maharddhih syād aṣtasiddhir-anuttamā*). But it adds that this is not for all. For the Brāhmaṇa may not make such a sacrifice. (*Brāhmaṇānāṁ narabalidāne nādhikārah*). And if he does so, he goes to Hell. Moreover according to K. B., who cites as his authority the Yāmala quoted in the Kālikalpalatā, the King alone can make such a sacrifice.

This leads one to point out that the Hymn has other than these gross (*Sthūla*) meanings. In Brāhmanism everything has three aspects—Supreme (*Para*),

Subtle (*Sūkṣma*) and Gross (*Sthūla*). Thus the nineteenth S'loka when referring to the sacrifice of various animals and of man himself intends according to the subtle sense the six great sins for which they stand, ranging from Lust (goat) to Pride (man). It is these which must be sacrificed by the knowers who are worshippers of the Mother, the age of material sacrifice, so universal throughout the world, having passed away. So again the word Paraśakti may refer to the Supreme S'akti or may be used in the sense of a S'akti other than the *svaśakti* or Sādhaka's wife who, may, in the case of the competent (*adhikāri*), be an associate in the worship on the principle stated in the Guhyakālikhaṇḍa of the Mahākāla-Saṁhitā.

" As is the competency of the Sādhaka, so must be that of the Sādhika. In this way only is success attained and not otherwise even in ten million years ".

Yādṛśah sādhakah proktah Sādhikā'pi ca tādṛśah
Tatah siddhim-avāpnoti nānyathā varṣa-kotibhih.

This principle rests on the fact that man and woman together make one whole and can only co-operate in the rites where the attainments or *Adhikāra* of each is the same. But this does not necessarily mean that such co-operation is by *Maithuna* in its sexual sense; quite the contrary. In the same way in the Vaidik ritual the wife is *Sahadharmiṇī*. But such ritual is only for the competent within the bounds of S'āstric injunction for, as the S'aktisaṅgama Tantra (Part IV) says,—" Though a man be a knower of the three times, past, present and future and though he be a controller of the three worlds, even then he should not transgress the rules of conduct for men in the world were it only in his mind ".

Yadyapyasti trikālajñas-trailokyāvarṣaṇakṣamāh.
Tathā'pi laukikācāram manasā'pi na laṅghayet.

But *Paraśakti* again may mean no woman at all, but Supreme S'akti or the Mother Herself whose forms they are and in such sense the union of the Sādhaka is with the "Woman" within himself—the Kuṇḍalinī S'akti who in Yoga unites with Her Supreme Husband Paramaśiva. (See *The Serpent Power*). The context must be known as in the misunderstood saying "*Maithunena mahāyogī mama tulyo na saṁśayah,*" which does not mean, as a recent English work on Hinduism suggests, that by sexual connection (*Maithuna*) the *Mahāyogi* becomes without doubt the equal of S'iva or God. This is on its face absurd and had it not been that such criticism is clouded with prejudice the absurdity would be recognised. How can sexual connection make any one God or His equal? The person spoken of is a *Mahāyogī* who. as such, has no connection physical or otherwise with women. *Maithuna* means "action and reaction" and "coupling" and sexual intercourse is only *one form* of such coupling. Thus when Mantra is said there is a coupling or *Maithuna* of the lips. In Yoga there is a coupling (*Maithuna*) of the active and changeless Principles of the Universe. The saying means that the *Mahāyogī* who unites Kuṇḍalī-S'akti in his body with Paramaśiva becomes himself S'iva.

So again it is said in an apparently alarming verse quoted by Tarkālaṁkāra, in his commentary on the Mahānirvāṇa.

Mātṛ-yonau kṣipet lingam bhaginyāh-stanamardanaṁ
Guror-mūrdhni padaṁ dattvā punarjanma na vidyate.

This verse in its literal sense means that if any one commits incest with his mother and sister and places his foot on the head of his Guru he is liberated and is never again reborn. But of course that is not the meaning. The first half of the line refers to the placing of the *Jīvātmā* in the triangle situated in the *Mūlādhāra* centre with the *Svayaṁbhuliṅga* in it which triangle is called *Mātṛ-yoni*. The *Liṅga* is the *Jīvātmā*. From this point upwards, after union with Kuṇḍalinī, the *Jīvātmā* is to be led. The union of *Jīvātmā* with Kuṇḍalinī is spoken of in the second half of the first line. Kuṇḍalinī is the sister of the *Jīvātmā* both being in the same body. The meaning of the last line is as follows:—after union of Kuṇḍalini and *Jīvātmā* the united couple are led up to the *Sahasrāra* or thousand-petalled lotus in the head which is situated above the twelve-petalled lotus which again is the abode of the Guru. When the Yogī is above the twelve-petalled lotus his feet may be described as being on the head of the Guru. Moreover it is said that at this point the relationship of Guru and disciple ceases. *Mātṛ-yoni* is also the term given to those sections of the fingers between the joints on which count of the Japa or recital of the mantra is *not* to be done. If *Mātṛ-yoniṁ* suggests incest, then this verse is a prohibition of it—*Mātṛ-yoniṁ parityajya viharet sarva-yoniṣu*. There are many other technical terms in Tantra-Śāstra which it is advisable to know before criticising it. One of the tests to which an intending disciple may be put consists in being questioned as to such passages. If he is a gross-minded or stupid man his answer will show it.

In order therefore that the Hymn may be understood in its various aspects I have given in the notes explanations of or in respect of its *Sthūla* or gross meaning. This is followed by the valuable commentary given to me, some years ago and now first published, by Vimalānanda-Svāmī which is called *Svarūpavyākhyā;* that is, it gives the subtle (*Sūkṣma*) or, as we should say in English, the inner sense or esoteric meaning according to the teaching of his own Guru Mahāmahopādhyāya - Rāmānandasvāmī - Siddhānta-pañcānana. The text books and Commentary are preceded by an admirable little essay of Svāmī Vimalānanda by way of Introduction to the *Vimalānandadāyini svarūpa-vyākhyā* on his " Lord of Hymns " which is commonly known as the Karpūrādi Stotra chanted by Mahākāla to, and in honour of, Dakṣiṇā-Kālikā. It, as also the inner-sense Commentary, is written for those liberation-seeking Sādhakas who, worshipping S'rīvidyā, meditate not on the gross form (*Sthūlamūrti*) but on the *Svarūpa-tattva* of Brahma-vidyā Kālikā. As such many will be glad, as I was, to read it and will derive benefit therefrom.

I may note here that the Svāmī while revising the Vyākhyā, has given a new interpretation of the line " *te Lakṣmī-lāsya-līlā-kamala-dala-dṛśah vāma - rūpāh bhavanti* " in the 5th S'loka and of " *rati-rasamahā-nanda-niratām* " in the 13th S'loka.

On the attainment of *siddhi*, ritual ceases. There is neither sacrifice nor worship, nor *yoga*, *puraścaraṇa*, *vrata*, *japa*, or other *karma*. For all *sādhana* ceases when it has borne its fruit in *Siddhi*. The Siddha - Kaula is beyond all rules.

For the meaning of these and other terms, the reader is referred to the Author's Principles of Tantra, (Tantra-tattva)," " S'akti and S'ākta," "The Serpent Power " and " Garland of Letters " which is a study on the Mantra - S'āstra ; and for other Hymns to the Devi, his and Ellen Avalon's " Hymns to the

Goddess," translated from the Sanskrit of the Tantra, Purāṇa, and the Devī-stotra of S'aṁkarācārya, which gives other specimens of the Hindu Hymnal, of which that now published is but one and a special type.

Puri JOHN WOODROFFE

30 May, 1922

---

* HYMNS TO THE GODDESS and HYMN TO KĀLĪ are now published together in this book. (PUBLISHERS' NOTE).

INVOCATION

AIM

I make obeisance to the Lord Guru, the wish granting Tree of Suras, eternal Consciousness and Bliss Itself, the highest of the highest, Brahman, S'iva Himself. I make obeisance to Her who by Her S'akti of three Guṇas creates, maintains, and at the end of the Kalpa withdraws, the world and then alone is. Devoutly I call to mind Her, the Mother of the whole universe, S'ivé Herself.

OM

Obeisance to the Supreme Devatā

Here follows an Introduction to the Vimalānandadāyini Commentary on that Lord of Hymns called the Karpūrādi-Stotra to S'rimad Dakṣiṇa-Kālikā.

All-good and all-powerful Parameśvara is without beginning or end. Though in Himself Nirguṇa He is the Ādhāra of the three Guṇas. Though Himself formless He creates, preserves and withdraws the world of extended matter (Prapañca) by means of the Āvaraṇa and Vikṣepa-S'aktis of His own Māyā which can make that possible which seems impossible. The S'vetāśvatara-Upaniṣad says that by meditation was seen the Sva-śakti of the Deva, who is the abode of all causes, associated with Kālatattva. In the Niruttara-Tantra S'iva peaks of the three-eyed corpse-like One,

Nirguṇa but also seat of Guṇas associated with S'akti. Though Himself without beginning, middle or end, He creates and is the material Cause of the world which has a beginning, middle, and end. For this reason the Tantras and other S'astras call Him Ādinātha, Mahākāla, Paramaśiva and Paramabrahman. It is this unlimited, undivided, beginningless, and endless Mahākāla who is imagined to be limited by the Sun, moon and Planets, and, as such, is called by the names of Kāla, Kāṣṭhā, Muhūrta, Yāma, Day, Night, Pakṣa, Month, Season, Half-year, Year, Yuga, Kalpa and so forth. It is He who divides Time into Kāla, Kāṣṭha and so forth, and as Vyaṣṭi is called by the name Kāla, and the rest. He is named Paramaśiva Mahākāla when creating, preserving and withdrawing the millions of worlds.

Apart from individual name and form, He exists as the Samaṣti of them and the Endless Supreme Greatness (Paramomahān). Viṣṇu-Purāṇā says that Bhagavān Kāla is without beginning or end. From him appears the limited in creation. Atharvaveda says that Kāla created beings (Prajā); He is Prajāpati. From Kāla was self-born Kaśyapa and Tapas. Mahākāla is omniscient since He is all-pervading, dependent on none, and the Ātmā of all. Kūrma-Purāṇa also says that he is the Supreme, imperishable, without beginning or end, all-pervading, independent, the Ātmā of all who fascinates (Manohara) all minds by His greatness. Kālamādhava cites Viṣṇu-dharmottara as saying that He is called Kāla because of his dissolving (Kalanāt) all beings, and He is Parameśvara because He is Himself without beginning or end. Mahākāla is Himself Nirguṇa and Niṣkriya, but his S'akti makes the Sun and other heavenly lights rise, stay and set.

It is by the Power of the S'akti of Kāla that men and other Jīvas are conceived in the womb, are born, attain childhood, boyhood, middle and old age and leave the world on death. In the S'āntiparva of Mahābhārata, Vedavyāsa says that it is through Kāla that women bear, that birth and death occur, winter, summer and rains come, and the seed germinates. Even Brahmā, Viṣṇu and Rudra appear, stay and disappear through the S'akti of Kāla. None can escape Its operation. Viṣṇu-Saṁhitā says that even those Devas who create and withdraw the world are themselves withdrawn by Kāla. Kāla or time is certainly then the stronger. Mahākāla is called Mahākālī because He is one and the same and not different from His eternal S'akti. It is She who is Mahāvidyā, Mahādevī, Mahāmāyā, and Parabrahmarūpiṇī. As Ādinātha Mahākāla is the first creator of the world so the S'akti of Mahākāla, the merciful Mahākālī is the Ādiguru of the world. Yoginī Tantra says that Mahākālī is the Mother of the world. and one with Mahākāla, as is shown in the Ardhanārīśvara Mūrti.

It was this Brahmavidyā who (Yoginī-Tantra, 10th Paṭala) at the beginning of this Kalpa was heard as a bodiless voice from the sky by Brahmā, Viṣṇu, and Maheśvara, who were then told to perform Tapasyā for the acquisition of creative and other S'aktis. It was this Aniruddha-saraśvatī who in the Satyayuga appeared in the Heavens before Indra and other proud Devatās in the form of a brilliant Yakṣa, and crushing the pride of the Devas Agni and Vāyu, in the form of all-beautiful Umā, taught Brahmatattva to Indra, the King of the Devas (See Kenopaniṣad 11, 12).

This Kālī again who is Parameṣtiguru and grants Kaivalya, compassionating the sensuous and short-lived Jīvas of the terrible Kaliyuga revealed the S'āṁbhavī-Vidyā. This, which was taught in the form of conversations between Devī and Īśvara, had been during the three preceding ages kept as concealed as a lady of high family from public gaze. It contained three sets of sixty-four Āgamas each, which revealed the path of Liberation for these Jīvas. Though She is Herself eternal and Saccidānandarūpiṇī, She at times out of compassion for Sādhakas assumes forms fitted for their Sādhanā. Similarly the Veda, Āgama and the rest though everlasting portions of the S'abda-brahmarūpiṇī are only revealed to Sādhakas at different times in the several Yugas.

When the Mahādevī who is Consciousness (Cinmayī) at the beginning of the Kalpa was pleased by the Tapasyā of Deva Rudra, floating on the Causal Waters, She assumed the Virāt aspect and became thus visible to Him. At that time by the command of Mahādevī the Deva Rudra saw in the Suṣumnā millions of universes (Brahmāṇḍa) and millions of Brahmās, Viṣṇus and Maheśvaras in them. The Deva, greatly wondering in the Heart-Lotus of Mahādevī, there saw the Mūrti of S'abdabrahman consisting of Āgamas, Nigamas, and other S'āstras (See Yoginī-Tantra, 9th Paṭala). He saw that of that Mūrti, Āgama was the Paramātmā, the four Vedas with their Angas were the Jīvātmā, the six systems of philosophy (Darśana) were the senses, the Mahāpurāṇas and Upapurāṇas were the gross body, the S'mṛtis were the hands and other limbs, and all other S'āstras were the hairs of that great Body. He also saw the fifty Mātṛkā (Letters) resplendent with Tejas on the edges and petals of Her Heart-Lotus. Within the pericarp of the Lotus of the Virātrūpiṇī He saw the Āgamas, brilliant as millions of suns and moons, replete with all Dharma and Brahmajñāna, powerful to destroy all Māyā, full of all Siddhis and Brahmanirvāṇa. By the grace of Mahākāli he fully mastered the Veda, Vedānta, Purāṇas, Smṛiti and all other S'astra. Later, Brahmā and Viṣṇu received this knowledge of Āgama and Nigama from Him.

In the Satyayuga Brahmā revealed the Smṛtis, Purāṇas and other S'āstra to the Devarṣis. In this way Brahmavidyā was promulgated to the world. This therefore is authority to show, that just as Brahman is everlasting, so are the Āgamas and Nigamas which tell of Brahman. Just as in the Satya and other Yugas, only the three twice-born castes, wearing the sacred thread, but not the S'ūdra and other low castes were entitled to worship according to the Veda, so in those three Yugas only Devarṣis, Brahmarṣis and Rājarṣis, who had conquered their passions and knew Advaita doctrine and Brahman, were entitled to the Āgama S'āstra which destroys all sense of difference caused by ignorance and grants knowledge of Advaitatattva.

By S'iva's command they kept it as secret in their heart as they would a knowledge of their own mother's illicit love. By Upāsanā they became liberated whilst yet living (Jivanmukta) and attained to Brahmanirvāṇa. At that time the Upāsanā of the Āgama was unknown to Sādhakas devoted to Karma. For this reason many people nowadays think the Tantra-śāstra to be of recent origin. Probably all know that in the first three Yugas Brāhmaṇa boys, after investiture with the sacred thread, used to learn the Karmakāṇḍa and Jñānakāṇḍa of the Veda orally from thir preceptors. The Veda was not then classified or reduced to writing.

Towards the close of the Dvāparayuga, S'rīkṛṣṇa-dvaipāyana Maharṣi Vedavyāsa divided the Veda into four parts and reduced it to writing. This however does not show that the Veda is a recent production. The Supreme Science (Para vidyā) which is contained in the Āgama was also handed down from generation to generation of Gurus in the first three Yugas and is being now similarly transmitted. Towards the end of the Dvāparayuga, and at the beginning of the Kali age, merciful S'iva impelled by compassion for humanity bound in the toils of ignorance, divided the Tantraśāstra, which is unlimited knowledge, into three sets of sixty-four parts each, according to the necessity of different Adhikārīs, and then told them to Gaṇapati and Kārtikeya the two beloved sons of Pārvatī. They repeated these Tantras to Ṛṣis of Siddhāśramas, and these last, in their turn, told them to their own disciples. Of the Ṛṣis who knew Āgama the chief was Dattātreya, an incarnation of Viṣṇu. At the beginning of the Kalpa the ancient Brahmavidyā contained in the Āgama appeared from out the Parameṣṭi-guru who is Mahābrahmavidyā and exists in man's heart unlimited and imperishable. If Sādhanā is done according to the instructions of a Sadguru it becomes visible in the Sādhaka's heart. Upāsanā, in the Vaidik form, predominated in the Satyayuga. In those days Brāhmaṇas, and other twice-born castes, impelled by a desire for wealth, progeny and so forth used to worship Indra, Agni, Vāyu, Sūrya, Soma, Varuṇa and other Devas presiding over particular S'āktis of Parameśvara in whom all S'aktis reside. But desire-free Brahmarṣis and Maharṣis did Sādhanā of Brahmavidyā the full and perfect S'akti. And so we see in the tenth Maṇḍala of the Ṛgveda-Saṁhitā that Mahādevī appeared in the heart of the daughter of Maharṣi Āṁbhṛṇī and so told the true nature of Brahmavidyā to Ṛṣis. This is the Devīsūkta full of Advaitatattva, the Hymn telling of the true nature of Brahma-vidyā in the Veda. In the Tretā and other Yugas the Brāhmaṇas and other twice-born devoted to the Karmakāṇḍa used to perform Yajñas and so forth, according to the Smṛtiśāstras of Manu and others. But Brahmarṣi Vaśiṣṭha (in Cīnācāra), Rājarṣi Viśvāmitra (see Gandharva-Tantra, First Paṭala), Videharāja Janaka, Bhṛgurāma the son of Jamadagni (see Kālīkulasarvasva), S'rī Rāmacandra and other high-souled men were worshippers of Brahmavidyā, the full and perfect S'akti. Again in the Dvāparayuga, despite the existence of Vaidik and Smārta cults, the Agnihotra Yajña and other rites used to be performed according to the Purāṇas. But high-souled S'rīkṛṣṇa the son of Vāsudeva (see Rādha Tantra, Devī Bhāgavata and Mahābhārata, Anuśāsana Parva, Ch. 14), the five Pāndavas namely Yudhiṣṭhira and others (Virāṭa Parva, Ch. 6), the high-souled Rājarṣi Bhīṣma, the great Muni Vedavyāsa, high-souled S'ukadeva, Asita, Devala and Brahmarṣis such as Durvāsā were worshippers of Mahāvidya the perfect S'akti. Of this the Mahābhārata and other books provide particular proofs. In the present Kaliyuga also the ten S'aṁskāras such as marriage and so forth of the twice-born, and the obsequial ceremonies such as S'rāddha are performed according to Vaidik ritual. Smṛti governs Cāndrāyana and other matters relating to Āśrama and legal affairs such as inheritance. The autumnal Durgāpūjā and other Vratas are performed according to the Purāṅas. But initiation, Upāsanā of Brahman with S'akti and various practices of Yoga are done according to the ritual of the Āgama S'āstra.

This latter is of three kinds according to the prevalence of the Guṇas namely Tantra, Yāmala and Dāmara. There are in all 192 Āgamas current, namely 64 each in Aśvakrāntā, Rathakrāntā, and Viṣṇukrāntā. Many Tantras were lost in Buddhist and Mahommedan times and the few which still remain with Sādhakas in different parts of the country are not shown by them to any but to their disciples, so that these also are about to be lost. The late Rasika-Mohana-Chattopādhyāya, with great effort and cost, saved some of these and the Englishman Sir John Woodroffe has done the same and I hope yet others will in future be rescued by him.

In the Yogini-Tantra, Īśvara says to Devī that the difference between Vedas and Āgamas is like that between Jīva and Ātmā, that is between Jīva covered with Avidyā and Īśvara who is full of Vidyā. Indra and other Devas who used to be worshipped as Īśvaras in Yajñas held under the Karma-kāṇḍa or Saṁhitā of the Vedas are, in Tantra-śāstra, worshipped as the Presiding Devatās of the Dikpālinī S'akti of Her who is all S'aktis (Sarvaśakti-svarūpiṇi). The three Īśvaras Brahmā, Viṣṇu and Rudra of the Vedas and Purāṇas are in Tantra-śāstra the presiding Devatās of the creative, preservative, and dissolving S'aktis of Mahādevī. As such they are worshipped as the supports of the couch of the Mahādevī. She in the Devīgītā says that 'Brahmā, Viṣṇu, Rudra, Īśvara, Sadāśiva are the Mahāpreta at my Feet. They are constituted of the five Bhūtas and represent the five different elements of matter.' 'I however' She says 'am unmanifested consciousness (Cit) and in every way beyond them.'

Again the Veda says 'All this is verily Brahman.' Despite this Mahāvākya, various distinctions are made, such as those of caste, Adhikāra of men and women and so forth. So a male Brāhmaṇa may say Vaidik Mantras but not Brāhmaṇa women. Distinction was again made between objects as between the water of the Ganges and a well. All such distinctions are wholly opposed to the Spirit of the Great Word (Mahāvākya). The Tantra-śāstra says that the supreme Brahman is both subtle and gross. In dependence on the truth of this Mahāvākya Tāntrik Sādhakas purify wine which is 'not to be taken and drunk' according to Veda. Considering it to be as holy as nectar, they offer it into the mouth of Kulakuṇḍalini who is Consciousness itself (Citsvarūpini). Again, in accordance with Veda, the Tantra holds food to be sacred and knowing that food is Brahman ordains the offering of it to Mahādevī. This offered food is Mahāprasāda and very holy and rare even for Devas, and whether it be brought by a Caṇḍāla, or even fallen from the mouth of a dog. The Vedas and Smṛti say that the Caṇḍāla and other low castes are untouchable. On touching them one must bathe, do Aghamarṣana and so forth. But the Tantra-S'āstra says that even a Caṇḍālā, who has a knowledge of Kula doctrine and Brahman, is superior to a Brāhmaṇa who does not know Brahman. The Tantra-S'āstra again says that during the Cakra all castes are equal. Since all are children of the one Mother of the World, no distinctions should be made at the time of worshipping Her. It is on this Tāntrik authority that no caste distinctions are observed in the matter of eating and so forth in the Virajākṣetra of S'rī S'rī Vimalā Devī. The Veda again prohibits the performance of Yajña or worship after the taking of food. Tantra-S'āstra however says that one should not worship Kālika whilst suffering from hunger or thirst ; otherwise She becomes angry. That is since S'iva and Jīva are really one it is futile to worship the Paramātmā saying 'I offer Naivedya' when the Jīva, who is one with It, is in want of food and drink. Smṛti again, which explains Veda ordains that the S'ālagrama stone which represents Nārāyaṇa should not be touched or worshipped by any but Brāhmaṇas. On the other hand, the Tantra-S'āstra ordains that the Bāṇaliṅga representation of the Brahman may be touched and worshipped not only by Brāhmaṇas but by S'ūdras, Caṇḍālas and women. In fact the Karmakāṇḍa of Veda contains many such ordinances opposed to Brahman-knowledge. For this reason Bhagavān S'rīkṛṣṇa has said in the Gitā that the Vedas are concerned with objects constituted of the three Guṇas (Triguṇaviṣaya) and bids Arjuna to free himself of the Guṇas. He says the Veda contains the Karmakāṇḍa but that he who seeks the Brahman-state above the Guṇas should abandon the Karmakāṇḍa and perform Sādhanā according to S'āstra by which Liberation is gained. In spite however of differences in worship and practice both Veda and Tantra S'āstras are one in holding that there can be no Liberation without Tattvajñāna. In the Nirvāṇa-Tantra S'iva says 'Oh Devī, there is no Liberation without Tattvajñāna.' According to Veda, a Sādhaka, in order to become fit for Nirvāṇa, must have first accomplished the fourfold Sādhanā. He must have acquired the faith that Brahman is alone everlasting, and have no desire for happiness either on earth or in heaven. He must possess the six virtues, S'ama, Dama and so forth, and must long for Liberation. He then discusses (Vicāra) and ponders on the Mahāvākya 'That thou art' (Tat tvam asi), and thus realizing the unity of Paramātmā and Jīvātmā, attains the knowledge 'He I am' (So'ham).

In Tāntrik Upāsanā the Jñānakāṇḍa is mingled with the Karmakāṇḍa. The Āgama teaches the ignorant Paśu, steeped in dualism, Vīrabhāva Sādhanā in which dualism and nondualism are mingled. It thus endeavours to raise them to the divine state of Jīvanmuktas, the state of pure Monism. Manu says 'Know dualists to be Paśus. Non-dualists are Brāhmaṇas.' Rudrayāmala says that Vīrabhāva is revealed for the development of Jñāna. After perfecting Jñāna and attainment of Brahmasiddhi, the Sādhaka becomes Devatā in a pure state of Sattva. The Vedānta and philosophic S'āstras are replete with instructions and arguments touching non-dualism. But they do not indicate the path by which one can be in actual practice non-dualistic. For this reason we see Vedāntic Pandits deeming it unclean to touch a low caste man such as a S'ūdra. They also observe endless distinctions as to what should or should not be eaten, and what should and should not be offered to Devatā. Tantra-S'āstra however says that non-dualistic Bhāva (Bhāvādvaita) should be accompanied by non-dualistic action (Kriyādvaita). The Yogavāsiṣṭha (Rāmāyaṇa) says that to the Muni who realizes non-dualism (Advaita) in Bhāva, in Kriyā, and in objects (Dravya), in all these three matters, the world seems but a dream.

According to the instruction of Tantra-S'āstra the Sādhaka rises in the early hours of the morning, and sitting on his bed, meditates as follows: 'I am the Devī and none other. I am that Brahman who knows not grief. I am a form of Being-Consciousness-Bliss, Whose true nature is eternal Liberation.' Again at noon sitting at worship he does Bhūtaśuddhi, and therein merging the 24 Tattvas beginning with earth in Paramātmā and thinking of the Paramātmā and Jīvātmā as one he meditates: 'He Ī am.' Gandharva-Tantra says that, after due obeisance to the Guru, the wise Sādhaka should think 'He I am' and thus unite Jīvātmā and Paramātmā. In all Sthūla-Dhyāna of Mahāvidyās, forming part of daily worship, Tantra-S'āstra everywhere enjoins meditation on the Mahādevī as not different from, but one with, the Sādhaka's Ātmā. The Kālī-Tantra says that, after meditating as enjoined, the Sādhaka should worship the Devī as Ātmā. 'He I am' (So'ham). Kubjika-Tantra says that the Sādhaka should think of his Ātmā as one with Her. Nīla-Tantra in the Dhyāna of Tārā says that meditation should be done on one's own Ātmā as one with the Saviour-goddess (Tārinī). In Gandharva-Tantra Mahādevī says, as regards the Dhyāna of Tripurasundarī that the Man who meditates on the unattached, attributeless, and pure Ātmā which is Tripurā as one with, and not different from, his own Ātmā becomes himself Her (Tanmaya). One should become Her by ever thinking 'She I am' (Sā'ham). Again in the Kālīkula-sarvasva S'iva says that whoever meditates on the Guru and recites the Hymn of the spouse of S'iva and thinks of Kālikā's Ātmā as one with his own Ātmā is S'rī Sadāsiva. Similarly Kulārṇava Tantra says 'The body is the temple of Devatā and the Jīva is Deva Sadaśiva.' Let the Sādhaka give up his ignorance as the offering (Nirmālya, which is thrown away) and worship with the thought and feeling 'He I am.' It is not only at times of worship and so forth that the Sādhaka is enjoined to meditate on Her who is Paramātmā as one with his own Ātmā S'iva teaches that our thought and feeling should be non-dualistic in all that we do, in eating, in walking and so forth. Hence in the Gandharva-Tantra S'iva says 'I am both the Deva and the food offered to Him, the flower and perfume and all else. I am the Deva. There is none other than Me. It is I who worship the Deva and I am also Deva of Devas.' Again it is ordained that at the time of taking Kāraṇa (wine) and the rest they should be offered to the Fire of Consciousness in one's own heart, uttering the Mantra, and thinking that Kula-Kuṇḍalinī extends to the tip of his tongue, let the Sādhaka say: 'The liquid shines. I am the Light. I am Brahman. She I am. I offer Āhuti to my own Self Svāhā.' He who does Sādhanā of the Mahāvidyā in Vīrācāra with such Advaitabhāva attains by Her Grace to Divyabhāva, and with the thought 'I am Brahman' becomes liberated whilst living, and on death is one with Mahādevī. In the Devīgītā S'rī S'rī Devī says 'He becomes Myself because both are one.' Again the Mahānirvāṇa-Tantra enjoins a similar non-dualistic feeling in the Mantra to be said when taking the Dravya (wine). The ladle is Brahman, the offering is Brahman, the fire is Brahman, the offering is made by Brahman and to Brahman he goes who places all his actions in Brahman.'

Saccidānanda Mahāvidyā, in undistinguishable union of S'iva and S'akti, can alone be worshipped with such non-dualism of feeling. Although Tāntrik worshippers are divided into five communities namely S'ākta, S'aiva, Vaiṣṇava, Gāṇapatya and Saura the first alone are all Dvijas since all worshippers of Sāvitrī (Gāyatrī) the Mother of the Veda belong to the S'ākta community. The Mātṛkābheda-Tantra says 'Sāvitrī the Mother of the Veda was born of the sweat of Kālī's body. That Devī grants the threefold fruit and is S'akti of Brahman.' Sādhakas belonging to the other four communities worship their respective male Devatās associating with them their S'aktis. Thus the S'aivas worship S'iva under the names Umā-Maheśvara, S'iva-Durgā, Kālī S'aṁkara, Arddhanārīśvara and so forth. The Vaiṣṇavas worship Viṣṇu under the names, Rādhā-Kṛṣṇa, Lakṣmī-Nārāyaṇa, Sītā-Rāma, S'rī-Hari and so forth. In the Nirvāṇa-Tantra S'rī Kṛṣṇa says 'To those who do Japa of Rādhā first and then Kṛṣṇa to such I, of a surety, grant a happy lot even now and here.' By uttering the name Sītā-Rāma (Sītā coming first) one utters the Tāra of Mahādevī, and for this reason it is also called Tāraka-Brahma. The Sauras perform their worship with the Mantra 'Obeisance to S'rī Sūrya accompanied by the S'akti who reveals.' Moreover the Māyā Bīja (Hrīm), which is the praṇava of Devī, is added to the Mūlamantra by every sect. This clearly shows that all these five sects are directly or indirectly worshippers of the Brahman who is S'iva-S'akti (S'ivaśaktyātmaka) both in his Nirguṇa and Saguṇa aspects. Kaivalyopaniṣad says 'By meditation on the three-eyed, blue-throated serene Lord (Prabhu) Parameśvara, who is without beginning, middle and end, who is one and pervades all things, who is wonderful, Cidānanda Itself, accompanied by Umā, the Muni goes to the Source of all being (Bhūtayoni) to the Witness of all, who is beyond all darkness.' Hence in the Tantra-S'āstra, S'iva has said that the S'iva-śakti-Tattva is the cause of Tattvajñāna and therefore Japa should be done by a Mantra in which they are united. That is one attains Tattvajñāna, which is liberation, by worshipping Brahman as Mother and Father. All Mantras being composed of S'iva and S'akti one should meditate on S'iva-S'akti as being one. In the Tantra S'āstra also S'iva has said that there is no difference between them who are inseparably connected (Avinābhāvasaṁbandha).

He who is S'iva is also S'akti and She who is S'akti is also S'iva. Fatherhood and Motherhood are merely distinctions of name. In reality they stand for one and the same thing. The Tantra S'āstra again says that S'akti, Maheśvara, Brahman all denote the same Being. Male, female, neuter are verbal and not real distinctions. S'akti, Maheśvara, Brahman; all three denote the one eternal Mahāvidyā who is Saccidānanda. Although the Mahāvidyā is in truth Nirguṇa and eternal, She assumes various Māyik forms, varying according to the Guṇas, for the fruition of the desires of Sādhakas. It is said in Candi that She ever appears to fulfil the purposes of Devas, and at such times She, who is Truth eternal, is commonly said to be generated. In the Devyāgama it is said; 'Mahāmāyā who is Cidrūpā and Parabrahmasvarūpiṇī assumes by Her grace towards Sādhakas various forms.' We may meditate on Mahādevī as either female or male, for these terms may be attributed to any gross body. They cannot however be attributed to Her in so far as She is Saccidānanda. Sādhakas of S'akti worship Brahman as Mother, for in the world the mother-aspect alone of Her who is Brahman is fully manifested. In the Yāmala, S'iva says:—'Devī may, My Beloved, be thought of as female or male, or the Saccidānandarūpiṇī may be thought of as Niṣkala-Brahman. But in truth She is neither a female, male, neuter being, nor an inanimate thing. But like the term Kalpavalli (a word in feminine gender denoting tree) feminine terms are attributed to Her.'

In fact the main cause of the birth and nourishment of men and animals is their respective mothers. Their fathers are merely helpers (Sahakārī). Every Jiva on issuing from his mother's womb, lives on her milk, and receives his first initiation with the Mantra 'Mā' (Mother). The first preceptor (Ādiguru) of every man is his mother. She is his visible Devatā. His first lessons are learnt of her. It is the mark also of the Earth to generate and nourish all Jīvas, like a mother, by producing for them all kinds of fruits and grains and holding them in her bosom. Hence we are not wrong in saying that the world is full of the Mother.

In mathematics zero has no value and is merely an empty formless (Nirākāra) thing, indicative of infinity until it is joined to an integer. But when joined to the figure 1 it converts it into 10. Similarly when She who is formless Brahman is joined to Her own Prakṛti, consisting of the three Guṇas, spoken of in S'ruti as 'the unborn one, red, black, and white,' then She assumes for the fruition of the Sādhaka's desires ten different forms (Daśamahāvidyā) whose variety is due to difference in the proportions of the three Guṇas. There are the ten Mahāvidyās who are S'iva S'akti (S'ivaśaktimayī). These ten forms are Kālī and Tārā, the Mahāvidyā Ṣodaśī, Bhuvaneśvarī, Bhairavī, Cinnamastā, Dhūmāvatī, the Vidyā Bagalā, the Siddhavidyā Mātaṅgī, and Kamalā. Some Tantras mention eighteen Mahāvidyās, but these are forms of the ten with slight variations. Of the ten Mahāvidyās, Kālī is S'uddha-sattva-guṇa-pradhānā, Nirvikara, Nirguṇa-brahma-svarūpa-prakāśikā. It is this primordial form which alone directly gives Kaivalya. In Yoginī-Tantra Devī says 'Now see my form (Rūpa) which is Brahmānanda and supreme. Listen, this form is the supreme state (Paramadhāma) in the form of Kālī. There is no Brahman-form higher than this.' In Kāmadhenu-Tantra S'iva says 'In the void is Kālī who grants Kaivalya'. Tārā is Sattva-guṇātmikā and Tattva-vidyādāyini; Ṣodaśī (Mahātripurasundarī),

Bhuvaneśvarī and Cinnamastā are Rajahpradhānā and Sattva-guṇātmikā and hence they grant Gauṇamukti in the form of Heaven (Svarga), Aiśvarya and so forth. The forms of Dhūmāvatī, Bagalā, Mātaṅgī and Kamalā are Tamah-pradhāna and hence their Sādhanā is done in Ṣatkarma, such as causing death to others and so forth. In short all the forms of Mahādevī give Enjoyment and Liberation directly or indirectly.

The forms of the Mahāvidya are divided into two groups namely the Kālīkula and S'rikula. So Niruttara-Tantra says that 'Kālī, Tārā, Raktakālī, Bhuvanā, Mardinī, Triputā, Tvaritā, Durgā and Vidyā Pratyaṅgirā belong to the Kālīkula. And to the S'rikula belong Sundarī, Bhairavī, Bālā, Bagalā, Kamalā, Dhūmāvatī, Mātaṅgī, Vidyā, Svapnāvatī and Mahāvidyā Madhumatī. Of all the Siddhavidyās Dakṣinā is, O my beloved, the Cause (Prakṛti).'

Kālī-kula is for the worship of Jñānis in Divya and Vīrabhāva, and S'rī-kula is for the worship of Karmins in Divya, Vīra and Paśu-Bhāvas. The Tantra-S'āstra gives an account of the Mantras, Yantras, mode of worship and so forth for all the ten or eighteen Mahāvidyās. But almost all Tāntrik writings hymn the greatness of, and give the highest place to, Kālikā the first Mahāvidyā for the others are but different forms of Brahmarūpiṇī Kālikā. The Nigama-Kalpataru says 'Of all castes the Brāhmaṇa is the highest. Amongst all Sādhakas the S'ākta is the highest. Of S'āktas he is the chief who does Japa of the Kālīmantra.' Picchilā-Tantra also says 'of all the Mantras of the Devas that of Kālikā is the best. Even the vilest can become Jīvanmukta simply through this Mantra.' In Yoginī-Tantra, S'iva says 'This Vidyā Kālikā is Mahā-Brahma

Vidyā, through whom even the worst may attain Nirvāṇa. Even Brahmā, Viṣṇu, and Maheśvara are her worshippers. She who is Kālī the supreme Vidyā, is Tārā also. The notion of a difference between them has given rise to various Mantras.' Again the Kāmākhyā-Tantra says ' Oh Parameśvari, seven lakhs of Mahāvidyās remain hidden. Of them all Ṣodaśī is said to be the most sublime. But Oh Devi, the Mother of the world, Kālikā is the mother even of Her.' Niruttara Tantra says ' Without knowledge of S'akti, Oh Devi, there is no nirvāṇa. That S'akti is Dakṣiṇa Kālī who is the own form of all Vidyās (Sarvavidyārūpiṇī).' The Yāmala again says ' As is Kālī so is Tārā and so are Cinnā and Kullukā. Oh Devi, thou, who art the supreme Kālikā, art also the Mūrti which is composed of these four. In the Vaidik system Sāgnika (fire-maintaining) Brāhmaṇas achieved their ends by the offering of oblations to the seven lolling tongues of fire named Kālī, Karālī, Manojavā, Sulohitā, Sudhūmravarṇā, Sphuliṅginī and Devī Viśvaruci' (1st Saptaka, 2nd Khaṇḍa, 4th S'ūtra).[1]

Another important characteristic of the Tantra-S'āstra remains to be mentioned. Although this Scripture is very liberal in matters of practice and worship and does not recognize distinctions of caste and so forth, it has yet repeatedly, enjoined Sādhakas to keep this Ācāra hidden from ignorant Paśus. Of Kaulas it says that ' they are at heart S'āktas, outwardly S'aivas, and in gatherings Vaiṣṇavas.' It also contains injunctions such as that the teaching should be kept as secret as one would the knowledge of one's mother's illicit love, and that if it is given out the Sādhaka's purpose is frustrated and so forth. In the Gandharva-Tantra,

[1] See *Muṇḍakopaniṣad, 1-2-4.*

S'iva says that only such men as are without dualism, have controlled their passions and are devoted to Brahman are entitled to this S'āstra. 'He alone is entitled, who is a believer, pure, self-controlled, without dualism who lives in Brahman, speaks of Brahman, is devoted to Brahman, takes refuge in Brahman, who is free from all feeling of enmity against others, and who is ever engaged in doing good to all beings. Others are not true Sādhakas (Brahmasādhaka). It should not be told to Paśus, to those who are insincere, or to men of shallow knowledge.' For this reason S'iva has used symbols in the teaching of all Dhyānas, Mantras, Yantras, and modes of Sādhanā of Devas and Devīs. The meaning of these symbols is not known to any but the Sadguru. Hence the secret mysteries are unintelligible even to the learned without the grace of the Guru. In the Kulārṇava-Tantra, S'iva says 'There are many Gurus who know the Veda, the S'āstras and so forth. But, Oh Devi, rare is the Guru who knows the meaning of the supreme Tattva.' Hence in order to know the true meaning of the Dhyānas and so forth, there is no other means than to seek refuge with the Guru who knows the meaning of all Āgamas.

It is owing to ignorance of the true nature of Devatā that even Brahmavidyā, who is subtler than the most subtle and Consciousness Itself, seems to be a gross thing. Even learned men do not shrink from saying that this Brahmamayī, whose desires are fully realized (Pūrṇakāmā) is fond of offerings of blood, flesh and so forth. In the Jñānasaṁkalinī-Tantra, S'iva says, 'Agni is the Deva of the twice-born. The Devatā of Munis is in their hearts. Men of small intelligence worship images. To the wise, Devatā is everywhere.' That is Karmin Brāhmaṇas worship

Agni as Īśvara, Yogīs see the Devatā in their own hearts, men of small intelligence (that is compared with the others) worship the Devatā in images, and high-souled seers of the Tattva see Brahman everywhere. In fact much as a teacher shows his little students, small globes and maps, in order to make them understand the nature of the great earth, so Gurus counsel Sādhakas of no great intelligence and of inferior Adhikāra to meditate on Sthūla forms in images and pictures so that their wandering minds may be rested, and they may learn the true aspects of Devatā. Unfortunately however, ignorant men consider the Sthūla form to be the true aspect of the Devatā. In the Kulārṇava-Tantra, S'iva says that some meditate on the Sthūla to still the mind, which, when so stilled, can fix itself on the Sūkṣma. The Sādhaka should first learn from the Guru what quality or action each limb of the image represents, and should then practise meditation on the subtle, otherwise the gross form will itself, become for him mere earth or stone. In Kubjikā-Tantra S'iva says ' Oh Lady of Maheśa. One should meditate on the Formless (here used in the sense as opposed to forms of images, etc.) along with the form. It is by constant practice, Oh Devī, that one realizes the formless.'

Hence Sādhakas who desire Liberation should always think of the Svarūpatāttva of Brahmavidyā-Kālikā. Of this Svarūpa the Devī says in Mahābhāgavata : ' Those who long for Liberation should, in order to gain freedom from the bonds of the body, meditate on that aspect (Rūpa) of Mine which is the supreme Light (Jyotih), Sūkṣma, and Niṣkala, Nirguṇa, the all-pervading, unbeginning, non-dual sole Cause which is Saccidānanda Itself. This is the Svarūpa of the Devī which is beyond all mind and speech.'

The Mārkaṇḍeya-Purāṇa says, 'The Mahāmāyā is Niṣkalā, Nirguṇā, endless, undecaying, unthinkable, formless and both eternal (Nityā) and transient (Anityā)'; that is, Mahāmāyā Kālikā is free from Kalā (Māyā) and free from Guṇas, without end, imperishable, eternal, and not transient as is the world (Jagat), formless, and hence, as such, is not the object of meditation. In the Kūrma-Purāṇa, Viṣṇu in the form of a tortoise says that the Supreme Devī is Nirguṇā, pure, white, stainless, free from all duality and realizable by the Ātmā only. This state of Hers is attainable only by Jñāna. In the Kāmadā-Tantra S'iva says 'That eternal Kālī who is supreme Brahman is one without a second either male or female. She has neither form, Ādhāra, or Upādhi. She is sinless and imperishable Saccidānanda, the Great Brahman.' She who is eternal Brahman has neither appearance (Āvirbhāva), nor disappearance (Tirobhāva), and being all-pervading, She cannot be said, like other Devas and Devīs, to reside in any particular Loka. Thus Brahmā resides in Brahmaloka, Viṣṇu in Viṣṇuloka, Rudra in Kailasa and S'rī Kṛṣṇa in Goloka, but Mahādevī is always and everywhere equally present; though for the fulfilment of the desires of Sādhakas, She appears in particular forms in their minds and hearts. It is clear therefore that her Sthūla aspect is Māyā-made (Māyāmaya) and transient (Anitya). For this reason S'iva, in the Gandharva-Tantra, says, 'That aspect (Rūpa) of the Devī which is the Supreme Bliss and the Great Cause of the worlds neither appears nor disappears'. In the Kulārṇava-Tantra, S'iva says 'It neither rises nor sets, nor grows nor decays; It shines

Itself and makes others shine without any help. This aspect is without condition (Anavasthā) and is being only (Sattāmātrā) and unknowable to the senses (Agocara).' That is, the Svarūpa aspect of the Māhādevī who is Supreme Bliss is the root-cause of this world of three Guṇas. This aspect has no appearance or disappearance and no growth or decay. 'It is self-manifest and manifests all other objects. It is beyond the states of waking, dreams, and sleep. It is unattainable by speech and mind and is Being itself.'

In fact just as fire which, though pervading all objects, does not show its power of burning and lighting, and cannot be put to use for cooking and so forth, until it has been generated by the friction of two objects, so although the Cinmayī is all-pervading, She does not become visible nor does She grant one's desire without the action of Sādhanā. Again just as the Sun, itself motionless in the distant Heavens, by its rays draws moisture from the earth, so the Mahādevī, who is the abode of all S'aktis, though in Herself changeless (Nirvikārā) creates (and the like) the world by means of the eight S'aktis, Brahmāṇī, Vaiṣṇavī, Māheśvarī and other Devatās, presiding as her creative and other S'aktis. For this reason in the Yantra of Mahādevī Kālikā (see Kālikopaniṣad) the Sādhaka worships the fifteen S'aktis, Kālī and others in the fifteen corners, the eight S'aktis Brāhmī and others on the eight petals, the eight Bhairavas and Vatukas Asitānga and the rest at the edges of the eight petals, the four Devatās, Viṣṇu and others, at the four corners of the Yantra, and the ten Dikpālas, Indra and others, in the ten directions as being the rays of Kālikā who is Herself a mass of pure light (Tejoghaṇa). The Mahādevī is worshipped as the

Mūrti consisting of S'iva-S'aktī (S'ivaśaktimaya) in the Bindu at the centre of the Yantra.

Although the Āgama-S'āstra, which grants Advaitabhāva and educes Tattva jñāna, has been revealed by all-merciful S'rī S'rī Bhairava and Bhairavī, it is still unknown to a mass of people. Many in fact to-day despise the Tantra because it contains Vīrācāra and Kulācāra, and some even refuse to admit that it is a Dharmaśāstra at all. If they had read the Tantra-S'āstra intelligently and learned its principles from S'ādhakas truly versed in it, they would have realized how mistaken were their notions of it and, instead of despising it, would certainly have admitted that this S'āstra is the only means of Liberation for the undisciplined, weakminded and short-lived. Seeing that wine, flesh, fish are consumed and sexual intercourse takes place in the world at large I am myself unable to understand why many people should shudder at the Sādhanā of Pañca-makāra to be found in the Tantra-S'āstra. Do these acts become blameable only if made a part of worship (Upāsanā)?

All know that ghee which nourishes and promotes longevity causes serious stomach-disease and even death if taken in too large quantities, whilst snake-poison, which kills, will yet cure and lengthen the life of a dying delirious man, if it be purified and given under suitable conditions with a cold bath, a diet of whey, and so forth. Similarly the Great Physician (Vaidyanātha) Himself has prescribed the Mantra of Ādyāśakti possessed of all S'aktis, and the invigorating Pañcamakāra as Sādhanā suitable for the cure of the malady of Existence (Bhavaroga) of the sinful Jīvas of this dark Kali age, and as a means whereby they may attain the supreme state full of eternal bliss, imperishable and immortal. All classes of physicians prescribe the use of wine, fish and flesh in measured quantities for the acquisition of strength by patients who are weak and have a low vitality. On that account the medical science does not deserve to be hated. Similarly the Tantra-S'āstra does not deserve to be blamed for prescribing the Pancha-makāra for the Liberation of Jīvaṣ suffering from the disease of worldly existence. S'iva has nowhere said that Sādhakas of S'akti should always drink wine, always slaughter animals and eat their flesh and always enjoy woman, and that thus they will attain Liberation. On the contrary, He has counselled various means for checking excesses in these matters, and He has in particular controlled licence by making these acts part of the worship of Īśvara. It is the degraded conduct of a number of great Paśus who pretend to be Sādhakas which is the cause of the public dislike for, and hatred of, the Tantra-S'āstra. In the Mahānirvāṇa-Tantra S'rī Sadāśiva says 'Wine is Tārā the Saviour in liquid form (Dravamayi). It saves Jīvas, destroying dangers and disease, and grants both Enjoyment and Liberation. But wine if drunk in contravention of rule (Vidhi), destroys the intelligence, reputation, wealth and life of men. Even a Kaula who has received Abhiṣeka an hundred times is to be deemed a Paśu and without the pale of Kuladharma if he is addicted to excessive drinking.' In the Kulārṇava, S'iva says 'Oh My Beloved, he who kills animals for self-satisfaction in contravention of S'āstric ordinance (Avidhānena) will dwell in a terrible Hell for as many days as there are hairs on the body of the animal.' These utterances of S'iva clearly show that He has nowhere ordained the free use of Pāñca-makāra by people in general. He has ordained Vīrācāra or Kulācāra only for Sādhakas of the Nivṛtti path who long for Liberation. Such Sādhakas, free from duality (Nirvikalpa) as they are, wish to see the Saccidānanda aspect of the Mahādevī, and S'iva has prescribed the Pañca-makāra to enable them to realize the Ānanda aspect. Just as a man who knows not sweetness is given sugar or honey to eat, so the Sādhaka is made to taste the fleeting objective (Viṣaya) bliss (Ānanda) of Pañca-makāra so that, thus controlling his six enemies for the time being, he may have a notion of the Eternal Brahman-bliss (Brahmānanda). This momentary taste of eternal Brahman-bliss makes the Liberation-desiring Sādhaka eager for and industrious to gain it. But after the attainment of this natural (Sahaja) Brahma-bliss he no more longs for the five Makāras and becomes gradually devoted to Divyācāra. If a Sādhaka takes wine in a limited way, after purification, the out-going of his senses is weakened, and the mind or inner sense is stilled so that he is thus fitted for Sūkṣma-Dhyāna. For this reason wine is called cause (Kāraṇa). In the Kulārṇava-Tantra, S'iva says, 'Ānanda is the Self (Rūpa) of Brahman and that exists in the body. Wine is its revealer and is hence drunk by Yogis. Wine and flesh are taken with Brahma-jñāna for the satisfaction of all Devas, and whoever partakes of them for self-gratification is a sinner.' That is Sādhakas do Sādhanā with Pañca-makāra for the satisfaction of the Devatās whom they worship and the development of Brahmajñāna in their hearts; but whoever takes them for his own enjoyment is doomed to a terrible hell as a great sinner. S'iva has also said in the Kulārṇava, 'One reaches heaven by the very things which may lead to Hell.' The fifth Makāra, that is, sexual intercourse, is the root-cause of the creation of the world of Jīvas. All

Jīvas, be they Devatās, men, beasts, birds, fish, insects or flies, are produced by the sexual union of their respective parents. In this world every male is an individualised (Vyaṣṭībhūta) aspect of S'iva, the Ādipuruṣa, and Caṇḍī says, 'all females in all the worlds' are part of the Mahāśakti. The Kūrma Purāṇa says, 'The Mahādevī is Herself One, present in many parts or divisions (Anekavibhāgastha), beyond Māyā, absolutely pure, Mahāmāyā, Īśvarī, eternal, stainless (Nirañjana), ancient, consciousness (Cinmayī, the First Puruṣa (Ādipuruṣa) of all Puruṣas.' The Gandharva-Tantra says, 'The male form (Puṁso rūpam) the female form, and any other good form—all this is undoubtedly Her supreme form (Paramam rūpam).' One Brahman, becoming dual appears as S'iva and S'akti, and that aspect in which there is union of S'iva and S'akti is the true aspect of Saccidānanda Brahman. It is from this aspect of Blissful (Ānandamaya) union that the world is created, and for that reason men and all other creatures ever seek happiness. The Bliss of the reproductive power of males and females manifests in their bodies only at the time of sexual union. At this time ignorant men remain intent only on gratifying their passion, but Sādhakas, possessed of the knowledge of Kula, then meditate on the Yoga-blissful (Yogānanda) form (Mūrti) of S'iva and S'akti present in the hearts of males and females and, calling to mind the meaning (Artha) of the Mantra of their Iṣṭadevatā, do Japa of it. In the Kālikulasarvasva, S'ri Sadāśiva says, 'By doing Japa of Mantra and by adoration of Bhagavatī, the consort of S'iva, at times of sexual union, a man becomes, like S'uka, free from all sins.' In another place He says, 'The consort of S'iva should be worshipped by becoming S'iva.' True S'akti-sādhanā consists in considering all girls and women, old and young, and of all castes, as the visible forms of one's own Iṣṭadevatā and (according to one's means) worshipping them with clothes, ornaments and so forth; or bowing to them as mothers with the Iṣṭamantra in mind and not treating them with neglect or contempt under any circumstance. In the Kaulāvali-Tantra, S'iva says, 'One should make obeisance on seeing a young woman of a Kaula family. One should bow to any female, be she a young girl, or flushed with youth, or be she old, be she beautiful or ugly, good, or wicked. One should never deceive, speak ill of, or do ill to, a woman and one should never strike her. All such acts prevent the attainment of Siddhi.'

At the present time a measured use of wine, flesh and so forth and a thorough respect for woman as for the Devatā are particularly seen in the civilized society of the West. Satisfied at this, the Mahādevi, who is the Queen of Queens, has granted to the people of the West the light of science and sovereignty over the whole world. S'rimat Ādinātha Mahākāla has, in the 'Karpūrādi Stotra' called the Svarūpa-Stotra, briefly described the Mantra, Yantra, Dhyāna and Sādhanā of S'rimati Dakṣiṇa-Kālika who is Parabrahman (Parabrahmarūpiṇi). This Supreme Tattva is hard to attain even by such Īśvaras as Brahmā, Viṣṇu and Rudra. Mahākāla Himself says, 'Neither Dhātā nor Īśa nor Hari knows Thy Supreme Tattva.'

However, in accordance with the teaching of my Paramaguru, Mahāmahopādhyāya and most worshipful Rāmānanda Svāmi Siddhāntapañcānana, the crest-gem of Tāntrikas, now gathered to the feet of S'iva, I write this Svarūpa commentary under the name of

'Vimalānandadāyini,' of this Karpūrādi Stotra, in consonance with the views of Tantra and other S'āstras.

PRAYER

AT THE FEET OF S'RĪ S'RĪ KĀLIKĀ

May the Mahā Devi who is called Kālikā,
Because She is without beginning or end,
Whose Body is imagined to be blue of colour,
Because like the blue sky She pervades the World,
And because She is Cidghanā [1] Sattvaguṇamayi
Who is imagined to be black,
Because She is colourless and above the coloured Guṇas,
Whose hair is dishevelled (Muktakeśi)
Because though Herself changeless She binds infinite numbers of Jivas by bonds of Māyā, symbolized by Her dishevelled hair and because She makes liberated (Mukta) Brahmā, Viṣṇu and Maheśvara who are Keśa, [2]

---

[1] This is a play on the word Ghana which means mass and black or dark blue cloud. Cidghana is massive, compact, unmixed, pure Consciousness (Cit). Again She is Nirguṇa and stainless but is also Meghāṅgi (cloud-bodied) because through Adhyāsa of the three Guṇas She appears varicoloured just as a cloud in itself colourless appears white, blue, and so forth by contact with the sun's rays. So Devi-Purāṇa says, 'Just as the uniform cloud appears as of many colours, so does She too through the instrumentality of the Guṇas.'

[2] Keśa=K+A+Īśa. And K=Brahmā, A=Viṣṇu' and Īśa=Rudra. The Niruttara-Tantra says, 'Kāli who is Aniruddha-sarasvati, is the great desire-granting tree, the sole Cause of Enjoyment and Liberation for Brahmā, Viṣṇu and Maheśa.'

Who is imagined as having the Sun, Moon and Fire as Her three eyes,

Because as the Virat, the Witness of the world past, present and future She sees everything,

Who is pictured as wearing the dead bodies of two boys as Her ear-ornaments,

Because as said in Āgama and Nigama the childlike and unperturbed (Nirvikāra) Sādhaka is very dear to Her, who being the sole Creatrix, Preserver and Destructress of infinite millions of Worlds, has on Her Body the mark of the Yoni signifying creation, full and high breasts denoting preservation, and a terrible visage signifying the withdrawal of all things,

Who is said to have large teeth, and a lolling tongue and to hold in Her hand a cup made of human skull,

Because the Cinmayī Mahādevī drinks the wine of delusion arising from the Tamas Guṇa of Her Sādhaka by means of Sattva-pradhāna rajoguṇa,[1]

Who is pictured as wearing a garland of severed heads,

Because She is S'abdabrahman (S'abdabrahmarūpiṇī) and the heads are the fifty letters,

Whose upper and lower right hands are seen to be making the Abhaya and Vara Mudrās,

Because She both destroys the dangers, and grants the desires of Sakāma-Sādhakās,

---

[1] White Teeth stand for the white Sattva Guṇa, the red Tongue stands for the red Rajo-Guṇa and Delusion is the Tamo-Guna. The meaning is, the Mahāvidya is represented with a lolling tongue because She first destroys the Sādhaka's Tamo-Guṇa by increasing his Rajo-Guṇa, and large teeth because by increasing his Sattva Guṇa and suppressing his Rajo-Guṇa She grants him the state of Nirguṇa-Brahman. In the Dhyānā of Tārā it is said, 'Ugratārā Herself destroys the *Jādya* (unconscious nature) of the three worlds by putting it in her skull-cup.'

Whose upper left hand is depicted as wielding a sword,
Because She severs the bonds of illusion for the
Niṣkāma-Sādhaka,
Whose lower left hand is seen to hold a human head,
Because She grants him Tattvajñāna,
Who is called Digambarī (space-clad)
Because being Brahman (Brahmarūpinī) She is free
from the covering of Māyā [1] and unconcerned
(Nirvikāra), [2]
Who is pictured as having a waist-chain of human hands,
Because hands are the principal instrument of work
(Karma) and at the close of a Kalpa all Jīvas with
their Karmas are merged in the Avidyā S'akti of
Mahāmāyā,
Who is seen standing on the breast of corpse-like S'iva,
Because the Supreme State (Paramapada) and Svarūpā-
vasthā or Mahādevī (one with Siva) is Nirguṇa
and changeless (Nirvikāra),
Who is seen in Viparīta-maithuna [3] with Mahākāla,
Because at the beginning of a Kalpa She who is ever
blissful (Nityānandamayī), and being united with
S'iva, feels pleasure in the work of creation which
She effects by bringing the changeless Paraśiva
under Her dominion (Vaśībhūta),
Who is again said to live in the cremation ground,
Because when at the end of a Kalpa all things in the
universe from Brahmā to a blade of grass are

---

[1] In the eighteenth century work of Kamalākānta called Sādhakaranjana it is said : 'Of the Nirākāra-Brahman, understand, Māyā to be the Ākāra' (Nirākāra brahmer ākāra dekha Māyā). The S'ūnya has no form until encircled by Māyā.

[2] Vikāra is also 'change'. She is then in Her changeless aspect.

[3] Coition in which the woman assumes the dominant role. S'akti is active and S'iva is the passive principle.

dissolved in Mahākāla, She is in and one with that Mahākāla, who may be thus compared to a cremation ground, and because at the death of Jivas She exists as the individual (Vyaṣti) Jīvātmā in the burning ground,

Whose Yantra for worship is composed of a circle symbolizing Māyā, an eight-petalled lotus denoting the eightfold Prakṛti, three Pentagons representing the fifteen Avayavas and a Bindu denoting S'iva-S'akti,

Because She is, as Paramātmā, in the gross and subtle bodies consisting of the three Guṇas and twenty-four Tattvas,

Whose Bija 'Krīm',[1] the Queen of Mantras is pure Sattva Guṇa, and consciousness (Caitanyamayi) and grants both Enjoyment and Liberation,

Who is worshipped as Dakṣiṇā because She alone grants the full fruits of all forms of Upāsanā and Yajña.

May She, this Mahādevī, who is Saccidānandarūpiṇī and forgiveness itself, pardon all offences committed by me in the explanation of this Her Hymn.

S'ambhu with His five mouths is unable to relate Thy qualities.

Pardon all my childishness. Be propitious.

Guard my life, guard my repute and guard my wife, sons and wealth.

And at death grant me Liberation.

O Mother of the World, obeisance.

S'RI VĪMALĀNANDA-S'VĀMĪ

---

[1] The S'vāmī also points out that the 'Kr' sound in this Mantra is also to be found in the word Christ and in the Mussulman's Karim. See Māyā Tantra Ch. vii for the Yavana-Bija.

HYMN TO KĀLĪ

(KARPURĀDI-STOTRA)

VERSE 1

O Mother [1] and Spouse of the Destroyer of the three cities,[2] they who thrice recite [3] Thy *Bīja* [4] formed by omitting from *Karpūra*, the middle and last consonants and the vowels, but adding *Vāmākṣi* and *Bindu*,[5] the speech of such, whether in poetry or prose, like that of men who have attained all powers,[6] issues of a surety with all ease from the hollow of their mouth, O Thou who art beauteous with the beauty of a dark rain cloud.[7]

Commentary

(inner sense)

With respectful obeisance to the beauteous feet of Svāmi Rāmānanda I write this Svarūpa-vyākyā named the Grantor of Pnre Bliss (Vimalānandadāyini). [8]

'Oh Mother' (Mātah)

The root Mā = to measure, to which is added the suffix tṛch = Mātṛ : that is, She who measures out or gives : She who grants enjoyment or Liberation according as the Sādhaka is desire-ridden or free from desires.

'Spouse of the Destroyer of the three cities'

The three cities are three bodies, gross, subtle, causal. She is the S'akti of Him who grants Liberation from these bodies. As the Power holder (S'aktimān) and His Power (S'akti) are one, it is She who is grantor of such Liberation. Kaivalya-Upaniṣad says, 'From the Ātmā, the root, the bliss, looking on all alike, who abides within the three cities, is born the multiple and various world and into Him these three cities are merged.'

'They who recite'

That is meditating on the same as being one with the Ātmā of the Sādhaka. Kālikā-S'ruti says, 'One should always think of Ātmā as Kālī. Those who do, attain the fourfold Puruṣārtha whether directly desired or not.' Todala-Tantra (Ch. vi) says 'Oh Devī, K grants Dharma, R grants Kāma, Ī grants Artha and M grants Mokṣa. Oh Beloved, the recital of these combined gives Nirvāṇa Mokṣa.'

'This (Etat)'

Thy Sattva saccidānanda aspect denoted by the Bīja 'Krīṁ'.

'Triple (Trihkritang)'

That is the triple aspect Sāttvika, Rājasika, Tāmasika.

'Bīja'

Denotes the aspect in which Thou art the Cause of the World. Although as Saccidānandarūpinī Thou art Nirguṇa when free of Māyā, characterized by the Karma of Jīvas and Kāla, Thou, becomest the seed in the creation of the world, what time Jīvas must enjoy the fruit of their Karma. In the Devīgītā, Devī says 'Then I who am Ātmā, Cit, Para-brahman and called the "One" assume the Bīja (seed) aspect through union with My own S'akti. The causal body of which I have aforetime spoken is Avyakta in which the world exists as seed (Bīja) from which issues the subtle body.'

'Karpūraṁ'

Saguṇa-Brahman, the Kalpaka or fashioner of the World.

'Omitting therefrom'

Omitting from Mūlaprakṛti composed of Sattva, Rajas, and Tamas Guṇas the middle Rajas Guṇa which is Ū and the last

Tamas Guṇa which is M. It is thus composed of Sattvaguṇa alone. The Jñānasaṁkalini-Tantra says, A 'is Sāttvika, U is Rājasa, M is Tāmasa. Prakṛti is these three.'

'Adding'

Powerful to give Nirvāṇa Mokṣa and by Māyā to grant the desires of Sādhakas; and in whom the pure Sattvaguṇa predominates. The Tantra Kalpadruma says, 'K on account of its brilliance is the Citkalā, Jñāna. 'Associated with the fiery letter (R) She is auspicious and full of all Tejas. As "Ī" She grants the desires of Sādhakas. As Bindu She grants Kaivalya.'

'Beauty of dark clouds'

Thou who should be meditated upon as of a dark (Nila) colour because Thou art Cidākāsa and dost possess the compact Tejas S'uddhasattvaguṇa. In the Nirvāṇa Prakaraṇa of Yogavāśiṣṭa it is said, 'Because S'ivā is Vyoma She is seen as black.' Tripurāsārasamuccaya says, 'As being Liberation, She who is attained by devotion (Bhakti) should be meditated on as being like the sky itself free from clouds.'

NOTES

[1] The Divine Mother of the World in Her aspect as *Dakṣiṇa kālikā*, that is, the beneficent Grantor of *Nirvāṇa*.

The *Kālikāhṛdaya* says: 'I worship *Kālī* the Destructress of *Kāla* the Shining One, who is the *Bīja Krīm*, who is *Kāma*, who is beyond *Kāla* and who is *Dakṣiṇakalikā*.' *Gandharva-Tantra* says: 'Hrīm, I bow to *Mahādevī* who is *Turīya* and *Brahman*. He who remembers Her does not sink in the ocean of existence.' *Caṇḍī* says: 'Oh Thou whose Body is pure *Jñāna*, who hast three divine eyes, who weareth the crescent moon, to Thee I bow for the attainment of all good.' (V)

[2] *S'akti* of Maheśa who destroyed the *Asura* named *Tripura* (*Tri* = three; *Pura* = city) along with his three cities in Heaven, Earth and the Nether regions (V).

[3] Recite (*Japanti*); utter repeatedly with mind fixed on the meaning of the *Mantra* (V). Lit, 'make *Japa*.' The word 'recite' is employed as the nearest English equivalent, but is not accurate, in so far as in *mānasa Japa* the action is purely mental,

and in *Japa* of the next lower degree (Upāṁśu) there is movement of the lips only, but no utterance.

[4] The 'seed' *mantra*. *Bīja* is seed, this cause of the *Mantra* body (V). According to the Nityā-Tantra, *Mantras* are of four kinds—*Pinda*, *Kartarī*, *Bīja* and *Mālā* according to the number of syllables, See as to *Bījā*, *The Garland of Letters.*

[5] That is, *Karpūraṁ*, less the vowels *a*, *ū*, *a*, and the consonants *pa* and *ram*= *Kṛ* + *Vāmākshi* ('the left eye' or long vowel *ī*), with the *Nādabindu* superimposed = *Krīṁ* which accomplishes all desire (Tantrasāra), is *Mantrarāja* (S'yāmārahasya-Tantra) (K. B.). Tantrarāja says, 'letter *Ka* is Thy form.'

[6] *Siddhi*, or success. *Siddhi* is that which is sought for (*Sādhya*) and is the result of *sādhana*, the training of the higher psychical and spiritual faculties. It includes the eight great powers, *Aṇimā*, *Laghimā*. etc., the power of motion 'and suspension in space, and others mentioned in the Skanda Purāṇa and other works. The Devī is Herself *Mahāsiddhi* (Lalitāsahasranāmam, v. 55).

[7] *Dhvāntadhārādhararucirucire.* Just as dark clouds, by shedding nectar-like rain, cool the earth parched by the sun's rays, so too dost Thou, by shedding the nectar of Thy Grace, give immortality to *Sādhakas* tormented by the three forms of pain (*Ādhyātmika*, *Ādhibhautika*, *Ādhidaivika*). The *Rudrayāmala* says, '*Devī* is Supreme *S'akti* and delivers from all difficulties. She is dark with the refulgence of a million suns and is cooling like a million moons.' (V).

[8] Vimalānanda is also the name of the Commentator.

VERSE 2

O MAHES'I,[1] even should one of poor mind[2] at any time recite but once another doubled *Bīja* of Thine, composed of *Iśāna*,[3] and *Vāmaśravaṇa*,[4] and *Bindu*;[5] then, O Thou who hast great and formidable ear-rings of arrow form,[6] who bearest on Thy head the crescent moon, such an one becomes all-powerful,[7] having conquered even the Lord of Speech[8] and the Wealth-Giver,[9] and charmed countless youthful women with lotus-like eyes.[10]

COMMENTARY

'*Maheśi*'

Possessor of the great Power of creating, preserving and withdrawing.

'*At any time*' (*Kadācit*)

Durgārāma-Siddhāntavāgiśa is of opinion that by the use of Kadāchit it is meant that unlike other religious Karma which can be done only in a state of purity (S'uci), Japa of the Mantra of Kālī can be done at any time whether one is in a state of purity or not (S'aucāśauca-kāla). Here he says one should not give up the worship if there be a birth or death in the house. The Tantra-S'āstra says that one should do Japa of the Mantra, whether one is in the state of purity or not, and whether walking, standing or sleeping.

'*Recite*' (*Japati*)

Meditate upon.

'*Of dual aspect*' (*Dvandvam*)

Having the dual aspect of S'iva-śakti. The Tantra-S'āstra speaks of the King of Mantras being generated by the union of S'iva and S'akti.

'*Another Bija*' (*Bījamanyat*)

Thy causal (Kāraṇa) aspect which is the Bija Hūṁ. In the Yāmala it is said, 'It is with the double S'abdabīja (which is Hūṁ) that She awakens the mass of S'abda.'

'*Iśāna*'

Is Īśvara. Kaṭhopaniṣad says, 'Puruṣa is the size of only a thumb. He is like smokeless fire, the Īśāna of what has been and will be. He is to-day and He is to-morrow. This is That.' Indu is immortality. Vāmaśravaṇa is the power of granting speech and of attracting forms (Rūpa). The Tantrābhidāna says, 'Ū is Bhairava, subtle, Sarasvatī....attractor of forms.'

Who dost grant Nirvāṇa liberation. The Mahānirvāṇa-Tantra says, 'The forehead of Her who is Nityā, Kālarūpā, Arūpā, and S'iva Himself is marked with the moon on account of immortality.'

'*Dost bear the half-moon*' (*Candrārddhacūde*) '*Earrings*'

Whose earrings (things very dear) are formed of two Sādhakas who are like Maheśvara and simple as boys; that is child-like simple Sādhakas who have true knowledge are dear to Her. In the Vivekacūdāmaṇi it is said, 'Just as a boy plays with toys heedless of hunger and other pain so the wise man plays, happy, unattached and selfless.' Such a Sādhaka attains all forms of knowldge and riches and can charm the whole world.

(*Mahāghorabālāvataṁse*)

There is however another reading given by Durgārāma-Siddhāntavāgīśa namely Mahāghorabāṇāvataṃse, that is whose earrings are formed of frightful arrows (Bāṇa).

Notes

[1] *S'akti* or *Maheśa* the Lord of even *Brahmā*, *Viṣṇu* and *Rudra* (V). The *Devī* as Īśvari, (Ruler), of the Universe and Spouse of Nirguṇa Maheśvara. Īśvara, according to the Liṅga Purāṇa, when associated with *Tamas*, is Rudra the Destroyer; with *Rajas*, the One born from the golden egg, Brahmā; and with *Sattva*, Viṣṇu.

[2] *Mandacetāh* who is not capable of devotion to thy lotus feet according to Commentator K.B.; for, as the Brahmāṇḍa-Purāṇa says, all sin is expiated by remembrance of the feet of the Supreme S'akti.

[3] That is, *Ha*.

[4] The 'left ear,' or long vowel *ū*.

[5] *Nāda-bindu*—that is, $H+\bar{u}+\dot{m}$ = *Hūṁ Hūṁ*. He who makes Japa of *Hūṁ* is more praiseworthy than Deva or Asura (Viśvasāra-Tantra) (K.B.)

[6] Worn by Kāli: reading Bāṇa instead of Bāla as to which see *post*.

[7] Viśvasāra (K.B.)

[8] *Bṛhaspati*, *Guru* of the *Devas*.

[9] *Dhanada*, i.e. *Kubera*, Lord of Wealth, King of the *Yakṣas*; according to one account the son, and, according to another, the grandson of Pulastya (see Muir, O.S.T. iv, 481, v, 488; v, 483; i. 492).

[10] That is, to them are given eloquence and learning, riches and beauty.

VERSE 3

O Kālikā, O auspicious Kālikā [1] with dishevelled hair,[2] from the corners of whose mouth two streams of blood trickle,[3] they who recite another doubled *Bīja* of Thine composed of *Īśa*,[4] *Vaiśvānara*,[5] *Vāmanetra*,[6] and the lustrous *Bindu*,[7] destroy all their enemies, and bring under subjection the three worlds.[8]

Commentary

' *Kālikā* '

Ka is Brahmā, A is Ananta, La is Ātmā of the universe, I is subtle, Ka is Brahmā, A is Ananta. (Tantrābhidāna). Thus it is said that Mahādevī is the subtle, beginningless and endless Ātmā of the universe. ' Thou who art Brahman without beginning or end.' In the Asitāstotra in the Adbhutarāmāyaṇa S'rī Rāma says, ' I bow to that Thine aspect which is Puruṣa without beginning and end, the unmanifest Kūtastha superior (to Thine aspect) as Prakṛti, the Ātmā of the universe appearing in multiple and differing forms.'

[Durgārāma-Siddhāntavāgīśa derives the word Kālikā as follows :—He who dissolves (Kālayati) the world is (Kāla or S'iva). And She who shines (Dīvyati) that is plays (Krīdati) with Him is Kālikā. Kāla + ikan + ā = Kālikā.]

' *With dishevelled hair* ' (*Vigalitacikure*)

That is one who is free from all Vikāras such as the passion for arranging the hair and so forth.

' *Stream of blood* ' (*Asradhārā*)

This blood indicates (the red) Rajas Guṇa. Mahādevī is without that for She is S'uddha-sattva-guṇa.

'*Recite* ' (*Japati*)

Meditate upon.

Of dual aspect (*Dvandvaṁ*)

The Bījā Hrīṁ is both S'iva and S'akti. In the Devīgītā Mahādevī says, ' H is the gross body, R is the subtle body, Ī is the causal body. I am Hrīṁ the Turīya.'

'Iśa'

Who is the aspect of subtle Bija.

'Vaiśvānara'

Which is full of Tejas.

'Vāmanetra'

That is, with Māyā consisting of pure Sattva-Guṇa.

'Indu'

That is, the S'akti which gives immortality.

Three syllabled Dakṣiṇē'

Dakṣiṇé is Dakṣiṇa in the vocative, and the latter is the Saccidānanda aspect which grants Kaivalya and is indicated, by the three-syllabled Mantra. Nirvāṇa-Tantra says, 'The Sun's son (Death) is established in the south (Dakṣiṇa). The name of Kāli makes him flee in all directions with fear. Hence She is called Dakṣiṇa in three worlds.' Kāmākhyā-Tantra says, 'Just as guerdon (Dakṣiṇa) given at the end of a rite, causes it to be fruitful and gives Liberation, so this Devi grants the fruit of all Karma and hence She is called Dakṣiṇa-Kāli.' The same Tantra also says, 'Puruṣa is on the right (Dakṣiṇa) and S'akti on the left. The left conquers the right and becomes the grantor of great Liberation. Hence She is called Dakṣiṇakāli in the three worlds.

[Durgārāma construes these words as follows: Dakṣiṇé tryakṣare ati (by Saṁdhi tryakṣare'ti) that is Dakṣiṇé ati tryakṣare. As Upasargas can shift their position 'ati' has been placed in the verse after Tryakṣare. Atitryakṣare is the vocative of Atitryakṣarā. Atitryakṣarā means Atikrāntah (Adhahkṛtah or placed under) Tryakṣarah (S'iva) yayā (by whom) She: that is, She who has placed S'iva under Her. The whole then means 'Oh Dakṣiṇé who dost stand on S'iva.' Tryakṣara literally means the three lettered one which is the Praṇava (Oṁ) and is used for S'iva. The Mahiṁnaśtotra (see *The Greatness of S'iva* calls S'iva 'Oṁ' and another Stotra calls Him Tryakṣaramaya.

The same commentator then says that there is a different reading for Dakṣiṇé tryakṣareti, namely, Dakṣiṇé Kāliketi which he explains in two ways (*a*) Dakṣiṇé Kālike'ti = Dakṣiṇé

Kālike ati=Dakṣiṇé atikālike. The last word is the vocative of Atikālikā which means Atikrāntā (Sadṛśikritā, made similar to) Kālikā (Meghajālaṁ; a bank of clouds) yayā (by whom) She—that is, She who looks like a bank of clouds; the whole then meaning 'Oh Dakṣiṇé who hast the appearance of a bank of clouds' (*b*) Dakṣine Kāliketi=Dakṣiné Kālike iti which means Oh Dakṣiṇa Kālikā. The word 'iti' is Svarūpārthaka that is simply indicates that She is addressed as Dakṣiṇa Kālikā. Examples of the elision of 'I' after 'E' in Saṁdhi are S'akuntaleti and Meghajāle'pi Kāliketi.]

NOTES

1 The Devī. See Mahānirvāṇa-Tantra, chap. xiii and chap. iv, verse 31: 'At the dissolution of things it is Kāla who will devour all, and by reason of this He is called Mahākāla; and since Thou devourest Mahākāla Himself, it is Thou who art the supreme primordial Kālikā'.

Kālikā is *Brahmarūpiṇi* (V).

2 *Vigalitacikure,* as is the worshipped *nāyikā*. See *post*.

3 *Sṛkkadvandvāsradhārādvayadharavadane*. Kālī is so represented as having devoured the flesh of the demons. The Māhānirvāṇa-Tantra, chap. xiii, verse 9, says: 'As She devours all existence, as She chews all things existing with Her fierce teeth, therefore, a mass of blood is imagined to be the apparel of the Queen of the *Devas*.' Esoterically blood is Rajas Guṇa.

4 That is, *Ha*, as to which see Kāmadhenu-Tantra, chap. ii; and Prānatoṣiṇi, 53 *et seq.*

5 Lord of Fire, whose *Bīja* is *Ra*.

6 'Left eye,' or fourth vowel long *ī*.

7 *Nāda-bindu*; the *Bīja* is thus *H+r+ī+m=Hrīṁ Hrīṁ*. In Svatantra-Tantra H*a* (*Vyoma*) is said to denote manifestation; *Ra* (*Vahni*) is involution; and Ī maintenance of the worlds.

8 The earth, upper and nether worlds (see Viśvasāra-Tantra and Phetkāriṇī-Tantra). *Tribhuvanaṁ*, that is *Devas, Men, Nāgas* and so forth inhabiting *Svarga* (Heaven), *Martya* (Earth) and *Pātāla* (Nether world) (V).

VERSE 4

O DESTRUCTRESS of the sins of the three worlds, auspicious[1] Kālikā, who in Thy upper lotus-like left hand holdest a sword ;[2] and in the lower left hand a severed head ;[3] who with Thy upper right hand maketh the gesture which dispels fear,[4] and with Thy lower right hand that which grants boons ; they, O Mother with gaping mouth,[5] who reciting Thy name, meditate in this way[6] upon the greatness of Thy mantra, possess the eight great powers[7] of the Three-Eyed One[8] in the palm of their hands.[9]

COMMENTARY

'Sword' (*Kṛpāṇam*)

The sword is knowledge (Jñāna) by which the bonds of ignorance of the desire-free Sādhaka are severed. See S'ivadharmottara.

'Severed head' (*Cinna-muṇḍaṁ*)

The human head is the seat of Tattvajñāṇa free of attachment.

'Terrible countenance' (*Prakatita-vadane*)

Her white teeth indicative of the white self-manifesting Sattva-Guṇa bite the red rolling tongue indicative of Rajas Guṇa and suppress both Rajas and Tamas by Sattva.

'Precious Mantrās' (*Manu-vi-bhavaṁ*)

The three 'Krīm' Bījas represent the Cidghaṇa aspect of Devī, the two Hūm Bījas the Sattya-Guṇa aspect and the two 'Hrīm' Bījas the Rajah-pradhāna-sattva-Guṇa aspect.

[Durgārāma-Siddhāntavāgīśa explains this in the following different ways: (*a*) Manuvibhava = the Vibhava or Saṁpatti (precious possession) of Manus or Mantras. This precious possession is the name in the vocative case 'Dakṣiṇé Kālike.' The meaning of the passage then is that those who recite Thy name Dakṣiṇé Kālike, which is the precious possession of Mantras, and meditate on this Thine appearance possess the Powers and so forth. (*b*) Manuvibhava is the Vibhava of the Manu that is the twenty-two syllabled Mantra of Kālī. This possession is the name Dakṣiṇé Kālikā. (*c*) Manuvibhava = Manu (Mantra) vibhava (Ghataka) of which (the Devī's body) is the body of which Mantra is the generator. The bodies of the Devatās are produced by their Mantras. The passage thus means that, they who recite Thy name Dakṣiṇé and Kālikā and meditate on this Thine appearance generated by Mantra possess the virtues mentioned above.]

See last Verse.

Kālikā (*Kālike*)

'*Three eyed one* (*Tryaṁbaka*)'

[The same commentator (Durgārāma) offers three explanations of the term Tryaṁbaka used for S'iva (*a*) He who has three Aṁbakas or eyes is Tryaṁbaka, (*b*) He who has three Mothers or Aṁbās is Tryaṁbaka. The Kālikapurāṇa says, 'As Hara is born of three Mothers He is known, even amongst Devas, by the title Tryaṁbaka. (c) Todala-Tantra says 'the Vidyā Bhuvaneśvari is in Heaven, Earth and the Nether world (Pātāla). He who delights in the Devī as threefold in three places is called Tryaṁbaka. He is with S'akti and is worshipped in all Tantras.']

Notes

[1] *Dakṣiṇé*, the beneficent grantor of *Nirvāna*. (V)

[2] *Khadga*, the peculiar heavy sword with the blade curved at the tip so named, used to behead the sacrificial animals.

[3] The Devī is the destroyer of the wicked.

[4] The Devī is the dispeller of all fear, and makes with Her hand the *mudrā*. The right upper hand makes the gesture of dispelling fear, or the gesture of assurance of safety (*Abhaya-mudrā*) and the right lower hand makes the gesture of granting boons (*Varamudrā*). (V). The *Sādhakā* seeks fearlessness, which is the great gift of the Goddess, who is *Bhayāpahā*, 'remover of fear.' 'If thou art remembered in times of difficulty, Thou takest away all fear' (Mārkaṇḍeya-Purāṇa). At the same time it is she who fills the ignorant with terror (*Paśuloka-bhayaṁkarī*)—that is, those devoid of the knowledge of non-duality, for 'fear comes when there is duality' (Br. Up. 1-4-2, Lalitā, v. 99).

[5] *Prakatita-vadane* (see '*Daśa-Mahāvidya Upāsanārahasya*,' by Prasanna-Kumāra-S'āstrī). *Vimalānanda* reads *Prakatitaradane*, that is, with big protruding teeth. The *Yoginī-Tantra* says, 'Supreme eternal, large-toothed, smeared with blood.' The *Tārākalpa* speaks of '*Syāmā* of the colour of a new (freshly formed) cloud, with large breasts, terrible with protruding teeth. (V)

[6] As stated, that is, *Krīṁ Krīṁ Krīṁ Hūm Hūṁ Hrīṁ Hrīm* which with *Dakṣiṇe* makes ten syllables.

[7] *Siddhi*—that is, *Aṇimā, Laghimā, Garimā, Prāpti, Prākāṁya, Īśitva, Vaśitva, Kāmāvasāyitā*; the power of becoming small, great, heavy, light, etc., which are inherent in Īśvara, and are attainable by Yogis who become Īśvara and gain *Āiśvarya*. By realization of the self, that Divine state which is the universal Self is manifested, as also the eight-fold manifestation of the Divine power.

[8] *Tryaṁbaka* or *S'iva*. According to Tarkālaṁkāra's Commentary on Mahānirvāṇa-Tantra, *Tryaṁbaka* means the father of the three *Devas*, Brahmā, Viṣṇu, and Rudra. The Ṛgvidhāna uses it as an equivalent of Mahādeva. The Mahānirvāṇa-Tantra says: 'As She surveys the entire universe, which is the product of time, with Her three eyes—the Moon, Sun, and Fire—therefore She is endowed with three eyes' (*Ullāsa* xiii, verse 8). The Moon, Sun, and Fire are the *Icchā*, *Kriyā*, *Jñāna* and other *S'aktis* (see the Ṣatcakranirūpaṇa of Pūrṇānanda-S'vāmī) and *The Serpent Power*.

[9] 'By him who carries a flower its odour is enjoyed without seeking. By him who looks upon himself as the universal Self the powers (of Brahmā, etc.) are enjoyed' (Commentary of Sureśvarācārya on the tenth *S'loka* of *Dakṣiṇāmūrti Stotra*).

———

VERSE 5

O MOTHER, they who recite Thy charming *Bīja*, composed of the first of the group of letters,[1] followed by *Vahni*,[2] *Rati*,[3] and beautified by *Vidhu*,[4] thrice, the *Kūrca Bīja*[5] twice, and thereafter, O Smiling Face, the *Lajjā*[6] *Bīja* twice, followed by the two *Thas*,[7] they, O Spouse of the Destroyer of the Deva of Desire[8] contemplating Thy true form,[9] become themselves the Deva of Love whose eyes are as beautiful as the petals of the lotus which Lakṣmī holds in Her playful dance.[10]

COMMENTARY

'*Whoever*' (*Ye, ye*)

Even the most sinful. The Kālikularahasya says, 'Whoever he be who remembers Durgā with or without reverence is delivered from evil and attains the supreme end.'

'*Recite*' (*Japanti*)

Meditate upon.

'*Thy Bīja*'

[Durgārāma Siddhāntavāgīśa calls it the nine syllabled Bija.]

First letter (*Vargādyaṁ*)

The aspect of Consciousness (Cinmayarūpa) which is the beginning of creation.

Placed on Vahni (*Vahnisaṁsthaṁ*)

Full of Tejas.

'*Associated*' (*Vidhu-rati-lalitaṁ*)

That is cooling and beautiful.

'*Thrice*' (*Trayaṁ*)

'That is the three aspects of Sattva, Rajas, Tamas.

'*Kūrca*'

Is S'abdabrahman.

'*Lajjā*'

Is Brahman associated with Māyā.

'*Two Thas*'

Svāha the revealing S'akti of Fire.

'*Smiling face*' (*Smitamukhi*)

Because She is always blissful.

'*Spouse of the Destroyer*' (*Smara-hara-mahile*)

S'akti of S'iva who is the Destroyer of passionate Desire ; that is She destroys the lust, anger and so forth of Her Sādhakas.

'*Thy true form*' (*Svarūpaṁ*)

That which is not different (in essence) from Jīvātmā. Svarūpa is explained here as the Rūpa of S'iva, that is Ātmā, meaning the Oneness of Paramātma and Jīvātma. Kālikā-S'ruti says, 'One should always think of Ātmā as Kālī'. Kālīkula-sarvasva says, 'He who worships the spouse of S'iva thinking that his Ātmā is Kālikā's Ātmā and meditating on the S'iva-like Guru is Sadāśiva Himself.' Yoginī-Tantra says, 'He who thinks, even if it were for a moment, "I am Brahman" to him the Devī gives unending fruit. One's own body should always be thought of as the body of the Iṣṭadevatā. And so the whole world should be considered as Her body.'

[Durgārāma explains Svarūpa in the following ways: (*a*) The true form is that indicated in the previous or following verses. (*b*) It is that of the nine-syllabled Mantra. (*c*) It is that indicated by the letters composing the Mantra. For instance Varadā-Tantra says that in 'Krīṁ', K is Kālī, R is Brahmā, Ī is Mahāmāyā, Nāda is the Matrix of the universe and Bindu is the Dispeller of Sorrow. In 'Hūṁ', H is S'iva Ū is Bhairava, Nāda means the Supreme and Bindu is the Dispeller of Sorrow. In Hrīṁ, H is S'iva, R is Prakṛti, Ī is Mahāmāyā, Nāda the Generatrix of the Universe and Bindu the dispeller of pain. Contemplation of Mantras constituted of these letters reveals their Caitanya. Japa of Mantra without knowing its Caitanya is useless.]

'*Become themselves*' (*Kāmarūpa bhavanti*)

They acquire the power of assuming whatever form they desire and of charming the whole world with their beauty.

Notes

[1] That is, *Ka*.

[2] Deva of Fire, or *Ra*.

[3] S'akti of Kāma, God of love, or long Ī.

[4] The moon, or *Nāda-bindu*. The *Bīja* is, therefore, *K*+*r*+*ī*+*ṁ*=*Krīṁ*.

[5] That is, *Hūṁ*.

[6] *Hrīm*; literal meaning of *Lajjā*, is modesty.

[7] Or Svāhā, S'akti of Agni. The *mantra* is, then, *Krīṁ*, *Krīṁ*, *Krīṁ*, *Hūṁ*, *Hūṁ*, *Hrīṁ*, *Hrīṁ Svāhā* or the nine-lettered *Vidyā*, or feminine *mantra*, which ends with *Svāhā* (see Viśvasāra-Tantra).

[8] *Smarahara* or *S'iva*, who destroyed Manmatha with fire from his central eye of wisdom when the latter sought to distract him by passion from his *Yoga*. The Devī, according to the Brahmavaivarta-Purāṇa, restored Manmatha to life (see as to this Bhāskararāya's Commentary on the Lalitā, verse 34).

[9] *Svarūpaṁ*, that is true form as described in the first and other verses (V).

[10] *Lakṣmī* is associated with, holds, and stands on the lotus, hence Her titles—Kamalā, Padmā, Padmālayā, Padmadhāriṇī (see Lakṣmīstotra in Tantrasāra, p. 577, Rasik Mohan Chatterjee's edition).

VERSE 6

O Devī [1] of full breasts, [2] whose throat is adorned with a garland of heads, They who meditating [3] recite any one or two or three of Thy very secret and excelling *Bījas* or all thereof [4] together with Thy name, [5] in the moonlike face of all such the Devī of Speech [6] ever wanders, and in their lotus-like eyes Kamalā [7] ever plays. [8]

Commentary

'Devī'

The self-manifest one.

" Full breasts' (Pīnastanādhyā)

The milk of these is the food with which She nourishes the world and the drink of immortality with which She liberates Her Sādhakas.

'Whose neck' (Muṇḍa-sragatiśaya-lasat-kaṇṭi)

She who is S'abdabrahman consisting of 50 letters. Niruttara-Tantra says, 'She is adorned with a garland of heads representing the 50 letters.' Kāmadhenu-Tantra says, 'In My throat is the wonderful Bīja of 50 letters.' Again 'I worship the Mother the source of the universe, S'abdabrahman itself, blissful.' Viśvasāra says, 'Blissful Brahman is adorned with S'abdabrahman and within the body is represented by all Mantras.'.

'Bīja'

Mūrti (appearance) in the individual aspect as Prājña, Taijasa, and Viśva and in the aggregate as Īśa, Sūtra and Virāṭ. Devīgitā says 'the causal self is Prājña, the subtle bodied one is Taijasa and the gross bodied one is Viśva.' Similarly Īśa is spoken of as Īśa, Sūtra and Virāṭ. The First is the individual (Vyaṣṭi) aspect and the second the aggregate (Samaṣṭi) aspect.

Eyes (Netra)

Not to speak of themselves being wealthy, the sight of them gives wealth to others. Bhairava Tantra says that Kamalā and the Devī of speech never forsake them for three generations downwards.

Notes

[1] *Devī* which comes from the root *Div* to shine, is the Shining One (V).

[2] *Pīnāstanādhye* (see also Bhairvīstotra in Tantra-sāra, p. 596). The physical characteristics of the Devī in swelling breasts and hips are emblematic of Her great Motherhood, for She is *S'rīmātā*. See also as to the former, (Durgā-*Dhyāna* in Devī-Purāṇa, which speaks of her large and rising breasts (*Pinonnata-payodharāṁ*); the Annapūrṇā-*Stava* (*Vakṣojakuṁbhāntari*); Bhuvaneśvari-*Stotra* (*Āpivara-stanatatīṁ*); and the Saraswati-*Dhyāna* (*Kucabharana-mitāṁgiṁ*). The Annapūrna-*Dhyāna* (*Annapradāna-niratāṁ stanabhāra-naṁrāṁ*) speaks of Her limbs as weighted by Her breasts. The Mahābhāgavata describes Her as naked, terrific, with fiery eyes, full and erect breasts, and dishevelled hair; and the Lalitā (verse 15) says: 'Her golden girdle supports Her waist, which bends under the burden of Her breasts, thrice folding the skin below Her bosom' (*Stanabhāra-dalanmadhya-pattabhandha-valitrayā*).

[3] *Bhāvayantah*, that is, meditating on the naked, full-breasted, black form with dishevelled hair as stated in Her *Dhyāna*, and which is the *Artha* of the particular *Mantra*. The *Bhūtaśuddhi-Tantra* says, 'A Mantra should be recited mentally meditating the while on the form of the *Devī* denoted by it' (V).

[4] Any one of the aforesaid Bījas or the whole, that is, the whole nine-lettered *Vidyā* in full, which according to the Kumārī-Tantra cited in Tantraratna is *Krīṁ, Krīm, Krīm, Hūṁ, Hūṁ, Hūṁ, Hrīm, Hrīm, Hrīṁ*. S'yāmārahasya quoting Kālikā-S'ruti, says that the whole *Vidyā* should be recited once, twice or thrice, or the whole *mantra* with '*Dakṣiṇe Kālike* between the Bījas.' (K. B.) Thus, *Krīṁ, Krīṁ, Krīṁ, Hūṁ, Hūṁ, Hrīṁ, Hrīm, Dakṣiṇe Kālike, Krīṁ, Krīm, Krīṁ, Hūm, Hūṁ, Hriṁ, Hrīṁ*.

[5] *Dakṣiṇe Kālikā*.

[6] *Sarasvati*. The Bhāradvāja-Smṛtī says Sarasvatī is She who ever resides in the tongue of all beings, and who causes speech.

[7] *Lakṣmī:* for them is all learning, weallth, and prosperity (see Mahānirvāṇa-Tantra, *Ullāsa*, vii, verse 50).

[8] In other words they become rich and learned.

VERSE 7

O MOTHER, even a dullard becomes a poet who meditates upon Thee raimented with space,[1] three-eyed,[2] Creatrix[3] of the three worlds, whose waist[4] is beautiful with a girdle made of numbers of dead men's arms, and who on the breast of a corpse,[5] as Thy couch in the cremation-ground,[6] enjoyest Mahākāla.[7]

COMMENTARY

Dullard' (*Jadacetāh*)

One whose mind is smitten with passion for the world.

'*Poet*' (*Kavih*)

A great Jñānī.

'*Meditates*' (*Dhyāyan*)

'Who in mental vision sees Thee who art Saccidānanda-rūpiṇī.

'*Whose loins*' (*Bāhuprakarakṛta-kāñciparilasannitambām*)

At the end of each Kalpa all Jīvas abandon their gross bodies, and existing in their subtle bodies in which their respective Karmas inhere, form part of the Avidyā which is in the causal body of the Brahmarūpiṇī associated with Her own Gūṇās (Svaguṇa) until they are liberated at some future time after the commencement of the next Kalpa. Hence the girdle adorning the loins, lower belly and generative organ of the Mahādevī virāṭrūpiṇī, capable of producing children, is fashioned of the arms and hands of dead Jīvas. For these arms and hands were their principal instruments for the doing of work (Karma). The S'āktānandataraṅgiṇī says, 'With Karma is a Jīva born, with Karma he dies and in the next body again that Karma is attached to him.' Devīgītā says, 'In Her at dissolution Jīvas and their Karmas are merged in undifferentiated mass, just as all which is done (Vyavahārā) merges in dreamless sleep (Suṣupti).' Again the Devī says, 'It is I who create the whole world and enter therein with Prāṇa, Māyā, Karma and so forth.'

'*Raimented with space* (*Digvastrām*)

Raiment is the covering of Māyā. She is without that and above Māyā.

Three-eyed' '(*Trinayanām*)

Having knowledge of the three divisions of Time, past, present and future.

'*Creatrix*' '(*Vidhātrī*)

She who at the beginning of the next Kalpa gives birth and enjoyment to Jīvas according to their respective Saṁcita Karma.

'*On the breast of a corpse*' (*S'avahṛdi*)

The corpse is Nirguṇa-Brahman. The couch is the support (Ādhāra). On Nirguṇa-Brahman as Thy Ādhāra, that is, established in Thine own state (Pada) as Nirguṇa Brahman. Gāyatrī-Tantra says, 'By the word corpse is indicated Brahman as the dead body (Preta).' Gandharva-Tantra says Sadāśiva is the couch on which lies the subtle Tripurasundarī.

'*In the cremation ground*' (*S'maśānasthā*)

The cremation ground (S'maśāna) is the great Ether (Mahākāśa) in which all creatures are merged as corpses in the Great dissolution (Mahāpralaya). In dissolution even the greatest of creatures are but corpses and hence it is a cremation ground.

'*Dost enjoy Mahākāla*' (*Mahākāla-surata-prayuktām*)

At the end of a Kalpa, there being no creation, She being inactive, and there being nought but supreme Brahman, She being inseparate from Paraśiva, experiences Herself as unlimited (Akhaṇḍa) Bliss.

NOTES

[1] The Devī is naked, as is S'iva, for, like Him, She is clothed with space, and is the great void itself (Mahāśūnya).

[2] *Trinayanāṁ*. The Three eyes are Sun, Moon and Fire (V). *Mahānirvāṇa-Tantra* says, 'Three eyes are attributed to *Kālikā* because She observes the whole world with such eyes as the Sun, the Moon, and so forth'. See as to the meaning of these three terms

which do not merely denote these luminaries and elements, *The Serpent Power* and *The Garland of Letters.*

[3] *Vidhātrim,* who provides Enjoyment and Liberation for all Jivas. (V).

[4] *Nitamba,* literally, buttocks but the girdle goes all round. Kāli is represented as so girdled.

[5] The corpse (*S'ava*) represents *S'iva* (V) because He is inactive whilst his *S'akti* it is who does everything. *S'avahṛdi*—that is, on the breast of S'iva (*Viparitarati*). The Devi is given the dominant position in her union with Her consort, because She is *Kartri* (actress), and He is *Bhoktā* (unacting enjoyer). According to Sāṁkhya, *Purūṣa* is neither producer nor produced, but passive, and a looker-on upon the actions of *Prakṛti.* It is not the *Puruṣa* who is active in the creation of the world, but it is She who, in the light of His gaze, dances the world-dance. So Kubjikā- Tantra says: 'Not Brahmā, but Brahmāṇi, creates; it is Vaiṣṇavi, not Viṣṇu, who protects; Rudrāṇi, not Rudra, who takes all things back. Their husbands are like dead bodies.' For in respect of power they are dependent on their S'aktis. As to the *Sādhana,* see Prāṇatoṣini 622, *Viparitaratau japtvā nirvāṇapadavīṁ vrajet.* Two corpses are sometimes pictured, the lower being the eternally quiescent S'iva, and the upper being the S'iva united with S'akti in creation. Similarly the Devi is represented as reclining on a couch made of five corpses, which are the Mahāpreta (see Bhairavayāmala, Lalitā, verse 174, etc). The *Mahāpretas,* whose *Bija* is is *Hsau,* are Sadāśiva, Iśāna, Rudra, Viṣṇu, and Brahmā.

[6] The site of certain forms of Tāntrik *Sādhana,* such as *S'avāsana, Muṇḍāsana,* etc., as to which the Phetkāriṇi-Tantra says that it is an excellent place for *Sādhana.* He who makes *japa* a number of times on a corpse in a cremation-ground attains all manner of success (*Siddhi*).'

[7] Parama-S'iva.

———

VERSE 8

THOSE who truly [1] meditate on Thee, the Spouse of Hara,[2] who art seated in [3] the cremation-ground strewn with funeral pyres, corpses, skulls, and bones, and haunted by female jackals howling fearfully; who art very youthful,[4] and art in full enjoyment upon [5] Thy Spouse, are revered by all and in all places.[6]

COMMENTARY

' *Meditate on* ' (*Dhyāyanti*)

That is see with unperturbed mind.

' *Spouse of Hara* ' (*Haravadhūṁ*)

Hara is He who removes (Harati) the threefold pains (Ādhyātmika, Ādhibhautika, Ādhidaivika) of Jīvas. His spouse is S'akti, that is She who grants Liberation to Jīvas and is Saccidānandarūpiṇi.'

' *Hast entered* ' (*Praviṣṭāṁ*)

Art established.

' *Flaming* ' *pyre* (*Prakatitacitāyāṁ*)

Cit-śakti On account of Her being self-manifested. Caṇḍi speaks of ' Her who pervades the whole universe as consciousness (Cit).'

' *Fearful* ' (*Ghorābhih*)

That is very powerful.

' *Jackals* ' (*S'ivābhih*)

That is Mahābhūtas which are auspicious (S'iva) before being made fivefold (Pañcīkṛta).

' *Skulls and bones* ' (*Muṇḍāsthi-nikaraih*)

The white colour of the skulls and bones indicates the white Sattva-guṇa. Hence associated with the Sattva and other Guṇas of the Jīvas dissolved in Mahāpralaya.

'Ever youthful' (*Atiyuvatīṁ*)

That is She is always the same, fresh, unchanging, and unwasting.

'Satisfied with enjoyment' (*Santuṣṭām-uparisuratena*)

She, after subduing Parama S'iva to Her will, has willingly enjoyment in the work of creation, preservation and dissolution. Nirvāṇa-Tantra says, 'The Vāmā (She who is on the left) is the Grantrix of Great Liberation after conquering the Dakṣiṇa (S'iva who is on the right).' Gandharva-Tantra says, 'She who is the Sun, Moon, and Fire and half of Ha (S'iva) puts down the Puruṣa and enjoys him from above.' Niruttara-Tantra says, 'When Nirguṇā Kali becomes Saguṇā She is engaged in Viparitarati.' The Yogavāsiṣṭa in the Nirvāṇa-Prakaraṇa says, 'Natural unity is S'iva. Creation is (compared with it) unnatural.' That is the Mahādevi is Nirguṇa-Brahman in Her Svarūpa aspect and the subversion of this Svarūpa is the cause of creation.

'Nowhere' (*Kvacidapi na*)

In no birth.

'Humiliated' (*Paribhavah*)

That is they are not subjected to birth, death, and rebirth and attain Nirvāṇa.

NOTES

[1] Commentator K. B.: where *param* is said to mean 'rightly,' or meditation alone without *japa*.

[2] *S'iva.*

[3] *Praviṣṭām.* 'Literally', entered.

[4] *Atiyuvatim.* She is without childhood or old age. The *Sāradātilaka* says, 'Although Thou art primordial, Thy youth is ever fresh'. (V)

[5] *Santuṣṭāṁ uparisuratena,* that is *viparītarati,* or *viparītavihāra* as to which see note 5 of last *śloka.*

[6] Commentator K. B.: Literally 'They nowhere suffer (*Kvacidapina*), that is, neither in this nor the next world defeat or humiliation.'

VERSE 9

WHAT, indeed, O Mother,[1] can we of so dull a mind say of Thee whose True Being [2] not even Dhātā,[3] Īśa,[4] or Hari [5] know ? Yet, despite our dullness and ignorance, our devotion towards Thee makes us talk of Thee. [6] Therefore, O Dark Devī, [7] forgive this our folly. Answer towards ignorant creatures such as we, is not befitting Thee [8].

COMMENTARY

'Mother'

Of us all including Brahmā, Viṣṇu, and Rudra. In the Devī-Sūkta, Viṣṇu says, 'One, subtle, and unchanged, and yet many, Thou dost give birth to millions of worlds. Who am I Viṣṇu, and who is the other S'iva and who are the Devas that we and they should be able to (fully) sing Thy praises?' In the Mārkaṇḍeya-Purāṇa, Brahmā says, 'When Viṣṇu, Īśvara and myself owe our appearance to Thee who has the power to (fitly) praise Thee ?' In Viṣṇuyāmala, Viṣṇu says to Devī 'Oh Mother none know Thy supreme aspect. The heavenly ones therefore worship that gross (Sthūla) aspect of Thine in the form of Kālī and the rest.' The Mahākāla-saṁhitā says, 'When Dhātā was not, nor Viṣṇu, nor Kāla, when the five Bhūtas were not, then Thou the Cause wert alone as the Supreme Brahman, the Being of all that is.'

(Asite) 'Unlimited'

She is not limited by the Guṇas and is Nirguṇā.

NOTES

1 *Jānāmi ;* origin of the three worlds.

2 *Paramaṁ,* or 'reality' (Commentator K. B.).

3 *Dhātā* is *Brahmā* who dispenses the fruits of *Karma.* (V)

4 *S'iva. Īśa : Rudra* who wields the power of *Īśvara-hood.* (V)

5 *Hari : Viṣṇu* who dispels the threefold sorrows of *Jīvas.* (V)

6 *Tathāpi tvadbhaktir mukharayati. Tathāpi :* still, despite our dullness and ignorance (V) *Tvadbhaktiḥ :* inclination to sing

Thy praises (V). *Mukharayati* : impels to utter words in praise of Thee (V)

[7] This is literal but According to V, *Asite* = unlimited one. *Mahākālasaṁhitā* says, ' Unthinkable, unlimited, *S'akti* Itself, which is That on which all that is manifested rests, beyond the *Guṇas*, free of the opposites (*Dvandva*) to be apprehended only through *Buddhi* : Thyself alone art Supreme Brahman.' (V)

[8] As one does not become angry with animals (Paśu or animal and ignorant men also called Paśu) because they do wrong, so do not be angry with us. It is moreover, the part of the great to overlook the faults of their inferiors (Commentator K. B.).

———

VERSE 10

If by night,[1] Thy devotee[2] unclothed, with dishevelled hair, recites whilst meditating on Thee,[3] Thy *mantra*,[4] when with his *S'akti*[5] youthful, full-breasted, and heavy-hipped, such an one makes all powers subject to him, and dwells on the earth ever[6] a seer.[7]

Commentary

'*Laya Yoga*'

Is here described in this and following verses. Gheraṇḍa-Saṁhitā says' 'One should become S'aktimaya by doing Yoni Mudra. One should be in Paramātmā with sweet S'ṛṅgārarasa (love sentiment) and being Blissful (Ānandamaya) should unite with Brahman.' The Gorakṣa-Saṁhitā says, 'Raising the S'akti with the Jiva to the Lotus in the head one should become S'aktimaya and uniting with S'iva should think of all forms of happiness and enjoyment.' The Tantra-Kalpadruma says, 'One should meditate on Devi Kuṇḍalini as Iṣṭadevatā, ever youthful, of the age of sixteen, full-breasted, dark, subtle, appearing as creation and in the form of creation, maintenance and dissolution (S'ṛṣti-sthiti-layātmikā).'

'*Thy devotee*' (*Bhaktah*)

Here the Divya Sādhaka who is a Yogin.

'*By night* (*Naktam*)'

That is, awaking in Brahmavidyā which (though Light) is darkness for all ordinary creatures. The Bhagavadgītā says, 'The self-controlled man awakes in what is night to all creatures.'

'*Naked*' (*Vivāsāh*)

That is, stripped of the covering of Māyā : that is awakened.

'*Dishevelled hair*' (*Galitacikurah*)

That is, with mind free from all restlessness. The word Cikura means both hair and restless.

'*Meditating*' (*Dhyāyan*)

On Thee as in enjoyment of Sāmarasya bliss with Paramaśiva.

'*Enjoying*' (*Ratāsaktām*)

By doing Laya of (merging) the Jīvātmā in Kuṇḍalinī-S'akti, the ever-youthful, all-pervading Genetrix and Preserver of all Jīvas. The creative and nourishing function of Kuṇḍalinī is indicated by the epithets 'heavy-hipped' and 'full-breasted.'

Notes

[1] *Naktaṁ.* At dead of night. The Phetkāriṇī-Tantra, 'By night, naked with dishevelled hair, in union with *S'akti*, by him is all *Siddhi*, gained'. The Kālikrama says, 'The *Paśu* devoted to his own *Ācāra* should recite his *Mantra* a lakh of times by day. The *Vīra* or *Divya* should recite it a lakh of times by night.' Kubjikā-Tantra says 'Such as are in *Paśubhāva* are but *Paśus*. They should not touch a rosary nor recite *Mantra* by night.' (V)

[2] *Bhaktah.* Here a *Vīra-Sādhaka.* Niruttara-Tantra says, 'The *Mantrin* who has received *Abhiṣeka* should do *Kulapūjā*. Oh Devi the *Mantra* of *Kālī* does not become *Siddha* without *Kulācāra.*' (V)

[3] *Tvāṁ dhyāyan.* Mentally seeing Thee in his heart as ever in the Enjoyment of union with *Mahākāla.* (V)

[4] Thy *Mantra* is the aforesaid great *Mantra.* (V)

[5] He is *Ratāsakta,* the meaning of which is as follows: *Sa mantraṁ japati yadā sa śobhanāṅgapratyaṅgaśālinyā manohāriṇyāyuvatyā śaktyā saha maithunāsakto bhavati.* Whilst in union (*Maithuna*) the mind must be concentrated on *Devi Kālī* and *japā* must be done of Her *Mahāmantra.* The devotee should not think of aught else.

[6] So also Phetkāriṇī-Tantra (ch. x) says:

> '*Rātrau nagnah śayānas ca maithune ca vyavasthitah.*
> *Athavā muktakeśash ca tena syuh sarvasiddhayah,*
> *Staṁbhanaṁ mohana-caiva vaśīkaraṇaṁ eva ca.*'

Here *Athavā* means if the *Sādhaka* is without a *S'akti*; then recitation of *mantra* with dishevelled hair gives the same *siddhi.*

[7] *Kavi* which has not here the limited sense of 'Poet.'

VERSE 11

O SPOUSE of Hara [1], should (a *Sādhaka*) daily [2] recite Thy *mantra* for the space of a year meditating the while [3] with knowledge of its meaning [4] upon Thee, intent [5] upon Thy union [6] with the great Mahākāla, above whom Thou art, [7] then such a knower [8] has every pleasure that he wills upon the earth,[9] and holds all great powers [10] in the grasp of his lotus-like hands.

COMMENTARY

'Spouse of Hara' (*Haravadhū*)

Charmer of Mahākāla.

'Mentally recite' (*Vicintya japati*)

The Kaulāvali says that mental (Mānasa) Japa is a hundred times more efficacious than verbal (Vācika) Japa.

According to Durgārāma the words may also mean 'recite' keeping in mind the Artha or meaning and so forth of the Mantra. For it is said that he who does not know the Artha of Mantra, the Caitanya of Mantra, and Yoni-mudrā is without success (Siddhi) even if he do Japa of the Mantra a million times.

'Unperturbed mind' (*Susthībhūya*)

The Kulārṇava-Tantra thus enjoins : 'Beloved ! when doing Japa of a Mantra one should be calm, pure, sparing in food, reverential, self-controlled, unaffected by the opposites (Dvandva), steady of mind, silent and self-disciplined.'

'Meditating on Thee' (*Vicintyatvām*)

The Kaulāvali-Tantra says, 'One should meditate upon the Spouse of S'iva before Japa and after meditation should again do Japa.' The Sādhaka who does Japa and meditation together soon attains success.

'Upon Him' (*Viparītām*)

(The original is 'Viparitah' in the first case and Durgārāma therefore makes it an adjective of the Sādhaka who he says unites with his S'akti in Viparita Maithuna. Vimalānanda however reads it as Viparītām in the second case making it an adjective of 'Thee' (the Devī) who is the object of meditation).

'*Great Powers*' (*Mahāsiddhinivahāh*)

Such as that by which is gained Sālokya, Sārūpya, Sāyujya and Nirvāṇa forms of Liberation.

Notes

1 *S'iva.*

2 *Sadā:* Means 'always' here 'daily' (K.B.).

3 *Vicintya,* that is, who has mentally thought of the letters of the *Bīja* and their meaning, which is mental *japa* (*Mānasa japa*), defined in Narasiṁha-Purāṇa (cited in the Āhnikācāra-tattva of Raghunandana) as the repetition in the mind, letter by letter, syllable by syllable, of the *mantra,* meditating at the same time upon its meaning.

4 That is upon *Varṇa-saṁsthāna* or placing of the letters and their meaning and so forth.

5 *Susthibhūya*—that is, whose senses are not directed to any other object (Commentary, K.B.).

6 *Atiśayamahākālasuratām.*

7 *Viparītām* (see *śloka* 7, note 5.)

8 *Vidvān* whose sole aim is *Mokṣa.*

9 Literally, 'wandering freely on Earth' (Commentary, K.B.).

10 *Siddhi* (see *ante*, p. 295.)

VERSE 12

O MOTHER, Thou givest birth to and protectest the world, and at the time of dissolution dost withdraw to Thyself[1] the earth and all things; therefore Thou art Brahmā, and the Lord of the three worlds, the Spouse of S'rī,[2] and Maheśa,[3] and all other beings and things.[4] Ah Me! how, then, shall I praise Thy greatness?

COMMENTARY

'*Dost withdraw*' (*Saṁhārati*)

That is dost make the world lose itself in Thy Causal (Kāraṇa) body.

'*Dhātā*'

She is the creative S'akti of Brahmā.

'*Husband of S'rī*' (*Srīpatiḥ*)

She is the preservative S'akti of Viṣṇu whose spouse is S'rī or Lakṣmī.

'*Maheśa*'

She is the dissolving S'akti of Rudra.

'*All things*' (*Samastaṁ*)

Thou art both the material and instrumental cause of the world. The Triputā-Stotra says, 'Thou art Earth, Brahmā, and Creatrix of the world. Thou art also Water, Viṣṇu, and Preserver of the world. And thou art Fire, Rudra and the Dissolver of the world. As the Air of the world thou art Aiśvarya.' Another Stotra says, 'She assumes three forms of body for the purpose of creation, maintenance and dissolution. The world being constituted of the three Guṇas, Brahmā, Viṣṇu and Rudra are Her Vikṛtis.'

NOTES

[1] It is commonly said that She destroys but not so. Devatā does not destroy (*Na devo nāśakah*). Man does. She takes back what She has put forth.

[2] *Viṣṇu,* husband of *Lak.*

[3] *S'iva.* The *Trimūrti* is, in fact, Her manifestation.

[4] *Prāyah sakalaṁ api,* that is, all moving and unmoving things (Commentary, K.B.). For the Devī is *Viśvarūpiṇi* in that form of the whole universe. She is the objective world, '*jadātmika*' (Lalitā, verse 90), as well as its Cause.

———

VERSE 13

O Mother, people there are who worship many other *Devas* than Thyself.[1] They are greatly ignorant, and know nothing of the high truth,[2] (but I) of my own uncontrollable[3] desire for Thee approach Thee, the Primordial Power,[4] who dost deeply enjoy the great Bliss arising from union (with S'iva),[5] and who art worshipped by Hari, Hara, Viriñci, and all other *Devas*.[6]

Commentary

'Deluded' (*Vimūdhāh*)

That is devoid of discrimination.

'Enlightened' (*Vibudhaih*)

The Bagalā-Stotra says, 'Oh four-armed, four-headed, worshipful Parameśvari, Oh Devi Aṁbikā who art ever worshipped with devotion by Kṛṣṇa, Oh Parameśvari who art worshipped by the Lord of the daughter of Himālaya, grant beauty, grant victory' and so forth.

'Ādyā'

Who art before and the beginning of the world.

'Union' (*Rati*)

Which is Viparīta as above described.

'Wine'

That is Rasa.

Notes

[1] That is, thinking that other *Devas* grant greater boons (Commentary, K.B.). Cf. also what S'aṁkarācārya says about the worship of other *Devas* in the fourth *śloka* of the *Devyaparādha-kṣamāpana-stotra,* and see Hymn to Jagadaṁbikā. V. 19., p. 142 *ante*.

[2] *Paramam,* that is, *Tattvaṁ.*

[3] For he is a devotee (Bhakta) whose desire for Her is so great that he cannot control but is controlled by it.

[4] *Ādyā.*

[5] *Rati-rasa-mahānanda-niratām.* The Devī delights in creation, which is the fruit of Her union with the *Puruṣa* (S'iva). 'Great Bliss,' for, as on the physical plane *yadrūpaṁ paramānandam tan nāsti bhuvanatraye* (Mātṛkābheda-Tantra, chap. ii), it is the counterpart on that plane of the ecstatic union which produced the Universe itself. It is the reflection of the higher Bliss attainable even here by the union of S'ivaśakti (in the form of Kuṇḍalinī) in the *Sahasrāra.* Some read *Rasikāṁ* for *Niratāṁ.*

[6] *Viṣṇu, S'iva,* and *Brahmā.* What, then, is the use of praying to *Brahmā, Viṣṇu,* and *S'iva* when they themselves worship Her? (Commentary, K.B.). Cf. also Devibhāgavata, *loc. cit.* The *Devi* is Mother of all, from *Brahmā* to the lowliest worm (*Ābrah mākhilajanani,* Lalitā 67).

VERSE 14

O KĀLī, spouse of Giriśa,[1] Thou art Earth, Water, Fire, Air and Ether.[2] Thou art all. Thou art one and beneficent.[3] What can be said in praise of Thee, O Mother ? Of Thy mercy show Thy favour towards me, helpless as I am. By Thy grace may I never be reborn.[4]

COMMENTARY

'Kālī'

Dispeller of the fear of Kāla or Death.

' Thou art Earth' (*Dharitrī kīlālangshachirapi samīropi gaganam*)

Guptārṇava-Tantra says, ' Thou art Earth, Thou art Water, Thou art Fire, Thou art the Air of the world, Thou art Ether, Thou art Mind as Manas, Ahaṁkāra, Mahat (Buddhi) and Thou art Prakṛti. Thou art also, Oh Mother, Ātmā. Thou art the Supreme. Nothing is greater than Thee. Oh Devī of terrible form showing Thy teeth, may my sins be forgiven me.' The Triputā-Stotra also says, ' Thou art the Ādhāra-S'akti and the Ādhāra. Thou dost pervade the world and the world is in Thee.'

' One ' (*Ekā*)

Without a second.

' Beneficent ' (*Kalyāṇī*)

Because She grants Nirvāṇa Liberation to Jīvas.

' Spouse of Giriśa ' (*Giriśaramanī*)

Spouse of S'iva. Or He who is in the Giri or Kūta is Giriśa that is Kūtaṣtha-Brahman ; His spouse or S'akti. Though changeless (Nirvikārā) Thou dost appear as the twenty-four Tattvas, namely, Earth and the rest through Thy Māyā. The Devīsūkta of the Ṛg-Veda says ' Thou who art one and many, subtle and the Vikāras (gross things) and giveth birth to millions of universes. '

' All ' (*Sakalaṁ*)

S'ruti says, ' Verily all this is Brahman '.

' Helpless' (*Agatikaṁ*)

On account of liability to rebirth despite Sādhana.

Notes

[1] The Lord who inhabits the mountain, whereas, *Giriśa* is Lord thereof.

[2] Liṅgapurāṇa says, Devī becomes matter' (*Kṣetra*). She is *Kṣetra-svarūpā*, that is, the field or matter which is known by the soul (*Kṣetrajñā*). See Lalitā Sahasranāmam (fourth hundred) for the Brahman who creates the visible world Itself enters into it (*Tat sṛṣṭvā tad evānuprāviśat.*)

[3] *Kalyāṇi*. According to the Padma-Purāna, *Devī* is worshipped as *Kalyāṇi* in the Malaya Mountain.

[4] *Bhavaṁ anu na bhūyān mama januh*, that is, liberated. The S'yāmārahasya reads *Bhavaṁ ananubhūyat*, using *bhavaṁ* as meaning *dukhaṁ* (pain), arising from *bhava* (the world) (K. B.).

VERSE 15

HE, O Mahākālī[1], who in the cremation-ground, naked, and with dishevelled hair, intently[2] meditates upon Thee[3] and recites Thy *mantra*, and with each recitation makes offering to Thee of a thousand *Ākaṇḍa* flowers[4] with seed,[5] becomes without any effort a Lord of the earth.[6]

COMMENTARY

'And' (*Tu*)

For Divya Sādhakas.

'Mahākālī'

Or Parabrahmarūpiṇī.

'Cremation-ground' (*S'maśānasthah*)

The cremation-ground is Parabrahman into which in the great Dissolution (Mahāpralaya) all beings go as though corpses. 'In the cremation-ground' therefore, means devoted to Parabrahman.

'Naked' (*Dikpatadharah*)

That is, free from the covering of Māyā ; whose Consciousness is untainted.

'Meditates on Thee' (*Dhyānaniratah*)

That is, upon Thy Saccidānanda aspect. The Rudrayāmala says, 'He who follows the Kula path should do Japa of Mantra seeking protection from Devī who is Consciousness, Bliss and Source of knowledge, who is all Tattvas, whose refulgence is that of millions of flashes of lightning.'

'Sunflowers' (*Arkānām*)

Flowers of feeling such as compassion, forgiveness and so forth which are functions of the Mind called the Sun in the Brahmarandhra. The Jñānasaṁkalinī-Tantra says, 'Oh Beloved, the mind is seated on the surface of the sun and life on that of the moon.' The Yājñavalkya-Saṁhitā says, 'The Moon is known to be in the Idā and the sun in the Piṅgalā (Nādī).

'*Self-produced Bīja*' (*Nijagalitavīryena*)

This Bīja is here the nectar which naturally flows from the thousand-petalled Lotus. The Mahānirvāṇa-Tantra says, 'The Heart-Lotus should be offered for seat, the nectar (Amṛta) shed from the Sahasrāra for water to wash the feet, the mind as the offering (Arghya), Memory (Citta) is offered by way of flowers, and the vital airs (Praṇa) as and by way of incense.' Jñānasaṁkalinī-Tantra says, 'Libation (Tarpaṇa) to the Supreme Liberatrix should be made from out the vessel of the Moon and Arghya should be given from out the vessel of the Sun. Compassion, wisdom, and forgiveness are flowers as is also control of the senses. So too are charity (Dayā) and religious merit. Non-injury (Ahiṁsā) to any being is an excellent flower. Bliss is a flower and so too is the worship of the Sādhaka. Whoever offers these ten flowers attains to the feet of the Liberatrix.' In this verse Savikalpasamādhiyoga is indicated.

Notes

[1] *Mahākālī, S'akti* of *Mahākāla.*

[2] *Susthah :* with undistracted mind. (V)

[3] *Tava dhyāna-niratah,* that is, Upon Thy form. (V)

[4] *Arka*=Sunflowers known as *Ākaṇḍa* (V) not the flower so called in English.

[5] *Nija-galita-vīryeṇa kusumaṁ.* Thus the offering is not only of the flowers of the *Ākaṇḍa* plant, ***yatah sādhakah devyai svavīrya-miśritārkapuṣpāṇi samarpayati.*** Durgārāma-Siddhāntavāgīśa cites the Mahākālasṁhitā as saying that the ***sūryapuṣpa*** should be offered in the same way with ***japa*** of the ***mūlamantra*** (***svavīrya-miśrita-sūryapuṣpāṇi***). The ***vīrya*** does not, refer to the sap of the plant. ***Nija*** refers to the ***sādhaka.*** 'Along with, that is dipped in or that is spread over with.' ***Mahākāla-samhitā*** says, 'A ***Kaula-Sādhaka*** in the cremation-ground, naked, dishevelled and with tranquil mind, should offer a thousand sunflowers with seed reciting the while his ***Mantra.*** After meditating and worshipping with great devotion he should recite the Hymn' (V).

[6] That is, king or *rājā.* So the Phetkāriṇī-Tantra says that wealth, strength, eloquence, intelligence, and the love of women (*Sarvayoṣitpriyah*) is gained.

———

VERSE 16

O KĀLĪ,[1] whoever[2] on Tuesday at midnight,[3] having uttered Thy *mantra*, makes offering even but once with devotion to Thee of a hair of his *S'akti*[4] in the cremation-ground,[5] becomes a great poet, a Lord of the earth, and ever goes mounted upon an elephant.[6]

COMMENTARY

'*Kāli*'

Dispeller of the fear of Kāla or Death.

'*Whoever*'

Here a Divya Sādhaka.

'*Midday*' (*Madhyāhne*)

At noon.

'*Devotion*' (*Premnā*)

That is Parabhakti.

'*Offers*' (*Vitarati*)

Merges in Thee, that is, attains Nirvikalpa-Samādhi. Pātanjala-Sūtra says that Nirvikalpa-Samādhi is attained by suppression of the Vṛtti of mind.

'*In the cremation-ground*' (*Citāyām*)

In thee as Consciousness (Cit).

'*Bīja*'

That is here nectar which issues on the enjoyment of the union of Kula-kuṇḍalinī and Paramaśiva. The Gandharvamālikā-Tantra says, 'Oh beloved One, the Queen of Devas unites with Paraśiva and in a moment, Oh Devi Parameśvari, nectar is forthwith produced. That nectar, Oh Devī, is like the juice of of lac. With it, Oh, Mistress of the Devas, libation (Tarpaṇa) should be offered to the supreme Devatā.

'*At home*' (*Gṛhe*)

In the thousand-petalled Lotus (Sahasrāra).

'Hair with its root' (*Cikuraṁ Samūlaṁ*)

The mind with its functions. It is such Sādhaka who gains both enjoyment and Liberation.

Notes

[1] *Kālī* is destroyer of *Kāla* (V).

[2] 'Whoever' is here a *Vīra Sādhaka.*

[3] *Madhyāhne.* Noon or (here) midnight. *Kakārakūtarahasya* says, 'Whoever naked and with dishevelled hair, on a Tuesday, at midnight, does *Homa* in the cremation-ground with hair, nails seed and whatever adheres to the *Sammārjañī* and offers them after having uttered the *Mūlamantra* and recited Thy name a thousand times attracts to him the Lord of the Earth' (V).

[4] The offering is stated in the words *grihe sammārjanyā parigalitabījam hi cikuram samūlang madhyāhne vitarati citayām kujadine.* These words have received various interpretations, of which the two chief alternatives are given. *Gṛhe* is by some translated as 'at home,' in distinction from the cremation-ground to which, according to this rendering, the *sādhaka* subsequently goes to make his offering. This, however, is said to be erroneous, as the *sādhanā* takes place not in the house but in the cremation-ground. Others (see Calcutta edition) translate it as the equivalent of *grihinī*, or wife. *Sammārjanī* is by them read to mean 'comb.' *Parigalita* is translated 'removed,' in the sense that the curling of the hair of the wife is 'removed or straightened with the comb. *Bījam* given either its primary meaning, or as the equivalent of *vīrya* is said to mean *kautilyam*, or curl of the hair. *Cikuram* is 'hair,' and *samūlam* qualifies it, meaning pulled out, taken off at the root. The meaning is, then, an offering is made of wife's hair, the curls (*kautilyam*) of which have been straighténed out with the comb (*sammārjanyā*), and some of which has at the root (*samūlam*). The correct rendering, however, is according to K. B. *S'aktisādhakayoh gṛhe maithunasamaye yoniliṁgasaṁgharṣavaśāt śaktiyonipatitaṁ vīryaliptaṁ loma devyai samarpitaṁ bhavati. Gṛhe* thus doesnot mean 'at home,' but *manmathagrihe.* The hair is from the same. *Saṁmārijanī* = *S'iśna. Samūlaṁ* qualifies *cikuram* in the sense of 'come off at the root' under the circumstances stated. *Parigalita* is 'dropped'—referring to the *vīrya.*

According to *Vimalānanda, Gṛhe parigalita-vīryaṁ,* is that produced by union with the *Sādhaka's svaśakti* or wife (V).

Of the words *Gṛhe sammārjanyā parigalita-vīryaṁ cikuraṁ samūlam* the Commentator Durgārāma Siddhāntavāgiśa gives the two following alternative expressions: (*a*) *Sammārjanyā* means with a comb with which the hair is put in order. *Parigalitavīryam cikuram* means hair of which the *Vīrya* or crookedness has been removed. *Gṛhe* means in the wife: for it is said the wife is the home. The whole phrase then means Wife's hair, root and all, combed out straight with a comb or (*b*) *Sammārjanya parigalita-vīryaṁ* means *S'ukra* produced by *Sammārjani* here meaning *Liṅga* of the *Sādhaka*; *gṛhe* means in the abode of *Kāma* that is *Yoni* of *S'akti* together with hair, root and all.

The English translation is somewhat abbreviated with the object of giving only so much as all renderings are agreed upon. But in practice *Vīrya* is used by most in its literal sense, this is the gross meaning. The inner sense is given in the *Svarūpa vyākhyā* which follows.

5 According to some, the offering is made on the built-up pyre, and, according to others, on the fire after the body has been consumed. *Citā,* however, is really used as a synonym for the burning ground (*Smaśāna*). The Niruttara-Tantra (Ch. I) speaks of two Kinds of *S'maśāna*:

S'maśānaṁ dvividhaṁ deva citā yonih prakīṛtitaṁ.

6 That is, he becomes a *Rājā,* and has no longer to go on foot like common folk.

VERSE 17

THE devotee[1] who, having placed before himself,[2] and meditated and again meditated[3] upon, the abode,[4] strewn with flowers,[5] of the *Deva* with the bow of flowers,[6] recites[7] Thy *Mantra*, Ah![8] he becomes on earth the Lord of Gandharvas,[9] and the ocean of the nectar of the flow of poesy,[10] and is after death in Thy supreme abode.[11]

COMMENTARY

'*Devotee*' (*Bhaktah*)

The Sādhaka who is a Yogi on Divya path.

'*The Abode*' (*Kusumadhanuṣo mandiram*)

The triangular Yoni Maṇḍala in the Mūlādhāra. Nirvāṇa-Tantra says, 'In the triangle, the abode of Kāma, the Liṅga is Maheśvara.'

'*With its own flowers*'

Adorned with the Svayambhu-linga which is compared to a flower. Gorakṣa-Saṁhitā says, 'He is truly wise who knows the supreme Tejas in the Yoni called Svayambhuliṅga. Others are but beasts of burden.

'*Lord of Gandharvas*' (*Gandharva śreṇipatih*)

A great singer. It is said 'there is nothing better than a song.'

'*Poesy*' (*Kavitvāmṛta nadi nadinah*)

He becomes like the great poet Kālidāsa.

Is great' (*Prabhavati*)

He attains Nirvāṇa on being united with Thee who are Saccidānandarūpā. Kūrma-Purāṇa says, Brahmavādis have learnt in all Vedas and Vedāntas the one, omnipresent, subtle (Kūtastha), immovable, absolute, endless, undecaying Brahman, the sole supreme Niṣkala-Tattva higher than the highest, eternal, auspicious, wondrous.' Devīgītā says 'Oh Mountain, he in whom Parabhakti is thus generated becomes merged in Pure Consciousness.'

Notes

[1] *Bhaktah :* here the *Vira Sādhaka* (V).

[2] *Purah :* that is with the *Maṇḍala of Kāma* before him (V).

[3] That is, with intensity. *Dhyāyan dhyāyan,* repeatedly meditating (V).

[4] *Kusuma-dhanuṣomandiraṁ.* The Deva with the bow of flowers is *Kāmā* whose abode is the *Madanāgāra. Tantrakalpadruma* says, 'He who recites the *Mantra* ten thousand times meditating on the flower-covered *Yoni* (*Svapuṣpairākirṇam*) of *S'akti,* of a certainty charms all with his poesy.' *Svapuṣpa* is called *Svayaṁbhukusuma* in *Tantra-śāstra*; *Mātṛkābheda-Tantra* says, 'Oh Lady of *Maheśa Svapuṣpa,* which charms all is the *Rtu* which first appears in a married girl (V).

[5] *Svapuṣpairākirṇam.* The word *svapuṣpa = svayambhupuṣpa*— mentioned in the Tantras. The word *puṣpa* has here, and in ordinary parlance, a figurative sense, as in English. For *puṣpaśabdena atra ṛtur ucyate, mātṛkābheda-tantra-pramāṇānusāreṇa anūḍhāyāh kanyāyāh, prathama eva ṛtur atra ucyate. Tantrāntare tu vivāhitāyā eva, bālāyā ṛtur atra vivakṣitah.* The S'yāmārahasya reads '*supuṣpa,*' which literally means pleasing fragrant flower, but which is possibly a misprint for *svapuṣpa.* The meaning of the passage is as follows: *Sādhakah svasya purobhāge śaktiṁ saṁsthāpya tasyā ṛturudhirasiktāṁ yoniṁ avalokayan san devīmantraṁ japati.*

[6] That is, *Kāma,* the *Deva* of Desire, whose bow and arrows are made of flowers.

[7] *Japati.* Recites ten thousand times (V).

[8] *Aho.* 'Ah' an exclamation of wonder (V).

[9] Celestial spirits (*devayoni*), who play and sing at the banquets of the *Devas.* According to the Viṣṇu-Purāṇa, sons of Brahmā 'born imbibing melody.' The *Sādhaka* thus becomes a master of dance, music and song. *Gandharva-śreṇīpatih.* He becomes a great singer and a master of melody. The *Sāhasānka* says, '*Hāhā* is called a *Gandharva* and singing also makes a *Gandharva*' (V).

[10] He becomes a *Paṇḍita* in all literature. The Kāli-Tantra, quoted in the Kālikalpalatā, says that in strength he becomes like

the wind, in wealth of gifts like Indra, and in the musical art like Tumburu (K.B.)—a *Ṛṣi,* master of music and inventor of the *tambūr*.

[11] *Paramapadalinah prabhavati,* that is, he attains *nirvāṇa* (K.B).

Prabhavati : becomes capable of creating and so forth on being merged with Thy Supreme Feet (V). The word literally means 'Excels.'

———

VERSE 18

He who at night, when in union with his *Sakti,*[1] meditates with centred mind[2] on Thee, O Mother with gently smiling face, as on the breast of the corpse-like S'iva, lying on a fifteen-angled yantra[3] deeply enlisted in sweet amorous play with Mahākāla,[4] himself becomes the destroyer of the God of Love.[5]

Commentary

'*Mother*' (*Jananī*)

The Progenitrix.

'*At night*' (*Naktaṁ*)

Midnight. Brahannīla-Tantra says, 'He who is intent on meditation at midnight or early dawn surely sees the supremely blissful aspect of Devī.'

'*Meditates*' (*Dhyāyet*)

'On Thee as not different from the Sādhaka's own Ātmā, who art Cidābhāsa in his body as a Yantra.' Gandharva-Tantra says, 'He who is in Advaitabhāva, and thinks of the self as Devatā in the three forms of body thinks of Her and his Ātmā as one. He should worship the Devi as Ātmā with the articles prescribed. The Yantra which is one's own body should be considered the best of all Yantras.' Again 'He who meditates on the Nirguṇa, unattached pure Atmā of Tripuré as not being different from his own Ātmā becomes one with Her.'

'*Thee* (*Tvāṁ*)

That is Brahmamayī.

'*Smiling face*' (*Smera-vadanāṁ*)

Because She is ever blissful, being Bliss itself.

'*On the breast*' (*Mahākālenoccāih*)

On the breast of S'iva who is inactive like a corpse. She divides Herself into two parts like a grain of gram, namely, S'iva and S'akti by means of Māyā associated with Iccā, Kriyā, Jñāna, whilst at the same time remaining established in Her Nirguṇa-Brahman state.

'*Fifteen-cornered seat*' (*Tripāñcāre pithe*)

This is the Sādhaka's own body conceived as the Yantra in which Avidyā is the encompassing circle, the eight-fold Prakṛti consisting of Earth and so forth is the eight-petalled lotus, the five Jñānendriyā, the five Karmendriyā and five Prāṇa are the fifteen Triangles and the Bindu which is Consciousness reflected in Māyā composed of pure Sattvaguṇa is the adorning Bija. The Gandharva-Tantra says, 'The Cakramantramaya is the Devatā's Supreme Body which is S'iva-śakti.' The Bhagavadgitā says, 'Earth, Water, Fire, Air, Ether, Manas, Buddhi, Ahaṁkāra, these Tattvas constitute my eightfold Prakṛti.' Gandharva-Tantra says, 'The subtle body composed of uncompounded (Apañcikṛta) Bhūta and equipped with five Prāṇas, Manas, Buddhi and ten Indriyas is the vehicle for Enjoyment. Unbeginning and undefinable (Anirvācyā) Avidyā is the causal Upādhi. Know Atmā to be different from the three-fold Upādhi.'

'*Deeply enlisted*' (*Madanarasalāvanyaniratām*)

Always united in the reverse (Viparita) way with Paramaśiva the Saguṇabrahman. The Gandharva-Tantra says, 'When that Supreme S'akti by putting that Puruṣa down, of Her will appears as the universe then She becomes passionate. And then becoming Herself active the Devi rises upon Bhairava and enhances Her own bliss with waves of natural pleasure."

'*Himself also enjoying*' (*Svayam api ratānandaniratah*)

Enjoying the bliss of union in Laya with Paramatmā by Yonimudrā and becoming S'aktimaya himself. The Gheraṇda-Saṁhitā says, 'He should do Yoni mudrā and himself become S'aktimaya. He should move in Paramātmā with the good S'ṛṅgārarasa. Becoming Ānandamaya he should be one with Brahman.'

'*Destroyer of Kāma*' (*Smarahara*)

The Advaita-sādhaka attains Kaivalya by being merged in Thee who art Paramātmā.

Notes

[1] *Svayam api ratānandaniratah*, of which the meaning is as follows: *yadā sādhakah śaktyā saha maithunakriyāsakto bhavati, tadā sa ślokokta-dhyāna-prakārānusāreṇa devim dhyāyati.*

[2] *Samāsaktah*, concentrated on Thee.

[3] Kālikalpalatā says it is a kind of *yantra* (diagram).

Tripañcāre pithe. The *Yantra.* The *Kāli-Tantra* says, 'First draw a triangle. Outside it put another. Next draw three triangles. In the centre draw the *Baindava-Cakra* adorned with the *Māyā Bija.* Draw a circle outside the six cornered figure. Next draw the eight petals attached to the outer circle and *Bhūpura.* He who knows this great *Yantra* surely attains liberation.' *Bhūpura* is the gross body composed of the five *Bhūtas* (V). It is made with five triangles superimposed.

[4] *Mahākalenoccair-madana-rasa-lāvanya-niratām.* *Mahākāla* is *Paramaśiva* (V). *Madana-rasa-lāvaṇya-niratāṁ* refers to *Viparitarati* (V).

[5] *Smarahara.* The destroyer of *Kāma* is *S'iva* Himself (V).

That is, he becomes *S'iva* Himself, who destroyed *Smara* the *Deva* of Love (Kāma), with Fire from His central eye, when the latter, by the excitation of desire (towards Pārvatī), sought to detract him from his *yoga.* Or it may be translated 'excels in beauty the God of Love.'

———

VERSE 19

O Dark One, [1] wondrous and excelling in every way, [2] becomes the accomplishment, [3] of those worshippers [4] who living in this world [5] freely make offering to Thee in worship [6] of the greatly [7] satisfying flesh, together with hair and bone, [8] of cats, camels, sheep, [9] buffaloes, goats, and men. [10]

Commentary

'Oh Black one' (*Asitā*)

Asitā means free from bondage. Sitā means bound. Asitā is therefore 'not bound' or eternally liberated. The root So, means 'to bind.' Amarakośa gives the meaning of Sitā as 'bound.'

'Wondrous' (*Apūrvā*)

Best.

'At every step' (*Pratipadam*)

In succession, step by step.

'All Powers' (*Sarvasiddhi*)

The five Siddhis which are the five forms of Liberation. The S'ivagita says, 'Sālokya, Sārūpya, Sārṣti, Sāyujya and Kaivalya. Know these to be the five forms of liberation.'

'The flesh of' (*Palalaṁ*)

These animals represent the Six Enemies (Ripu) or Vices which are specially characteristic of the following animals: The goat stands for Lust (Kāma) 'as lustful as a goat (Chhāga),' the buffalo, Anger (Krodha) 'as angry as a buffalo (Mahiṣa),' the cat, Greed (Lobha) 'as greedy as a cat' (Mārjāra), the sheep, Delusion (Moha), 'as stupid as a sheep' (Meṣa), the camel, Envy (Mātsarya) 'as envious as a camel' (Uṣtra), Man, Pride (Mada) 'the Pride and arrogance of man' (Nara).

The Ānandakalpa says, 'Worship should be done by making offering of lust as goat, buffalo, and so forth'. Offering is made to Thee who art Cidrūpā of lust and other vices as articles of offering (Upacāra) in worship with the object of ridding oneself of them. Bṛahannila-Tantṛa says, 'In the fire of Ātmā which flames with the ghee (Havih) of Dharma and Adharma, I ever offer in Homa by the Suṣumnā path, with the mind as ladle, all the functions of the senses—Svāhā.'

'*In worship*' (*Pūjāyām*)

In mental worship according to the manner prescribed.

'*With hair and bone*' (*Loma, asthi*)

That is the whole without omitting any part. Such Sādhakas attain the Sālokyā and other forms of liberation.

NOTES

[1] *Asitā*: That is Kālikā *v. post.*

[2] *Pratipadam.* The S'yāmarahasya-sārasaṁgraha reads *pratidinam.* (every day) (K.B.), which seems preferable, for, as K.B. says, the worship (*pūjā*) is the general daily *pūjā*, upon which daily advancement in *siddhi* would follow.

[3] *Siddhi*: success in work; accomplishment of all which is desired (V).

[4] *Sat*, that is, *sādhu* (wise, good, pious). *Satāṁ*=*Sādha kānām* (V).

[5] That is, among men.

[6] *Pūjāyāṁ api* (see note 2), *ante.*

Pūjāyāṁ: *Naimittika* or occasional worship (V). The force of the particle *api* is that the offering is not confined to special *Sādhanā* but is made in ordinary worship also. (K.B.)

[7] *Param* (K.B.).

[8] That is flesh and all.

[9] *Maiṣaṁ.* The S'yāmarahasya-sārasaṁgraha gives also *mauṣam*, of rat's flesh. The Phetkāriṇi-Tantra has both sheep and rat's flesh (K.B.)

S'yāmārahaysa says, 'To him who makes offering of the flesh of cats, sheep, camels, and buffaloes together with bone, hair and skin *Dākṣiṇe* is ever beneficial like a Mother.'

[10] As to this human sacrifice, K. B. says that Kings alone, and not any other, are entitled to make human sacrifice, citing the Yāmala quoted in the Kālikalpalatā (*Rājā naravaliṁ dadyān nānyopi parameśvari*). For inner sense see Svarūpa-vyākhyā *post.*

———

VERSE 20

O Mother, he who, being a controller of his passions,[1] eats *haviṣyānnaṁ*,[2] and, being proficient in meditation on Thy feet, rightly recites[3] Thy *mantra* a hundred thousand times by day, and he who afterwards[4] naked at night, when united with his *S'akti*,[5] rightly recites Thy great *mantra* another such hundred thousand times, becomes on earth like unto the Destroyer of Smara.[6]

Commentary

'*Naked*' (*Nagnah*)

That is free from the covering of Māyā ; Nirvikāra.

'*Amorous play*' (*Nidhuvana-vinodena*)

That is enjoying the bliss of union between Ātmā and Parāśakti. The Kulārṇava-Tantra says, 'That is coition (Maithuna) in which there is the bliss arising from the union of Ātmā and Parāśakti. Others are but Enjoyers of women.'

'*Becomes*' (*Syāt*)

That is, becomes liberated whilst yet living (Jīvanmukta) like S'iva.

Notes

[1] *Vaśī*. The first part of this *S'loka* refers to *Paśvācāra*.

[2] That is, one who has undertaken the *Puraścaraṇavrata*, and eats pure form of food known as *Haviṣyānnaṁ* (K.B.).

Haviṣyāśanaratah: that is after the recitation (V).

[3] Makes *japa* (see *ibid.*).

[4] *Paraṁ*: that is, when he has been *Abhiṣikta* into *Vīrācāra*.

[5] *Naktaṁ nagno nidhuvana-vinodena*, the meaning of which is *yādā sādhakah śaktya saha maithuna-kriyāsakto bhavati, tadā sa mantraṁ japati*.

[6] *Smarahara* or *S'iva* (see note 5 to *S'loka* 18, *ante*). The Tantra-kalpadruma says, 'He who eats *Haviṣyānnaṁ*, who keeping

Devi in mind recites the *Mantra* a hundred thousand times by day and is at night united with his *S'akti* becomes the Lord of the earth.' (V).

VERSE 21

O Mother, this Hymn of Thine is the source from whence originates Thy *mantra.*[1] It sings of Thy real self, and contains injunctions for the worship of Thy two lotus Feet. He who reads it at midnight or at time of worship[2] even his random talk[3] becomes the nectar juice of poesy.

Commentary

' *Thy real self* (*Svarūpākhyaṁ*)

Speaks of the Dhyāna of both Thy gross and subtle aspects.

' '*Reads*' (*Paṭati*)

That is recites aloud. The Viśuddheśvara-Tantra, 'Oh Devī, the reading of a Hymn (Stotra) mentally, or the recitation of a Mantra loudly is as ineffectual as water in a broken jar.'

' *Nectar of Poesy*' (*Prasarati kavitvāmṛtarasah*)

He becomes full of the sweetness of Poesy. The Kālikula-sarvasva says, 'All whose difficulties and dangers are destroyed by a single reading, as it were flies in a flame. His speech flows like the Ganges full of prose and poetry.'

Notes

[1] *Manusamuddharaṇajanuh*—that is, cause of *mantroddhāra*: formation of Mantra of Devī. The *mantra* is made known, and then impressed with the life and consciousness (*caitanya*) of the *sādhaka* (*mantra-caitanya*).

[2] *Pūjā.*

[3] That is, even his meaningless delirious talk, as in fever or madness, etc. (K.B.).

———

VERSE 22

NUMBERS of women with large eyes, like those of the antelope,[1] impatient for his love, ever follow him. Even the King becomes subject to his control. He becomes like unto Kubera[2] himself. An enemy fears him as if he were a prison. Living in continuous bliss[3] the devotee is liberated when yet living, and is never again reborn.[4]

Here ends the Hymn by S'rī Mahākāla, entitled *Karpūrādistotra*.

COMMENTARY

'*Liberated*' (*Jīvanmukta*)

And on death gets Videhamukti.

'*No rebirth*' (*Muktah pratijanuh*)

He gets Nirvāṇa in Brahman. The Mahākāla-saṁhitā says, 'Whoever constantly and with devotion reads this Hymn originating from Mahākāla, is free from danger, disease and death and in the end attains Kaivalya liberation.'

Here ends the Hymn named Svarūpastotra of S'rīmatī Dakṣiṇa-Kālikā by S'rīmān Mahākāla.
Here also ends its annotation and Svarūpavyākhyā entitled Vimalānandadāyinī.

NOTES

[1] *Kuraṅga*, which has beautiful large eyes.

[2] Lord of wealth.

[3] *Kelikalayā*, by the various entertaining acts (*parihāsādinā*) of which there are sixty-four. The meaning here is that there is continuous bliss.

[4] *Kelikalayā ciraṁ jīvanmuktah sa bhavati ca bhaktah pratijanuh.* The translation in the text reads *pratijanuh* to mean as K.B. says, *Janmanivritti* or cessation of birth. But *Pratijanuh* may also mean 'birth after birth.' According to this translation *jivanmukta* would not refer to the state immediately preceding *Kaivalya* but, as K.B. says, *Jīvadavasthānubhūtadevatā-sākṣātkāramukha* in which case the

translation will be, He living in continuous bliss obtains direct Experience of the *Devatā* and is reborn life after life as Her devotee. According to the translation adopted complete liberation follows and in the other case some lower though happy state.

Obeisance

To Kāli the spouse of Kāla, who destroys all sin and is Kāla.[1] She who is Tārā the Saviour, the Supreme Brahmavidyā, who is adored by the lotus-born Deva.[2]

She who is S'rīvidyā, desirous of the welfare of Sādhakas on the path of Liberation, to whom Hari and Hara[3] make obeisance.

May that Devī the Mother, who appears in the form of all things, bring forth benefits for all such as sing Her praises.

Colophon

Of this King of Hymns wherein Mahākāla has described the true self of Kālikā, the Karpūrādya Hymn, untainted by worldly desire, which gives bliss to Devotees, the aforesaid Annotation containing its simple interpretation, as well as the Svarūpavyākhya (Commentary) which gives pure joy was prepared by me Vimalānanda Svāmī for the enlightenment of Sādhakas in the Saka year 1837. Mayest Thou reside in the throat of him who reads it.

OṀ, TAT SAT, OṀ

---

[1] The first Kāla is Mahākāla and the second is the produced Kāla.

[2] Brahmā.

[3] Viṣṇu and Rudra.

Talking Cinema

Bhawana Somaaya has been a film critic for over thirty years and has contributed columns to publications like the *Hindu, Hindustan Times, Pioneer* and *Sunday Observer*. She is the former editor of *Screen* and has authored many books on cinema. Her last book, *Mother Maiden Mistress*, was published by HarperCollins in 2012. Some of her other books include biographies of Hema Malini and a trilogy on Amitabh Bachchan: *The Legend* (1999), *Bachchanalia* (2009) and *Amitabh Lexicon* (2011).

She is a film expert with 92.7 BIG FM and writes weekly columns for *Pravasi, Hans India* and the *Indian Express* (North American edition). She has served two terms on the advisory panel of the Central Board of Film Certification. *Talking Cinema* is Somaaya's twelfth book.

Talking Cinema

Conversations with Actors and Film-makers

Bhawana Somaaya

HarperCollins *Publishers* India

First published in India by
HarperCollins *Publishers* in 2013

HarperCollins Publishers India, Cyber City, Building 10-A, Gurugram,
Haryana-122002, India
www.harpercollins.co.in

2 4 6 8 10 9 7 5 3

P-ISBN: 978-93-5029-645-5
E-ISBN: 978-93-5029-646-2

Typeset in 11/ 14.3 Arno Pro
Saanvi Graphics Noida

Printed and bound at
MicroPrints India, New Delhi

This product is made of FSC®-certified and other controlled material.

HarperCollins Publishers, Macken House, 39/40 Mayor Street
Upper, Dublin 1, D01 C9W8, Ireland

To the technicians; movies and actors would never be the same without their expertise

Contents

Section 3
Director's Cut

Section 4
The Specialists

The Magnificent Obsession

Just as there is a mood for a song and a dance and a mood for a cry and a fight, there is one for an artiste and a journalist to engage in a conversation on cinema.

For most artistes, an interview is an occupational hazard they have to go through mechanically. They also have to, during the interview, stay disconnected from the distractions around them. During this process, however, unknown to them, comes a moment when the artiste ceases to treat the exercise as a task. He begins to enjoy the thought process for, in all probability, this is the first time that the actor has paused to reflect on his characters and it is cathartic!

This magical moment is, in many ways, similar to what the actor perhaps experiences in front of the camera between the commands 'action' and 'cut'.

As audiences we have, over the years, watched our favourite actors transform into diverse characters and wondered how they inhabit roles so contradictory to their persona. We have wondered how these portrayals affect the actors' psyche and how they endure the suffering for so many years. Is it all as painless as it seems or do the characters affect the artiste's personal lives? What are the creative and the disconnecting processes and do they even exist?

Talking Cinema attempts to capture these magical moments as actors shed their inhibitions and discuss their anxieties as performers. It draws directors to confess their conflicts and vulnerabilities while the making of a film. The book is a testimony of their passion for cinema and, more important, their obsession with their craft.

In the centenary year of cinema, it is the right time for me to recapture milestone moments with actors and film-makers I have interacted with for over thirty years. I choose artistes who were then at the crossroads of their careers.

Anil Kapoor and Madhuri Dixit, after ruling as a romantic pair in the 1990s, were travelling different landscapes – Kapoor was the angry politician in *Nayak* and Madhuri was Chandramukhi in *Devdas.*

When Kamal Haasan turned director with *Hey Ram,* he was weighed down with the scale and the expectations of directing. Waheeda Rehman was anxious about fitting into show business when she returned after a long break in *Om Jai Jagadish.* Rani Mukerji was at a turning point as an actor post *Saathiya* and Abhishek Bachchan was elated when he broke the jinx with *Dhoom.*

Tabu spoke about how she lost and found Ashima Ganguly in her first international film, *The Namesake,* with Mira Nair.

Kirron Kher described shooting *Khamosh Pani* during troubled times in Pakistan. *Guddi* Jaya Bachchan was facing the camera after decades in *Hazaar Chaurasi Ki Maa* and narrated how she identified with her character Sujata.

Shabana Azmi discussed the dividing line between the actor and the activist, between Indian and international cinema and nobody speaks as passionately about acting as she does. She said Indian cinema would change in the twenty-first century and it has.

Rekha was enacting her first deglamourized role as the midwife and mother in *Lajja* and, even though she was pushing fifty at that time, she was the first choice of film-makers looking for a heroine to be cast in a courtesan's role in *Yatra*.

I was privileged to spend quality time with many generations of directors. I interviewed Hrishikesh Mukherjee after *Jhooth Bole Kauwa Kaate* and Yash Chopra after *Veer-Zaara*. I didn't know at that time that *Hu Tu Tu* would be the curtain call for Gulzar as a director and mark a new innings for the lyricist who made his debut in 1960. Gulzar is today the oldest and most successful songwriter of Hindi cinema.

The new breed of directors like Karan Johar and Sanjay Leela Bhansali were then young and restless. *Kuch Kuch Hota Hai* for Karan and *Hum Dil De Chuke Sanam* for Sanjay had raised the bar and both were anxious to live up to the expectations of producing good cinema after the success of *Kabhi Khushi Kabhie Gham* and *Devdas*.

The elusive Mani Ratnam was disillusioned by the Hindi film industry after *Yuva*. He felt disheartened by the critics and, for the first time, let his guard down and spoke from the heart. I interviewed A.R. Rahman, the only music composer featured in the book and someone who is forever inaccessible, at the Gateway of India, Mumbai, during the music release of *Swades*. It was a surreal moment and Rahman was at his spiritual best.

Amitabh Bachchan features as a subject in Anurag Kashyap's story in Bombay Talkies, which celebrates a hundred years of cinema, because it's difficult to exclude an actor who has been active for forty-four out of those hundred. Yet, in 2000, film-makers were unsure of what roles to cast the fifty-eight-year-old superstar in. He was too charismatic to play ordinary father roles and too loved to be accepted as a villain so it took several trials and errors for the audience and the camera to figure out how he would play his next innings. Some film-makers, surprisingly, still perceived him as a cop even if director Govind Nihalani's Dev in the eponymous film was diametrically different from Rajkumar Santoshi's Anant Srivastav in *Khakee.* Sanjay Leela Bhansali conceived him as a teacher for the disabled in *Black,* a role Bachchan had not played in his long career.

Amitabh Bachchan analyses his stardom and says the pressures have lessened because the responsibility of how the film fares at the box-office is on the hero and he is in a more comfortable position today. Shah Rukh Khan, after over a decade in films, had launched his production company. He had seen the highs and lows as an actor and as a star. He was loved, hated, hounded and attacked by the media and turned into a recluse. Khan discussed his roles, friends, perceptions and anxieties as an actor.

These conversations reflect an era and a mindset. This was a phase when the old, leisurely way of doing things was giving way to corporatization of cinema, when promotions did not yet determine content and entertainment was not limited to a marketing exercise. Actors were yet to become brands, the pace of life and work was no longer laid-back yet not quite rushed as it is now, cinema was not yet all about designer looks and Rs 100 crore clubs! This was an era of flux, and many of these conversations probably mirror the uncertainties that mark any period of change from one way of life to another.

Bhawana Somaaya

Section 1

An Actor Prepares

I had a teacher who said to me, 'If an actor has forgotten what it is like to play as a child they should not be an actor.' What the child sees is transformed by imagination. The pattern in a carpet can become a world; a staircase, a mountain; and everywhere there are secrets.

Simon McBurney, theatre legend

Kamal Haasan

Acting is about trusting your instinct

Do you feel relieved now that *Hey Ram* has been released?

After being with the film for almost a year it's not easy parting with it, and yet parting is essential. It's when the artiste has exhausted all possibilities and given his best, that the art is ready for exhibition. As a film-maker I did all I could within my capability and was on edge till the prints reached the cinema halls. Now it is no longer in my control – so whether good, bad or indifferent, I'm relieved that it is over.

It's difficult to believe that you can be even slightly indifferent to your art.

That's true , I'm too much in love with the craft to be indifferent. In fact, my problem is that I cannot be satisfied with anything but the best. By temperament I cannot tolerate mediocrity.

The interview was conducted in 2000 before the release of *Hey Ram. Vishwaroopam* (2013) was Kamal Haasan's last release.

And how would you define mediocrity?

Any form of art delivered without passion or energy is always mediocre. Anything that is not from the heart and lacks conviction is usually a compromise. Anybody who is complacent is bound to be mediocre.

How does an artist protect himself from becoming complacent?

If I'm conscious I will be able to fight complacency. If I am selective about my assignments I will be able to resist the temptation of money, and thus will not compromise. It is eventually about trusting your instinct and not feeling insecure even if a good role slips through your hands.

Instinct can sometimes let you down. Look what happened to your Tamil film *Marudhanayagam*.

Marudhanayagam is not a mistake and I'm very sure about that. The film has been shelved temporarily, but that doesn't mean it will not be made. It may take a few months or a few years and God forbid, even if the film is not made, I will never regret the decision. I'm extremely proud of whatever I have shot and time will prove this. The best part of following instinct is that I'm responsible for my actions.

Does that include the accolades and the brickbats you may receive for *Hey Ram*?

Of course, I'm the director but the fate of the film does not reflect my ability as a film-maker. The box-office may dismiss the film, but it cannot crush me as an artiste. I'm very certain that history is going to remember this film. I have worked extremely hard for a very long time and the effort shows in every frame of the film. It's still too early for me to view the film objectively but I will do so in future. Feedback from the audience is precious and reviews matter as long as it is constructive criticism. I take my critics seriously, so they better do a good job!

What about the feedback from within the family?

Their opinion is, of course, paramount for I know they will not lie. I can count on them to tell me the truth and at the same time save me from hurt.

A lot of your family members feature in the film.

Yes, my older brother Chandra Haasan makes a debut as my ageing son and Gautam, my nephew, plays my grandson. My older daughter Shruti features in a passing shot when walking with Sardar Patel in the Gandhi Ashram and also sings a duet with me. Akshara, the younger one, has dubbed for one scene and Sarika has done the costumes, so it is a family production.

When you launched your film banner did you anticipate you would one day turn director?

I knew I would become a director the day I joined films. I have been obsessed with films since childhood and when I finally got into them, I was certain that I was never going to get out. I started as a choreographer and since then it has been a long journey of dreams and making them come true.

Dreams of making films like *Appu Raja* and *Chachi 420*?

Yes, among many others. Somehow an actor feels closest to his last character. So at the moment, I'm consumed by Saket Ram and *Hey Ram* is the ultimate film for me.

Your detractors are describing *Hey Ram* as an anti-Gandhi film – do you agree?

I am tired of explaining that *Hey Ram* is not anti-Gandhi. The message is so simple that I'm surprised people are misinterpreting it. The tragedy is that the younger generation does not know history and their confusion stems from ignorance. It's very sad and something to think about.

They are saying that the film is grossly over budget too.

A film like this cannot be made on a shoestring budget. The canvas and the scale encompass three generations and six decades. The expenses are huge because there is no compromise on quality. There are compensations though when Gandhi's grandson Tushar Gandhi agreed to appear in a cameo. It's his first brush with acting, but he's so convincing. Every time I see the scene where he says, 'I'm just the grandson of a great grandfather,' I choke up.

A female fan features in the film as well.

An old woman had been hanging around the sets to meet me. When she finally met me, she touched my hand and said a dream had come true for her that day! There was something arresting about her face. I felt she would look terrific on-screen so the next day, when I spotted her on my sets again, I asked her if she would like to do a role in the film and she agreed – simple.

What next after *Hey Ram*?

Let's see, the mind is ticking and so are the computer keys. Some of them are locked in my laptop and travel with me wherever I go. I'm noting ideas – giving shape to stories but I'm not sure which of them I will finally pick.

After writing/producing/directing your own films is it difficult to submit to someone else's vision?

It is and more as one gets older, but it's not impossible if what is offered is extraordinary and gets your adrenaline flowing. Then it is very easy to surrender. The best thing about being an artiste is that as long as you are excited, you can submit to almost anything.

Waheeda Rehman

Acting is getting your lines right

You are returning to acting after almost eleven years. What made you say yes to *Om Jai Jagadish*?

Yash Johar came home with his son Karan and insisted that I do *Kabhi Khushi Kabhie Gham.* My heart wasn't in it because both my mother-in-law and husband were unwell at that time. I opted out when my husband became critical. He passed away after a few days. A month after his demise, Anupam Kher came over with producer Vashu Bhagnani and signed me for *OJJ*.

It is strange that you should come back with a new director. What made you say 'yes' to Anupam?

I have worked with several new directors, be it Bappi Soni, Pramod Chakravarty, Dev Anand, Niranjan or Akhtar. Experience has nothing to do with success – the best banners can produce flops

The interview was conducted in 2000 before the release of *Om Jai Jagadish* (2002). *Dilli 6* (2009) was Waheeda Rehman's last release.

and an unknown film-maker can deliver a superhit. Showbiz is a gamble, and true artistes learn to surrender to fate because no matter how talented or clever we may think we are, destiny rules everything. If Dev Anand had not taken a risk with me in *CID* there would have been no Waheeda Rehman today.

What were your feelings on the first day of the shoot?

It was a difficult time for me because I was recovering from a tragedy. The thought of facing the camera after such a long break was weighing me down when, three days before the shoot, Anupam called to say that he had invited the entire unit – all the artistes and technicians – for tea on the sets. He wanted his actors to get familiar with each other and their surroundings, which is the best thing a director can do to help his actors shed their inhibitions. So for three days all of us met for tea and discussions where Anupam spoke extensively about the characters and we listened. I was relieved to discover that everybody was as anxious about starting a new film as I was.

Did Anupam Kher share his anxiety too?

No, a director must never do that. He is the leader and has to be in charge all the time, particularly when it is his first film. It is interesting how all new directors on some level feel insecure about senior actors because they fear they will try to control them. When they realize it is not true, they lower their defences. I have experienced this so many times with so many directors in my long career that I have now begun to feel protective towards them.

What are the advantages of working with a first-time director?

The passion that a debutant exudes can never be replaced by a seasoned director. During the shooting of *Lamhe*, Anupam would often joke that if he ever became a director, he would cast me in his film. When he finally did, his passion had not diminished. Actors-turned-directors are all the more special because they have been on the other side and are always adding to your performance.

Irrespective of what happens to the film I can guarantee you that all the performances will be praiseworthy. And for this the credit goes to the director. He has paid individual attention to all the characters, taken care to portray dialogues as conversation, not as lines spoken by actors, so that the audience is involved in the thought process.

What is the most difficult thing about performing for you as an actor?

Crying is the easiest, while laughing with perfect timing is the most difficult. Screaming is difficult because it means straining your vocal chords and, later, matching the intensity during dubbing. I'm paranoid about getting my lines right, for you can always tell when an actor is taking an emotional pause and when she is struggling to recall her lines. I would hate to be caught on the wrong foot even in the smallest scene.

Is it because writers are very demanding?

Some writers are obstinate about actors not missing out a single word of the dialogue and this puts too much pressure on the performer. While emoting you cannot make concessions for egos. The success of a scene is a joyous moment for everyone involved, and nobody should feel offended because of a slight change as long as the meaning and the message is not misinterpreted.

Would you say actors today are less spontaneous as compared to those from the olden days?

Actors change with technology and changing is a positive sign. In the olden days, we worked at a slower pace. It was unthinkable to start a new scene on the same day. It was always a fresh scene with a fresh mind the next day. Today, several disconnected scenes are shot on the same day – sometimes actors shoot for different films on the same day and it works. Not just that, film-makers do post-production simultaneously. The pace is faster today but it hasn't taken away the magic of films. Actors do terrific work even today, yet something is missing. It's as if everything is touching you but only superficially. The needle that must travel to your heart and sew up your wound all the way up is not there. The pain is missing!

That is unusually articulate – you don't sound like an actor who has been out of touch with her craft.

I have been in exile but I have not stopped feeling. Observation works overtime when I'm watching films. All of us know that eventually acting is about relating to human emotions. The slightest overconfidence or insecurity in a performer is visible on the screen. The camera is too sharp and misses nothing.

What about the actor's frame of mind?

It is very important. An artiste always performs better when he feels reassured. Anupam and Vashu Bhagnani made the shooting a special experience for me. And this was important, because I was in a difficult phase of life at that time.

Looking back, do you think you crossed over to mother roles too early in your career?

I knew I had to make the transition some day. I could have postponed the decision by a few years, but not beyond that. A time came when suddenly all the big banners were only offering me mother roles and I knew I had to make a cross over. Sometimes though, I feel I gave in too easily or maybe times were different back then. Now heroines who are much older are refusing to wear white wigs and I applaud their courage. Our generation didn't have the confidence to say 'no' so convincingly.

Was that the only reason?

I'm sure destiny plays its part. When accepting or rejecting a film, an actor never knows whether he is striking gold or if he is making a mistake. Sometimes, a good role comes your way and you don't recognize it. I refused Nutan's role in AVM's *Milan* because I wanted to play Yamuna's role and the director didn't want that. Sometimes, you are not allowed to take on challenging roles because of pressure from your producers. My film-makers felt that doing a supporting role would be detrimental to my career. That is also the reason why Yash Chopra deliberately didn't cast me in Nirupa Roy's role in *Deewar* because he felt it would hamper my image as Amitabh's wife in *Kabhi Kabhie*, which was made around the same time. Interestingly, there are no such restrictions on the hero.

Was gender discrimination an issue with your generation of heroines?

Even if it was, nobody ever expressed it. It was a given that heroes got more money and their names appeared before the names of the heroines in the credit rolls. I don't know what it is about showbiz but here a man worships a man. The film-maker and the hero are full of praise for the heroine, but are reluctant to give her equal status – just as in our society. If at a public gathering the heroine got more attention than the hero he sulked like a child. The irony of life was that off screen, careers of all heroines, including mine, were governed by women – mother, aunt, sister. As a result the producer/director had to perpetually seek her out so that his film progresses.

How friendly were you with your colleagues and film-makers?

I was familiar, but not friendly. I did not entertain any calls from anybody after 9.30 p.m. and was fortunate not to encounter any ugly incidents throughout my career. When any of my colleagues won awards, I sent them congratulatory telegrams but seldom received the same appreciation when I won accolades. With the exception of Nanda, I wasn't friends with any other heroine. Probably because we were all very busy and heroines back then didn't mingle as freely as they do today. At the same time, we didn't look upon each other as rivals because all of us had a distinctive image and were identified with specific roles.

You were mostly cast in roles of the traditional simple girl.

Yes, film-makers said I had a trusting face that inspired confidence. Strangely nobody seemed to remember that I played a vamp in my very first film *CID*. Later, I played a nautanki dancer in *Teesri Kasam* and, much before that, a prostitute in *Pyaasa.*

You played a prostitute in *Pyaasa* – how much did you understand your characters?

I was seventeen when I did *Pyaasa.* So when Guru Dutt told me that I was to play Gulabo, a streetwalker, in my mind I thought of Gulabo as a street sweeper. The day we were to shoot '*Jaane kya tune kahi…*' Guru Dutt said I had to lure clients and take them home. I asked him innocently why I had to take the clients home. He was too embarrassed to elaborate and asked my mother to explain while he checked on the lighting. My mother took the easy way out and advised me to follow what the director instructed. Exasperated, Guru Dutt just asked me to look into the camera – smile, look down, smile and look away – and that's exactly how I have done it.

In *Kaagaz Ke Phool* the actress is involved in an illegitimate relationship.

When I did *Kaagaz Ke Phool* I was nineteen and during the shooting of the film I lost my mother. I was in a very fragile condition at that time so Guru Dutt saab did not bother explaining the character to me. On the day of shooting the scene, he provided me with appropriate cues and I reacted accordingly. During the confrontation scene with Baby Naaz, he said, 'Think of yourself as all alone in this world where you have no one to call your own or depend upon…' That was enough for me to break down!

What gave you the strength to do path-breaking roles like the ones in *Mujhe Jeene Do* and *Guide*?

I strongly believe that every disadvantage has an advantage. Not having a secretary and not socializing with others in the film industry worked to my advantage. I got no criticism from anybody and, free from their prejudices, I followed my heart and made my own decisions. Do you know that I was the first mainstream actress to do an NFDC film in Malayalam and Hindi? The film was *Trisandhya* but nobody knows this. I accepted *Guide* and *Mujhe Jeene Do* because I found the characters to be out of the ordinary. I have never laid emphasis on the length of a role because what matters to me is the content. The audience must come out of the theatre thinking about the character.

Have you found yourself thinking about any of your characters after the film is over?

I don't think I identified with a single character completely. There may be shades of them in my personality but never a complete image. The fact is, after all these years I'm still discovering myself. I am certainly not the traditional girl I portrayed in my films. At over sixty years of age I would say I'm progressive and fun loving but also reticent. None of the characters haunt me, but I often think about the single mother in *Phagun* who unintentionally intrudes into her daughter's married life. I have learnt restraint from her. I tell my children that when they get married, I don't want to live with either of them. In our caring, we occasionally destroy their dreams and *Om Jai Jagadish* is about this aspect of a relationship. It's something all of us have to learn and accept. No matter how deeply attached I am to my daughter, I wouldn't give up my independence for anyone.

Om Jai Jagadish focuses on the crumbling family. What are your views on the joint family system?

Considering that most women are working today, we need the support of our elders to run an efficient home and take care of the third generation. Their presence instills the right values in our children and, in time, they will need our concern and care. When you live separately you lose the ability to adjust. Crisis is always surmountable when you are together as a family. Unlike the West, we are not prepared to put our parents in old-age homes. Therefore a joint family is the only solution.

As a senior star you are all the time put on a pedestal. Do you like it?

No, I don't want to be put on a pedestal and worshipped. I want to be treated naturally and be allowed to make mistakes. I don't want to be a saint and go to heaven. I'll die of boredom with so many virtuous people around me.

Anil Kapoor

Acting is disconnecting with the character when the film ends

How does an actor know that he is making the right choices?

Nobody knows that he is making the right choices until they are made. All of us realize our decisions only in hindsight. I have made my decisions following my instinct and I'm fortunate that most of the time they have worked in my favour.

Your recent films address social issues, are you making a conscious effort for change?

Most of the time actors choose roles depending on the phase they are going through. When I was younger, I was drawn to more self-centered characters and liked playing roles that emphasized power and ambition as in *Tezaab* and *Ram Lakhan.* They were the right

The interview was conducted after the release of *Nayak* (2001). *Race 2 and Shootout at Wadala* (2013) were Anil Kapoor's last releases.

roles for me at that time and lend me an image that the audience identified with.

Are you suggesting that you have now outgrown the angry Munna image?

The anger and violence I portrayed so many years ago was real. That anger does not exist in me any longer. If I have to play an angry man now, the role will have to be written differently and portrayed differently like in *Trimurti,* which I rate among my mature performances. It was necessary for Munna to mellow down because, over the years, the audience has changed as well.

What is your self-image as an actor?

(*Thinks*) Someone who is credible, someone who is consistent, and someone who will not compromise on quality. I have never believed in short cuts, either in my career or in my relationships.

How would you describe yourself as a person?

As somebody who will stretch himself to the maximum for a given task because I don't want to regret that I didn't put in my best effort. I have met many distinguished personalities in my life who have been masters in their fields but proved to be irresponsible life partners and parents. I have taken extra care not to repeat the same mistakes in my life.

Over the years how much has the actor influenced the person and vice versa?

Eventually the human being gains more from the actor; that has at least been true for me. In my case, the actor has disciplined the person, taught him generosity. I shudder to think what kind of a person I would have been had I not been an actor. It would have been a boring life without the arc lights.

What are the significant lessons you have learnt from some of your characters?

This one is difficult to answer, but let me try. From Prem Kumar Patiala in *Woh Saat Din* I learnt that life is a smile and innocence, a rare virtue. The hero smiles through all his struggles and emerges a winner. *Eeshwar* in a way is an extension of *Woh Saat Din,* he is a misfit in society but depicts a rare courage that most of us lack.

The hero of *Hamara Dil Aapke Paas Hai* is larger than life and the film melodramatic. How do you come to terms with such exaggerations?

The exaggerations are justified when your co-star is as beautiful as Aishwarya Rai. Jokes apart, one can never predict how an individual will react under any situation until one is in that space. Melodrama is a part of our culture and films, and my job as an actor is to strike the right chord under all circumstances. It is not important for the actor to always identify with his character and sometimes it happens without making an effort. In *Viraasat,* the hero chooses responsibility over love. I would do the same and, with time, transform my responsibility into love.

Have you realized that most of your romantic films are marital love stories?

If you don't want to run around trees, marital romance is the only option. I'm privileged that all these stories – *Judaai, Viraasat, Hum Aapke Dil Mein Rehte Hain, Biwi No. 1* and *Hamara Dil Aapke Paas Hai* – lent a different flavour and message. In show business, when something clicks, the performer is offered the same kind of roles. I have resisted stereotyping by consciously playing drastically different roles like the one in *Lamhe* in the olden days and the one in *Nayak* more recently.

Has any particular character haunted you long after the film was over?

Yes, the commander in *Pukaar* was a troubled soul and portraying him was very painful. I was anguished during the shoot and thought about him even after the shoot had concluded. Actors are sensitive souls and contrary to what they project, it is not that easy to detach oneself from the character when the film ends. *Pukaar* is based on a real-life story and there are innumerable unresolved cases of such innocent victims. This is common in times of war and other crises. As a Third World country, we are easy targets of corruption and repression.

Which other character you played has made a place in your heart?

The musician in *Taal* was interesting. He is the other side of me, the side I have taken care to suppress over the years. Initially, it was very difficult for me to let the arrogance surface. I was uncomfortable unleashing him and holding back, but director Subhash Ghai had worked very hard on the character and that helped immensely. My performance in the film is a reflection of my trust in my director.

The hero of *Taal* is a bad loser, how do you react to failure?

Eventually every one of us has to lose in life – whether it is youth, stardom or our near and dear ones. That's life. I feel privileged that so far I haven't lost anything precious, or at least what I consider important to me in life, which is family and work. It's been a fulfilling journey and I have no complaints.

You sound philosophical.

My wife is attending Bhagwad Gita classes these days and I'm the passive recipient of all the knowledge imparted to her at the lectures. The spiritual teaching instills a positive energy and has a calming effect on me.

When you are feeling low, where do you derive your strength from?

I believe that distraction is the best therapy, so the minute I sense I'm feeling depressed I head to my gym. Sometimes I read though, let me tell you, it's difficult to concentrate when you are disturbed. These days I'm hooked on to Anthony Robins, a mesmerizing speaker and a master on all subjects. He was the one who inspired Bill Clinton to confess about Monica Lewinsky.

What is more important – mental or physical health?

Both go hand in hand. An actor cannot perform under duress and he looks horrible if he is not fit. I sweat it out at the gym or I feel so guilty I cannot sleep. If something is bothering me I talk to my wife and she always has a solution.

You have often said that an actor needs inspiration all the time.

A self-preserving artiste must reinvent himself all the time. That is the only way to grow and learn.

Madhuri Dixit

Acting is the character's taking over of the individual

How would you analyse your last few releases?

Lajja was a satisfactory experience not just for me, but, I think, for all of us involved in the film, and that is apparent in the final product. I look back on my role and the message of the film with a lot of pride.

What about your forthcoming films?

Well, _Hum Tumhare Hain Sanam_ has been in the making for a long time, but there is a refreshing angle to the story. Unlike what everyone assumes, it is not the regular love story and offers new insights into marriage. Shah Rukh plays a suspicious husband who cannot express himself while I play the archetypal wife who is oblivious to her husband's need for romance. Salman is my

The interview was conducted in 2002 before the release of *Devdas*. *Aaja Nachle* (2007) was Madhuri Dixit's last release and *Gulab Gang* is expected soon.

childhood friend who wants to share everything that goes on in his life and in the bargain oversteps, creating chaos in my marital life.

If a similar situation were to occur in real life would you be able to deal with it?

I'd hate to believe that something like that could happen in my life. I'm optimistic by nature and believe if there is basic trust and confidence in a relationship, there is no room for problems. This is a hypothetical question and human beings never know what they can deal with unless they are faced with a crisis. I believe it's the same with challenges.

Shah Rukh and you share a special chemistry on screen. How would you describe your relationship with him?

We are comfortable as co-stars and there is a mutual affection for each other, which probably filters into our scenes. He is naughty and I'm wary of his pranks, but there is a healthy give and take of ideas as well. Acting isn't about competition but about making every scene work and this isn't possible without camaraderie between actors. The audience must be able to identify with what's happening to the characters on the screen.

Do film-makers have a convincing theory as to why they offer you a particular role?

Well, the conscientious directors do because they love their scripts more than anyone else and cannot bear to see anything going wrong with their project. In certain films, the roles are such that it doesn't matter who plays which role. In this case, when the director offers you a choice, he isn't being insincere.

What was Sanjay Leela Bhansali's explanation in offering you Chandramukhi and not Paro in *Devdas*?

Sanjay was upfront. He said there are two heroine roles but he would like me to play Chandramukhi because that was how he had imagined me in the script. He felt my training in classical dance and abhinaya would be more appropriate for the character. I agreed with him and trusted his judgement.

If you had the choice would you have preferred to play Paro?

I don't think so because I have played shades of Paro in my earlier films except that they were not period films. On the other hand, I had never played a courtesan and Chandramukhi's role had all the potential of projecting the nava rasas. In her devotion for the man, the courtesan transforms into a devotee, which I find very appealing.

Whose sacrifice between Paro and Chandramukhi according to you is greater?

That's a very tough question to answer but let me try... Paro was ahead of her time, but in today's context she seems perfectly reasonable. Chandramukhi was the more selfless of the two. It isn't easy to love as selflessly as she did. She made too many sacrifices and assumed responsibility for somebody who never loved her in return. Just the thought is so daunting and painful. A love story like that is not practical today.

How did you research for a role that is so far-fetched?

It was not difficult because the director was very clear of his projection. Bhansali views Chandramukhi as an extension of Meera whose love for Krishna remained unrequited till the very end. That was the emotional process. For the physical one, I had the elaborate costumes, the magnificent sets and the extraordinary choreography. Playing the role was like playing out a fantasy. When I walked into the sets, I actually felt the part.

Do you follow a specific process in creating your characters?

I don't think so, at least not consciously. I don't believe that such a formula exists. Most of the time actors merely follow their instinct.

Sometimes the director provides layers of subtext as in the case of *Devdas,* where Bhansali was always available to facilitate my performance in every way. The trick, if at all there is one, is to let the real person withdraw and let the role take over. The process happens so quietly that the only person apart from the performer who notices it is the director. That is because he has seen the film in his head before actually making it.

It's the first time you have attempted playback singing?

It was just a few lines and you can hardly call it singing. In dance terminology they call it kavita or chhand but I enjoyed it and it was an experience I will always cherish.

Now that you are training as a singer would you say singing is easier than acting?

I think nothing is easy. Besides, I'm hardly in a position to draw comparisons between the two. I was fortunate to grow up in a home resonating with the ragas every morning. Maybe that is the reason I'm so appreciative of music, of the purity of Lata Mangeshkar's voice, of Asha Bhosle's vivacity and Alka Yagnik's prolificacy.

Some years ago, you seemed completely detached from your contemporaries.

That's not true. Progress of art in any form is appealing to me. I didn't articulate my appreciation because I'm not demonstrative. Also, when you are in the limelight, everything you say and do runs the risk of being exaggerated or misinterpreted. That's the price of stardom and the only way to survive is to remain discreet. Now I understand why most successful stars are described as reserved. It's more out of self preservation than temperament.

How much has marriage changed you as an actor and as an individual?

I don't think the actor can change, just as a doctor or an engineer does not change as a professional, just because they are married. As an individual everybody changes. Those close to me say I have become more talkative now. I feel I have become more demonstrative. I was expressive as a child but changed after coming into films, or maybe I was so busy working that there was never any time for communication. I don't know but I rather like my new self and so does my family.

How has your family adjusted to your flying visits to India?

They miss me when I'm not around and I miss them tremendously because we are so used to being with each other. We talk a number of times a day and I am always thinking of what they would be doing at a certain time of the day, just as they think of me all the time. My parents are now a retired couple, happy that all their children are well settled. I'm fortunate to have such special parents and can never thank them enough for making so many sacrifices for me. My career demanded keeping crazy schedules but they never complained. I value that tremendously and can never repay their affection.

What about your adjustment in your new home? Have you made friends with the city?

Yes, initially I was scared but if you have the desire and are ready to push yourself to your optimum level, you can do it. I was frightened to drive, to cook but I have made friends with the electrical appliances, the innumerable knobs and the alien roads. In fact, now I shop at the local supermarket, carry lunch to my husband at the hospital, browse in the shops, you can say I rock! What finally matters is happiness in one's personal life and I have found that in my partner and my dwelling place.

Shabana Azmi

Acting is not like a sprinter's race

What, in your view, makes a truly great actor?

Versatility, I imagine. Like someone once said, 'Acting is not like a sprinter's race where one who runs the fastest in the shortest period of time emerges the winner.' A most definitive Hamlet can turn out to be a disastrous Macbeth. An actor who can do a wide variety of roles with equal felicity would qualify as a great actor in my book.

In recent times, which performance have you truly admired?

Russell Crowe in *A Beautiful Mind* is outstanding. He perfectly blended technique and pure ability in delivering the role. He inhabits John Nash's world, calibrates the stages of schizophrenia and ages unnoticeably in the film. His performance has taken the

The interview was conducted post *Makdee* (2002) for the Locarno Film Festival. *Matru Ki Bijlee Ka Mandola* and *The Reluctant Fundamentalist* (2013) were Shabana Azmi's last releases.

benchmark for acting a notch higher than where it is possible for actors to go.

You are rated among the best actors in our country. How do you evaluate yourself as an artiste?

I am nowhere near achieving the ability exhibited by the really great performers. I have just enough in my repertoire to qualify as an actor. Like a writer must at least know the alphabet to qualify as one, I am capable of being sometimes good, sometimes bad and sometimes average. I need to be pushed hard to rise to the level of the potential I believe I have. I approach every part with anxiety and a hopeless sense of inadequacy. To really shine, I need an excellent script, a talented director and terrific co-stars. Film is such a collaborative medium that one department cannot excel without active contributions from the other departments.

What about theatre? You've done a number of plays in India and abroad.

When on stage you are on your own. Theatre is much more an actor's medium than the director's. When I did The *Waiting Room* at the National Theatre in London or *Nora* at the Singapore Repertory Theatre, I realized that deep down, I am more a film than a theatre actor. Many years ago, when I agreed to do *Sufaid Kundali,* and later *Tumhari Amrita,* I knew it would be demanding for me as a performer, but I agreed because I think it's healthy for actors to work in both the mediums. It keeps them on their toes. Believing in one's own greatness is the biggest stumbling block towards an actor's growth. Mercifully, my family will never allow me to fall into that trap. I come from a family of artistes who are either hugely critical or hugely appreciative, so my sanity remains intact!

Your training as a professional actor at the Film and Television Institute of India followed the Stanislavski school of method acting. Does that enable you to play any part with complete honesty?

Yes, but after playing complex roles where characters are forever struggling against injustice and oppression, a time came when I could no longer treat acting as a nine-to-five job. The residue of the characters' lives that I had inhabited started leaving their mark on me and, unconsciously, I began to get involved with their concerns.

Is that normal?

Every artiste's resources must be drawn from life itself if they are to reflect the truth. If the purpose of art is to create a climate of sensitivity then it's normal to get drawn into the process that protests against these injustices.

You've often said *Paar* is the film that stirred the social activist in you. Can you elaborate?

I function as an actor by trying to find a person who is close to the character I am playing as this helps me to understand her mindset. During the shooting of *Paar* I struck a rapport with a slum dweller and modelled my character Rama on her. A couple of days later, she invited me to her house – a 150 square foot hut with no water or electricity where she lived with eight members of her family. I was amazed that a woman who lived in such subhuman conditions had never once complained. She had the generosity to assist me in whatever I asked of her without expecting anything in return. I felt if I returned to my world without doing anything for her, it would be a betrayal of the trust she had placed in me. This was the turning point for me and I joined Nivara Hakk, an organization which fights for the rights of slum dwellers in Mumbai.

That is not unusual considering your background – your father, Kaifi Azmi was a member of the Communist Party of India and wrote inspiring poetry all his life.

I suppose so. Till I was nine-years old, we lived in a commune. All the comrades (there were literary giants like Ali Sardar Jafri, my father and others) were allotted one room per family. The tiny balcony was converted into a kitchen and the bathroom and toilets were outside, and common for all eight families living there. The drawing room, called the Red Flag Hall, was reserved for party meetings. There was a lot of naare baazi, talks about revolution and inspiring speeches on the rights of labourers. Then I think, at some point as a teenager, I drifted away from all this. I immersed myself in acting and took pride in the fact that I didn't even read the newspapers. It is to my father's credit that he never pushed me and never revealed his disappointment. Perhaps, it was because he was confident that the soil was so fertile that the plant was bound to take root. And that is exactly what happened.

Arth followed close on the heels of *Paar*. How was it working with Mahesh Bhatt?

Mahesh is a fabulous director for an actor. The story of *Arth*, although inspired by the comedy-drama film *An Unmarried Woman*, was largely based on Mahesh's own life and the film was his tribute to his wife Kiran. Mahesh was at a heightened state of sensitivity and had the ability to infuse his passion into all the characters of *Arth* – particularly me. It was as though he would push a button and I would produce a reaction. In the film, there was one particularly traumatic scene when I had to beg my husband (Kulbhushan Kharbanda) to give me one more chance to revive our marriage. I was uncomfortable enacting the scene because it is much easier to do parts that require you to be noble. While actors feel good projecting virtues that they may not demonstrate in real life – begging is a humiliating experience and I had to get in touch with my suppressed emotions and make them come alive on screen! I had to beg and, at the same time, retain my dignity. It was an excruciating experience and I was inconsolable for a long time after the shot was over.

Arth turned you into a crusader of women's rights, were you prepared for it?

Not when we were shooting the film because at that point I was only concerned with my part. When the film was released I was unprepared for the overwhelming response I received. Suddenly, I had women walking into my house who did not regard me as fans do a star, but viewed me as a sister. They expected me to resolve their marital conflicts. Though I was humbled by their faith in me I was also apprehensive. Slowly I rose to the occasion and became more aware of causes related to women. I started getting invited to seminars where initially I had very little to say. That was when I began reading feminist literature, interacted with women's organizations and realized that actors have a social responsibility because people trust and idolize them.

Would you attribute this change to your screen roles or to your background?

Not just my father but his entire generation of artistes believed that art should be used as an instrument for social change. But it took me a while to become aware of this myself. However, my roots never left me and when I started working in films I was drawn to subjects fighting against social injustice. Unknowingly, I began asking questions. I guess the purpose of art is in making you look beyond yourself.

Is that not the case in mainstream cinema?

Mainstream cinema doesn't allow your sensitivity to be nurtured. It does not allow you to look for resources from life. The only form of acting that exists here is inspired from other films and actors. The responses are imitations from Hollywood or other Hindi films. Here stars are forced to inhabit an alternate world which helps them hone skills that qualify as a 'star' – a toned body, dancing prowess, physical abilities, an accent and, most important, appearance. It is very important for the actor to look good. Hindi cinema is larger than life and you are rarely required to pull your reference points from life itself.

Hunger-strikes, padyatra, fighting for riot victims... How does your family cope with the pressures you go through for your convictions?

Before I went on the hunger strike I had sought my husband Javed Akhtar's advice. He had warned me that I would face a lot of flak because my action would be projected as a publicity stunt. It meant not attending the screening of my film, *Genesis*, which was an entry in the competition section at the Cannes Film Festival. Those days my mother was unwell and my brother was angry with me for imposing this additional strain on her. On the day I was leaving, my mother looked devastated, but she didn't once say, 'Don't go'. Instead, she came along to the slum and even shouted slogans. My father, who was in Patna then was informed of my decision and he sent me a telegram saying, 'All the best, comrade!' My family and friends were extremely supportive. But their anxieties grew as days passed by because they were worried about my health and safety. Looking back, I agree it was quite traumatic.

What about the peace padyatra? That must have been a difficult experience?

When I first mentioned my decision to go on the padyatra, my well-wishers said it was dangerous for an actress to be found roaming the streets of Uttar Pradesh, claiming that the political parties were exploiting me. I was very emotional the evening I was to leave. My brother, who is not at all demonstrative, hovered around me. He had prepared a first-aid kit for me to carry along. My family was so encouraging that I had tears in my eyes as I left for the airport. My father knew that deep down I was scared and he said, 'You are a brave girl, nothing will happen to you.' His eyes were fearless and that gave me a lot of strength! It was an uncomfortable experience since we did not have adequate beds, bathrooms or changing facilities, but when you are committed to a cause, you can endure anything.

You are the only Indian actor to work with so many international directors. How exactly did the opportunities come your way?

One day, out of the blue, I got a call from producer Robin Dalton who told me that Ruth Jhabwala had suggested my name for a part opposite Shirley MacLaine in John Schlesinger's *Madame Sousatzka*. When she described the part to me over the phone, I suggested she look at a video home system of Shyam Benegal's *Mandi*. Five hours later, there was another call saying that John wanted to meet me. I flew to London and fell in love with John in one-second flat, a feeling I think was somewhat mutual! I had no free dates in my diary and convinced John to let me return to India thrice to complete my assignments. It is hard to imagine that he would agree, but he did, though he could not understand how any sane person could work in more than one film at a time. It was the writer's and the director's decision to portray the mother-and-son duo as Indian rather than Jewish, as it was in the original. John believed that Asians were now so much a part of the British social fabric that they needed to be visible in cinema as well. If only more film-makers were sensitized to this reality!

What were the adjustments you had to make as an actor working on foreign soil?

I think and speak in English with greater ease than I do in Hindi. I think it comes from my schooling. However, in the UK studio, where I was surrounded by so many authentic English accents, my English stood out pitiably. In fact, John would often tease me about my sing-song accent. At the same time, he didn't want me to alter my diction. The other adjustment was more emotional and temperamental. When I did *Sousatzka* I was well established in Hindi cinema and in danger of becoming complacent. I deliberately took on the project despite my fears because I believe that it is important for actors to risk failure and thereby push the parameters of their tried-and-tested abilities. In India, we have a bad habit of blaming the audience for our failures whereas it would be much simpler to accept that the film just didn't work!

And what was the experience of working in such close proximity with Shirley MacLaine?

Oh, Shirley MacLaine was a generous co-star. I remember rehearsing one scene with her from 9 a.m. to 7 p.m. with just an hour's lunch break. At 8 in the evening, the doorbell of the flat rang once again (I was staying at John's home those first few days) and there was Shirley, clinging to her script, asking ever so sincerely 'Shabana, I've thought of a new interpretation, can we try one more rehearsal?' I was exhausted and ready to fall asleep. Finally, John persuaded her to take a break and have a drink.

Those who work with you say you are equally obsessed with homework and rehearsals.

Yes, in fact, what I miss most in Indian cinema is never having enough time for rehearsals. We don't have the concept of preparation. I have all through my career arrived on a set that doesn't remotely reflect my character. Next, I'm introduced to two awkward boys who are to play my children in the film. It would be so much simpler if the cast could come together for an induction or a workshop. Shyam Benegal does this, Vijaya Mehta does it, and to some extent I pushed Sai Paranjpye to do it for *Saaz*. The actor and the director have to earn the trust of the children. It cannot happen by just handing over the dialogue sheet before a shot. Children absorb the anxieties of the adults and are terrified of making a mistake. You need a Chetan Anand *(Akhri Khat)*, a Shekhar Kapur *(Masoom)* and Mira Nair *(Salaam Bombay)* to understand the psyche of kids. During the shooting of *City of Joy* it worried me that the slum children swimming in the pool of the Grand Hotel in Calcutta with Patrick Swayze would have to face their own reality once the film was over! But these kids displayed amazing resilience. Their acting tutor constantly reminded them that this was real only till the shoot lasted, and they seemed to take it in their stride.

As a slum dweller in *City of Joy* you speak fluent English, doesn't that create a problem for an actor?

Of course, the spoken word is probably the most difficult thing that an actor is made to portray – to give the appearance of the first time – as if the line is not a result of painstaking rehearsal but rather the result of an impromptu thought process in the character's head. Not enough attention is paid to this in Hindi cinema. There are so many constraints on the actor's time that if you can deliver your lines without making a mistake, it is accepted as satisfactory! In that sense *City of Joy* was bizarre and I needed to convince myself that the film was working as a translation or else we could never have had a *Hamlet*, a *Julius Caesar* or any other classic. It is unfortunate but we still have to accomplish a film that has been able to resolve its language complexities with clarity.

What made you agree to an insignificant role in *Son of Pink Panther*?

My agent told me that Blake Edwards would like to meet me in connection with a part and I went to meet him without giving it much thought. Blake's office was on the eighteenth or nineteenth floor of a plush hotel in New York. When I entered the office, Blake was sitting on his chair, his eyes covered with shades, which he refused to take off. I found this very offensive. There was something about the manner in which they were conducting the interview that was off-putting. I suddenly didn't care whether I got the role or not and therefore there was a natural arrogance in my response at the interview. By the time I got back to India, there were eight calls from their office within six hours. From the casting agent, who was going completely mad, to my personal agent, everyone was pestering me to say 'yes'. I wasn't convinced so I called an English friend and sought his opinion. Next, I spoke to Shyam Benegal. Whenever I'm confused, I speak to Shyam. Everyone said, 'Do it. It's a cameo but you are also getting big money.' So I said 'yes'.

What is your frame of mind when you begin shooting a new film?

I get withdrawal symptoms, more so now since I have reduced the number of assignments I do. I start getting cramps in my stomach since there is always the danger of not being able to balance my assignments. Earlier, when I did substandard work I was always confident that I would have other better performances at the same time. Now, because I'm doing fewer films, I worry more. I create all kinds of fantasies in my head about how I will convince the director to drop me and take on somebody else. Then ultimately, out of sheer fright and not having the guts to tell the director, I surrender.

And what propels such exaggerated anxiety?

The anxiety comes out of creating a character. The biggest and the best actors have denied thinking about their roles. Ask any actor and he says he doesn't do any homework. I do. I think about what the character will wear, how she will speak and walk. Maybe, the other actors are capable of competent performances from whatever alternative realities they are functioning in. But for me, it's very painful and a lot of hard work. I think I'm an extremely hard-working actor.

You have won five National Awards – three in consecutive years. Which out of these has made you particularly proud?

When I won my fifth National Award for *Godmother* I was surprised that it brought me as much joy as my earlier awards. Still, my favourite performance is *Khandhar;* it was in competition with *Mandi,* which was more touted for an award. *Mandi* demanded a lot of histrionics and I enjoyed playing over the top. On the other hand, Jamini of *Khandhar* is so quiet that she's almost unnoticeable and therefore I was grateful when I got the award for *Khandhar.* That is not to say that I did not enjoy my work in *Mandi,* but to me the character Jamini is a creature of poetic sensibilities.

Would you say this has anything to do with you being Kaifi Azmi's daughter?

I would agree with that. *Khandhar* made me discover myself. Jamini is somebody I have tremendous respect for. Normally, acting is a two-way process; the character gives to the actor and the actor gives to the character. This time, however, it was the character that lent me her strength and helped me play her not as a victim, but as a person who was tragic and yet possessed an infinite dignity.

And *Godmother*?

Vinay Shukla, the writer-director of the film, is also a dear friend and wanted to offer me a 'star vehicle'. He was convinced that Rambhi-behn, my character in the film, should be a larger-than-life role while also retaining credibility. My main conflict, of course, came from the issue the film raised – a larger representation of women in the political system. Here was a film showing a woman traversing the same path that men had before her. I have always believed that when women become empowered, they will transform the notion of power to one that is based on sharing and not on abuse. That's not how the director viewed his film. He felt I was looking at it from a narrow perspective, seeing it through the point of view of women's emancipation. His motive was to highlight the dangers of community mobilization for vote-bank gains. Rambhi poses an important query to her husband. She asks, 'A community unites the tribe but alienates it from the rest of the society, is this right?'

Are you drawn to politics? There are speculations that you will be contesting elections.

I haven't done so in the last three terms though the grapevine keeps writing about it. The media hasn't stopped asking me this question. Politics don't interest me, but people change and I don't see why one shouldn't change one's mind if one is convinced. At the moment I'm more interested in organizing people together, forming programmes which would aid in bringing about a change in the country.

Between the actor and the activist, whose contribution to society is greater?

The activist's, most definitely! A few years ago, I was arrested for demonstration in a slum and was held up at the police station when I had a show the same evening. I had to make a choice between the actor and the activist and fortunately everything worked out fine in the end, but the dilemma I went through was nightmarish! The actor, as understood in Hindi cinema, has a limited role but an artiste who is truthful to his work is of greater consequence to society than an activist who isn't.

Does the actor in you ever feel overshadowed by the activist in you?

Not overshadowed but limited and it was discomfiting. It was a period when I was very intense about my new consciousness and my political ideology was colouring my choice of roles as an actor. I had begun to look at the most innocent lines with deep scepticism and this was constraining me. That's when my friend and director, Aparna Sen, pulled me up and said I was limiting myself as an actor and she was right. So when Deepa Mehta signed me on for *Fire*, I surrendered myself completely to the character of Radha. Acting is really a fulfilling profession and pushes you to use your potential as a performer to the optimum level. This is one of the reasons why I continue to be an actor.

What are your concerns about Hindi cinema today?

We still haven't been able to make one truly crossover film. Satyajit Ray won an Oscar for Lifetime Achievement and was hailed as one of the ten best film-makers in the world by the British Film Institute, yet his work has been accessible to only a select few in the world. Mira Nair, more recently, has made headway following the success of *Monsoon Wedding* abroad but Hindi cinema still has a long way to go. What's unfortunate is that we make about 800 films a year, twice the number that Hollywood makes, and yet the international circuit discards all our films as run-of-the-mill melodrama. India is a country that lives in several centuries simultaneously, and it is up to our film-makers, writers and artistes to make the world aware of her complexities and strengths, and help steer her away from the 'third-world-exotic-despite-famine-and-drought' stereotype.

Amitabh Bachchan

Acting is freezing the mood and the moment

Did you ever imagine you would flourish as an actor after sixty?

All these years my career was managed and regulated by others. I diligently followed what I was told and the outcome was satisfactory. In 1990 it was suggested that I didn't need to work and could take a long sabbatical. I did but soon realized that a life without work is dull and uninteresting. I would have continued being in that stagnated state had economic circumstances not compelled me to get back into action once again.

It was a difficult phase of your life, what lessons did you learn from the experience?

I learnt to take control of my life and career, even in areas I did not understand. I learnt to question what I could not fathom but most

The interview was conducted on the sets of *Khakee* in 2003. *Aarakshan* (2011) and *The Great Gatsby* (2013), where he has a cameo, were the last releases of Amitabh Bachchan.

important, this was the first time I was making decisions for myself, and right or wrong, I was responsible for them.

You mean career choices?

That's right. It's a liberating feeling to know that you are responsible for your choices. Today, I want to work as long as I can. I feel hesitant to say 'no' to friends, to turn down youngsters. Their enthusiasm is infectious and I want to, if possible, participate in their dreams. Someday, I know, I will have to press on the brakes. There will come a time when my face will not appeal to the camera, or the audience will get tired of watching me. But for as long as I can, I would like to pursue acting with the same passion.

And after that?

I've always wanted to learn languages or learn to play an instrument. I am also inclined towards gardening or maybe just looking after the home. It can be quite recreational, you know.

Your wife says you make an excellent housekeeper.

That's because after the traumatic experience we went through with our company I have begun to look into the finances of running a home. I've made it a discipline to check the expenditures at the end of the day, because I don't ever want to be in the same kind of financial mess again. I'd rather be cautious than embarrassed. The memory of the crises we endured is too painful and I want to protect the family from such a menace forever.

The crisis has changed you – you are less guarded now.

Yeah, we have shed a lot of baggage. We are shy to admit this but economic security instills a lot of strength. I've become less guarded because I'm less defensive now. My self-assurance also comes from the fact that today I'm old enough to be forgiven if I make a mistake.

Nobody is willing to forgive you for doing *Boom* and neither have you accepted it as a mistake!

My character of a don in *Boom* is repulsive because he is an obnoxious man. If people do not like the character, I'd say it is a deficiency on the part of the screenplay. However, if they have not liked me as an actor, they are justified in their backlash and I accept blame for letting them down. I take their outcry as a compliment because it is a gesture of affection for my betterment.

How much of your success do you attribute to destiny?

Destiny throws us opportunities and it's up to us to take up these challenges. *Mohabbatein* and *Kaun Banega Crorepati* were opportunities I accepted and, to my good fortune, they proved to be fruitful decisions.

You are viewed as a brand today?

The world around us has changed. We are living in a consumerist society. In the olden days nobody mentioned brands but today every celebrity worth his name is endorsing some product or the other. I'm fortunate to be lured by so many offers because this enables me to clear my debts and rise above my financial crisis. No matter how the public perceives me, at home, I'm the provider of the family and it is my responsibility to fulfill their wishes. That they don't desire or demand too much is a blessing and I'm privileged to have a family that is not overly ostentatious.

If they were, would you indulge in the extravagance?

My philosophy is that I work hard and I should be allowed to spend my money as I please. We lead a comfortable life, according to some this may appear as excessive, but one has strived for it. So if the extravagance brings joy to my family, they should be indulged.

When you do anything for your loved ones you are never counting the expenses.

What about expenses for yourself?

I'm not demanding by nature and there are no deprivations as such, but if there was something I cherished, I would not exercise unnecessary self-control. Life is beautiful and all that comes with it should be valued.

You are being conferred with a new title everyday, how do you react to so many felicitations?

Gratitude, it's all very overwhelming. I accept people's appreciation for my work with humility but there is also a sense of shock. I'm not sure if I deserve so much adulation.

Do you sometimes fear it will all go away?

I do, in fact, all the time. And I know it will go away because that's the law of nature. Nothing lasts forever and no matter what anyone says, nobody is ever prepared to lose it. We sense change from the reactions of the audience at different seasons of our career, but no artiste is ever sure or ever completely secure.

How different is the current success from what you experienced in the seventies and the eighties?

I don't think I was conscious about it then since all my time was spent working. Today I don't have the mega successes I had then, which is in a way an advantage because the pressure is less. I was expected to perform better with every new release earlier, which can be very stressful. Today the responsibility of how a film fares is on the hero and not on me so I'm in a far more comfortable position.

So are you enjoying yourself much more now?

Most certainly, for this is a time when you have finished paying dividends as a professional. Unfortunately, a major part of an individual's life is spent in aspiring for success. When you are just out of college you are frustrated because you are not sure if you have chosen the right career. You are also not sure if you are courting the right choices and, after the entire struggle, you are not sure if you are going to succeed. That's not all. When you finally succeed, you are never sure how long it will last. It is an exhausting process but once the frenzy subsides, there is peace! It is the law of nature that tranquility follows storm.

This reflects in your commercials, earlier there was a certain shyness but now you appear less inhibited.

I'm shy even now, there are butterflies in my stomach every time I face the camera, but I'm shooting ads more frequently now so I'm able to disguise my awkwardness. It is because I have understood the craft. In cinema, we have the luxury of delivering a message in three hours but in advertising, we have to sell the product in three seconds, which is a big challenge.

As the patriarch in *Mohabbatein* to the autumn romance in *Baghban*, how much on the screen is contributed by the actor?

I would feel defeated as an artiste if I'm denied expression. Communication is part of a creative process and its beauty absorbs everyone involved in the exercise. As actors we listen to story narrations, rehearse our lines; some of us spend private time in the bathroom or bedroom acting out the scene in front of a mirror. But when one is on the set, in front of the camera, a new world takes over. When you hear the clapboard, an entire new identity takes over and what you do at that moment is entirely different from

what you had imagined. That is why I shy away from rehearsals, for I'm always frightened of losing the moment.

What are your other recurrent fears as an actor?

I'm always nervous when I'm beginning work with a new director because it means I'm going to be tested again. It's bad enough to attempt to deliver a convincing performance, but it's worse when you have to stand up and emote in front of a stranger. There is a possibility that he feels he is as much on trial as I am but as we are not sharing notes, the discomfort persists till we arrive at a creative understanding and recognize each other's comfort zone. Once that is accomplished the nervousness settles down.

Must an actor restrict himself to his role or make suggestions during the shooting?

It depends on your equation with the film-maker. In the early stages of my career I didn't. Now I feel it would be dishonest to not articulate something I feel strongly about though it is the prerogative of the film-maker to accept or not accept my suggestion. Still, that does not give me the credit of structuring a scene. Santoshi has a unique ability as a director to explain a scene to his actor without insisting on them doing it his way. Only in extreme cases, and for valid reasons, he urges you to do the scene the way he has conceived it.

Have you been through moments when you have had second thoughts about your scenes?

Of course, and on such occasions I have always expressed them to my directors the following day. During *Khakee,* Santoshi was very forthcoming of the suggestions I made. There were times he disagreed too and I respected that. I am conscious of my responsibility as an actor and unless I have a very strong alternative,

I would not recommend it to him or any other director. Such communications can only occur when there is mutual trust between the director and his artiste.

What about moments when you wanted to suggest an alternative and held back?

Yes, there have been such occasions as well and I've regretted them. There were times I held back because I didn't want to be misunderstood or because I was feeling lazy, and felt miserable later. Now I feel I should have listened to the artiste inside me and asked for a retake. Today, if there is an irritant I prefer to express myself rather than leave it for posterity. I'm at a phase in life where I don't want to hold back, so whether it's a scene or a song, a film or an argument I disapprove of, I make myself heard. I didn't in the past but I do now and feel much lighter. What's heartening is that people accept it sportingly; life is so much better this way!

You sound like your character in *Baghban*.

For whatever reason, the character has struck an emotional chord with the audience. The film has evoked social debates in countries all over Asia. Parents are reviewing their relationships with their children and children are revisiting their priorities. The younger generation in our country is unsure of what to do with the older generation. Unlike the West, where they put parents in old-age homes, we tend to safeguard them, sometimes to the extent of disabling them. Inadvertently, we closet them away from the world whereas abroad, the retired lead a more challenging life. The process of fending for themselves fills them with zest, whilst back home, with our mollycoddling, we take away their spirit to survive.

When you grow old which of the two lives would you prefer?

I may not get there. Don't forget, I take my daily dose of Chyawanprash (*laughs*).

Rani Mukerji

Acting is about focus and concentration

Two of your films *Yuva* and *Hum Tum* are releasing back-to-back. Does this make you feel anxious?

Yes, in the mornings when I drive to my shoots and see huge posters staring me in the face, I feel all knotted up inside. The media and the distributors create so much hype that one is always scared of letting down people who have invested so much hope in you. I guess this is the reason why how a film fares at the box-office is important. Success brings about collective happiness; when a film is a hit the entire unit celebrates.

Was it difficult shooting for such diverse roles at the same time?

Shashi of *Yuva* is lower-middle-class and uninhibited in expression. Rhea of *Hum Tum* is urban and emancipated. They are not just

The interview was conducted before the release of *Yuva* (2004). *Talaash* (2012) and *Bombay Talkies* (2013) were Rani Mukerji's last releases.

diverse in their backgrounds but also in their romances and relationships. In *Yuva,* it is a very physical, almost violent romance with Abhishek while the character in *Hum Tum* projects restraint. It's not difficult getting under the skin of any character once you have understood the mindset. Of course, you have to be alert all the time, for the slightest preoccupation on the part of an actor reflects on screen.

Playing Rhea must have been comparatively easier.

Yes, she is like any girl my age. She is modern but her values are in place. She is carefree but not frivolous. Relationships matter to her but she will not allow them to distract her from her career goals. On the other hand, I don't know anyone remotely similar to Shashi but I have faint memories of my mother talking in whispers to our maid when I was growing up. It's funny how an actor stores memories and brings them out at the right time. I think Shashi has similarities with that maid.

Mani Ratnam and Kunal Kohli are directors of different sensibilities. How was the experience of working with both of them?

It was my first film with Mani Ratnam and all of us on the sets were completely in awe of him. It's difficult to believe that someone as accomplished as him can be so normal. The best thing about him is that he shoots the most complex scenes very casually. It's only when you watch the film that the enormity of the moment dawns on you. With Kunal Kohli it was my second film after *Mujhse Dosti Karoge,* so it was a more informal relationship and I was conscious when I was giving suggestions.

Yuva is your second film with Abhishek Bachchan after *Bas Itna Sa Khwab Hai* and the two of you share a great chemistry.

I have loads of affection for Abhishek so I'm able to portray fondness without making an effort. We share a comfort level as co-stars where we are not self-conscious when performing an intimate scene. Mani Ratnam understood this and exploited it to the fullest. The chemistry emerges from mutual trust as co-artistes.

You've been in the profession for almost a decade, would you say you are happy with the way your career has shaped up?

I think so. I didn't join films with any great aspirations. My father had suffered his second heart attack and the family was feeling insecure. I had just completed my twelfth standard and was looking for an alternative to studies. It was at that time that Salim uncle (Akhtar) suggested I do his film and I said 'yes' more as an escape from studies than for the joy of acting. It's only when I got into it that I realized how much I was enjoying it.

Enjoying being an actor or a star?

Both, for the survival of one depends on the survival of the other. Today, happiness for me comes from those around me: my family. Sometimes I feel that they enjoy my stardom more than me because, while my life is restricted to the studios and outdoor locations, they are my windows to the world and my only anchor. They blossom when I'm appreciated and wither away when I'm sad. When my film fails they suffer more than me.

Does that create a lot of pressure on you?

Not at all, it is not as if they withdraw affection every time I fail. On the contrary, I'm able to overcome hurdles because of their support. If I aspire for success it's not out of external pressure but because I'm an achiever. In the final analysis though, I would give more emphasis to a happy day spent at work with friends than in chasing unrealistic goals.

Do you sometimes wonder what you would have been had you not been an actress?

I would have been a housewife like my mother, worrying about her husband and children all the time. But I had to be an actress. There has to be something burning inside you to be able to survive here. My grandmother tried to make an actress out of all her four daughters but only the youngest, Debashri maasi (Roy) succeeded. She was the only one who had the determination and I'm like my aunt.

Do you regret picking all the wrong projects in the early stage of your career?

No, they were learning experiences and I had to go through those mistakes to become what I am today. Whether they were wrong choices in films or in people, they helped me understand myself better. I know for sure that I would not make the same mistakes today.

Has it occurred to you that you are the only actress of your generation to play a wife in as many as seven films?

Yes ... It could be because I'm the kind of girl guys like to take home to their moms (*laughs*).

Seriously, do these portrayals offer any insight into real marriage?

They are merely roles and the situations are hypothetical so I'm not looking for lessons of life. In *Kuch Kuch Hota Hai*, for instance, I'm urging my daughter to find a new mom for herself. I'm not sure if I can be as large-hearted in real life.

Ten years ago, when you did *Raja Ki Aayegi Baraat*, did you understand the issue about dowry deaths?

Not as much as I understand it now. At that time, I was too wrapped up in the excitement of my first film to be bothered about the message of the film. Today, I'm more socially aware. I would not want to be a wrong role model for my fans.

What about all those erotic scenes with Kamal Haasan in *Hey Ram?* Did you understand the implications?

(*Smiles*) If I did, I would not have agreed to those scenes. It's difficult for an actor to protect herself in situations like these unless you have had sufficient exposure. Today, I'm in a position where I can make put down a precondition of what I will or will not do on screen and it will be accepted provided my request is reasonable. When issues are clarified beforehand everyone is comfortable. But to argue on the sets after signing the contract is unprofessional.

Chori Chori Chupke Chupke addressed surrogate motherhood.

Yes, it is a sensitive issue but the script was fair to all the characters – the husband, wife and the other woman. There is nothing undignified about either the wife or the prostitute. I just went with the flow of the story. Today I wonder why the writer didn't think of a test-tube baby option.

Saathiya and *Chalte Chalte* are stories about commitment and responsibility in marriage. How important are these qualities to you in a relationship?

Without commitment there is no relationship and relationships are based on the foundation of responsibilities. I look for both these qualities in my partner. Actors lead a high-profile life. On the sets we do love scenes and, at parties, we hug and kiss our co-stars. There is a familiarity in our daily interaction, which can be misleading to an outsider but that is not the reality.

And how do actors retain their sanity in an unreal world?

By learning to decipher between fact and fiction, by not getting carried away with all the praise that comes your way and giving your best shot to every role no matter how inconsequential some of the scenes may appear during shooting. I do that.

Like '*Aati kya Khandala…*' in *Ghulam* and the screaming heroine in *Bichhoo*?

They are regular formula films and are enacted as per the instructions of the director. So if Vikram Bhatt asks me to smile all the time in *Ghulam*, I do, and if the director wants me to scream at the slightest provocation in *Bichhoo*, I obey.

How much of these characters do you take back home?

You will be surprised but all my characters stay with me whether it is just standing in a frame with Govinda in *Hadh Kar Di Aapne* or shooting in an unbearable climate with Anil Kapoor for *Nayak*.

With so many characters residing in your heart, how do you make space for new characters like *The Rising* or *Black*?

The new characters occupy a special place and rule my heart. There is nothing more stimulating than working with great talent. I'm fortunate that I'm at a phase in my career when I'm working with exceptional actors like Aamir Khan and Amitabh Bachchan who are conscious not just about their own performances but also their co-stars'. The slightest false chord in your portrayal and they are quick to correct you. I'm fortunate to have the guidance of able directors like Ketan Mehta and Sanjay Leela Bhansali. The kind of passion and research they lend to a project is inspiring. Ketan is highly energetic and Sanjay will not rest until he has pushed you to your optimum level. There were times when I was frustrated with a scene and wanted to give up but he never let me.

In this frenzied life of shoots and parties, how do you relax?

By watching films, it's the only way I can de-stress myself and you'll be surprised that most actors feel that way.

Shah Rukh Khan

Acting is a complex exercise, different formulas, different times

Three releases, a dubbed film, and a world tour of concerts – that's a lot for one year, aren't you exhausted?

I'm all right; I make sure I grab my breathing space in the middle of the various commitments I have. The pace of work is not an issue. It has always been this hectic. I've always had three releases a year, but, yes, the associated activities have multiplied so the schedules get tighter. But I'm okay, in control.

How do you divide your time between commercials, film shoots and musical shows?

The shows are chalked out over a span of two years. This time the gap was four years because of my back surgery. The commercials

The interview was conducted before the release of *Paheli* (2005). *Jab Tak Hai Jaan* (2012) was Shah Rukh Khan's last release. *Chennai Express* is expected soon.

are not in the least bit demanding. I endorse just four products and the shootings take about two or three days. So roughly it works out to a total of twelve days in a year, which is not difficult to organize. Also, the agencies don't define any fixed dates for shoots. The campaigns are according to seasons and therefore flexible. I usually try and combine the brand shoots with my outdoor shoots to save time.

And film shoots?

Film shoots have never been so professional. All the film units are thoroughly prepared before going on floor. Actors allot bulk dates to a film, so on an average a regular film is completed within ninety to a 100 shooting dates. Add to it another extra week for music and TV promotion, which still leaves me with sufficient time to go on holidays with my family. Of course, when my children are on vacation they travel with me wherever I go.

What about your innumerable friends, where do their happy and sad moments fit into all this?

One always finds time if one cares. One learns to prioritize. There are times you extend yourself because the person or the moment is important to you and there are times, when, despite your best intentions, you are unable to reach out to them, or reach late. These are occupational hazards and those who care for you have to learn to accept it.

Fourteen years ago, when you came into films, they called you a brat. Today you have mellowed considerably.

I don't agree that I was a brat. I have always spoken my mind. Earlier, because I was new, people were reluctant to accept it. Today they are more accommodating. It's natural because that's how perceptions are created. All of us categorize people into good or bad, generous or evil. Those who didn't communicate with me put me in a specific category. I never disregarded anybody but I wouldn't have been obedient just to create a good impression. As far as I know, there has not been any drastic transformation in my personality. I still speak my mind but I don't overstep, I don't think anyone can say that I'm irreverent.

You believe that?

I'm absolutely certain that I don't misbehave and I don't tolerate badtamizi from anyone including my children. I have very clear notions about right and wrong. I accept that I'm often naughty but I am never insensitive. When somebody provokes me I'm forced to respond tersely. Recently, when we returned from the Sri Lanka tour, the electronic media hounded us as if it was a celebration of the tragedy. A young reporter asked me the most offensive questions in a tone that was almost accusatory. I wanted to tick her off. When I was younger it may have been inappropriate to reprimand her. At thirty-nine I have earned the right but I held back because the moment was so fragile. I didn't want to say something I was going to regret later.

Do such incidents occur often?

You will be surprised but quite often. Strangers try to enter my studio and when stopped from doing so drop names of doctors and lawyers. To spare them embarrassment, I let them in but they overstep and take further liberties. Sometimes, out of excitement, fans say things out of turn and sometimes professionals say wrong things too. My wife Gauri says I should give them a long rope because when people meet me for the first time they become awkward. I don't accept that. I am willing to make concessions for a fan but not for someone who aspires to work with me.

In moments of conflict who do you rely on for guidance?

I listen to everyone but do what I think is right. While shooting for *Swades,* Ashutosh Gowariker told me, 'Shah Rukh, now you will have to listen to me. I'm the director.' That's because we have a long-standing joke on the actor-director equation. Of course, by now, Ashu is used to my whacky sense of humour.

Are statements like 'Aamir Khan has the range and I have the height...' a part of the same humour?

I'm sufficiently familiar with Aamir to know that he will not mind such a comment coming from me. Our camaraderie is beyond such interpretations. We have spent enough time together for him to be familiar with my tongue-in-cheek comments.

And the passing reference to Simi Garewal in your episode on *Koffee with Karan*?

I cannot remember what I said on that show. Simi came up in our conversation because the profile of Karan's show is similar to Simi's *Rendezvous* but there was nothing wicked about the comment. I wouldn't dream of disrespecting someone as senior as Simi Garewal.

The top is a lonely place but you seem to have accumulated hordes of friends. How many of these would actually be there if you lost your stardom tomorrow?

All of us want to believe that our friends are there because of us and not because of our status. The truth, of course, has been proven over a period of time. Not everyone who is seen around me, or introduces himself as my peer, is an insider. I don't make friends easily. After fourteen years in films I have just four friends. There are several relationships from the heart with strong ties, but there

is a difference between the two. A friend is someone I call when I'm distressed. These people have been there with me before my stardom, even before I came to Mumbai. There have been a few additions to the list and they are precious to me. They are not turned on by my success. They don't flatter me after watching every film of mine, they tell me the truth.

You have three releases this year, which out of your forthcoming film characters do you identify with the most?

Let me think. I nursed a crush on my school teacher so there are similarities between Ram in *Main Hoon Na* and me. Veer of *Veer-Zaara* is selfless and surrenders his entire life to a woman. I'd like to believe I'm as devoted as him. That leaves Mohan Bhargav of *Swades.* Mohan is too idealistic, I would want to be like him, but I'm not.

And how would you rate your performances in all of them?

Main Hoon Na was a fun film and all of us had a great time during the shooting. *Veer-Zaara* called for me to play a much older man and the disability had to be reflected in my posture and speech, calling for slower reflexes. In *Swades,* physically, I'm an extension of what I look like or do in real life – drive cars or tinker with gadgets. It's more or less the same lifestyle minus the ideals. It all looked very simple on the surface but it was only when I began shooting that the character seemed unattainable.

What is your reaction when you watch your film for the first time?

I don't know about other actors, but the first time I watch my film, I detest everything about it. Then, a little later, when I watch it again, I find myself to be a little better and the third time a lot better. I think one needs time and a certain distance to absorb a new image.

Then, over a period of time, I slowly outgrow the role. In the olden days, the process took longer but now, with more assignments, the detachment sets in faster. For years, every time I was asked about my favourite role, I'd say *Dilwale Dulhaniya Le Jayenge.* Now I say, 'the next one'. It's because the actor is always hoping and waiting for a better performance to come his way.

What is your definition of a good performance?

This may sound like a cliché but I don't think there can be a fixed definition. My opinion changes because I'm changing all the time. All I can try to do is to not lose focus till the film is complete. Acting is a very complex exercise and different formulas work for different people. I'm often criticized for being Shah Rukh Khan in all my films. My argument is that even if I dare to bare all, is it about being different or about being yourself? For fourteen years I have exhibited bits and pieces of me on celluloid. The day I feel I have exposed myself completely and have nothing more to offer I will pack up. Such a time can be described as creative salvation or it can be called a burn-out!

And how would you know which one it is?

I don't know and this obviously means that I have not reached that point as yet. The precaution is to watch oneself, to preserve your muse. The film is the director's journey. My job as an actor is to project the director's vision aided by the locations, costumes and the words he provides me with. I play my role within the constraints of his script. Depending on the sculptor I'm sometimes competent, average or bad in a film. Unfortunately, cinema is the only medium where creativity is judged by commercialism, but irrespective of whether the film succeeds or fails, the person always gains from the actor.

Out of the many characters you have played, which ones have you carried home?

I admire the Gandhian character *Dada* in *Swades* but to follow in his footsteps would be a fantasy. My character Mohan Bhargav can aspire to be like him because he is the hero but it's very difficult to be so heroic in real life. I said yes to *Swades* because I was attracted to the message of the film. Everyone wants to be virtuous, but to say that I'm an infallible patriot would be overselling me.

How different was the experience of shooting with Gowariker compared to a Chopra or a Johar?

Out of the numerous films I have done in my career only six have been shot with the Johars and Chopras. The rest of my work belongs to various other film-makers, but people tend to have a selective memory about this. This is probably due to the commercial impact of those films or my personal relationships with the families and I cannot do anything about these impressions. After my recent narrow escape in the bomb blast in Sri Lanka, I have discovered that life is too precious to waste over negative emotions.

You have success, fame, family, money… What more would you want out of life?

Honestly, all I want is to be able to say 'thank you' to the millions of people who have given me a place in their hearts. That night when I returned home after the nightmare, there were huge crowds outside my house only because they wanted to be reassured of my safety. It was so overwhelming! What happened wasn't my fault but I feel responsible. I'm grateful that I'm not scarred but I'm suffering for those who lost their lives. What happened should not have happened!

Abhishek Bachchan

Acting is learning to relax before the camera

When you watch *Refugee* today, is there anything you would like to change?

Sure. I would like to change everything: my appearance, my walk, my dialogue delivery and my performance. Today, when I watch the film I cringe in embarrassment. I find myself grossly inadequate and unprepared to be working with a film-maker of the calibre of J.P. Dutta.

Were you conscious about this at that time? Did your detractors say so?

Everybody did, including the media and relentlessly so, Friday after Friday. I should have appreciated their suggestions, but I was on a different trip. I was so excited at the prospect of working in films, of shooting everyday, that their criticism fell on deaf ears.

> The interview was conducted before the release of *Dhoom* (2004). *Bol Bachchan* (2012) was Abhishek Bachchan's last release.

You were young and defensive.

Most certainly, I was. I felt that because I was earnest, my efforts should have been appreciated. It was only later that I realized that show business operates on results. The box-office is not concerned with an actor's journey no matter how arduous or inward. All that matters are the collection figures.

How painful was your journey? Were you as diffident as your character in *Refugee*?

Not to the extent I should have, I admit. And it's because I was so thoroughly pampered on the sets by the entire unit. There was no feeling of deprivation for either Kareena Kapoor or me. We were treated like kids and we enjoyed it. I feel guilty about all this now. I feel like I let down my director.

Did J.P. Dutta express feeling let down?

Never, this was my perception and I tried making up for it in our next film together, *Line of Control,* and was gracious that he was appreciative. When I was dubbing for the film, he said, 'You've learnt a lot.' The fact is, that no matter how much I improve, I know I can never match up to his standards.

Would you agree that you were overconfident in *Tera Jadoo Chal Gaya*?

Nobody said that to me, but I'm willing to accept the observation. In hindsight, though, I wonder if the overconfidence was perhaps an extension of the love and reassurance from my producer Vashu Bhagnani. I did *Tera Jadoo Chal Gaya* for two reasons: The first was Vashu Bhagnani, I would do anything for him. Second, the story and the character were in complete contrast to my debut film and I felt it would make an appropriate second release.

You wore a bizarre costume reminiscent of Aamir Khan in *Rangeela*, was this deliberate?

Not at all. The costume happened completely by chance. We were ready to shoot the scene but the costume had not yet reached the sets. In a desperate move, Vashu Bhagnani and I just walked to the costume shop at Ramoji Rao Studio where we were shooting and picked up the gaudiest set on the shelf. It was perfect for the character, something he would have picked up for a special occasion.

You performed a difficult dance number in this film.

Yes, '*Humne to kaha saubaar sanam…*' choreographed by Saroj Khan. The steps were very difficult and we were shooting in the middle of summer in Agra. Saroj Khan made us dance till our feet ached. During this song I learnt that in cinema it's not sufficient to be a technically competent dancer. What's more important is to enjoy dancing. The film industry's three best dancers – Hrithik Roshan, Govinda and Arshad Warsi are superb not only because they know their steps but because they enjoy dancing and this shows on screen!

You share a good equation with most of your co-stars.

It's not just me, my entire generation shares a healthy equation with their colleagues. The current crop of stars is friendly and interactive on the sets. During *Om Jai Jagadish,* Urmila and Fardeen would give me constructive tips. I'm told actors were not as friendly in the olden days but there is no politicking among the present lot. In our generation, there is no politicking as well as power play.

No discrimination on the sets vis a vis a big star like Aishwarya Rai during *Dhai Akshar Prem Ke*?

My flops hadn't started at that time. I was shooting simultaneously for *Refugee, Tera Jadoo Chal Gaya* and *Dhai Akshar Prem Ke.*

Aishwarya has always been a supportive co-star and Raj Kanwar is among the few directors who had faith in me before my debut release. I was quite chilled out during *Dhai Akshar* and believed that what's meant for me cannot be taken away.

Bas Itna Sa Khwab Hai was about an ambitious man who loses his conscience on his journey to success. Do you ever fear losing your inner voice?

I will never lose my conscience because I've had the fortune of playing Suraj in *Bas Itna Sa Khwab Hai.* In front of the camera I saw what greed led him to do and what he lost in the process. Let me share something with you. During the making of this film, something similar happened to my friend Goldie and me. We had started out with a lot of honesty but as the shoot progressed we got confused, we were scared of failing and in the process added irrelevant tracks to the film. We compromised and lost our conviction and this showed in the film.

When did you realize this?

We felt something was going wrong but the fact that we had cheated on our intentions, dawned on us much later. The audience can never be won over by dishonesty. The film was a learning experience. Its failure was poetic justice.

What about *Shararat*?

I stand by the message of the film. I think director Gurudev Bhalla did a splendid job. Probably the timing of the film was wrong but I enjoyed the experience of working with a marvellous cast like Amrish Puri, Daisy Irani (aunty) and others. The long outdoor shoots spent with the senior stars made me realize how young they were and how old I was. The film took a long time to release; it was a victim of my bad phase.

How bad was the failure phase?

Very bad. Every Friday morning I woke up with a sinking feeling as one more disaster got added to my list. It was happening rapidly and after a while I became numb. I began watching the whole process from a distance, like an outsider.

Had you ever envisioned that pursuing a career would be such a battle?

The irony is that I didn't think of it as a battle. I genuinely thought everything would just fall into my plate. When it didn't, I turned defensive. I shunned help from everybody including my parents. It was because I wanted to do it on my own, wanted them to be proud of me, little realizing that by alienating them, I was hurting them and making more mistakes.

So what made you rethink your stand?

It was a stray comment from a colleague. He said, 'So what do your parents say?' I drew a blank. Later, as I thought it over, I realized for the first time how foolish I was. I had the best actors of show business at home and I wasn't consulting them. By this time, some more films of mine bombed and I completely lost confidence. One day, I was on the sets to execute a very crucial scene and I just couldn't do it. I phoned dad and said, 'I need help'. That's it. Within twenty minutes dad had folded his shoot and was by my side. We spoke in my van and I was ready to shoot again.

Did you regret not seeking him out earlier?

Yes I did, because I felt so reassured instantly. His sheer presence was so calming. I felt all my suffering was unnecessary. I was trying desperately to give them a moment of glory, little realizing that they already believed in me. They didn't want the glory, they wanted my happiness, wanted to be a part of my journey, and it's unfortunate that I realized this so late. But once I did, I surrendered.

Haan Maine Pyar Kiya had all the ingredients of a masala movie, including the steamy love scenes. Why do you think it failed?

I feel we tend to analyse our films far more than the audience does. I'm not sure if so much analysing is constructive. The man visiting a cinema hall comes with the good intentions of enjoying, even liking a film. But very often he doesn't, and has no explanation for this. As an actor I'd prefer to rely on my instinct and not worry about the consequences. I believe that irrespective of the fate of my film, I'm never the loser because I'm always learning from the character I portray.

What did you learn from Jagadish, the youngest of the three brothers in *Om Jai Jagadish*?

Jagadish was young and restless, quite similar to what I was going through in my life at that time. I felt empathy for him. But my character is not the only reason I did this film. Before I joined films I did a workshop with Anupam Kher who taught me the magic of acting. To be directed by him was an opportunity to grow as an as actor. Anupam taught me how to relax before the camera. He taught me how not to be conscious of my surroundings while emoting. It is a priceless contribution.

So are you uninhibited shooting any kind of a scene anywhere now?

Well, more or less.

Are you embarrassed when your parents watch your love scenes on screen?

Yes, I feel shy if we are watching the scenes together. If they are watching it when I'm not with them, it's alright. Maa has watched Paa romance all his leading ladies for years, so maybe they'll get used to my love scenes too, but I'll continue to feel slightly awkward, I guess.

Was it a difficult decision accepting a special appearance in Sooraj Barjatya's *Main Prem Ki Deewani Hoon*? How does an actor going through a lean phase feel when paired with an actor riding high?

I'd like to put it on record that *Main Prem Ki Deewani Hoon* is not a special appearance but a second lead. I hate the term 'special or friendly appearance'. It denotes a disassociation with the film, which I don't think is fair to the project. If I'm acting in a film then I'm accountable for it. To be fair, Sooraj Barjatya was very gracious. He told me that in the circumstances he could only offer me the second lead and would respect whatever decision I took. I didn't go through any conflict and said 'yes' immediately. There was something so honest and appealing about him that I could not refuse him. Besides, I liked my character Prem. He is similar to what I'm like in real life. On the sets there was no discrimination either from the unit or my co-actors. Don't forget, Hrithik, Kareena and I have all grown up together.

How important is a conducive working atmosphere for you?

It's very important. I'm completely rattled if my surroundings are not harmonious. I may not show it but I get deeply affected by even the slightest tension or negativity around me. I think it's the duty of every film-maker to create an atmosphere on the sets that enables his artistes to deliver their best. A happy workplace atmosphere always reflects on the screen.

You looked nourished and nurtured in *Mumbai Se Aaya Mera Dost*.

It's because all of us were happy shooting. The director, Apoorva Lakhia, is a close friend and there was a mutual trust that helped. Away from Mumbai, it didn't matter that my films were failing at the box-office. I was determined to not let cynicism creep into my

work. It wasn't easy but because I was conscious, I was able to fight the demons.

From AB Corp's production assistant during *Major Saab* to sharing screen space with Ajay Devgn in *Zameen*, how was the experience?

Ajay Devgn is like an elder brother to me and no matter how casual we may be with each other, I can never forget that my first job was under him. He was an unrelenting support to our family during the making of *Major Saab* and there is no doubt in my mind that our outdoor stint in Australia would not have been accomplished without him. Our family can never forget that. What's further remarkable is that when we began working together in *Zameen,* he treated me like an equal.

So when did the wheel of destiny turn for you?

Gradually I guess. Paa always said it would and when I least expected it. He said I must not attach undue importance to success, and instead concentrate on continuing to work, giving everyday and every scene my best shot and effort and someday, I will strike the right ball and then I would be able to swing it. I trusted him and he proved right. *Bluff Master* happened out of the blue.

Rohan Sippy and you went to the same university and later did two films together, *Kuch Na Kaho* and *Bluff Master*. Is working with a friend an asset or a pressure?

I'd say a bit of both. Rohan understands me very well and that always helps. On the other hand, because he is a friend, I want to give the film my best and not let him down. When you are working with a friend, you feel concerned about how the film fares. We were fortunate that we made up for the failure of the first with the super success of the second venture *Bluff Master*.

Yuva got you many accolades as an actor. Had you ever imagined the film would be so significant in your career?

Never. Mani Ratnam sent a word with his assistant Shaad Ali that he wanted to cast me in his next film. When we met, he began narrating the story and then suddenly stopped to say, 'I'm sorry, I forgot to ask you if you will do my film?' That is Mani sir, never taking anybody for granted. Later, when I was shooting *Run* in Chennai, he would drop by in the evenings at my hotel and we would talk at length about my character Lallan Singh.

Rani Mukerji says you were Mani Ratnam's favourite actor on the sets.

I don't think he played favourites intentionally, but perhaps, Lallan Singh was Mani sir's favourite character and that reflected in his interaction. I like Lallan Singh too. He's the only character I've played so far, who has no shades of gray for everything is either black or white for him. There were six stars in the film but it's extraordinary how Mani sir could shift attention from one character to another. His ability to explain a scene and extract emotion from actors even though he is not comfortable with the language is admirable. Also, he is a keen observer of human relationships. He saw the comfort level between Rani and me and used it to the maximum in our love scenes.

Phir Milenge was your first, and so far only, film with a woman director. How different was the experience?

It was very interesting working with Revathi ma'am. It made me realize that men and women are temperamentally different. It's always an advantage working with a director who is an actor. When the actor is a woman, there is a double advantage. Revathi ma'am gave a lot of space to her actors. She let you enact the scene your way, then gently suggested a new gesture and said, 'How about this?' In the final take, she urged you to combine both the versions and it always worked. Her simplicity was so touching. My favourite scenes in the film are the romantic ones between Shilpa and Salman. They were so refreshing, so subtle and sensitive.

Dhoom got you into a different league, which is your favourite scene in the film?

The bike chase, undoubtedly. It was so suave and, what's more, all of us enjoyed ourselves thoroughly.

Your character Jai is similar to the cop played by your dad in his old films. What was your brief from the director?

Before we started shooting *Dhoom*, the entire star cast was assembled before the producer, Aditya Chopra. Adi explained very clearly that *Dhoom* was not designed to win awards. It was meant to be a roller-coaster ride to entertainment and that's how it should be treated. Nobody understood this better than the director, Sanjay Gadhvi. Sanjay was so well tuned to the expectations of the producer that he did not once digress from his brief. Such restraint is hard to find in a new director.

Ram Gopal Varma offered you *Naach* at a time your career wasn't exactly flourishing.

I have no idea why he did that. I was shooting for *Yuva* in Chennai when late one night, Ram Gopal Varma phoned to say that he had watched just one scene in *Main Prem Ki Deewani Hoon* and decided to cast me in his next film. I didn't know what to say. One, because Ramu seldom makes the effort to watch another director's film, and two, because he was casting me in a romantic film. But that's Ramu. Nobody can understand what he does and why.

You played a struggler who becomes a star – Abhinav was quite a complex character.

I would say *Naach* is RGV's most personal film so far. The philosophy of the film is probably his philosophy of life. My only conflict with the film was the climax. I felt the character was far too internalized to express so much at one go. I felt that he should have been able to contain himself.

He is a contrast from the small-town boy Rakesh you projected in *Bunty Aur Babli?*

Oh yes, but contrary to the mood of the film, let me confess, it was a nerve-wracking experience to shoot for the first time with Dad.

It didn't seem so either in *Bunty Aur Babli* or *Sarkar*.

There is a reason for this. Because he is my dad, he helps me ride out my anxiety but that does not mean that the anxiety doesn't persist. He handles the double role, of a father and an actor, much better than I do. I'm awkward and unsure long after the shot is over. But I'm improving, gradually learning to relax. The experience was less traumatic during *Sarkar*. The underlying fact is that I cannot take Amitabh Bachchan for granted just because he is my father.

You are together at public functions, at home and now more and more on the sets. Doesn't the proximity sometimes get suffocating?

My mother says when I was a little boy I hovered around my dad when he returned from work. I looked forward to the occasions when I would just hang around on his sets and office. I may have shot up in height but the little boy hasn't changed. Even today, I'd rather spend my time with my dad than do anything else. When we are shooting together, we travel in the same car and eat lunch

together as well. It's never suffocating being with him because I don't want the space.

Watching you with Sanjay Dutt in *Dus*, one wonders if you miss having an elder brother.

I don't because Sanjay is like my big brother. Besides, I have an elder brother, Nikhil Nanda, my brother-in-law. When there is genuine affection between actors, the scenes always exude that extra energy.

Section 2

Character Speak

I studied a lot of military manuals, paramilitary books and isolated myself in the jungles … I was training and dieting, doing everything in my power to harness ferocity … I did everything possible to keep away from all distractions … including sex.

Adrien Brody, on his transformation into a muscleman for his role in *Predators*

Jaya Bachchan on *Hazaar Chaurasi Ki Maa*

Sujata fights within the confines of her home

Has the portrayal of women in cinema changed over the years?

It has come a long way from the way women were presented in the olden days. The present image is double-layered. In the first, the woman is still portrayed as getting a raw deal and, in the second, she is depicted as generating a lot of power. I would say that *Mrityudand* is a perfect example of the second, where Shabana Azmi and Madhuri Dixit rise above oppression.

Which bracket does *Hazaar Chaurasi Ki Maa* fall in, the former or the latter?

Sujata of *Hazaar Chaurasi Ki Maa,* despite appearing to be the conventional wife, is not one. She protests against her husband and

The interview was conducted before the release of *Hazaar Chaurasi Ki Maa* (1998). *Laga Chunri Mein Daag* (2007) and *Drona* (2008) were Jaya Bachchan's last releases.

children from within the confines of her home and that, according to me, is her strength. What we tend to forget is that most women don't have options and can only express themselves within the space provided to them.

It is interesting that the actress who made her debut in *Guddi* in 1973 returns as a mother in '97.

Isn't that natural? It has been twenty-five years since my debut and Guddi has grown up both on and off screen. In fact, I'm on my way to becoming a grandmother.

By choosing to return as a mother, haven't you limited your choices as an actor?

When I came into films, people said about me 'If she can, so can the others.' I took that as a backhanded compliment. I have always maintained that show business is not the prerogative of just the bold and the beautiful, ordinary people can have their say too. As a young girl I was attracted to the craft of acting and had the courage to follow my dream. I joined the Film and Television Institute but I had no clue what the future had in store for me. I never planned my career, it just happened. When I was in the family way I decided to quit and when I felt I was ready again, I came back. These are instinctive decisions.

Do you see yourself fitting into the regular commercial films?

Why not, as long as the role is well defined I'm open to all kinds of roles. The only kind I'm not attracted to is an all-positive or an all-negative one. It is important for me that the message and the motive of the film are noble.

Have you considered a sequel to *Abhimaan* with your husband?

The story focused on marital conflict and in the end the couple resolved their differences so what more can be left to say in a sequel? Also, the satellite channels have been showing the film so often that the magic has worn off completely.

All those years, when you were not active on screen, how did you exercise self-expression?

All artistes are accustomed to channelizing their energies into productive activities. Self-expression is imperative but it can be of a different kind. Just like M.F. Hussain paints horses, the goddess and also Madhuri Dixit, similarly, I have found an outlet in my home and children. Sometimes, I agree, a film I watched made me nostalgic but most of the time they didn't. Sometimes my husband would come home from work and describe his co-star's role as 'Jaya-Bhaduri type', adding 'I miss her presence'. That was enough to reassure the artiste in me.

How do you nourish the artiste in you away from the camera?

It happens naturally without one being aware of it. Films, books, conversations, everything makes a contribution. I travel a lot and therefore observe a lot. The artiste is unconsciously always storing information for future use. I may not use what I absorb immediately or in the exact form or situation, but the sentiments linger. How an artiste works is quite a complex and interesting process.

Can you give an instance?

Let me try. Yesterday, we shot a scene where the police ransacked my deceased son's room. Director Govind Nihalani had discussed the scene with me, but I was not sure how exactly I was going to perform it. When we began shooting I was more or less blank but as I walked into the room, I was overcome with sorrow and was full of despair. When the shot was over, Govind came to me and said that's exactly what he wanted and was curious to know what I was thinking when I shot the scene.

What were you thinking?

I was thinking about my deceased son, his daily routine and the time he must have spent in this room. I was reliving his presence by touching his belongings. I was angry and upset with all these strangers parading into his room and invading his space. As an actor I can portray a lot of emotions but how it is projected depends entirely on the director.

Are you a confident actor or do you ever have self-doubts?

By temperament I'm not an unsure person. I take swift decisions and don't dwell on matters for long. Therefore, even as an actress, I'm quick to react. There are times I disagree with the director and ask questions. My interpretation of the role does not have to match the director's interpretation a 100 per cent but if we can come close to ninety, the remaining 10 per cent can be compensated with technology.

Are you usually satisfied with the final cut of your films?

Every time I watch myself on screen I cringe because I know there is so much room for improvement. I wish I could do it all over again. I think this happens because actors find everything about themselves monotonous. As a rule I hate everything I have done and want to do it again. I think this happens because actors find everything about themselves predictable. Frankly, it is a torture to watch oneself on screen; in fact, it is the worst part about being an actress.

How would you describe the experience of working with Govind Nihalani?

Govind is very sensitive about not putting any pressure on his artistes and I value that greatly. As a director, he gives you a lot

of space but is always in the background in case you need him. He wants you to give your best and will push you to the optimum level. I would say he is a serious person and seldom smiles because he dislikes distractions. Nowadays though, he is changing, he has begun to smile and even laugh heartily on the sets.

Out of all your directors who do you think has brought out the best in you?

Isn't it obvious? Gulzar bhai and Hrishi-da.

Rekha on *Lajja*

Ram Dulari is doomed and she knows it

What attracted you to accepting the role in *Lajja*?

The fact that the director was completely convinced of the subject motivated me as an actress. Everyone knows that the film was inspired by a real-life incident but just how deeply Rajkumar Santoshi was affected by the tragedy was evident when we began shooting the film. I was happy to be a part of this experience.

How do you usually decide on your films?

It depends, if it is a director I have already worked with, like Rakesh Roshan, then I don't need much coaxing. In that sense, Raj Santoshi is a new name, because until I agreed to do *Lajja,* I had not seen any of his films, not even *Damini.* The last time I saw him he was assisting Govind Nihalani during my film *Vijeta* and I never heard him speak a single word throughout the shooting, so

The interview was conducted in 2001. *Sadiyaan* (2010) was Rekha's last release. *Krrish 3* is expected soon.

you can imagine how shocked I was to get a narration of this film from him.

And how was the narration?

Flawless. He explained he was depicting the five faces of Sita, which are in fact the five phases in a woman's life. He elaborated every character and it was all very enthralling. He had an unusual graph for the script, which is the journey of one woman but portrayed in four images – Vaidehi, Maithili, Janaki and Ram Dulari – all faces of Sita and all fascinating.

Were you given a choice in picking your role or was it always Ram Dulari?

To be honest, I was more drawn to playing Janaki, essayed by Madhuri Dixit, but the director felt that I should play Ram Dulari because I was most appropriate to represent the opening outcry '*Amma humko bachai le, ye dushman humka phuk de...*', his inspiration and reason for making the film. That was the director's projection of me. I wasn't completely convinced but I consoled myself that while I had done shades of Janaki in my earlier films, this was a new expression and a new challenge for me as an actress.

When does the process of acting begin for you, when you listen to the story or when you begin shooting?

I have not studied acting and I have not done theatre, so there is no definite method for me. When I was new I was indifferent to my work and didn't give a damn whether I got the scene right or wrong. Later, as I evolved I didn't want to understand the method because it takes away the magic. Acting is more of a spontaneous reaction. Eventually, of course, the moment of truth for all actors is when the director calls 'Start camera'. What happens prior to this happens at a subconscious level. It could be something I have watched from my car window and stored in my memory bank for years. It's different each time.

And what is your frame of mind as the shooting date approaches?

I become anxious. A week before we were to commence the shooting of *Lajja* I asked the director to describe his vision of Ram Dulari. He said 'I know my vision. I'm keen to know what's going on in your head.'

And what was going on in your head?

I was extremely nervous because even though I had played a gaon ki gori in numerous films earlier, she was never the authentic rural woman. I had never spoken Avadhi in its purest form and was terrified of not getting it right, but Rajji is excellent with research and that is what put me at ease.

You did a test shoot before the filming, were there disputes on the look of the character?

Not disputes, but healthy discussions. I was carrying both bright and dull-coloured saris. He discarded all the brighter shades and settled for the dull ones. I had plastered my hair with oil to give it a rustic look but he made me shampoo my hair and said '*Hawa chal rahi hai na,* so let your hair fly.' The photo shoot was a good decision because it put both of us at ease and I felt confident to surrender to him as an actor.

Do you usually surrender so easily?

I'm obedient. It is a result of not going through any kind of formal education and therefore, for me, the film-maker is the teacher and the studio, my school. There are some actors who become unsettled when a director enacts a scene for them. I don't mind it, I distill his projection and absorb what is to my advantage.

Why do most actors describe the first day of a new film traumatic?

An actor, who is about to get under the skin of a new character, is like a bride adopting a new family after an arranged marriage. You are under a microscope, judged by everyone on the sets. It can be very unnerving! And for some sadistic reason, the director always picks the most crucial scene for the first day. Directors do this deliberately, to go full steam into the film. Or perhaps it is their way of ensuring that the actor does not get complacent.

What were you thinking when you did the highly dramatic browbeating scene?

I was thinking about the complete helplessness of the character. Ram Dulari is doomed, and she knows it. Only a thoroughly dejected person would beat her brow the way she has. It's a very disturbing moment in the film.

Do scenes like these affect the performer?

Personally, it does not affect me any longer because after so many years, one is able to switch on and off. However, the yelling and the shrieking is a matter of concern because it is a nightmare to reproduce the same effect during the dubbing. The climax shot in the film was also my last shot. We had been shooting all night and had to complete the scene before sunrise! This was not how it was in the script. Rajji changed his mind at the last minute and shot the scene with the available light. He is an easy director and lets his actors emote without giving too many instructions.

Was shooting the rape scene traumatic?

It's too private for me to elaborate on it, but I will say this much, just knowing that someone is lusting after you is humiliating. Men will never be able to understand the feeling because they've never been raped! They suffer a minor loss in business and fantasize jumping out of their window while women go through so much and continue with life.

Would you say *Lajja* has altered your way of thinking?

It is the first time I wanted to lend my voice to a cause. It's the first time I understood how activists feel. *Lajja* has made me aware of just how important it is to bond with my own gender. The film is as significant for men as it is for women. Men should watch *Lajja* to understand their women and women should watch the film to celebrate womanhood.

From a don in *Khiladiyon Ka Khiladi* to a princess in *Zubeidaa* to a midwife in *Lajja,* what next?

Anything... I'm ready for any role of any length and character. I'm even willing to play a man, change my walk and voice, provided the director is confident to take the risk.

Ajay Devgn on *Company* & *The Legend of Bhagat Singh*

Mallik terrorizes, Bhagat Singh inspires

What made Ram Gopal Varma offer you *Company*?

Originally, I wasn't supposed to do the film. Ramuji approached me to narrate an entirely different subject. He said he would start shooting with me eight months later, after he had finished his current project. Then, as is Ramuji's habit, he began narrating the story idea of *Company* to me. The next day, he phoned to say he saw flashes of Mallik in me and would like me to play the lead. Earlier, he had planned to take a new face but changed his mind later.

So how do you work on a character like Mallik because you have never interacted with the underworld?

One doesn't have to because whatever information I required to know about the character was provided to me by Ramuji's research

> The interview was conducted in 2002. *Himmatwala* (2013) was Ajay Devgn's last release.

team. Also, it was not as if we were rigidly following Dawood or Chhota Rajan. The joy of working with a director like Ramuji is that if you concentrate on his first narration, you almost get it right. This is remarkable considering Ramuji never works with a bound script. He came to meet me for ten minutes but stayed on for three hours. It was an exhaustive narration complete with shot divisions. I have merely followed his instructions and therefore the credit for my performance goes to the director.

But the projection comes from the actor and you must have a method of preparing for a role?

This may sound strange but the only way I can prepare for a role is to switch off. I have to be completely blank and absorb the character like a sponge. It is a silent process for me. If the director is competent, he can trust me to give a competent performance. If not, I have to rely on my instinct.

All actors talk about instinct but very few are able to articulate the process of emoting.

I agree there is a definite process and a rhythm to it, but it is all very abstract and differs from performer to performer. I'm always anxious for the first few shots. Then, as the scenes progress, I unconsciously hit the right chord. The trick is to recognize the signal.

And what was that 'signal' moment in *Company*?

I was lucky because we began shooting with my introductory scene with Vivek Oberoi where I ask him '*Kitna lega*?' That's my first meeting with the young boy and I knew I had to convey my superiority through my body language. Ramuji was very clear that Mallik's character would not get aggressive under any provocation.

He made me understand that it was a character that talked less and listened more. A man who read faces and made decisions about them. I internalized that. Everything Ramuji said is reflected in my performance, particularly the scene where Antara Mali pleads with me for Vivek's life.

How confident are you as an artiste? Do you need constant reassurance from your director?

I'm confident about myself but I can give my best only when the rest of the cast performs to the level of the director's expectations. It's when the collective effort is superior that the film becomes memorable. Reassurances from the director or the cinematographer always help but I wouldn't feel insecure if the director didn't pat my back after a good shot. Once he has explained the character graph to me, I wouldn't want to demand more from him. Sometimes too much discussion creates confusion and a little distance is necessary to reflect and garner your creativity.

How would you describe Ram Gopal Varma as a director?

He is very flexible and does not believe that the written word is law. He is open to suggestions, to constructive inputs from anyone in the unit. Our equation is completely devoid of ego. When in disagreement, either he convinces me or I convince him.

And your equation with Rajkumar Santoshi during the shooting of *The Legend of Bhagat Singh*?

Again, I wasn't Santoshi's first choice for the role. During the shooting of *Lajja* Santoshi told me he was writing the script for *Bhagat Singh,* which he planned to make with a newcomer. Santoshi was very happy with my weight loss and said if he did not find a suitable newcomer, he would cast me in the role. A few months later, when I lost some more weight and Rajji had not found his newcomer, he cast me. Once I said yes I was bombarded with research material from his office. Their homework was perfect and I was charged up just by observing their level of preparation.

Bhagat Singh was your first historical portrayal, were you nervous?

I was nervous in the sense that there was a lurking fear of doing injustice to a leader whom history had already wronged. Bhagat Singh was an extraordinary character and this is apparent in the small and big things he accomplished in his life. He fasted for eighty-three days and inspired his cell mates to do the same. When we had to shoot the starvation sequence, my colleagues had not eaten for three days to get into the mood. As a result, on the day of the shoot, they were literally breaking down. It was a very emotional moment!

What about you?

I didn't even attempt to starve because I'm not a method actor. I believe I don't have to feel hungry to portray hunger but I was conscious of what my co-actors were going through. It's when you play a hero like Bhagat Singh that you realize how inadequate you really are, you realize you have not accomplished even a fraction of what they strived for. It was a very humbling experience.

Does playing a noble character transform an actor as a person?

How much of these noble thoughts one can put into practice I don't know, but I definitely started thinking differently. It made me realize that Bhagat Singh's saga has got more to do with humanity than patriotism. History was unable to value him as a human being.

It is unfortunate that corruption has become a way of life today. The violence and the restlessness in our society is proof of that.

Who is to be blamed for this loss of idealism?

All of us, I guess. All of us have become impotent in the face of the rising social injustices around us. Whenever something goes wrong, we say, 'What can I do?' And nobody does anything. The frustration persists.

Frustration provokes revolution too.

That can be relevant for larger issues but not on a personal level. As an actor I cannot give my best if I'm not at peace with myself. I would do anything to diffuse pressure and strive for calm.

Were there any self-doubts before saying yes to a negative role?

The role was fascinating. I had never been offered an evil character before and I just could not say no. The interesting bit was that after I said 'yes', no hero was willing to do the positive role. Four leading men were signed on, but backed out of the project after saying yes. Ultimately Akshaye Khanna said 'yes' and he was perfect for the part.

It was a complex role that needed tightrope-walking as an actor. Did you at any time fear losing the character?

Not the character, but I was unsure whether I would be able to sustain my stammering or not. On consulting a speech therapist I was told that when a patient with a speech disability is stuck at a word, he or she will automatically alter it and move on. That's what I did with my character as well.

Did you feel the need to consult a psychiatrist to portray the role more realistically?

I did meet a psychiatrist, not during the film but after, and that too by accident. I shared my portrayal of a split personality with him and he agreed with my projection.

You sometimes give the impression of being too complacent, are you?

There are two theories to this. I appear complacent because I'm not displaying my restlessness or ambition. The other, more important, reason is that when I'm in front of the camera I never cheat. So if I'm able to convey my sincerity without getting bogged down by it nobody should complain.

How did your fans react to your negative portrayal?

You will be shocked but people empathized with my character. This is a common problem when a star plays a negative role. When I beat up the girl, the audience got up and cheered. It's very disturbing to discover that we are living in a warped society!

Kirron Kher on *Khamosh Pani*

Ayesha heals her scars and finds happiness

How did you come in contact with film-maker Sabiha Sumar?

This is strange but one afternoon I was lounging at home when I got a phone call from a stranger, she said she was a documentary film-maker and was planning her first feature film in Pakistan. She briefly explained the story of a Sikh woman who gets left behind in Lahore during Partition. She asked me if I'd be interested and I instantly said 'yes'.

Are you usually that easy to persuade?

On the contrary, unless I'm totally convinced of the subject or familiar with the director's body of work, I take a very long time to say 'yes'. But there was something I liked instantly about Sabiha.

The interview was conducted in 2003 before the release of *Khamosh Pani*. *Ajab Gajabb Love* (2012) was Kirron Kher's last release. She was also seen as a judge on a reality show, *India's Got Talent*, on TV.

She was focused, sincere and it was the manner in which she presented the idea that made me say 'yes'.

So when did the two of you meet?

Only after a couple of weeks – she informed me she was visiting Delhi and asked if I could meet her there. She requested me to stay with her rather than in a hotel so that we could have more time to discuss the film. When I reached her house, the first thing she did was to hand over the script to me. 'We will speak after two hours of your having read it,' she said. After two hours, I understood why Sabiha had chosen me for the part. I was the right age and from the right region to play the character. Sabiha later told me that she saw a lot of her mother in the role.

The film is inspired from a real story.

Yes, but I'm certain it's not the story of just one woman, but many like her. It is a reflection of that era. Of the turbulent times both the countries cannot forget.

What attracts you most about the character?

Her spirit, which survived under all circumstances; her strength in denying death and taking a chance with life; her wisdom in absorbing sorrow and, most important, cherishing her memories without pain. There is a scene in the film where Shabnam, Ayesha's friend asks her if she misses her husband and Ayesha, almost philosophically, responds that time heals all scars. This is not entirely true and yet Ayesha finds happiness in life. I appreciate that.

Was it difficult to portray Ayesha's angst?

I hope I'm not sounding pompous when I say a role like this could not be performed, it had to be lived. Here I would give full credit to my director and writer for providing me with the fodder. It is a very well-researched script and because Sabiha is essentially a documentary film-maker, her eye for detail in ambience and content is remarkable.

Were you worried about the political pressures because the relationship between the two countries has always been strained?

Yes, our army was on the border fighting at Kargil and it's a mystery how Sabiha got me the visa. It was complicated to land directly in Pakistan so all of us had to arrive via Dubai. The entire crew was under an oath not to disclose that we were shooting for the film. Anupam, as my husband, had the right to know and was extremely supportive. He has always maintained that if you believe in a cause, you must lend your voice. I deliberately did not inform my son Sikander till the day of my departure. He was devastated at the thought of my being in Pakistan. I was nervous too but something inside me just pulled me along.

Was this your first trip to Pakistan?

Yes, I had always wanted to go to Pakistan and could never make it. As children, my sister and I played badminton at the national level and she represented India in a tournament to Pakistan where I was not selected. This remained a big regret for me. My mother often spoke about her childhood friend Suraiya, who stayed back in Lahore after Partition. So, in a way, Suraiya aunty was my only anchor in a foreign country.

Were you subject to any hostility during your stay and did the shoot involve emotional adjustments?

I wasn't an outsider within the film crew. We worked like one big family, shot for twelve hours at a stretch and at the end of the day, sang Hindi film songs. All the younger actors were from theatre and therefore very competent and spirited. Everyone understood that I needed to be protected. I think the persecution between the two countries is more imaginary than real. Whether it was the police department or the doctor treating me for a torn ligament in my ankle, their curiosity about India and Hindi films in particular is insatiable. When I went shopping, nobody would take money from me because I was a guest in their country and yet there was so much friction on the border. The contradictions were very confusing and disturbing.

Is it true that the film was originally to be made with a Pakistani actress?

Technically, yes. Sabiha's husband is a Sri Lankan and had put together a French, German and British collaboration. They had signed a Pakistani actress and even shot for a few days. Then 9/11 happened, followed by Afghanistan and the crew fell apart. The film was shelved temporarily. As circumstances improved, Sabiha made some forays again and contacted me. We began shooting the film but there was still no money for post-production. But Sabiha went along, confident that money would come when the time was right, and it did.

Did you expect the film to fetch you international accolades?

I was satisfied with the film and my performance but I didn't expect the reactions to be so overwhelming. The Locarno Film Festival was particularly moving because the festival director joined me for dinner the previous evening and opened a bottle of champagne in my honour. I didn't see this as an unusual gesture until I was told that it was a tradition to announce the winners a day before the closing. It was a special moment to share the platform with Holly Hunter. By the time the Cape Town and Karachi Film awards came, my cup was full to the brim.

When you see the film today do you notice any mistakes?

Yes, I regret the director cutting out a scene involving my friend Shabnam and her husband because it has a link to the story. In my performance I regret two scenes. One, where I sign the money order in the post office and push the pen back to him – this is an urban gesture. My character would have left the pen where it was. Two, I disapprove of the way my duplicate stands with her feet apart before her final exit in the climax. If I wasn't injured, I would have shot the scene myself – with my feet together.

Do you agree with the morbid end?

Those were tragic times. The film is essentially about the choices Ayesha makes in life. As a child she refuses to obey her father because she loves life. Later, she chooses to marry her abductor and when he is no more, makes a living out of teaching the Quran the Sufi way. It is only in the end, when she learns that she has lost her son and her best friend that she musters up courage to make a dignified exit.

The film imparts a bigger message.

Khamosh Pani is about the sub-continent – India and Pakistan, the rural and the urban, where men make a majority of the choices for women. It's because the right people don't voice their concerns that we are forced to deal with fundamentalists. Our ancient society was more emancipated than the present one. Previously women did not cover their heads; there were no veils, men and women mingled freely. It was only later, post 1978-79, when under the guise of religion, we exploited and abused tradition and gender.

Do you anticipate the film getting released commercially?

If it were a Pakistani production it would have been impossible but since it is a French, German and British collaboration it is marketed in a special slot. The message of the film is more important than its nationality. Cinema does not belong to any one region. It belongs to the world. After doing *Khamosh Pani* I'm very clear that I will not play second-fiddle roles. My presence must lend a voice to a cause, if not, I have the luxury of refusing offers because my husband runs the kitchen. I'm not under any compulsions to work.

In which case, how do you explain a film like *Devdas*?

My character makes a difference to the script no matter how small the part. Sanjay Leela Bhansali is a vibrant film-maker and I enjoyed being a part of the lavishness. I enjoyed dressing up and dancing. I have come full circle from where I started on stage.

Do you miss doing theatre?

I'm still performing *Saalgirah* with Anupam Kher and accompanying my husband on his tour for *Kuch Bhi Ho Sakta Hai*. When I was young I thought I could never do theatre because it called for too much hardwork. Yet when the time came, I became obsessed with it. Theatre provides immediate responses which is very thrilling and also very scary because there are chances that you will slip up. Films, on the other hand, are fragmented, but for posterity. Right now, I feel passionately about both and want to do everything.

Amitabh Bachchan on *Dev* & *Black*

Dev Pratap Singh is intense, Debraj is daunting

Govind Nihalani has said that both of you had been trying to work with each other for the last twenty years.

That's true, ever since *Ardha Satya.* Sometimes an actor gets restricted because of the expectations from the box-office. He appears to have great power but the fact is that his position prevents him from taking risks, because his decisions inadvertently affect his other projects. Perhaps that's what happened with me, but finally I'm at a phase where I can afford to take risks; I can do different kinds of roles without being bogged down by the pressures of an image or how the film will fare commercially. We intended to work together a long time ago but I guess these things happen when they have to, and better late than never ...

> The interview was conducted in 2004. Amitabh Bachchan was last seen in *Kaun Banega Crorepati* on TV and in a cameo in *The Great Gatsby* (2013). *Satyagraha* is expected soon.

Do you regret that it didn't happen earlier?

I don't know, one can never predict such things. There is a possibility that had we done a film at that time, it would have been a different kind of film. An actor always wonders about projects he could have done and didn't since he was guided by commercial constraints. But these are delicate decisions dictated by destiny. An ideal situation would be where one can combine the art house with the mainstream but it's not that easy.

What attracts you to Govind Nihalani as a film-maker? Are you familiar with his body of work?

Yes, I have seen most of his films and *Ardha Satya* in particular remains my favourite. He is a great technician and has a penchant for hard-hitting subjects. All his films have been about social consciousness. He takes up burning issues, which is very inspiring for me as an actor.

You have said you are keen to work with all art-house directors.

Yes, I maintain that. I am privileged to be associated with meaningful cinema. Today, I'm fortunate to be working with a rare mix of young and senior directors belonging to all genres of cinema like Farhan Akhtar, Vikram Bhatt and Sujay Bose, as well as Ravi Chopra, Ramesh Sippy and Govind Nihalani. The seniors bring experience and the youngsters are all extremely goal-driven.

They all seem overawed by you and mention you in superlatives.

I don't know why they do that... I would rather they treat me normally. A lot of them do, it's only in print that they talk about me in superlatives.

After so many portrayals as a police inspector, what makes *Dev* different?

The fact that I'm playing a sixty-two-year-old cop and that I'm being directed by Govind Nihalani are the main differences. The film gives a lot of emphasis to details – the dialogues, the costumes, the sets and the information that is imparted. It is evident that the writer has first-hand information regarding the police system and the fact that we had a police officer present on our set at all times to guide us was a big boon. It was the same with *Khakee.* The cop on duty made sure that there were no mistakes in our projection. It is very reassuring for an actor when the director takes all these precautions. The entire unit had done their research well and that facilitated my performance.

How would you compare the cop in *Dev* to that in *Khakee*?

Govindji used a very appropriate word to describe the two films. He said while *Khakee* was an explosion, *Dev* is an implosion. Anant Srivastav of *Khakee* was a loser. Dev Pratap Singh is certainly not a loser. He's an achiever and, even under adverse circumstances, takes a stand. They have the same concerns but their way of fighting the system is completely different.

Anant Srivastav was a loser; how would you describe Dev Pratap Singh?

Dev is certainly not a loser. He is intense and searching. You can say he is idealistic but understands that he has to draw a line somewhere. He accepts there are flaws within the system but he has to abide by them because that is the constitution.

After crusading against social evils for three decades in your films where do you draw inspiration for a new character?

The inspiration comes from the film itself. New stories and new characters provide the fodder. As opposed to my regular formula films which look for escapism, serious cinema strives for realism. Under the given circumstances, I cannot play my usual larger-than-life hero but a protagonist who combines both weak and strong moments. The motivation comes from the convictions of the character.

And how does an actor transform into the character?

By learning his lines provided in the script, by staying connected to the sequence of events in the film, by remembering the previous and the following scene and, finally, by staying alert to the continuity of the character.

You make it sound very simple.

It is simple if you stay focused, and difficult if you are distracted. Acting is all about concentration.

And when the film ends, is there a specific process of disconnecting with the character?

I have never carried my characters home but I guess creative artistes need their private space to unwind. It may be a different process for different actors. I need my moments of quietude to walk away and slip into a new character again.

Do some characters leave a hangover; do they affect your real life?

I don't become a smuggler because I play one and I certainly cannot become a police officer without the qualifications but, yes, one does reflect over their qualities, be it a forthcoming film or one that has already been released. I may have played a cop in various films but I still find something intriguing about Dev Pratap Singh. It could be his perseverance or his sense of uprightness but the character lingers in my thoughts.

Govind Nihalani has said that Amitabh Bachchan is not starring in *Dev* but he is Dev. Do you feel the same way?

That's very flattering for me and I hope I have been able to live up to his expectations. I hope there has been no digression from his original concept. When a character is as close to the director's heart as Dev is to Govindji it becomes a huge responsibility for the actor.

This is the first time you are working with Om Puri. How important is coordination between co-stars?

Without a good co-star you can never aspire to give your best no matter how brilliant the script. The slightest disinterest or distraction on his part can ruin your scene. It is very important for co-stars to be on the same wavelength. In fact, it is the dream of every artiste to work with an actor who understands as much about the medium as he does. Only then can there be a healthy relationship of give and take. Fortunately, Om Puri and I struck the right balance from the very first day and if my performance is appreciated, part of the credit should be attributed to Om Puri.

The two of you are friends-cum-colleagues?

Yes, but there comes a time when there is conflict in the relationship. They have to choose between loyalty and ideology. They have different perspectives and it is disturbing to see how they come to terms with it. A lot of the scenes in the film are very

hard-hitting and therefore very disturbing, both as an actor and as a citizen of the country.

Which was your most difficult scene?

It comes towards the end of the film where I'm with my wife and introspecting over the event. She is beside me but it seems more like I'm talking to myself. It's an outpouring of a quiet kind. It was a very complex and long scene. I requested the director to take it in one shot because it's difficult to sustain that kind of intensity. When we finished the scene, I was completely drained.

Actors describe Govind Nihalani as a very demanding director, do you agree?

He may be demanding but what he offers in return to his artistes is much more than what he takes away from them.

In the olden days, you worked with Hrishikesh Mukherjee who was a director-cum-editor. Then, Rajkumar Santoshi who is a writer-cum-director and now Govind Nihalani, who is cinematographer-cum-director. What are the advantages or disadvantages of working with directors who have dual responsibilities?

I cannot think of any disadvantages because when the captain of the ship is multifaceted it can only be an asset. Besides, Govindji isn't just the cinematographer/producer/director of the film; he is also the date manager, the costume designer, the spot boy, the crowd controller and even the counsellor on the sets. He goes over the lines with the actor and even paints blood on my face when he isn't happy with what the make-up man has done. That's his level of involvement. He is a man of all seasons.

You have moved from the young hero to middle-aged and now senior citizen's roles.

At my age I'm fortunate to be getting as many roles as I do. The transition has by no means been easy. As a character artiste, you don't get the adulation you did as the hero. On screen, younger actors overpower you because the screenplay provides them with better footage. In public gatherings, there is a bigger uproar for the upcoming hero but these are changes one has to accept gracefully. It has happened to superstars before me and it will happen to others after me. There is no guarantee that the highs or the lows will not return. One has to have the fortitude to face them. One has to learn to be content and move on. The advantage of the current phase I am in is that I'm no longer watched by the hawk-eyed box-office like I used to be earlier and that is very liberating, both as an actor and as a human being.

What about *Black*?

Sanjay Leela Bhansali called me and said he had a subject for me. I was shooting in Nasik at the time so he came over to the location. He was dressed in a crisply ironed kurta which reflected his character in a way. He said his narration would take about three and a half hours and that I'd have to be patient. We met in the evening after pack-up. Sanjay arrived in my room carrying a beautifully bound script with golden lettering. These small details are indicative of how passionately a director feels for his craft.

And what was your impression after the narration?

Well… we didn't get there. Sanjay began narrating the story to me but stopped halfway because he felt he was not doing a good job of it. He apologized, said he was not a good story-teller and suggested that I read the script on my own. I did and I was overwhelmed. It was an extraordinary script. I can safely say there is not a single scene in the film that I have projected as an actor earlier. The role was an opportunity for me to explore areas within myself that I didn't know existed. I was very excited and also extremely frightened. I didn't want to fall short of my director's expectations. I knew it wasn't going to be easy and was prepared for the challenge.

Does method acting help in situations like these?

All the trained actors might not like this but I don't believe in method acting. It has been my experience that whenever one tries too hard, one destroys a spontaneous expression. The magic is in not knowing. Somehow, the idea of mulling over a scene has never worked to my advantage. I'm not denying that it happens subconsciously without my being aware of it but when I'm performing, it has to be an emotional response. I have to feel the moment and express it.

And what is the process for that?

Well, there were many stages and phases in the preparation, some conscious and some unconscious, some mental and some physical. There were certain issues I needed to work out in isolation and some that needed to be discussed with my director because I had to understand his perspective. Sanjay introduced me to the school for the blind and sent a tutor home to teach me sign language. It was an arduous process to become familiar with the signs but it was well worth it. The real preparation for any role, of course, begins when you start shooting. The first day on the sets of a new film is always traumatic! Slowly you become acquainted with the ambience and your character but even then every shot is an acid test. An actor may do his best but what finally unfolds before the camera is a mystery nobody has been able to unravel.

How important is the chemistry between co-stars?

It is very important and the magic has always reflected on the screen. Rani is a tremendously gifted and spontaneous artiste. This is our second film together after a few scenes in *Kabhi Khushi Kabhie Gham*. The chemistry between the director and his team is equally important and when you watch *Black*, you will notice how well connected the captain is with his entire team. Sanjay is an exceptionally sensitive and intense director completely obsessed with his art. He is a man driven by passion.

So would you say you are completely satisfied with your performance in the film?

An actor is never satisfied and always wants reassurances from his director. Only the director is the right judge of his performance, because only he sees the complete picture. However, it's important for me to also enjoy the experience, and working on *Black* was very special. It matters to me how I'm given my call sheet, how they present my make up room and Sanjay gave personal attention to all this. It was a privilege to be directed by someone as gifted as him, a privilege to watch his commitment and obsession for details, his pursuit of perfection. All his films are labours of love!

And what did you learn from your character?

That touch is the most important gesture of human expression. It transforms relationships.

Tabu on *The Namesake*

Ashima Ganguly has the will to survive under all circumstances

What was your reaction when Mira Nair offered you *The Namesake*?

Mira and I had been meeting from time to time and bouncing off ideas, but nothing concrete came out of them. We came close to finalizing a subject but even that didn't work out. Then, one day, while I was shooting in Hyderabad, Mira, who was all set to roll *The Namesake* with another actress, telephoned to say that the casting had fallen out and asked if I would play the main part? She wanted to know if I had free dates. I did but before I said 'yes' some basic formalities had to be worked out between us.

It did not bother you that you were not her first choice?

No... because these things are not as simplistic as we make

The interview was conducted in 2007. Ang Lee's *Life of Pii* (2012) and *David* (2013) were Tabu's last releases.

them out to be. There is a larger perspective, a bigger message to the moment. Also, nobody was forcing me to say 'yes'. If it had bothered me, I would not have agreed. These issues are trivial as destiny plays a part as well. The role was meant for me and probably that is why the last-minute changes. I had read the book and loved the character of Ashima Ganguly. I feel Ashima was seeking me as an actor as much as I was seeking her as a character.

That's an interesting perspective.

I like Ashima's honesty, her complexity and her will to survive under all circumstances. The story is ordinary but what makes it spectacular is the manner in which the characters unfold. Based on Jhumpa Lahiri's novel by the same name and screenplay by Sooni Taraporewala, it talks about an immigrant couple trying to make a home in New York City. Despite their best efforts they are at all times dreaming about Kolkata. This is true of so many people. My own aunts living abroad are perpetually dreaming about Hyderabad and Mumbai.

Did you require to do any homework for your character?

Not particularly, because I'm familiar with the Bengali culture. All my friends are Bengalis and live in Kolkata. I didn't have to worry about my appearance because I knew that Mira would have worked out the details. I didn't want to over-prepare and lose my spontaneity. Mira made the entire team undergo a two-week workshop before we began shooting. It was her idea that we first shoot in Kolkata on Howrah Bridge, later in Agra at the Taj Mahal and, finally, in New York. This was my first experience of shooting with an all-international unit on a foreign location and the first time that I travelled to an outdoor location without my entourage: the make-up man, the spot-boy and the hairdresser. I was, in the truest sense, baggage-free!

Did you enjoy the experience?

I did but there were times I missed being pampered and felt terribly homesick. Particularly on days when it was very cold and I longed to eat hot Indian food. At the same time I liked having my private space and utilized it productively reading books or listening to music. I had made friends with the unit and often hung out with them. The hotel where we were put up was in the heart of Manhattan so it was very easy to just stroll into a theatre, restaurant or a Broadway show whenever we felt like it.

And how was the atmosphere on the sets? Is Mira Nair a demanding director?

I have known Mira for a long time now but she is always surprising me. She is highly energetic, goal-oriented and has fascinating observations about human beings and life. Her personality is evident in her interactions with her actors and technicians. She is not hard on them at all and believes in making shooting an enjoyable experience. On the sets, she would deliberately underplay dramatic scenes so that her actors didn't get worked up. I nicknamed her 'David Dhawan of USA' because her motto is to be happy all the time.

That's a revelation.

Exactly, it is so easy for someone in her position to get carried away but Mira is so grounded. It is because she values people as human beings. She has the rare ability to make everyone around her feel special and is highly appreciative of the slightest good work that you deliver. It's the first sign of a competent director and so reassuring for the actor.

Do you feel frustrated while working with incompetent directors?

Thankfully, I have reached a stage where I don't need to work with directors I don't get inspiration from, but, yes, I think all good actors are frustrated when they have to work with incompetent directors. The inspiration always comes from the director and the team is always taking the cue from him. The day we had our movie premiere was America's coldest day and we were worried about attendance. But we had a full house. Mira is a great organizer and does everything with a touch of class. The premiere was a memorable event for me as an actor.

Had you not done the film would you have regretted it?

I cannot view it so dramatically. I'm grateful that I had free dates and was not committed elsewhere when Mira got in touch with me. A role belongs to the actor who plays it. It was the right film at the right time in my life. I was looking for emotional space and shooting far away helped me connect with myself. This was the first time I stayed back on location after completing the shoot. It was the first time that I travelled without an escort, lived in a service apartment and commuted by tube. It was a liberating experience.

Weren't you scared of interacting with complete strangers?

No, why should I be? They were aware that I am an actress in India but since they didn't watch Hindi films they didn't understand the enormity of it. This made me feel comfortable. I discovered that there's more to life than just Mumbai and films. I realized that the only way to enjoy life is to drop your guard. I needed that after a demanding performance like *The Namesake*.

Section 3

Director's Cut

I was only twenty-nine when *The Sixth Sense* released. The film earned $660 million worldwide and I was propelled to the category of an A-list Hollywood director. Then, I don't know why but I stopped getting it right. In fact, the fact that my name was on a film spelt doom! I took into account the advice of all my peers and consciously worked at stories I felt ecstatic about.

M. Night Shyamalan, film director

Shekhar Kapur

If a film can raise concern, the effort has been worth it

You appear disillusioned with all the controversies related to *Bandit Queen*.

(*Sighs*) Yes, but this feeling of being weighed down was expected. It is a time when all possibilities get exhausted. It is like you have been through the grind and you start asking yourself if it was worth getting into it in the first place…

Was it?

(*Thinks*) I guess it was despite the gloom and the despair; it was worth it because the overall feedback to the film, to the victim, has been positive. A family friend – a poet – phoned me to say his son has been in a state of shock ever since he saw the film. He has been badgering his father about the injustice inflicted on the

The interview was conducted in 1994 before the release of *The Bandit Queen*. *New York, I Love You* (2008) and *Passage* (2009) were Shekhar Kapur's last releases as a director.

lower castes. If the film can make you question and show concern, then the effort has been worth it. The elders react with compassion but also resignation, a certain helplessness that comes from not being able to initiate change, but if the younger generation feels motivated I think there is hope.

Will the recent injunction on the film destroy its chances of an entry for the Oscar Awards?

No ... no ... There is no such danger. The print has been delivered to the Oscar Awards' committee and it must already be under consideration. The judgement is not enforceable in London.

The subject of the film, Phoolan Devi, complained that she had not yet seen the film. Is this true?

We invited her to watch the film at the Cannes Film Festival but she refused. Now my producer refuses to let her see it unless she withdraws the case. She is justified in wanting to watch the film pre release, but as the director I cannot overrule the producer's decision. Quite frankly I'm tired of these never-ending accusations. I'm bored with Phoolan Devi, with Bandit Queen, with the concerned lawyer, with everything! Can you imagine a film gets honoured in twenty-three countries, it features in *Time* magazine's list of the ten best movies, but in your own country they don't value its worth? If the festival authorities wanted, they could have fought for the film. They didn't and that is what is so depressing.

You sound bitter.

I'm plain exhausted. I'm exasperated with my subject and her family forever changing their statements. I'm tired of Phoolan Devi's husband's changing perceptions; tired of the claims to justice and law, of rhetoric, of lies, of praise; and mostly of people taking positions and stands.

That's unfair, are you not taking a stand by protesting against censor cuts to your film?

My stand has been straight and it hasn't changed in all these weeks. The film is a work of truth, of art. All I'm asking is to release the film as I have made it, or forget about it. The Censor Board made concessions for *Schindlers List* with their explanation that it had relevance. My argument is that *Bandit Queen* has relevance too.

The Censor Board follows guidelines.

A guideline of turning women into a symbol of the middle-class virtue of modesty, ha! Does Phoolan fall into this slot? Is her life, the story of an ordinary woman? Why should guilt be imposed by force? Why is everyone thrusting shame upon her? What is wrong with anger? That is an emotional expression as well.

Phoolan Devi is entitled to react the way she wants, surely you cannot control that?

I don't believe that is how she feels. It is the people around her who are provoking her. The middle-class intelligentsia is imposing their morality on Phoolan, which is ridiculous. Her protest is so out of character. She has become a weak woman from being a strong one, by denying her past.

People change, she was a dacoit but is a domesticated wife today.

(*Smiles*) Okay, but the woman who has been domesticated is not the woman I have made a film on. My heroine is the one who was subjected to violence and is oppressed. The new Phoolan is no longer oppressed. The woman who went to jail was a proud woman but today there is a loss of pride. I'll tell you what, the bottom line is very simple, everyone is looking for their little place in the sun, be it Phoolan's lawyers, the politicians, the biographer's and perhaps even me!

So what has the experience taught you?

I learnt a lesson I already knew. Every time there is a revolution, they shoot the intelligentsia first. People don't like being told the truth. Pirated copies of the film are already in the market and are being sold for two hundred rupees. If the film is not going to be released, one might as well see it on the cable, so what if it is a pirated copy?

Hrishikesh Mukherjee

Lean on me and I will sail you through this

Are you disappointed that *Jhooth Bole Kauwa Kaate* didn't fare well at the box-office?

I give every film my best shot and work extremely hard; I do everything within my ability to nourish the subject, but coming from where I do, it is not my job to monitor the release and other trade-related formalities. I'm told other directors do it and that is the norm today. I come from a different school where there is a clear demarcation of duties. The director concentrates on the creative processes and the producer on the marketing. My equation is with the audience, on whether I'm able to communicate and engage them with my story-telling.

The interview was conducted before the release of *Jhooth Bole Kauwa Kaate* (1998), which was Mukherjee's last release. He died on 27 August 2006.

Ten years is a long time to stay away from the camera; what are the changes you see in your craft and in the system?

It has been a long break from the big screen, but it wasn't as if I was disconnected with the medium. I made a tele-serial *Hum Hindustani* comprising eighty-four episodes, which amounts to ten films. I always wanted to make short films but never got down to doing it. The serial fulfilled my desire of shooting the body of work of distinguished writers. I thoroughly enjoyed my experience on television because when you shoot episodically there is no question of a compromise. No producer can push you to add songs in a sequence; you don't have to create a situation for a dance or a fight sequence. Television projects life as it is.

What about cinema ? Do you feel out of place with the new trends and technology?

This is a question you ought to be asking the actors, not me. They are the ones who have to make new adjustments. We technicians are always behind the camera. The changes are tremendous, and for the better. Today you can watch the shot on the monitor and the director does not have to look through the lens. There are machines to facilitate continuity, editing, in fact the entire post-production process is smoother and easier now. During *Jhooth Bole Kauwa Kaate* I never felt we were shooting a film, except during the outdoors when we shot for ten hours at a stretch, but then that's my style of working. I am by temperament a very economical director. If you don't believe me check with all my producers and they will confirm that I use the minimum raw stock, probably one-fourth of what other directors use. My films have no junior artistes, no background dancers performing PT exercises; if such things don't happen in real life then why show them on the screen?

It is said you never allowed your actors including Amitabh Bachchan any retakes.

I'm against the practice of retakes. Do as many rehearsals as you want, but only as many retakes as the director asks. Amitabh and I had a standing joke during all our films. Whenever he asked for a retake, I'd say, 'Provided you pay for the raw stock.' During *Jhooth Bole...* when Amrish Puri insisted on a retake, I said, 'Provided you pay for the vouchers.' He backed out. All artistes are restless souls. They are seldom satisfied with what they deliver. I have a simple theory as a film-maker: I tell my actors that either they convince me on how they can improve their shot, or leave the decision to me.

Would you agree that you are an autocratic director?

If that was so I wouldn't be able to repeat so many actors in my films. Amitabh Bachchan has done the maximum number of films with me, and that too, when he was at the peak of his success. He never heard the story, never discussed the price and never checked his dates, he just said, 'yes'. I'm sure of my craft but that does not make me autocratic. On the contrary, I tell my artistes, 'Lean on me and I will sail you through this experience quietly. If the endeavour fails, I take the blame. If it succeeds, you take the credit' and I mean this wholeheartedly.

Why is guilt a recurrent emotion in all your films?

People who have a conscience nurse feelings of guilt. Extortionists, criminals, murderers, even small-time thieves don't suffer any guilt. If they did, they would not be able to make a career out of their vices. So there is nothing wrong if my hero and heroine suffer pangs of guilt time and again. They feel the way they do because they are sensitive and filled with remorse.

The women in your films are always the moral guardians, is that fair to the man?

One, I don't think this is always true. Amitabh in *Bemisal* never wavers from his path and, in fact, protects both Raakhee and Vinod Mehra from trouble. Gender is not to be equated with morality. A woman can be loyal in bed, but cold and unresponsive emotionally.

On the other hand, there can be a woman who isn't monogamous but is wholesome and compassionate in her responses to her man; would you condemn such a woman? I don't think so. Even mythology makes concessions for this complex category. They are called panch kanya – Ahilya, Draupadi, Tara, Kunti and Mandodari – even though all these women were victimized, they were very special women.

Women appear oppressed in your films: Leela Naidu in *Anuradha* is oppressed by her husband and Sharmila Tagore in *Anupama* by her father. There are other examples as well like Rekha in *Jhoothi* and Raakhee in *Jurmana*.

In *Anuradha,* the protagonist feels she is oppressed but the fact is that her husband is weighed down by larger issues. He has neglected her but has neglected himself as well. If he takes her for granted it's because he considers her a part of him. Critics had debated this issue when the film was released and I'm surprised that after so many years you raise this question again. My answer is, 'What do you expect from the wife? That she breaks up her marriage and pursues her career? Will that resolve their conflict?' I don't think so. Their marriage suffers because Balraj Sahni does not follow the norm, he does not express love to his wife. Leela Naidu expects some kind of demonstration from her partner. She loves him but does not fully understand him and, in marriage, understanding is more important than love.

Would you say Uma understood or loved Subeer in *Abhimaan*?

Both, she is a sensitive, evolved person, more mature than her husband, and that is why she takes the decision she did – to refrain from singing. Subeer loves Uma as much as she loves him and it is because they understand each other that they are able to resolve their conflicts even if it happens after a lot of heartbreak.

It is sad but nobody makes this kind of cinema any longer.

At a time when onions cost forty rupees and potatoes twenty rupees, how do you expect the common man to survive? The audience is looking for an avenue to escape and there is no harm if he can laugh and enjoy while watching an entertaining film. No one would be interested in listening to bhashans these days. We are living in turbulent times and our middle class is the most burdened. They need an emotional release and if my film can provide that without gimmicks, violence or vulgarity, I take that as a compliment.

The middle class is no longer visible in our films. Where has that person disappeared?

Everything changes with consumerism. This is inevitable. My granddaughter watches a slim model in an advertisement on TV and stops eating because she wants look like the model. We have fallen in our choice of role models. Mahatma Gandhi said we must not bolt our doors so tight that the breeze cannot come in – at the same time, we must not open our windows so wide that you can get swept away. It's very sad that we have been swept away.

Which of the film-makers and artistes in recent times have impressed you?

Mani Ratnam is talented but concentrates too much on the form. Gulzar's films are always touching, Adoor Gopalakrishnan is easily the best in India. Shyam Benegal and Govind Nihalani make films that satisfy them, while jokers like me make films to satisfy the audience.

It has been a long time since you have worked with your old favourites Amitabh Bachchan and Amol Palekar; do you miss them?

One cannot miss people who are among us. I miss those who are not amid us today like Dr Rahi Masoom Reza and Rajendra Singh Bedi. A director spends a lot of time with his writers while making a film. When the film is complete you feel a vacuum. Unfortunately, this vacuum will never get filled again. I will always miss these two friends.

If you were provided an opportunity which of your films would you like to rework?

If I had the chance I would have preferred not to make some of the films I made. I will refrain from naming them because that would damage them further. My films are like my children. Not all can past the test; some are superior, some have a genetic deficiency, some a character deficiency; some make me proud, some disappoint me, but they are all mine. Good, bad or mediocre, I cannot disown them.

If a film is to be made on your life which actor would you like to play Hrishikesh Mukherjee?

I wouldn't like a film to be made on my life. Parts of me have already been projected in some of my films. *Satyakam* reflects my idealism, *Chupke Chupke* my humour and *Alaap* my pessimism, while *Bawarchi* was about my father. Tapan Sinha made a film on him in Bengali and I adapted the idea in Hindi. He was a multifaceted, multi-talented genius and his dynamism is reflected in Rajesh Khanna's charisma. I wouldn't want anybody to play me on screen. If I feel the need, I'll recreate my life in my own words in my autobiography.

Gulzar

Music has to be a part of the story-telling

Ready to release a new film but your office hasn't changed much in all these years.

(*Looks around*) That's true; it means there has been absolutely no growth (*laughs*).

It signifies stability?

Perhaps, I'm not a great one for change. Not in my immediate surroundings, at least. In thinking and writing you have to change, or you are going to be left behind. But I'm not someone who likes too many new things around me. I don't reshuffle my furniture and don't add new things to my table; anything extra on it disorients me. My table is reassuring, it instills a certain continuity and an emotional attachment. I feel connected to the smallest paperweight on my table.

The interview was conducted in 1999 before the release of *Hu Tu Tu*. *Jab Tak Hai Jaan* (2012) was Gulzar's last release as a lyricist.

What happens when the paperweight breaks?

(*Laughs*) Then it will have to be replaced, but I make certain that it will last for a long time. I'm careful with my possessions; I don't allow them to be damaged so easily. I would like to believe that I am loyal to all of them till the very end.

That is very endearing, almost romantic.

These are labels given to me by the media. I just do my work. My most romantic song according to me was, '*Mora gora ang lai le…*' from *Bandini* in the sixties. I was in my twenties at that time and yet to discover love. Nobody bracketed us into categories then. The media revolution came about much later, after a decade or two, perhaps.

How would you describe your three-decade journey?

Training under Bimal Roy, discipline was part of our psyche. I have had the privilege of participating in stimulating discussions among stalwarts, sometimes heated arguments as well. Burman-da and Bimal-da were always at loggerheads, but it was always a constructive argument and for the betterment of the film. We were very young at that time and never allowed in the room, but we were curious and watched them from the fringes. Then I was merely penning lyrics for Bimal-da, it was later when he employed me as an assistant, that I was given the opportunity of writing dialogues, then screenplays and finally emerged as a full-fledged director. It has been a long, steady journey.

Yash Chopra and you are the only directors from your generation to survive the changing trends, have you ever wondered why?

Ten years ago there was a lull in my career. None of the parallel-cinema directors were making films but Yash Chopra continued to make films even at that time. There were two reasons for this. First, he had his banner to produce his films and the second, a more relevant reason, was that Yashji always made romantic films and love is immortal and transcends all generations. My films, I would say, are about human relationships. Other things happen in my stories as well, but my camera remains focused on the human angle, or at least that's what I feel about my films.

Maachis was a turning point in your career.

Absolutely, I was doing a film after almost ten years. The stars' prices had shot up to dizzying heights and I was out of touch with the numbers game. I had a new producer and I had no choice but to take newcomers. It is my good fortune that the music and the story of the film were in tune with the climate of the country and it worked. I'd say *Maachis* was the right film at the right time. It touched a raw nerve.

And *Hu Tu Tu*?

The film reflects the changing times in our country. *Maachis* was about Punjab. *Hu Tu Tu* has a Maharashtrian flavour. The sutradhar is a Dalit folk singer inspiring revolution among the people. It blends the message with music and I like the way the songs are choreographed. It's very rare that a film-maker is able to weave music as part of his story-telling and the songs don't stick out like a sore thumb.

Was it difficult working with a temperamental actor like Nana Patekar?

Not at all, on the contrary, Nana was a sheer delight to work with. It's the first time Nana has done a full-fledged dance number in a film; where he performed *powda* or lok natya, a dance form he's familiar with. Nana gave me no cause for complaint, except that he was busy playing cricket on the sets sometimes and I had to persuade him to get him back to the shot.

And Tabu?

She is ravishing. What can I say about her beauty or talent that the world does not already know? She has a beautiful face and a beautiful existence. I have no doubts about her talent and feel she's improving by leaps and bounds with every film.

What made you cast Suhasini Mulay as the politician when any of your old favourite heroines would have done the role?

You're right. Jaya, Rekha, Hema, Shabana, even Sharmila Tagore are heroines I've worked with in the past, but I was very clear that I didn't want a star with an image in that role. Suhasini had the perfect posture and the dialect for the character. Besides, she also came without any baggage. The audience had forgotten her after *Bhuvan Shome* and there were no expectations. She lived up to my expectations and gave a marvellous performance.

You appear angry in *Hu Tu Tu*, is that how you are feeling?

No, I'm not angry but my films have always projected unrest, whether individual or societal. *Mere Apne* portrayed students' unrest, *Achanak* was about marital tension, also about betrayal and deceit. It's all about perspective. Just because Hema Malini in Meera is peaceful and is able to transform her obsession for Lord Krishna into devotion, her character is about love and loss. While Tabu's journey of anguish in the film transforms into hostility and alienates her from her loved ones. I have great faith in the new breed, I trust their spirit and courage and I feel *Hu Tu Tu* reflects that. Old guards say that the youngsters are irreverent, I don't think so. They have questions and it's up to us elders to provide their answers. If they've gone astray, we have failed somewhere.

What next?

I'm taking a sabbatical but I'm sure I'll be back behind the camera soon. In times where my guru Hrishikesh Mukherjee is still all charged up and making films I cannot afford to be laidback.

Karan Johar

My actors are my prime concern

You've said that in your first film you sought acceptance and in the second you seek appreciation. How important is approval to you?

Extremely important. It always has been since childhood. I always wanted reassurances from my parents and friends. When I made my first film *Kuch Kuch Hota Hai*, I was confident of the product, confident of my craft, yet I sought approval from everybody. There is probably a little boy inside me that refuses to grow up and that is why I'm always so wired-up and hyper.

What could be the reason of your being so on edge?

Temperament, I guess. Even today, after I confirm a shot, I find myself watching the expressions of my assistants. If it's not what

> The interview was conducted in 2001 before the release of *Kabhi Khushi Kabhie Gham*. *Bombay Talkies* (2013) was Karan Johar's last release as a director.

I'm expecting, or if their degree of involvement is lower than my expectations, it is an indicator for me that something is missing. Those on the sets are the first recipients of the content and if the scene does not touch them, there is little hope that it will touch the audience.

Are you as hyper in your interactions with your actors as well?

Never, they are a sensitive and fragile breed, and I would not burden them with my neurosis. What I'm going through is a discreet, unobtrusive process of survival, more a constructive than a destructive exercise. As a director, raising the comfort zone of my actors is my prime concern. I wouldn't do anything to destroy their concentration, but at the same time I cannot deny my anxieties either.

Your father Yash Johar is an extremely calm producer, so do you attribute your anxieties to your mother?

My mother is hypersensitive and my father and I refer to her as a tap. The slightest emotion triggers a flood of tears so we have to always be extremely careful. Dad is extremely sensitive as well but internalizes his emotions. His calm exterior is more a defence, and those close to him know when he is suffering. My father can be depended upon in a crisis and my mother on her judgement. I pretend to be calm in the wake of a problem but have inherited a sixth sense from my mother. Something in the pit of my stomach always tells me when a happy or a sad moment is coming.

So were you happy or sad when as a child you were sent to boarding school?

I was twelve years old and overheard Dad tell Mom that Dimple aunty was dropping Tina and Chinky to Panchgani. I was an awkward adolescent at that time, weighing hundred kilos, forever ridiculed by my friends in my building. At that age peer pressure is paramount. I think I was looking for an escape and my parents accepted my decision. A grand farewell party was organized for me but within just three days of my arrival in the new school, I realized it was a mistake. My only friend in the school, Tina Khanna, told me that the only way a student could escape from school was by rolling down the hill. So I rolled down the tall hill and bruised myself before being picked up by the school security. Dad was summoned and I returned home.

And how did your friends react to this? Did they make fun of you?

That's the interesting part... I was so happy to be home with my parents that I was suddenly free of all other baggage. My mother maintains that the boarding was a life-altering experience for me. Nobody could bully me any longer and by the time I was in the tenth standard I represented my college at inter-collegiate debates. It's strange how children know what they want and can resolve conflicts without adult intervention.

You've portrayed that in *Kuch Kuch Hota Hai.*

Yes, though I have to admit it happened unconsciously. Little Anjali makes her own decisions – what to buy for her father and where to spend her summer vacations. When she wants something, she's willing to manipulate her father, grandmother and even convinces Salman Khan into shifting affection from Kajol to her favourite TV anchor. In the climax it's more her silent tears than the hero's that coerce Salman into sacrificing his bride-to-be for Shah Rukh Khan.

Kuch Kuch Hota Hai packaged old values in a new bottle.

I think everything that is internalized, like our basic values and sense of justice, everything relating to roots and family, is traditional. Everything external, like our appearance and ambience, everything we project, is a culmination of influences gathered from what we read and watch. In my case, I feel I'm a product of cinema. I've grown up on a diet of Hindi films and all my reference points are from Yash Chopra films. The subtext comes from Raj Kapoor and the packaging from Sooraj Barjatya and Aditya Chopra.

Isn't it about time you break the umbilical chord with Yash Raj Films?

Yash Chopra would have been an even bigger influence on me if he were not a part of the family. He is a father figure and I cannot be in awe of him. Intimacy does not permit adulation. Years ago, when I was still a child and had never seen him, but only watched his films, I had stayed awake all night because he was coming home for dinner. When I finally met him I said to myself, 'But he looks exactly like my father.' This is strange but Yash uncle and Pam aunty even structurally resemble my parents. Ours is an extended family and I doubt I will ever be able to break the umbilical chord.

Visually and musically you are forever borrowing from his films.

Musically all of us are borrowing from somewhere unless one has learnt music or can create one's own notes. I admit that *Kuch Kuch Hota Hai* is a continuation of Yash Chopra films, but in *Kabhi Khushi Kabhie Gham* I have deliberately broken away from the mould. I have used warmer tones and done away with the vibrant colours and the sporty apparel associated with Yash Chopra's films.

Is that because you have outgrown the bubblegum phase?

I feel older, more mature and my films reflect this. *Kuch Kuch Hota Hai* said friends could be lovers while *Kabhi Khushi Kabhie Gham* has simple moments that occur in every home. When I watched *Monsoon Wedding* I felt I knew all the characters because the film-maker makes you feel as if you are a part of the family. My film says if you feel love, express it. We waste so much time discussing so many things, but hesitate to tell people we care for that we love them. The youth is going to identify with both Hrithik and Shah Rukh's characters.

Which of the two heroes do you identify with?

I'd say there is a little of me in both the characters but more significantly, I identify with the subject. Contrary to the impression generated, non-communication isn't just a rural problem. About 99 per cent out of the so-called urban nuclear families don't ever express their affection through words. I know I don't, though I'm changing now. My film has emphasized its importance to me.

Lagaan and *Dil Chahta Hai* released earlier in the year have proved path-breaking. What should one expect from your film?

I'm scared of preconceived notions. There are high expectations from the box-office. It's too much responsibility. In my opinion, rather than get into comparisons, we should celebrate diversity in Indian cinema. Today, cinema is like a well-laid banquet where the audience can pick and choose.

You have worked with the most illustrious star cast. What have you learnt from them?

Let's see, from Amit uncle (Amitabh Bachchan) I've learnt about discipline and drive. The humility with which he listens to a fresher like me is moving. From Jaya aunty (Jaya Bachchan) I learnt the ability to be at ease once the camera is switched off. Kajol has that quality too and that is the reason both of them were sparkling on my sets. Shah Rukh Khan has extraordinary qualities and the more time I spend with him the more I learn from him. His energy is infectious.

You've left out Hrithik Roshan and Kareena Kapoor?

Hrithik is obsessed with his work, we all are, but while the rest of us give a 100 per cent, he gives 300 per cent. From Kareena I learnt nothing, but I have taught her instead. It's interesting for me to observe that today Kareena is at the same stage where Kajol was during *Kuch Kuch Hota Hai*: completely spontaneous and magical.

Trade pundits say *K3G* is the most over-budget film to be released to date.

It's because I am a mad man when it comes to my frames. I am not willing to make the slightest compromise in quality and I have an equally obsessed father who is willing to indulge every whim of mine. In fact, he is the wings that help me fly…

Sanjay Leela Bhansali

You don't need money to make a film, you need passion

Had you ever imagined that your film would be premiered at Cannes Film Festival one day?

Never! These were news items one read in the papers and associated with doyens like Satyajit Ray and Mrinal Sen. The dream was too far-fetched for a boy growing up in a chawl in Bhuleshwar and yet cinema was part of my youth. My father was a small-time film-maker; he made films like *Lootera,* so fantasy was a childhood companion. There was always something burning within me, a craving to do something different, something special.

Did you have a lonely childhood?

Not lonely, but there were disturbing phases when one wanted answers and there were none. I wasn't unhappy, but my life wasn't

The interview was conducted in 2002 before the release of *Devdas*. *Guzaarish* (2010) was Sanjay Leela Bhansali's last release as a director.

peaceful like that of my friends'. There were great highs and great lows. My father would take my sister and me to Opera House to watch *Mughal-e-Azam* again and again, and enlighten us on the finer points of the film like the scale, the grandeur and Bade Ghulam Ali. Today, all those lessons are of immense use to me. My father was a different person when he took us to watch movies and a different person when he was at home. He wanted us to stay away from the film world, get educated and pursue a normal life.

You have unresolved issues with him, which is evident even in the opening credit of *Hum Dil De Chuke Sanam*.

I never got along with my father as long as he lived. He was an awesome personality, but circumstances didn't provide him the opportunities he deserved and that destroyed him. Every time I think of him I can only remember his last days at the hospital. He was in a coma and in that unconscious state I saw him reaching out for my mother's hand. That one moment, when their fingers locked, compensated for all her suffering over the years. I didn't realize it then but that immortal moment was the beginning of *Devdas*.

What draws you to make *Devdas*, a film made so many times before?

No other piece of literature has lent so much dignity to a woman, so much compassion for the characters, as Saratchandra's novel *Devdas*. My father died from excessive consumption of alcohol; my mother has to this day preserved his last unconsumed bottle in her cupboard. It's her way of remembering him, preserving his memories. Incompleteness is fascinating. I understand Devdas, his restlessness, his pain. The sad thing is nobody can resolve his demons for him. He is haunted by his memories and not even Chandramukhi can help him.

Do you think this is a right time for your subject?

I'd say that Hindi cinema is returning to its roots. There are bigger opportunities today because screenplay writing is evolving. Producers, after a long betrayal, are learning to trust their directors again. The audience is in a receptive mood after a long time. Hindi cinema is changing because the audience is changing. The public is rejecting mundane stuff and asking for adventure. This is the right time to make a lavish, passionate film like I'm making.

Your first film, *Khamoshi – The Musical*, raised a social concern. Your second, *Hum Dil De Chuke Sanam*, is a love story and the third one, *Devdas*, is a tragedy. How do you decide on your subjects?

I take a very long time to decide but once I do, I stay committed. After *Hum Dil De Chuke Sanam*, I met several writers and heard innumerable subjects but my heart wasn't in them. Then one day I was all alone at home and, for no particular reason, picked up the novel from my bookshelf. I was reading the book for the second time but it consumed me completely. I made up my mind right then. Everyone advised me against it, felt it would not work but I was adamant. My argument was that barring the fact that *Devdas* was a period film it was about human anguish, about passion and while some people like Nana Patekar and Seema Biswas in *Khamoshi* take life as a challenge, some like Devdas succumb to it.

It is your interpretation of the classic.

Naturally, as a reader of the classic I have my own fantasies and I should be allowed to interpret the story as I see it. In my vision, I want to retain the intensity and the layers provided by Bimal Roy but I also want to add the drama and energy of Raj Kapoor. I don't view these changes as taking liberties but extending my sensibilities to the subject. Reinterpretation is always about reflection not imitation. If that was not the case I could have just distributed copies of the old *Devdas* to everyone and forgotten about making it myself.

Did the earlier versions of the film haunt you? Were you at any time during the shoot filled with self-doubt?

You have asked the right question. It is not easy to run away from the past. It is also natural to wonder if one is on the right path, but by the grace of God, I was very upbeat throughout the shoot. I didn't reshoot scenes and didn't do patchwork either. Yes, I often went home feeling I could have done better but that enabled me to perform even better the following day. By temperament, I'm not overly confident but I like it that way. I like my restlessness; it keeps me alert and alive.

Do you feel calmer now that the film is almost complete?

I'm never at peace, the calm is to disguise my restlessness; I let it simmer while at work but when I go home I crack up. My mother has the most unusual way of restoring my sanity. She has a special equation with the Almighty, and recurrently absolves me from crises. It's because I return home night after night to innocence that I remain uncorrupted. *Devdas* has taken two-and-a-half years in the making, which is two hundred and seventy-five days, and in all these months, I have not met friends, not gone out, not watched films or read any books. I only read my script, watched my rushes, and listened to my music. My friends said I'd go mad, I feel that it is self-preservation. Interacting hampers my creativity and it is my choice to remain isolated.

Which of the three characters – Devdas, Paro and Chandramukhi – do you identify with?

I would say there is a lot of Devdas in me. He lets opportunities go by, he is weak inside. He thinks he can rectify his lapses in judgement but he cannot. There is an inherent sadness in him and there is also hope.

The description sounds more like your father than you.

You are right again. I see my father in Devdas and I want his soul to rest in peace. Whenever I think of him I feel his pain. I want both of us to be free of the suffering, and that can be possible only if I relive his anguish. I chose Shah Rukh for the role because he has sad eyes and a madman's energy. The character calls for languid movements and it also calls for a very special ability to shirk off twelve years of a certain rhythm and adopt a new body language. Shah Rukh has managed to do that effortlessly. I just love the way he has portrayed Devdas.

What have you learnt from your trio of protagonists?

Why just the trio, I learn from all my characters in all my films. Ajay Devgn, who played Vanraj in *Hum Dil De Chuke Sanam*, could have turned bitter, instead he rises to the occasion and helps his wife find her beloved. Similarly, Salman also has the grace to let Aishwarya go. If I ever make a sequel to the film, I would concentrate on Salman's story. Would he have found another love or would he have turned into another Devdas? The fact is that all three – Paro, Dev and Chandramukhi – love with honesty. I disagree that Devdas is a coward, he is child-like. He hits when he is denied a candy and runs away when the family reprimands him. He expresses without manipulation. Paro symbolizes strength and Chandramukhi, patience. Even after she gives up the kotha she returns to it with the hope of finding Devdas visiting her someday. The sad thing is that Devdas believes he can resolve all his anguish. He wants time, and time runs out on him.

Are you going to let time run out on you too or are you going to settle down someday?

Celluloid is my beloved and I cannot have two wives. My films are my grandchildren. My honest confession is that I don't want to settle down. I want to explore, have this continuous love affair with the camera. When I was waiting at the laboratory for the first print of *Hum Dil De Chuke Sanam* it was like going through labour pangs and when the distributors collected the prints for the release it was like giving away my daughter in marriage. It was heart-wrenching!

So how would you sum up the experience of shooting a 50 crore bonanza?

There were days when we thought we would not be able to can a single shot. There were scenes that required forty generators, 500 light men and 2500 lenses, and we didn't even have ten rupees in the production kitty. My assistant directors and technicians were not paid for weeks, and I was looking for a special fabric for my curtains. My unit stood by me through all this. I don't know whether they begged, borrowed or stole but they reproduced whatever I asked for, without any complaints, indulging every obsession of mine. They have seen me break down and rise again. They have seen me come out of all problems to inspire them. My producer Bharat Shah has been through hell but kept up our spirits and asked us to not stop shooting. Whenever I was particularly low and sensed all doors closing on me, my father appeared in my dreams and assured me, holding my hand that everything will work out. I strongly believe that you don't need money to make films.

You need passion. We have been able to pull through this because we were driven by Bharat bhai and Sarat babu's passion.

There is a superstition that gloom stalks everyone who attempts to make *Devdas* and the ominous clouds disappear when the project is complete.

I believe that now. I have died a thousand deaths during the two-and-a-half years of the making of the film. Bharat Shah has been in and out of hospital and jail; humiliated and slandered. It has been a traumatic time for Shah Rukh with his new house and sudden health problems; Aishwarya went through a tumultous relationship. Saratchandra wrote the novel when he was only nineteen, but the anguish hasn't subsided in all these years nor has the passion. There were times when I felt like a lone ranger galloping on a horse, unaware of my destination. I was lonely despite being amid crowds, but I endured it all. If you want to make *Devdas* you have to be ready for the suffering. That is the boon and the curse of the character.

Vishal Bharadwaj

Cinema stems from reality, music is pure fantasy

When did you first realize you wanted to be a film-maker?

It was in the year 1996. I was attending the International Film Festival in Thiruvananthapuram with Gulzar saab where *Maachis* was being shown in the Panorama Section. While watching the retrospective of Polish director Krzystof Kieslowski, something churned in my heart. One of the films included ten short films based on the Ten Commandments from the Bible, but adaptable in our daily life. The impact was mesmeric. I realized that film-making is the most expressive medium of all fine arts and I was going to be a part of it.

Is desire sufficient to make a dream come true?

Most certainly, without desire there are no dreams. I had been writing for as long as I could remember. Stray thoughts, verses

The interview was conducted before the release of *Makdee* (2002). *Matru Ki Bijlee Ka Mandola* (2013) was Vishal Bharadwaj's last release as a director.

scribbled on papers and preserved in files, some ideas developed into short stories, some into screenplays. Around this time my friend Hansal Mehta was making a series on love stories for Zee TV and asked me to recommend new writers. I sent him a couple of my stories under a fictitious name. He selected one story, *Highway*, for an immediate telecast and I knew the time had come for me to reveal my true identity.

Were you as secretive about wanting to become a music composer as well?

No, because I grew up attending music recordings with my father, Ram Bharadwaj, an eminent poet and lyricist. Rhythm was so much a part of our daily environment that as a child I studied my lessons in musical notes. That's when I realized that I could become a composer. When I was still in the twelfth standard, my father mentioned to music director Usha Khanna that I had composed a tune. Ushaji asked me to play it and used it in her film *Yaar Kasam*. Later, A.V. Mohan gave me a break in *Wahem*. I was in my second year of college when I recorded my first song with Asha Bhosle. It was my most complicated tune because when you are eighteen you are dying to show off!

Then what took you so long to pursue your dreams?

My father died in 1984 and for a long time I could not leave Delhi. Domestic responsibilities forced me to remain there even though my heart craved to be in Mumbai. I obtained a job as a recording manager. A few years later, I suffered another tragedy and my boss, R.V. Pandit, I think, on emotional grounds, transferred me to Mumbai. One thing led to another, I met Gulzar saab who asked me to compose *Maachis* and five years later, when Pandit wanted to make a film on the Amritsar riots, I got my break as a music composer in *Maachis*.

How was it working with Gulzar?

During the making of *Maachis,* Gulzar saab included me in the brainstorming sessions. Not that I contributed much but I was their bouncing board. In a way that was the beginning. He always said, 'If you want to become a film-maker, you have to write your own script.' I remembered that and whenever something touched me deeply, I remembered to write it down. Some years passed by and while I composed music for *Satya, Chachi 420* and *Godmother,* in my free time, I continued to write stories.

Did you narrate these stories to your film-makers?

Not in the beginning because initially I was co-writing with my two friends, Raju Patel and Kannan. Soon I realized that co-writing was not practical, so I opted out of the team. I wrote *Barf,* which Ajay Devgn was to produce, but two weeks before the launch the project was shelved because his home production *Raju Chacha* had bombed. I was shattered. I tried to revive the project with other producers but nobody was willing to touch it. For six months I knocked on many doors. I felt like a prostitute luring a client, desperate for acceptance.

All debutants go through the same anxieties…

I don't know how they cope. I was completely frustrated. I heard the sound of the camera in my dreams and I craved the smell of a studio set. I decided that if I made a film for any government body the exercise would be relatively easier and contacted the Children's Film Society India, little aware that the problems would multiply! I withdrew my film from the CFSI and, with help from friends and a trusting partner, completed the post-production of *Makdee.* All the technicians in the film: cameraman Hemant Chaturvedi, art director Sameer Chaddha and others contributed eleven thousand rupees each as a gesture of support, which I can never forget. The lead star of the film, Shabana Azmi, has not charged a single penny, a gesture I can never repay.

How did you convince Shabana Azmi to work in your film?

I guess I was just destined to work with her. I had always fantasized about casting her and when I was on a location shoot for *Godmother* in Jodhpur I mustered up the courage and asked her. She said she would listen to my subject on our flight to Mumbai. On board, I bounced off a few ideas. She liked one, a hard-hitting story of a politician but a few days later phoned to say that as a Rajya Sabha member, the plot would be too close to reality and that's when I narrated the idea of *Makdee.*

Wasn't she offended that you offered her the role of a witch?

On the contrary, she was vastly amused. Within two minutes of hearing the concept she said it was a challenge to play a part so out of ordinary. Her confirmation boosted my confidence as a director. Just as music directors cannot make a mistake with Lata Mangeskar, directors have to be prepared with their homework to work with Shabanaji. It's amazing that after all these years and multiple awards, she feels so passionately about her work.

How did you conceive this never-before-seen Hindi screen character?

This has to be said on record that the entire credit of creating the visual image of the witch goes to Shabana Azmi. There are no references to similar characters in Hindi cinema and it was her idea that she should be an ageing, portly, frizzy-haired, hunch-backed witch. We were very clear that we should break away from the stereotype and give her the contemporary look. Shabanaji requested tech-savvy friends to visit sites and send her print-outs.

These were jumbled with her own pictures, picking out different features from different visuals to lend drama. The long legs and clawed hands were again her suggestion. She consulted three costume designers and finally settled for the most outlandish one.

Getting ready for the shoot must be a nightmare.

The make-up process took three hours and I had been warned that she is very impatient but she was as sincere as a student. We suffered a setback when, due to a personal calamity, her make-up man Vipul Bhagwat had to be replaced with a less competent artiste. Shabanaji broke down and retreated completely. A few hours later, when we salvaged the crisis, she blossomed again and the transformation was almost childlike. It's because she has been able to retain her anxieties that there is still a magical quality to her performances.

It is not very common for music composers to turn film-makers, what motivated you to change track?

You are right. Except Kishore Kumar in the past, who made a couple of films, and composer Salil Choudhary, who made *Pinjre Ke Panchhi*, I'm the only one. I think I was able to do it because I was a dormant writer, because my father was a poet, and an active musician and because he was also a lyricist. Making a feature film was my ultimate dream but every time I came close to my goal, something would go wrong. I guess things happen when they have to.

I'm sure you are aware that *Makdee* is inspired by many Gulzar films.

He is my mentor and I cannot deny that. He is responsible for turning me into a music composer, writer and, now, a film-maker. He has been the strongest influence on my creative growth. In poetry, Dr Bashir Badr's body of works influences me. In fiction writing, I look up to American film director Quentin Tarantino of *Pulp Fiction* and *Reservoir Docks fame.* Then there is Premchand, Sharad Joshi and among Indian film-makers, Shekhar Kapur, Mani Ratnam and Mahesh Bhatt.

How different is composing music from directing a film?

There are no comparisons. As a director, I have the liberty to make a film without songs, but as a composer, whether it is for a video album or a feature film, I will still need a director. Cinema stems from reality while songs are pure fantasy. Even if I make the best music in the world I will continue to be a creative slave, whereas the most mediocre director enjoys complete artistic control. The only common factor between the two is rhythm – whether it is dialogue, action or a song, every art form calls for special timing.

What about the stress levels?

Creating music is recreation, creating a film is both a high and a low. Do you know that a recent survey in *Time* magazine revealed that among pressures endured by professionals, the bomb dropper's is the highest and the film-maker's the second highest. Direction is about people management and understanding actors. It's not easy motivating a sleepy child to laugh before the camera but it has to be done and effectively. There are times you want to murder your cameraman who is obsessed with a particular lighting or your assistant director who has bungled the continuity shot, but when the film is completed, everything is forgiven.

Now that you have become a film-maker, producers may not hire you as a music composer.

I was warned about this and it has happened. When I wrote my first script, people assumed I was no longer interested in music, which is ridiculous. Sadly, a music composer in our industry is looked upon as a general store that provides some happy, some sad and some situational tunes and I wasn't prepared to cater to that. Osho says, 'The mind does not allow you to live in the present because it is forever either in the past or the future.' I didn't want to die with regrets so I lived my dream.

Rajkumar Santoshi

Films I make must inspire society

How different is the feeling every time before a new release?

The anxiety pangs are more or less the same. Sometimes you are more confident of your product, sometimes you need assurance but your association with the film doesn't change till the end. As the day of the release draws closer, you are like an expectant mother, restless to deliver because after a point you just cannot carry the creative baggage. Also, the more demanding the subject the more drained you feel.

What inspired you to make *Khakee*?

When Govind Nihalani was making *Ardh Satya*, I was assisting him and was overawed by his sense of detail and level of research. I have wanted to make a film on the police force since then but never got

The interview was conducted in 2004 before the release of *Khakee. Ajab Prem Ki Ghazab Kahani* (2009) was Rajkumar Santoshi's last release as a director.

the opportunity. When it was decided that Amitabh Bachchan and I would do a film together, I decided that I wanted him to play a cop. Coincidentally, my co-writer of the film, Shridhar Raghavan, narrated an idea to me that I liked immensely. It was about the struggle of the men in uniform, their hardships and travails. No matter how much we criticize the police force we cannot ignore their sacrifices.

So is your film an ode to the police force?

Well, it is about policemen who go beyond the call of duty for justice, but eventually they are human beings too. They have not dropped from Mars or Venus and are part of the same society that we live in, governed by the same systems so they reflect the same contradictions as the common man. Circumstances compel their actions. Some people flow with the tide and some fight against it. My film is made up of all kinds of cops – the good, the bad and the indifferent. One cannot generalize, for different people have different temperaments and weaknesses. *Khakee* is about their effort to overcome these failings.

Amitabh Bachchan has played a cop in so many films, how can your film be different?

His character Anant Srivastav is a loser; he is at the tail end of his career but has never won any laurels. Finally, he gets an opportunity to prove himself. It is a do-or-die situation and he takes up the challenge. Bachchan may have played a cop in many films but he was always a winner. What makes my film different is that he is not larger than life. It was a revelation to work with Amitji. He has contributed to the film more than just as an actor. There were times he made suggestions regarding the structuring of scenes and they were priceless moments.

The film features a mega star cast?

Yes, the roles deserve the actors. Besides, I'm used to working with lead actors in all my films. I've never considered that a pressure, on the contrary it is a privilege to have a charismatic star cast. They have implicit faith in me and some of them, like Ajay Devgn and Akshay Kumar, agree to do my film without even hearing the script. This instills a sense of further responsibility in me because it means I have to justify their trust.

How difficult was it adjusting to so many egos and attitudes?

I don't have to adjust to anyone's eccentricities because everyone adjusts to the script. I've worked with two superstars in *Andaz Apna Apna* and five heroines in *Lajja,* and there were no problems. The insecurities arise when the director has not done his homework or plays favourites. My actors know that I'm always prepared and that I will not play favourites.

How does a film-maker divide his creative and administrative time?

All the production work involving meetings and co-ordination happens during the day. Preferably post lunch, because I start my day leisurely and then carry on till dusk. After that, I reserve my time and energy only for creative work. I can only write at night because that is the only time I know I'm not going to be disturbed.

All your films are co-written, isn't it difficult to adjust to another sensibility?

On the contrary, it is a tremendous advantage because, first, he translates what I'm thinking and feeling and, second, when he expresses the futility of a scene, I accept his argument without discussion because I know that it has traversed all the possibilities so we are saving on creative energy. But the best thing about having a co-writer is that I constantly have someone to check me, someone to mirror my failings. It's very stimulating to work with self-respecting writers whose worldviews I respect, like Anjum Rajabali in *The Legend of Bhagat Singh* and Shridhar Raghavan in *Khakee*.

How different is your working style compared to your father P.L. Santoshi?

My father died when I was nineteen. Before that, when I was in school, he went through a bad patch in his career and was not too active. I have very fragmented memories of him as a professional. My son is comparatively more involved with my career and the know-how of the technical jargon associated with film-making, and is also more inspired. During the making of *The Legend of Bhagat Singh* my son was so influenced by the character that he would bombard me with questions. For a long time, he turned completely anti-angrez and refused to wear imported jeans or eat burgers. He'd insist on being served only Indian food.

When you were a young boy did your father's films influence you as much?

Sadly, I only remember his lean phase. If there were questions bothering me about films or the world at large I never mustered the courage to express myself the way my son does. I didn't ask my mother either. We were all proud of *Hum Panchhi Ek Dal Ke* and *Barsaat Ki Ek Raat* but there was no sharing with him. In my formative years, Govind Nihalani has been the strongest influence on me. He is the only director so far to have the confidence to blow up Om Puri's face on a thirty-by-forty billboard. I learnt from Govindji that strength is courage. That the face of an actor is only secondary and power comes from the story.

And what's the most important thing about story-telling?

Observations are important ingredients for any creative journey. In one lifetime it is not possible for one man to go through so many experiences but by choosing to read what you do, listening attentively and watching inspiring films you can nourish yourself. It is like a maestro storing innumerable notes in his bank and reproducing them at an opportune moment to strike the right chord. Akira Kurosawa said he never moved anywhere without a paper and pen, and whenever he read or watched something that touched him, he instantly scribbled it on paper. A few years later, he discovered that he had a wealth of ideas.

Do you follow the same practice?

Not consciously but one is able to recognize glimpses that stem from intimate observations. There are so many of them in several films of mine. I don't believe that one has to go to Bosnia to make a film on hunger. If you are insensitive, you are unaffected and if you are affected you are bound to reflect the concern in your work. Knowledge is responsibility. I believe that whatever films I make must inspire society.

Interestingly, your films are as much about the female gaze as the male gaze.

I am first and foremost a human being and a socially conscious citizen, and therefore it is not sufficient to say that I care and not show it in action. It is not right to criticize and not make any efforts to rectify the failing. If respectable people are going to shy away from voicing their protests, we deserve to be ruled by goons.

Have you considered joining politics?

I hadn't all this while because I felt my world belongs to cinema. But viewing the turbulent times our country is going through, I feel it is about time strong willed, concerned citizens came forward and assume responsibility, and that includes me. It does not mean, however, that I will divorce myself from film-making; I cannot. Cinema is my lifeline.

What according to you is your strength as a director?

My strength is inadvertently also my weakness. To tell my story with complete honesty is my strength but that is also a weakness because I'm not willing to compromise. During the making of *The Legend of Bhagat Singh,* I was lured with choices for the heroine and the music, but I resisted these temptations. That is perhaps why I've never had a mega success. The struggle is always to convince a producer to trust my dream. It is easier convincing actors because they don't make financial investments.

And what is your strength as a human being?

My emotions without doubt, and my heartbeat. They nurture the writer and the director in me. My emotions are also my weakness for I'm constantly frightened of being manipulated. Somebody once asked me that I make hard-hitting films but don't reflect that in my personal life. Charlie Chaplin revealed after the World War that tragedy beyond limits turns into comedy. I have the ability to laugh at myself, at life. I'm a great admirer of R.K. Laxman, who is my companion over a cup of tea every morning.

How does the family fit into your crazy life of one film after another? Do they complain?

It is difficult, I agree, but cinema is my passion and my dream, and my loved ones have to accept them with me. I cannot compromise on my creativity but I'm not insensitive to their anxieties either. I try my best to compartmentalize the two worlds but it's not always possible. Just like I miss my family when I'm on long outdoor shoots, ideas brim in my head during my domestic moments. The overlap is natural and unavoidable. Artistes live on different planes and are comfortable with parallel communications: one within them and one outside. Unless I feel the humiliation of Damini I cannot project it through a film; it is the same with Janaki's oppression in *Lajja.* I'm fortunate to have a family that is supportive of my creative journey. Had it not been for them it would have been very lonesome.

Mani Ratnam

The thrill is in crossing your threshold, in taking a leap

It has been almost seven years since *Dil Se*. What took you so long to make another Hindi film?

I was busy with two films – *Alai Payuthe* and *Kannathil Muthamittal*. *Kannathil*, particularly, could not be made in Hindi as it is too rooted in the south but *Alai Payuthe* was, as *Saathiya*, by Shaad Ali. However, I don't see making films in Hindi as any different from making them in any other language. I don't think of cinema from the linguistic point of view but as a need for self-expression. A film is my baby and I dress it with the colours and emotions I'm capable of.

How does it feel when the baby is rejected like in the case of *Dil Se*?

When a film does not work there is a simple theory: there's a flaw in the story-telling.

The interview was conducted in 2004 before the release of *Yuva*. *Raavan*, Mani Ratnam's last bilingual film, released in 2010.

Did it demoralize you when the critics described your film as '*Dil se*... not *dimag se*!'?

(*Laughs*) Did they say that? I don't read reviews so it does not make a difference. As long as criticism is constructive and offers insights to the film-maker, it is enriching. But when they pan your film for the sake of criticizing or because they have praised your earlier films and need to strike a balance, it is unfair. Why must the critic equate the quality of a film to how it fares at the box-office? They behave more like exhibitors and distributors than analysts. Even their questionnaire is more about the budget and the expenditure than the craft. It's something our interviewers and critics need to think about.

What made you cast Ajay Devgn, Abhishek Bachchan and Vivek Oberoi for the three roles in *Yuva*?

The three actors represent three diverse attitudes to life. Ajay Devgn plays Michael Mukherjee. He represents hope and faith in mankind. Abhishek plays Lallan, who gives a damn about the world because he feels the world gives a damn about him. He has no moral compulsions. Finally Vivek Oberoi, alias Arjun Bal Krishnan, is an urban, chilled-out guy, who wants all the good things in life without working for them.

And which out of the three is your personal story?

All of them are my stories. The best thing about writing a film is that you can play all the characters – I'm the opportunist and I'm also the idealist. I build dreams and I break them... so I'm allowed to express anguish, anger and ambition. Isn't that marvellous?

Okay, can you tell us which of the six roles you identify with?

(*Laughs*) You are not going to get any confessions out of me. I identify with all of them otherwise I would not be able to write them. They all have their strengths and weaknesses and reasons of why they are and where they are. As a director all I'm trying to do is weave a pattern out of their highs and lows, and create fiction.

Handling one star pair is demanding enough, how did you cope with six stars together?

You'll be surprised that the younger stars don't carry any baggage. They work as equals and are more focused than actors of the previous generation. I enjoyed working with all of them thoroughly and did not find them in the least bit demanding.

What kind of person were you in your youth – reckless or responsible?

I guess I was a bit of both. The fact that I was sent away to boarding school during my adolescence is proof that I must have been reckless. And the fact that my life has shaped up the way it has at present, endorses the fact that I must be reasonably responsible.

When in doubt, who do you rely upon?

I rely on my instinct.

Even instinct can go wrong at times.

Sometimes, yes… Then one has to stop for a while and mull things over or perhaps seek the opinion of somebody you trust.

Is it possible for a film-maker to always be confident of his scenes?

Not all his scenes, but his craft, yes. I may not get it the exact way I want to but I know where I'm heading. Self doubt usually appears in your first film when your mind is overcrowded and fuzzy. Gradually, as you make more films, you discover that the thrill is in crossing your threshold… in taking a leap and in excelling.

It is very difficult but one can accomplish it if one is always checking oneself.

And how does one do that?

By creating an environment that encourages objectivity. It means surrounding yourself with people who mean well, not sycophants. By being open to criticism but not losing your convictions. For instance, despite the box-office verdict on *Dil Se* I stand by the film. After fifty years of Independence we must have the maturity to be able to discuss terrorism.

Do you regret not directing *Saathiya*, the Hindi remake of *Alai Payuthe*, which won a lot of acclaim?

No, I had already done it once in Tamil and don't have the patience for a repeat run. I felt the film was in safe hands since Shaad Ali had been a part of *Alai Payuthe* and was the right director to nurture the baby in Hindi.

It calls for a lot of generosity to be able to give away your film to another director for the remake.

The fact is that Shaad did a competent job. As a creative artiste you have to let go. You cannot part with your muse and yet cradle it. That's unfair to the film as well as to its caretaker.

Crisis of conscience is a recurrent emotion in all your films. Is the accident in *Saathiya* from a real-life incident?

(*Takes a long pause*) Something similar could have happened to anybody you've known. All of us have been in a situation where we worry about a loved one not returning home. I didn't want to admit this in print but you are very perceptive, there are moments in the film which are borrowed from real incidents.

Your films directly or indirectly reflect a social consciousness, but off screen you are not associated to any causes.

I believe that you must not take up anything that you cannot give your best. I don't lend myself to a cause because I'm consumed by films. My wife Suhasini takes up a lot of issues though. I have great admiration for people who can do it. The only way I can contribute to society is to make films that make a difference to humanity.

All your stories portray a deep understanding of man-woman relationships. Does chemistry between lead stars contribute to it?

Chemistry adds a sparkle not just between the lead pair but also between the director and the actors, the director and the cinematographer and the director and the film's music director. An able director should succeed in creating chemistry between his artistes even when co-actors don't share a healthy friendship.

The love scenes in your films are always insightful and original.

All the scenes that a film-maker portrays on screen are a collage of images from his memory storage. They come from films, books or people one meets in daily life or sometimes from your own experiences. Over the years there are many additions and deletions but unfortunately this storage is limited. That is why very often you repeat some images, sometimes consciously and at other times without being aware of it. Sometimes you feel the need to bounce off an idea, sometimes you feel you work best in isolation. There are myriad moods and moments.

When you need a bouncing board, who is the creative partner you seek?

My wife Suhasini for she is my severest critic and also because she gives her opinion from the female point of view. We function well together since we work in the same medium. I may not always agree with her suggestions but I will listen to her in all earnestness.

You sound like the hero in your films: indulgent but obstinate.

No… no… don't equate me with any of my characters. I'm not that romantic. In fact, I'm quite an ordinary guy.

That's not what your cast and crew say.

Is that so? None of them has ever said such a thing to me and if you ask me I feel all of them appear too self-assured to be bothered about being impressed with me.

From Aishwarya Rai in *Iruvar* to Rani Mukerji in *Yuva*, all of them complain that you never give any feedback.

It's not in my nature to be effusive. The actors are paid to do the job and they are hired because they assure results. It's not as if I am restraining my responses but I sincerely feel that as professionals they should know when they are good and when they are failing to rise to the level of their potential. I cannot speak about them in superlatives because praising them inadvertently means praising myself. I'm always wary of what I say in print because I don't know how it will be presented in print.

You have always been wary of the media?

See, I must have something substantial to communicate and that is possible only before or after a new release. Some of them ask

irrelevant questions while some want you to participate in their thought process. I'm not sure if the exercise is always productive and therefore I'm selective about whom I talk to.

So what are you planning for your next film?

In my head my next film is already shot but in reality it is still to happen on paper. There are many ideas buzzing in my head but first I need to take a holiday and catch up with the world.

Govind Nihalani

Violence in my films is always as an undercurrent

You must be very persistent to pursue a dream for two decades.

The idea began in 1984, soon after *Ardha Satya.* One day Jaya Bachchan called me for a meeting with Amitji at their home, Pratiksha. He was the reigning star at that time while I was working with art-house films. I was preparing to go on floors with *Party,* and *Tamas* was brewing on the backburner. Maybe he was expecting something from me immediately and I was unprepared so we parted on the note that whenever I found a suitable subject for him I'd get back to him.

And in all these years there was no suitable subject?

After *Tamas* I was in the mood for a bigger canvas and approached him with a period subject. Jayaji liked it but Amitji said he would be

The interview was conducted in 2004 before the release of *Dev,* Govind Nihalani's last release as a director. The Marathi movie *Anumati* (2013) was his last release as a cinematographer.

more comfortable doing a contemporary film, so we dropped the idea. Then, about five years ago, he called me and narrated a subject close to his heart. I liked it too, but on second thoughts, both of us felt it lacked spark. Another few years went by. Meanwhile, I did *Hazaar Chaurasi Ki Maa* with Jayaji but never gave up on him. Last year, Meenaxi Sharma, my assistant narrated an idea to me and something clicked. I asked her to put it on paper. It was a hard-hitting subject and had to be made without songs.

Did that pose a problem in finding a producer?

Absolutely, but Manmohan Shetty, my long-time friend, was always by my side to support me. I knew I could depend on him. For years, he had been urging me to make *Ardha Satya II.* I felt the title would be misleading but a sequel in spirit would be fine. I narrated the idea to Shetty. He was ready to back it. My next stop was Amitji. I had made up my mind that if he said 'no', I would drop the subject. When I met him, he was geared for a narration but I'm a poor story-teller so I offered him the concept and character note. He promised to read it and get back to me. He got back within a week to say he was game.

How long did it take you to get ready to shoot?

We got cracking and were ready with the final draft in three months. I had warned him that I had to complete the film within a year and he assured complete cooperation. There were minor hiccups in between. Before we went on floors he said he was doing two more films as a cop – *Khakee* and *Lakshya* – and if I wanted I could substitute him with someone else. I asked if my film had similarities with others and he said no. The second delay came when his father turned critical. He had cancelled all his shoots and his schedules went awry. He phoned to say there was a possibility that he would not be able to honour his commitments and if I wanted it, he would withdraw from the film. I appreciated his gesture both the times. It was very courteous and professional of him to do so.

The mahurat of the film created a stampede at Rajkamal Studio.

Yes, and I wasn't prepared for the chaos. The media almost hijacked the event and had it not been for Amitji's timely interference in controlling the mob, it would have been difficult to commence the shooting. For the guests it was yet another event but for those involved, it was an anxious day. Fortunately, for me, both my actors – Amitji and Om Puri – were well prepared and I appreciated that. On the very first day of the shooting, I learnt something about Amitji. When the camera rolls, he offers nothing but his best. Unless you have that killer instinct, you cannot be a superstar.

As a film-maker what qualities attract you to an actor?

Passion, when Amitji and I first began talking of doing a film together, he said, 'I want to do a role where I lose my sleep.' I was taken aback, I said, 'Let's not be under so much pressure. Let's do a film that is effective and at the same time we can have a little fun.'

That's untrue because your films seldom project fun.

It depends on what your definition of fun is. My films are meant for a certain audience. *Dev,* I agree, has no place for comedy. It talks about riots… about how the police handle what happens to people.

Why are all your films so violent?

Now that's really unfair. There is more violence in real life than we show in our films. Violence exists in my films, I agree, but never as an item or to provide entertainment. *Ardha Satya* was made twenty years ago. Corruption is still there but the police now have to subvert to communal ideologies. There is no glamourization of violence in my films, no stylization. On the contrary it is always as an undercurrent. Most of the time it's gurgling underneath and that is why it is so much more terrifying.

Looking back, what do you think went wrong with *Thakshak?*

I was making a film after a long break and a lot had changed in the interim. There was a lot of pressure on me to aim for a mainstream film and I began with small compromises till I came to a point where I felt completely trapped in the system. *Thakshak* is an antithesis of the message of Lord Hanuman who is a symbol of loyalty. We have grown up listening to stories of the deity tearing his chest to show pictures of Lord Ram and Sita. *Thakshak* related the story of a different kind of friendship, between two underworld men. The idea didn't work.

Casting Amitabh Bachhan and Om Puri together is a strange idea?

Both are brilliant artistes and it's my privilege to have them together. They are highly professional and share a similar attitude to work. Both are disciplined and come prepared on the sets. I have never seen Amitji refer to his paper ever once he is on the sets. When he needs to prepare for major scenes, he goes to his van. Om Puri has a slightly different technique, but because I have done so many films with him I'm familiar with his rhythm. He says I'm a very greedy director because no matter how good the shot is I will always insist on an extra take. He is right because somehow, I always feel that maybe, the actor will be able to give me something better in the next shot.

But that can be very frustrating for the actors.

Not when they sense that the director is connected with them. Then they understand that it is for the improvement of the scene. In a moment like that everyone is above personal inadequacies. The set is charged with intensity and everyone is working towards a common goal. Often a director has no explanations for why he asks for retakes, it's only when he gets what he wants that he is able to articulate what was missing.

Can you give an example?

We were shooting a scene with Kareena Kapoor and Fardeen Khan where she is pleading with him not to get involved in violent situations. It was a very simple scene but as experts will agree, the most difficult scenes are the simple ones. After several trials, during which time Kareena and Fardeen were not able to reach a level of synchronization with their gestures, they managed to do so, suddenly, in the fifth take. These are poetic moments when nothing matters except the truth and actors recognize them. They don't need reassurances from the director. Besides, I believe that the best communications on screen are when the actor is awkward and inarticulate. Every actor has a way of discovering his truth, a specific method of working. Some blossom with rehearsals. Some fade away and become mechanical. The combination scenes are testing times for the director. He has to be careful so as to be able to balance the strengths of all. As they say, direction is more about management than creativity.

Does familiarity between a director and actor harm or help chemistry?

Om Puri has done the maximum number of films with me and it has helped. I know I can depend on him for the most difficult scenes. He does his homework but does not carry the baggage on the sets. On the other hand, I'm not familiar with Amitabh Bachchan but there is a foundation of trust and that helps. One day before the shooting of an important scene Amitji and Om Puri were horsing around and I was a bit worried about whether they would be able to get into the adequate mood, but once the camera started rolling, the shot was perfect.

What about younger actors like Kareena Kapoor and Fardeen?

Kareena is a natural and spontaneous. When she does not understand the subtext, she questions the interpretations. She relies on her instinct. She has only one talkie scene with Amitji but she is brilliant in it and was all charged up on the day of the shoot. On the other hand, Fardeen is a director's actor. He is attentive and patient. You guide him and he will follow you like a child, holding your hand. There are so many special moments in scenes between them that were contributed by the actors.

Would you agree that women in your films are always oppressed?

That's a somewhat simplistic description of my women. My women characters may begin as victims but finally emerge emancipated, be it in *Drishti* or *Hazaar Chaurasi Ki Maa.* I agree their empowerment comes from certain compromises and, to an extent, a certain unhappiness as well, but their concerns are real. Deep down, they are strong-willed women.

Yash Chopra

Cinema is my life and passion

Hum Tum, *Dhoom*, and *Veer-Zaara* on its way. How does it feel having hits raining in your backyard?

I feel scared every single time and I say that: it is all because of the blessings of the Almighty. I feel truly humbled by this showering of good fortune. I often wonder if I deserve so much affection from him. I'm fortunate to be connected to a medium I enjoy. Cinema is my life and my passion.

There has to be some secret formula that the Chopras have mastered and the others haven't. What is the secret behind so many successes?

I don't think any such formula exists. I have been honest and extremely hardworking. My banner has never believed in setting up

The interview was conducted in 2004 before the release of *Veer-Zaara*. *Jab Tak Hai Jaan* (2012) was Yash Chopra's last release as a director. He died on 21 October 2012.

proposals. We made films because we saw potential in the subject, and this transparency in intention and our undying passion for our art reflects in the product.

After so many years and films is it possible to remain objective about your work? What is your barometer to check that you are on the right track?

There is an art to watching a film but this art mysteriously deserts you when you are watching your own creation. I'm less attached to films I produce but I cannot be objective about the films I direct. Film-makers all over the world, I'm sure, feel the same way. But despite the underlying web of emotions, there is a method of checking that you are on the right track. The barometer varies from project to project. Sometimes something clicks during a story narration; sometimes during the shooting; and sometimes when you watch the final print. An inner voice always warns you when you are making a mistake.

And what does the inner voice tell you about your forthcoming film *Veer-Zaara*?

The inner voice guides me on creativity, not commercial success. It tells me that I have given it my best shot and I'm thoroughly satisfied with the product. I have no regrets.

Did you expect *Hum Tum* or *Dhoom* to become such huge successes? What do you think clicked about them?

None of us expected it and we are still recovering from the shock. Both the films were meant to be moderate-budget quickies. *Hum Tum*, a love story, was launching Saif Ali Khan as a lead and *Dhoom,* an action film, was a non-starrer, but its business has already crossed six crore in Mumbai itself. Nobody can analyse success. It's a mystery and if one could, there would be no failures.

To what extent do your hits and flops affect your family?

I guess as much as any normal family in any other business. We are a small unit of five members and our anxieties and joys are linked to each other's fortune and future. It's only natural to feel concerned.

What role has Aditya Chopra, your elder son, played in the growth of your banner?

When I launched the banner many years ago I lent it my passion, credibility and stability. Three decades later, my son lends his modern vision and vast knowledge of technology to the banner. We have different styles of working, but we work well creatively. On the administrative front not just us but the entire staff has clearly demarcated duties to avoid confusion. We have capable heads in every department, in every city, and they perform their duties with commitment.

How is work divided between you and your sons?

I concentrate on the distribution offices in India and abroad. The music company and the studio need more attention because they are still new firms. Aditya takes charge of the film productions: everything from the concept to the marketing and exhibition of every film. It was my idea that he launched his own production company. He works so hard, he deserves a separate title. So after much resistance, he agreed. *Hum Tum* and *Dhoom* are Aditya Chopra Productions, which is a part of Yash Raj Films. I remain the presenter of all films produced under the banner, his as well as mine. My younger son, Uday, is an actor but when he is not shooting he participates in all creative discussions.

What happens when there is a conflict of interest or ideology?

Conflict is necessary for any kind of growth. We disagree on several issues but because we live in the same house we have ample opportunities to vocalize our thoughts. To be honest, I had not expected either *Hum Tum* or *Dhoom* to work commercially but Adi was convinced that there was novelty in the attitude. He was so confident that I trusted his conviction.

Any other instance when you were apprehensive and his reasoning convinced you?

Dil To Pagal Hai was his concept and title. We were to originally make *Maine To Mohabbat Ki* penned by Javed Siddiqui and Honey Irani, but Adi felt the story was a bit outdated. He suggested we postpone the shooting dates for some time while he worked on the story. We agreed and the decision proved fruitful.

When Aditya launched as a director, his *Dilwale Dulhaniya Le Jayenge* resembled Yash Chopra classics. Then Yash Chopra's *Dil To Pagal Hai* resembled Aditya's debut film. Later Aditya's *Mohabbatein* was reminiscent of Yash Chopra's *Deewar* drama. So who is influencing whom?

When my son made his debut as a director, I opted to be the production controller because I wanted to make sure nothing went wrong on the sets. My contribution as a producer was a 100 per cent but as a creative person, zero. *Dilwale Dulhaniya* is solely Aditya's baby. Today, when I'm making my lavish project *Veer-Zaara*, my son and I have reversed roles. He is the co-producer as well as my first assistant. He says, 'Papa, whatever you need, just ask. You don't have to go hunting for locations and props. It will be made available to you on your desk, in your air-conditioned cabin.'

Would you say cinema has changed a lot in recent years?

I don't feel so, perhaps because my banner has remained steadfastly active. It was systematic even in the earlier days, when I assisted my brother B.R. Chopra. Bhaisaab was an extremely organized worker. Today, I notice there is greater discipline on the sets and technology has proved a great facilitator. Whether it is costumes or auditions, everyone is so focused. The younger generation does not leave anything to chance and their paperwork is perfect. Every department has a blueprint of schedules so there are no miscommunications on the sets.

How was it adjusting to sync-sound camera and screen monitors telling you that a take is okay?

Monitors were helpful but sync-sound was a bit difficult to accept initially. One is used to the sound of the camera, which in a way helps everyone to concentrate on the shot. The chilling silence on the sets was intimidating but one got used to it after a while. It is all about a mindset, I learnt that one does not have to belong to a particular region to understand that culture. Art director Sharmishtha Roy, for instance, has never been to Lahore or Chandigarh but with travel and research, created a perfect set for *Veer-Zaara*. It was the same with costume designer Manish Malhotra. Adi has never been to Pakistan but has scripted a love story about a Pakistani girl and an Indian boy.

What made him write a legendary love story set in Pakistan?

When we were planning our new film he was adamant that we must not set one more love story in urban India or abroad. He was very clear that the surroundings had to be different. Then one day, when my wife Pam, my daughter-in-law Payal and I were in the room, he announced that he had an idea! He said he'd narrate two scenes to us. We loved what he read and asked him to elaborate further. A month later, he narrated the entire story to the family and all of us were convinced that it was the right subject.

How much was the decision influenced by India's recently reformed relationship with Pakistan?

I have read in the papers that my film was conceived to facilitate Indo-Pak relations but there is no truth in these stories. My film does not propagate war, religion or the pain of Partition. There is an inherent drama in the film provided by the locales, which inadvertently define the tone of the film. The music and the moments in *Veer-Zaara* are very different from those in my earlier films.

This is the first time you are working with a writer who is not just your son but also your chief assistant, how claustrophobic can that get?

He was perpetually present on the sets, so I could not alter his lines in the slightest way. In the past, none of my writers, Salim Javed, Dr Rahi Masoom Reza or Javed Siddiqui, have ever been on my sets during shoots. That was the biggest difference. Adi is an organized worker. He has no problems reworking the scenes but would like you to approve before going on the sets. Once on the sets, he will not allow any second thoughts. To be fair to him, it was equally trying for him for this was the first time he was parting with his screenplay and handing it over to another director with whom there was no chance or scope of overstepping, his father.

Why couldn't he have directed the film himself?

I suggested it to him but he declined. He said he could write it because emotions are universal but to direct it, he had to be familiar with the ambience. He felt the subject called for maturity and I was more appropriate for the film. He was right, *Veer-Zaara* is a mellow, understated, love story. Lahore and Punjab have been a part of my formative years and I was ready to make an eternal love story.

You had a consultant on your set to guide you on the culture and customs of Pakistan...

Yes, Chinni Rehman, our consultant conducted extensive workshops with the lead actors on their dialect. She was always present on the sets to give feedback on costumes and sets. Before we went on floors, I took presentations from all the department heads. The film entails a lot of detailing. None of the characters wear jewellery unless there is an occasion of celebration. The entire process of the shoots, whether it was underwater, in the snow or in a hilly region, was a sublime experience.

Your last release was a long time ago, didn't you miss shooting all these years?

I did. It has been seven years since the release of *Dil To Pagal Hai* and eight years since I shot it. I was dying to make a film and I was nervous too. People have high expectations and you cannot measure expectations just in the way you cannot measure emotions.

Was Aishwarya Rai the original Zaara replaced from the film because of her fall out with Shah Rukh Khan?

I don't indulge in such stories. I signed Aishwarya Rai soon after she won the Miss World title but have not been able to use her ever since. Adi used her very briefly in *Mohabbatein* but my commitment of casting her is still pending. There are absolutely no problems between us and we will work together as soon as I find the right role for her.

It is the first time you are working with Rani Mukerji and Preity Zinta, how was the experience?

When I had heard just two scenes of the narration, I phoned Rani and told her that she was playing the lawyer in my film. It's an outstanding role and nobody could have played this except her. I thought of Preity as Zaara because she has so far not been projected in traditional roles. I auditioned her complete with make-up and costume and, only after the results, confirmed her for the role. She was so thrilled to be roped in for a Yash Raj Film that she didn't bother to hear the story. She said it was her mother's long-cherished dream that she work with our banner.

Your banner has, over the years, brought rival stars together.

As far as I know, the rivalry does not exist. If there are undercurrents, I'm not involved as long as it does not interfere with my film. I've worked with the biggest and the best from Sharmila-Raakhee in *Daag* and Rekha-Jaya in *Silsila*, to Madhuri-Karisma in *Dil To Pagal Hai* and Rani-Preity in *Veer-Zaara*, and let me tell you, none of the stars have ever given me any reason to be alarmed.

Eleven years ago, you launched Shah Rukh Khan. Today, he is a raging superstar. Have the equations altered between you?

Eleven years ago, he did *Darr* because he wanted to do something different. He didn't even hear my story. On the contrary, he narrated to me his other negative roles so that there was no overlapping in the films. Today, Shah Rukh does films with my banner because he has bonded with us as family. He still does not listen to the stories, and says that he trusts Adi and me. He never discusses payment, he says, 'Give what you want.' Our relationship has become stronger with time.

How much has he transformed over the years as an actor and as a person?

His stardom is indisputable and overseas he is even a bigger draw than at home. As an actor, he has surpassed himself in *Veer-Zaara.* His detractors will not find any residue of the old image. As a person, I feel his children have transformed him completely. He is a great father and is obsessed with spending quality time with his kids. Before confirming dates with any producer, he first checks his children's calendars to make sure that he is not giving away their vacation dates. This thoughtfulness has to be appreciated.

You have grown up on *Mughal-e-Azam* and now share a release with the re-release of the classic…

My release date was confirmed irrespective of who was releasing their film on that day. After forty-four years I still feel emotional about *Mughal-e-Azam,* like everybody else of my generation. But to expect that just because one's favourite vintage car is going to be on the road, no other car should drive on the highway is not fair. There are four releases this Diwali and I'm certain everyone will find sufficient audiences.

While most of your contemporaries have packed up, you are the only director of your generation to still connect with your audience. What's the secret?

I don't know, maybe it is because I don't have any distractions from my work or maybe I don't take my talent for granted. I've never thought about this.

The Dada Saheb Phalke Award, a rocking banner, so many titles and so many hits, what more does Yash Chopra want?

More films, I guess. Over here, you are judged by your success, not good films.

And how good is *Veer-Zaara* by your estimation?

Aditya's work is extraordinary in the film. Just as *Deewar* cannot be mentioned without crediting the dialogues, similarly *Veer-Zaara* cannot be appreciated without acknowledging the dialogues. Because he is my son, I cannot take away credit from him.

Aren't you underplaying your own contribution?

I wouldn't do that either. In all modesty, I'd say I have enhanced his script.

Section 4

The Specialists

They say Hollywood is obsessed with youth so actresses past forty need to consciously work on a new image. My film-makers have always cast me as a sex symbol but now there is going to be a shift. I'm going to now play more mom roles than a sex symbol and I intend to prove that older women have just as much strength in Hollywood as younger women and men.

Catherine Zeta-Jones, Hollywood actress

Shyam Benegal on Women

Women emerge stronger because they are survivors

Why are women in your films always oppressed?

A universal set of qualities applies to men which doesn't to women. Conventionally and traditionally, women cannot do certain things that men can and this evokes strong responses against social inequality.

Laxmi, in *Ankur*, hurling stones at the zamindar is not a social response but a feeling of anguish.

That's right. Her outburst is personal, but the little child throwing the pebble in the end, shows the transference of a wider expression. The child rebels against the system, in the climax he rebels against oppression, and his strength emerges from watching her in pain.

> The interview was conducted in 1993. *Mammo* (1994), *Sardari Begum* (1996), *Hari Bhari* (2000) and *Zubeidaa* (2001) were Benegal's other women-oriented films. *Well Done Abba* (2009) was his last release as a director.

Laxmi is oppressed on many levels. On a personal level, she is abandoned by her husband, who she is not sure will return. She is attracted to the young zamindar and pursues a tentative relationship with him even though she knows the relationship has no future. This tells us a lot about her sexuality, she is without defences.

The headmaster's wife Sushila, in *Nishant*, gives coy glances to the zamindar in the marketplace. Surely, she isn't all that innocent?

My films recognize different facets of a woman's character. Experience has taught me that human beings react differently under different circumstances. Some of them may appear out of character but does this gives us the right to be judgemental? My films have refrained from making judgements. Laxmi may have failed according to tradition but for her survival, the answer may be no.

Your women characters are never hung up on morality...

It's because they are human. Sushila, for instance, has no complaints against her husband, Girish Karnad, and leads a dull life absorbed in domesticity. She is unable to, and has perhaps never tried to, express her sexuality to her man. The landlord's son spots her in a marketplace, fancies her and abducts her. He recognizes her sexuality, an honour he will not bestow upon his wife.

She chooses to run away with her abductor in the climax when she could have returned to her husband.

Yes, because she is responding to life. She feels protective towards her abductor in the wake of the riots and feels secure with him.

Junoon was in a way a reversal of roles for Shabana Azmi.

That's right, in *Nishant,* the other man (Naseerudin Shah) is obsessed with her. In *Junoon,* her husband is obsessed with the other woman (Nafisa Ali). The only difference being Shashi displays the tradition of honour towards the phirangi hostages—mother, Jennifer and daughter, Nafisa, and Naseeruddin Shah defies tradition and follows his heart. Women emerge as the stronger sex because they are forced to fight for survival. Society puts that pressure on them. Life is full of complexities and women are a part of life.

Ramli of *Manthan* is the only character in your films who does not stray. She stands her ground, not losing focus from the real issue.

It's because she functions within the boundaries of tradition. It is revelatory how much stronger a woman is if she remains tradition-bound. She is secure and therefore will not falter.

How would you describe the character in *Bhumika*?

Urvashi lives life on her own terms, exactly the way men do. She is financially independent and entitled to more choices. Still, there is a void. She is searching for happiness in every relationship and discovers that there are terms of endearment. Eventually, she accepts her loneliness. The end is poignant; she is doomed to be desolate and accepts it.

What inspired *Kalyug*?

***Kalyug* is the Mahabharata set in modern times. The Mahabharata is the greatest epic ever written and after centuries we are still borrowing from its plot and its characters. Set against the backdrop**

of an industrial family, the film focused on the intricate politics within a large joint family. It's about the dominance of women. The eldest bahu of the family, Supriya, played by Rekha, enforces her strength by proxy. All the women characters – and there are many in the film – tread upon complex, delicate emotions.

Women seem to have played a strong role in your formative years?

That's right, all the women in my formative years have had a positive influence on me. My mother, sisters, their friends and various girls I knew in school and college and, in later years, women I worked and interacted with, and finally my wife and daughter. It is my observation that openly or subtlely all women are oppressed. Some discuss it, some joke about it, some condemn it, but they are all victims. It made me realize that gender discrimination is an attitude like the caste issue, and we need to rise above the traditional hierarchy.

Trikaal was an intriguing film but very dark, was Ingmar Bergman an inspiration?

Bergman deals with protestants. *Trikaal* was about the Goan Catholics and their old values. It's a story about a family that has lived in a mansion for three hundred years and carries its legacy. The best way to describe the family is to compare it with a Ming vase. You can either perceive it as an ordinary vase or view it as a relic of the Chinese dynasty.

And how would you describe *Mandi* – a township of prostitutes? How did you think of this unusual story?

Most men prefer their women not to work even today. The upper class 'allows' them if it's a cultural indulgence. The middle class compromises under economic pressure and the lower class doesn't know any other way. The prostitute is the only one who functions without classification or discrimination. *Mandi* told the story about one such township, which, despite constant pressure, rises above crisis. Rukminibai and her girls face the upheavals and establish themselves; somehow women have that kind of power to survive in the worst situations.

At the end of twenty-five years, how does it feel to be discovering so many talented actors?

They are not my discoveries and I'm not being modest. If it hadn't been me who gave them a break, it would have been someone else. From Shabana Azmi to Annu Kapoor, they were much too talented to rust away.

In all this celebration, do you miss Smita Patil?

I do, we did so many films together and could have done a few more, though I'm not sure how active she would have been as an actor were she alive today. For a while she would have been busy with the baby but coming from the family she does, she would have been an activist.

Yash Chopra on Love

Love is the most important thing in life

Dhool Ka Phool was about an unwed mother succumbing to societal pressures and abandoning her child. A nobleman enters her life, offers to marry her and accepts the baby. The song *'Tu Hindu banega na Musalman banega...'* picturized on Manmohan Krishnan, is an immortal tribute to anti-communalism relevant in today's turbulent times. The story idea was by bhaisaab (B.R. Chopra) and in keeping with his banner's tradition of socially relevant films. Pandit Mukhram Sharma, an unusually systematic writer of his times, wrote the screenplay. The lighter moments in the film were my inputs. I lent a philosophic tone to the romance.

In a five-decade career spanning twenty films, Yash Chopra made ten unforgettable romantic films presenting love's different seasons. The interview was conducted post *Veer-Zaara. Jab Tak Hai Jaan* (2012) was Yash Chopra's last release as a director.

There was a scene where the bicycles of the hero and the heroine collide into each other. I was asked to delete the scene by the censors because they found it vulgar. Today our definition of vulgarity is different. Morality changes with times and our films stand testimony to that.

Mala Sinha is the victim in the film and Rajendra Kumar the culprit. Nanda, Rajendra Kumar's wife, is the innocent recipient of her partner's crime. Ashok Kumar, the most important character of the quadrangle, is the crusader. I was only twenty-six when I made this film and had to brief Nanda about childbirth. She was amused and said, 'How do you know so much about delivery, you've never been pregnant, have you?'

The film was a runaway hit. We went to Hooghly for the silver jubilee function and there was a stampede. We were asked to come out on the theatre balcony and wave to the audience. As far as the eye could see there were only faces, it seemed like the whole city had come out on the streets that day. It was a terrifying feeling. I was scared of the future, scared of whether I'd be able to sustain the magic.

Dharmputra was based on a novel by Chatursen Shastri and it reflects on the perils of Partition. A Muslim girl gets pregnant and gives away her child to her Hindu neighbour. The child grows up to be a fanatic. When the truth is revealed, he suffers an identity crisis.

It was the most controversial film of that time and both communities threatened to burn down theatres if the film was released. The exhibitors weren't willing to release the film and to give them confidence, Shashi Kapoor, Deven Verma and I sat in the manager's room for all the shows every single day, but the box-office returns weren't encouraging. All of us were heartbroken. Around this time I attended a film function where Prithviraj

Kapoor, Meena Kumari and Mehboob Khan were full of praise for my film. Dilip Kumar was present at the function too. He sensed I was low and, after the party, took me for a drive in his car. We drove aimlessly on the streets of Mumbai till the wee hours of morning. I don't remember what he said, but his words were like a balm to me and offered me solace. When I returned home, I learnt that *Dharmputra* a had won the National Award for Best Film. This was some consolation after the box-office rejection.

Waqt was about a family separated in an earthquake, the first lost-and-found film of Hindi cinema. It was written by Akhtar Mirza, the writer of several hit films and the father of Saeed and Aziz Mirza. Our original casting was Prithviraj Kapoor and his three sons Raj, Shammi and Shashi. Papaji (Prithviraj) was enchanted by the idea, but wanted to reserve the novel casting for the RK banner. Bhaisaab was disappointed but then he met Bimal Roy and he said it would be a mistake to sign on real family because the audience will not accept their separation and the casting would be more damaging than helpful to the film. He was right.

We retained Shashi Kapoor and signed Sunil Dutt for the second brother. Rajendra Kapoor declined the middle brother's role because he was doing a similar role in L.V. Prasad's *Beti Bete*. Raj Kumar, who had earlier dropped out of *Dhool Ka Phool* because he had reservations about working with a new director, was confirmed for the role of the eldest brother on condition that there would be no discussions on the sets. Any query regarding his role or character would be addressed off the sets directly with the writer of the film and both of us honoured the agreement.

Waqt was the BR banner's first colour film and it was very generous of bhaisaab to trust me with the responsibility despite my two earlier flops. The film had sprawling sets and elaborate costumes, two consistent factors in all my films. Dress designer

Bhanu Athaiya, Sadhana and I personally shopped for Sadhana's wardrobe for the film.

A few days prior to the release, there was a black out in the country. Those were the days of the Indo-China aggression and the audience wasn't inclined towards entertainment. Well-wishers advised me to delay the release but the prints were already delivered. Finally, with the help of an air marshal friend I managed to retrieve the reels and weeks later, when the political clouds had cleared, we released the film.

It was India's first multi-star film and received a stupendous opening. On the morning of the release, we performed a havan at home, a tradition practised to this day for all our films. The entire unit was present for the puja. From there all of us headed to the press show at Naaz Theatre followed by lunch where all my artistes played hosts to the media. In the evening we met again for the premiere. The men were dressed in identical suits tailored from the same fabric while all the women were dressed in white.

After the show, we travelled to Mumbai's Hotel Sun'n'Sand, drank till late in the night and dined at dawn. At 5 a.m., all of us jumped into the swimming pool wearing what we had worn to the premiere. Soaked to the skin, we drove to a local restaurant for tea but our party wasn't over yet. We then drove up to a newspaper vendor and purchased the new copy of the cinema weekly *Screen*, and were delighted to look at the pictures and news of our premiere. Such camaraderie can never be regained.

Ittefaq was done as a quickie. When we were at the tail end of the shoot of *Aadmi Aur Insaan*, I felt the climax needed to be reshot but, unfortunately, our heroine Saira Banu was in London undergoing a surgery. We had no choice but to wait for her. During this long break, we went to watch a Gujarati play *Dhumas*. We were so impressed by it that the following day we watched the play again with our entire story department. *Ittefaq* was scripted in seven days and shot in twenty-eight days in chronological order. It was edited and mixed simultaneously and released within a record three months. The film had a number of firsts to its credit. It was the first non-song, two-hour Hindi suspense thriller to be released without an interval and again love was the undercurrent of the film.

Our first choice for the heroine was Raakhee but she was under a contract with the Rajshris for *Jeevan Mrityu.* Nanda got to hear of the role from her brother-in-law who was working with us and showed an interest in playing the part. We needed someone with a traditional image and signed her on. Rajesh Khanna was under a contract with United Producers and so was available to us. On the last day, I still remember, I shot for twenty-eight hours at a stretch and when I went home I was exhausted but couldn't sleep because I was so excited.

Ittefaq released and proved a roaring success. Saira Banu was back from London and ready to reshoot the climax. The film addressed corruption in the public sector. Initially, we had thought of a sequence where the dam bursts. But, later, we altered the plot around the public sector issue to narrate a story of two friends – one honest, the other dishonest.

Mumtaz wasn't a conventional heroine; she was beautiful but not traditional. As the film progresses, however, you discover that she has a heart too; it's just that her priorities are different. Human emotions are inconsistent; it's how you feel and what you say that makes all the difference.

I had just got married and moved out of my brother's nest. I was keen on launching my own banner and had met author Gulshan Nanda who had an interesting subject – *Daag.* While on my honeymoon, I thought of a unique treatment for the film and discussed it with Gulshanji on my return. He approved of it instantly. I summoned my creative team and we got cracking. Three friends stood by me like a rock: Sharmila Tagore, Rajesh Khanna and Raakhee. Raakhee returned my signing amount, saying, 'Keep it as a loan and return it to me when your film is a hit.' I can never forget her gesture.

Daag was a libelous subject and we expected problems with the censors, but they gave me a clear certificate. While I was returning from the censor office, Rajesh Khanna was on a horse on his way to his wedding mandap. The distributors were sure that the film would fail and released it with just eleven prints in Mumbai. Almost a dozen of Khanna's films had flopped in a row and they predicted doom! But within just four days, eighteen more prints were ordered. The film received an unprecedented opening.

One day Salim-Javed narrated a subject about a dock worker in a shipyard who becomes a don. Inspired from the life of the underworld don Haji Mastan, the story had spark. Every detail you see in the film was in the script. *Deewaar* was a perfect screenplay with perfect casting, made at the most opportune time.

Essentially a family story of two brothers, the film also told the story of their lady loves. Amitabh, an outlaw, is attracted to a call girl while Shashi Kapoor, a police officer, is involved with a girl from a good family. Their concerns and the undertones of their relationships are different. The brothers love their partners, but their first love is their mother.

Kabhie Kabhie was a love story I had been obsessed with for several years. I often wondered what happened to lovers married to different partners. Life could either be happy or a compromise. The film was about two such lovers, Amitabh and Rakhee. Rakhee, who is married to Shashi Kapoor, lives happily, while Amitabh who is married to Waheeda Rehman, becomes a bitter man. Amitabh played a poet in the film and my distributors felt it was a mistake to cast him in such a role in the wake of *Deewaar*, but I disagreed.

The wedding fever in cinema was initiated by *Kabhie Kabhie*. The opening song is the crux of the story and the deflowering of the bride on the suhaag raat, the ultimate erotic scene that is still talked about after all these years, was borrowed from a crude phrase – nath utarna – except that I presented the process aesthetically.

The first rush print had Amitabh in a long shot watching the couple take the nuptial rounds and with every round, there are inter-cuts of his fantasy involving Rakhee. When I was rerecording, my sound recordist Mangesh Desai commented that the scene was too artistic and could be misinterpreted so we changed it to Rakhee visualizing Amitabh lifting her veil during the song. I wanted her eyes to reflect the pain of her beloved and therefore deliberately placed the camera at an angle whereby Shashi Kapoor could not watch her face except in the end.

Trishul was about an illegitimate son settling scores with his father, a traumatic story of love-hate relationships, and romance was not the focus of the story. The film is about the family, the other relationships are incidental.

One day, during the shoot, producer Gulshan Rai mentioned that film-maker Mushir-Riaz's new release *Meera* was a disaster at the box-office. Javed Akhtar, co-writer of *Trishul*, was present in the room and in his characteristic humour joked, 'That's because we've still to release *Trishul*...' Javed wasn't joking. We had shot more than three-fourths of the film but all of us agreed that something was amiss. We stalled shooting for a while, reworked the screenplay and reshot for almost twenty to twenty-five days. The change was worth it. Even Javed acknowledged that. He said Salim and he should only partly be credited for the screenplay for all of us had given our inputs to *Trishul*.

We attach so much importance to the form of a film that we often overlook the soul. In my opinion, no matter how fabulous the structure, unless the soul is stirred, the audience isn't moved. *Kaala Patthar* lacked soul! With a number of hits in a row we were flying high on our success and were swept off our feet. We believed that whatever we touched would become successful until *Kaala Patthar* proved us wrong. The film had a terrific opening, but it wasn't a grosser. It wasn't a losing proposition either.

Kaala Patthar was the victim of the star system. My banner had a halo around it. I got carried away, hiring technicians from Hollywood for the special effects, but failed to capitalize on the charisma of a great star cast. Romance is not a priority in the story and sometimes I regret that.

Silsila had inherent tensions because of the casting coup. If I was confident of the project it was because all three artistes had individually assured me that there would be no problems at their end and they kept their word. It was the first film on extra-marital relationships and I developed cold feet at the last minute. The original ended differently but I changed it to the hero returning home to his wife. When and why I changed the ending I don't know, but I did so because I felt that the audience wasn't ready. I was wrong because the audience didn't buy what we offered them either.

The film is special because it has immortal moments. For Rekha's husband I wanted Sanjeev Kumar but he had reservations. After *Sholay* and *Trishul* he wasn't willing to play second fiddle to a script that focused on Amitabh Bachchan. He wasn't willing to even listen to the story, but I insisted and followed him to Bangalore. We were halfway through the narration and I was telling him about the restaurant scene when Rekha and Amitabh take the dance floor and Sanjeev interrupted me. He phoned his secretary to check his dates and confirmed that he would do the film.

For *Mashaal* I wanted Kamal Haasan as the younger hero. We thought we would make him a South Indian character finding his bearings in Mumbai. When we spoke to him, however, he declined, saying he wanted a role equal to Dilip Kumar's. Anil Kapoor was the star on the rise those days and we took a gamble. He was very excited with the offer, more so because it gave him the opportunity of working with Dilip Kumar. There were times he got carried away and Dilip Kumar had to take him aside and calm him down.

The best moment in the film is when Waheeda Rehman dies and Dilip Kumar is pleading for help. We shot two versions of the scene over four days and eight shifts, but when you watch the film you cannot sense the breaks. That's the brilliance of the actor. We put up Dilip Kumar at Hotel Taj to facilitate his travel to Ballard Pier, where we shot all night. He was appreciative of our thoughtfulness, said his reflexes were slow and thus he needed that much more time to recuperate. Kamal Haasan attended the premiere and said had he known the role was so good, he would never have turned it down.

Sometimes the director turns obstinate and pays a price for it. *Faasle* was the price I paid for being stubborn. I was in the mood to make a film with newcomers. Then, suddenly, I had second thoughts and contacted Anil Kapoor. He had no dates but promised to accommodate me. In the interim I changed my mind again – call it vinaash buddhi or destiny, but the damage was done. Some blamed the debacle on my hero Rohan Kapoor, some on the characterization of Sunil Dutt. Critics said no matter how bad a son-in-law is, no father-in-law would whip him. The sad thing about a film's failure is that even the good things go unnoticed. There were many beautiful things about the film that went unsung.

Faasle portrayed the seasons of love. Raj Kiran abuses his woman despite the sanctity of marriage while Sunil Dutt nurtures his mistress without the pressures of society. Farha is the abused wife while Rekha is the unmarried recipient of undying love from her beloved.

Vijay was a rehash of *Trishul*. In everyone's life there comes a phase when everything goes wrong. This was my phase and the films I made during this time are a proof of that. I'm not proud of these films, but I cannot deny them since I made them. The only consolation being that everyone connected to the film made money. It set me thinking, however, and I made a promise to myself that no matter what the pressures, I would now only make films I believed in.

Writer Kamna Chander had given me a story on the basis of which I had signed Vinod Khanna, Sridevi and Rishi Kapoor. On the day of the mahurat, however, as I peeped through the lens, a wave of depression overcame me. It was a premonition that I had made a mistake. Here were three dashingly good-looking stars and what I had in mind for them was a regressive story. The next day I summoned my writer and my artistes and informed them that I was changing the story. The first half would remain the same since everyone had confirmed dates but the second needed rewriting.

While we left for a shoot abroad I got my team to rewrite the second half but even then I wasn't completely satisfied. One day, I was watching the final rushes and stopped at Vinod Khanna's action scene. I felt a sudden bitter taste in my mouth. I contacted Vinod and Sri and told them I wanted to revisit the sequence. The office sequence, where Sri hitches a ride from him, was an afterthought. *Chandni* marked the saturation point of violence in formula films. My distributors didn't agree though. One opted out of my film because I changed Vinod's entry scene and another did so because he disapproved of the music. I was confident that they would come around and they did.

The idea of a younger man being in love with an older woman and not being able to accept her marrying someone else had been haunting me for years. In my imagination the news of her death comes through a knock on the door. In the film, we show her sinking in the hospital. *Lamhe* was shot in two schedules, in London and Rajasthan. We shot the second schedule first. The novelty of the romance in *Lamhe* is that when the heroine is young, the hero is old and when the hero is young, the heroine older. Sridevi and Anil Kapoor complemented each other beautifully, but the highlight of the film were the dialogues by Dr Rahi Masoom Reza. They don't make writers like him anymore.

Parampara was about the sacrifices our ancestors make to honour tradition. Anil Kapoor was signed for the role but a few days before the shoot he backed out. I was in trouble and contacted Vinod Khanna, who was upset with me for not taking him in *Lamhe* and, now, was having to come in as a replacement. He could have refused, but he agreed.

With the hero in place, I now had a new problem: my heroine, Ashwini Bhave. She was riding high on the success of *Henna* and had signed on to pair with Anil Kapoor. She wanted to opt out because Vinod Khanna fell into the older bracket of heroes. After that it was a chain of events going wrong. Ramaya's character of a gypsy didn't make sense but it was too late to make alterations. I continued shooting but deep down I sensed that the damage was done. I knew it the day I began shooting the film and my fear was confirmed the day I saw the first trial.

Darr was about obsessive love and what it can drive you to do. Aamir Khan was my first choice for the role, then Ajay Devgn, Sanjay Dutt and finally, Shah Rukh Khan. When I called Shah Rukh over to my house I told him it was a negative role. He said he was already doing two negative roles in *Baazigar* and *Anjaam* and narrated the plots of both. He said if my film offered him another shade he was willing to do it.

Shah Rukh's role was very small, but the impact of the character was tremendous. After the release of *Darr* many women confessed about similar traumatic experiences from anonymous callers. Selective stammering was part of Rahul's characterization. Rahul is a normal boy, but gets hysterical only when he utters Kiran's name. When I saw the rushes I felt Shah Rukh had overdone the stammering, but he dissuaded me from altering it during the dubbing. 'You don't know what a powerful film you've made,' he said, and he was right. The audience applauds Sunny Deol for killing Shah Rukh, but in an inexplicable way misses him when he is no more because they are attracted to his intensity.

Dil To Pagal Hai was conceived as a simple idea that there is someone for everyone in the universe. You have to only look for the signs to recognize that special person. The original title of the film was *Maine Mohabbat Ki*. My son Aditya felt that the title was too serious and we should either alter the story or the title. I liked the plot of musical shows and didn't want to alter the story so we altered the title for a more breezy effect. Today, any other title seems inappropriate for the film.

This was my first film where the characters don't carry the baggage of backgrounds, except perhaps Madhuri, who is the most stable character in the film. Karisma's role was offered to every actress in Hindi filmdom and turned down by Kajol, Juhi, even Urmila Matondkar. When I met Karisma for the film, I said to her, 'Don't refuse outright. Think about it for twenty-four hours before you say "no".' She said she didn't want to think. She said 'yes' right away and never regretted her decision.

I had been aching to make a classic love story and not liking anything offered by my story department. Finally, Aditya gave a concept about a girl in Pakistan and a boy in India and I jumped with joy. I was confident about the film from the day I heard the first narration and as the days went by, I felt more and more connected to my characters. Every actor cast in the film is appropriate for the character. Nobody but Shah Rukh would be able to play Veer and nobody except Rani Mukherjee could do justice to the lawyer's role. I auditioned many heroines for Zaara including Preity Zinta. The experience of shooting *Veer-Zaara* was sublime and cannot be explained in words. The real star of the film, however, is late Madan Mohan's melody. I'm grateful to Madan Mohan's son Sanjeev Kohli for offering me his father's unused tunes, for *Veer-Zaara* would never be the same without his compositions.

Amitabh Bachchan on Cops

Cops are human beings too, they have strong and weak moments

Your journey as a cop began with *Zanjeer*. Did you ever visit a police station or meet a real-life police inspector while preparing for a role?

No, I just followed the script and my instinct and that's how it has been all these years. The beauty of working with writers like Salim-Javed was that being performers themselves, they worked to the actor's advantage. Of course, the silences, the pauses and the emotional gaps had to come from the performer but it wasn't so difficult because the magical moments were all there on paper.

Out of the over 100 films that Amitabh Bachchan worked in his four-decade career, he played a cop in fifteen. *Khakee* (2003), *Dev* (2004) and *Bunty Aur Babli* (2005) were among his last releases as a cop.

Zanjeer was the first angry young hero of the Hindi screen.

Yes, but not that we analysed it at that time. I was an out-of-work actor those days. When the subject was narrated to me, I was drawn to it instantly. What was appealing about the character was that despite his seething anger and the justification of a turbulent past, his demeanour was calm. That is why his outburst makes such a strong impact. There was no conscious effort to adopt a particular body language. Whether it was pushing the chair or threatening the goonda, it was all in the script.

It is the only film where you wore your hair really short.

Yes, because I wasn't doing any other film at the time so there were no problems related to continuity in other films.

In *The Great Gambler*, you played a suave and flirtatious cop. The film was also your first double role, how did you differentiate between the two characters?

I played an officer in plain clothes and this was more because of commercial reasons than the demand of the script. There were no marked differences in the appearances of the two characters except for their wardrobes and their leading ladies. That's formula films, and part of the charm of doing double roles is to create confusion over identities. The audience loves it! As an actor, all I was worried about was whether the film would work at the box-office. Beyond that, I have to admit, there was no serious introspection involved as a performer.

That is strange considering you were playing at least one cop role every year.

Yes, but at the time one didn't view it like that. I related to the character from a wider perspective rather than just narrowing it down to his profession or background. The message of all my cop films was always bigger than my role or my stardom.

How would you bracket *Parvarish* and *Ram Balram*?

The social message of these films and the morality of the characters set them apart. *Parvarish* was unusual in the sense that I played an adopted son following in the footsteps of his foster father while his biological son (Vinod Khanna) grows up to become a smuggler. The message of the film is that upbringing is more important than genes. It was the same message in *Ram Balram*. Dharmendra and I are reared by a wicked uncle who abuses us for vested interests. We do as he says and don't realize the damage till much later. Both the films were more about family relationships than crime and justice.

The cop of *Dostana* rates friendship higher than love. Do certain roles create conflict in ideology?

It is unfair to equate real life with the world of make-believe. Unfortunately, such things happen only with us actors. Because of the nature of our work we are vulnerable victims of perceptions. My professional ethics can only dictate to me what is to be done on the sets, what happens beyond the studio gates is my life and my prerogative and I don't owe it to anyone to articulate my thought process. When you are playing so many characters, conflict is natural and it is for the performer to define his creative guidelines. There are many actors who find it difficult to go against their ideological/social/political/moral stand in their portrayals. In such cases it is important that actors define the boundary lines to avoid professional conflict. It should be very clear in their contract what they will or will not do.

What are the things you will or will not do on the big screen?

I have, from the very beginning of my career, stated that I will not to do kissing scenes and even though over the years there have been several occasions when the scene demanded it, I have refrained from doing it. Not because I'm being moralistic but simply because I'm uncomfortable.

What else?

Nudity, I have never done it and will not in future. Besides these, there are some unspoken areas where my sensibilities as a human being are offended and I will not perform those scenes on camera.

Can you give an example?

This is an indirect example but relevant to our discussion. We were shooting the climax of *Deewar*. I was on the run with Shashi Kapoor chasing me. The original script demanded that he fire three bullets at me. During the take, however, Shashi reasoned, that it went against his sensibilities to fire three bullets at a man who is unarmed and who is also his brother. Shashi felt that just one fatal firing was sufficient. There was a discussion and eventually Shashi had his way. I guess, if a human being is gravely affected by something and altering it would not really affect the screenplay, the sentiment should be respected.

In *Mahaan* you played a triple role. How would you differentiate the introvert cop from the tormented father and the entertaining twin?

The effort was to make all the three characters as different as possible and at the same time retain some similarities. So while the father is upright he has a funny side to him as well. One of

the twins inherits his father's humour and the other, his serious temperament. The problem about performing a triple role is that at any given time you are portraying at least two characters and are dealing with not just the physical attributes like the beard and the moustache but also their character traits. Timing is important but so is retaining eye contact. I made sure to fix my gaze on an immovable object among the props. Once the director was clear about his shot division, we'd record the entire scene with movements. Next we played the soundtrack and I would lip-sync like we do in songs, which balanced the movements. Shooting the film was very strenuous and despite all these precautions I remain dissatisfied with so many moments in the film.

Do you think singing-dancing cops like the ones you played in *Geraftaar* or *Inquilaab* exist in real life?

Why not? Cops are human beings too and have both strong and weak moments. There's no harm in singing and dancing. In *Inquilaab,* the officer's ultimate goal is to wipe out corruption from the country and to accomplish that he has to sacrifice some personal relationships and he is prepared for that. The film professed that the country is bigger than personal triumphs. It was a noble thought and I have complete faith that such characters exist in real life as well. The hero desires to become the chief minister not for personal gain but because that's the only way to clean up the system.

In *Aakhri Raasta* you oppose your father. Would you be able to rise above personal attachments in real life for the call of duty?

Such comparisons, though inevitable, are unfair. I don't let the characters I play take over my life. The script demanded that the son oppose his father but I don't view it so much as a conflict between father and son as that between a criminal and a cop. The film emphasized that the justification of a crime does not make you innocent and that duty is sacrosanct because, like personal relationships, it calls for commitment.

Nobody liked the corrupt cop played played in *Shahenshah* and were relieved when the true identity was revealed.

The film came close on the heels of my contesting the 1988 elections and unconsciously reflects the various influences and interactions with my constituency members. The role was different on paper but I felt that if we used the Avadhi dialect the character would work as a sharp contrast to the vigilant hero. What was interesting about these portrayals was that even the buffoon cop was not real. I agree with your observation of the corrupt cop but we need to remember that even he was only impersonating, biding his time before playing his card.

Cops portrayed in *Indrajeet*, *Akayla* and *Insaaniyat* were not effective; what do you think went wrong?

Roles become memorable because of the box-office success of a film. It's not as if these characters had nothing new to offer, they had. The heroes began as losers and emerged as winners eventually. In *Indrajeet*, I donned the disguise of a young man to avenge my daughter's murder while in *Akayla* I accomplish my mission despite being expelled from the police force. *Akayla* professed that it's not always possible to fight the system from within the legislation, that all problems are recurrent unless destroyed at the root. Shashi Kapoor endorsing the hero's actions due to lack of proof was a new expression in Hindi films. I have no memory of *Insaaniyat* as it was only a guest appearance.

Was it boring to be dressed in the cop uniform time and again for so many films?

No, because every time the measurements kept changing (*laughs*). And to try and avoid monotony, the script concentrated as much on the officer's social life to avail of ample opportunities to dress him in normal clothes and also featured in a love interest for an opportunity to include song and dance.

After playing a cop in over a dozen films would you say you are well informed about their ranks and rights?

Not much unfortunately. We try to be as authentic as possible but I'm sure there must have been areas where we went wrong. The closest we got to authenticity was with *Major Saab* and that was because the costumes were personally supervised by the Defence Academy.

Would you agree that the officer's trademark stick has become somewhat of a cliché?

There were times when the stick helped a scene but, yes, you're right, the prop by itself has become extremely clichéd. It calls for a lot of imagination on the part of the actor to use it effectively each time and, after a point, no matter how differently one uses it, it appears the same. That's the time to do away with it completely.

In *Bade Miyan Chhote Miyan* Govinda and you played double roles, one of which was a cop and the other a buffoon; it must have been crazy doing this film?

The film was a fun caper and I played the older of the duo. The most significant part of the characterization was that every time we played the buffoons, our performances had to go deliberately over-the-top. The film was a juxtaposition of situations and emotions

leading up to a hilarious climax. Govinda and I played cops but I think the buffoons got more claps from the audience.

The cop of *Aks* was dramatically different from any other cop you have portrayed so far.

In packaging, content and my appearance the role of a cop in this film stands apart from the those I have played in my previous films. The character has his idiosyncrasies and ideologies. He is a normal, happily married man with a child until an untoward incident changes the course of his life. He is assigned to nab a serial killer who has committed a string of heinous crimes. The film deals with paranormal experiences but it's not about spirits, it is about the soul. The Indian ethos has been eternally obsessed with the soul. That's why we pray for the departed soul and believe that while the body may have perished the soul remains.

A.R. Rahman on Compositions

I have refrained from being typecast

Are you really as unsocial as everyone makes you out to be?

I'm shy but not unsocial. I have my close group of friends with whom I let my hair down. But yes, I'm not overfriendly. My work calls me to meet all kinds of people and I'm used to interacting with strangers but how I deal with them depends entirely on my mood and circumstances. Sometimes you can have the best conversations with people you don't know.

Film-makers refer to you in superlatives. What is your assessment of yourself and work?

I deliver my best but it is not fair to give me all the credit for my tunes. My team works equally hard and so does the director who

The interview was conducted post *Swades* (2004). A.R. Rahman has since then been awarded two Oscars and a Golden Globe for original score and song in *Slumdog Millionaire* (2008). *Jab Tak Hai Jaan* (2012) was his last film as a composer.

projects my creation on a visual medium. I'm open to constructive criticism and encourage my team to tell me when they feel a particular tune is not working, and they do that. My assessment of my work stems from their responses and from the approval of my film-makers. I make sure I provide variations for every tune I compose so there is scope for discussion and selection. What they eventually accept or reject is what shapes the music of a film.

How do you decide which film-makers you will work with?

It's very tough and it's becoming increasingly difficult with time. Earlier, it was easier because I was not well known and could rely on my instinct. Now, there are greater expectations from me so one is perpetually frightened of making the wrong choice. The easiest way out is to continue working with people you've already worked with so there is a comfort zone like in the case of Mani Ratnam and, now, Ashutosh Gowariker. The credibility of the director and the lyricist is paramount otherwise at this stage of my career it is embarrassing to be attached with people who don't deliver. In the past, I have trusted every producer and delivered innumerable tunes but, after all these years, several of them remain in the cans. It is a colossal waste of time, energy and effort of my team and I'm not comfortable with it.

It's difficult to believe that any producer in current times will not fulfill a commitment made to A.R. Rahman.

I'm not saying that they do it deliberately or out of manipulation, it's the circumstances. They probably lack the finances or are facing some other problem. Let me give you an example: a few years ago, two directors approached me around the same time. The first was an established banner and the second, talented but new to the business. Both wanted compositions immediately and were ready to take tunes from my bank. The first, by my own admission, was an average composition and the second, above average. On instinct I gave the average composition to the established banner that transformed it into a chartbuster. The second, which was in fact the better tune, never got released. It's something I have always wondered about. There is a possibility that had I exchanged the tunes between the two film-makers, the superhit would have been an even bigger success.

There is a possibility that it may not have worked at all.

Sure, there is that possibility too. Till the tune is ready and finalized by the director, the music composer is never completely satisfied with his creation. He can never enjoy his own music until much later, sometimes, maybe even years later.

All your compositions, whether in Hindi or Tamil films, have an unmistakable Rahman touch, would you say that is an advantage or a disadvantage?

I have to admit that it is not deliberate but if it still exists, I take it as my identity. As long as my identity does not come in the way of my versatility I'm okay. There is a difference in being characteristic and in being typecast. So far, I think I've refrained from being typecast.

Film-makers seek inspiration from you, where do you seek your muse?

From life, from faith... I don't know and I'd rather not know. I don't think about it and I don't want to analyse too much. Sometimes reflection takes away from the natural process of journey. I guess it's about faith, and my faith stems from my religion. Nothing is possible without His will, neither my talent nor my innumerable compositions. He is secretly guarding it all and guiding me in my pursuits. The only time I feel I'm all alone and nobody can help is when I'm before a live audience at my concerts (*laughs*). I have done so many shows but I'm terrified every time I'm on stage and grateful that the Almighty guides me through it every single time.

You are deeply religious.

I surrender to my religion. It believes in one God. That is why I converted to Islam. My growing-up years were turbulent times for the family. My mother and I were seeking an anchor and we found it in Allah. By embracing a new religion I felt I had acquired a new identity. It was a liberating feeling and a tremendous opportunity to get rid of the excess baggage I had collected over the years after my father's demise. It's a decision I have never regretted.

Swades is your second film with Javed Akhtar and Ashutosh Gowariker after *Lagaan*, are you satisfied?

It is for Ashutosh and Javed saab to say if they are satisfied. I think it's a sincere effort on my part. Ashutosh has been very cooperative and encouraging. It has been a very healthy relationship of give-and-take between us as film-maker and music composer. He has spent days with me in Chennai and I have spent days with him on the sets in Panchgani.

Swades tells the story of a common man. How does someone who lives in an ivory tower associate with the sounds of everyday life?

The ivory tower makes the same demands out of me for a living as it does out of a slum dweller. We see the same skyline from our window at the end of the day and hear the same bells tinkle. I'm not out of touch with reality. I go out wherever my heart beckons me, be it to a restaurant for a meal or to a dargah for a public prayer. An artiste gets noticed in public only if he wants to be noticed. With my height I'm quite inconspicuous and by the time people recognize me and approach me, I have usually accomplished my mission and I'm out of that space.

Subhash Ghai desribes you as mercury – unattainable and unconquerable!

I'm not sure what Subhashji was thinking when he said it. This must have been during *Taal.* He could not be referring to my temperament because I'm very calm and far from mercurial. He probably meant someone you cannot hold on to – in which case he is right because even I cannot predict why I do certain things and when.

So you admit you are inaccessible?

Well, I'm attending this music release and I'm also talking to you right now, so I am accessible (*laughs*).

They say if you want to work with Rahman – you have to be prepared to park in Chennai and stay awake all night.

Look, I'm not forcing anyone to work with me but if I live in Chennai, that's where they will have to come. About keeping awake, I'm comfortable working in the nights but that does not mean that the film-makers have to stay awake as well. Shyam Benegal didn't during *Netaji Subhash Chandra Bose* or even during *Zubeidaa.* He would be in the studios till midnight and then arrive next morning to listen to the compositions. But Subhash Ghai, because he is a music lover, wanted to wait and watch the creative process during *Taal.* So it's their individual choice.

How did you get into the all-night pattern of work?

Many years ago, when I was working as a music arranger, my day was devoted to my employers and the only time I could call my own were the nights. That's when I played instruments and created my own compositions. I loved the stillness of the night when I could create peacefully without interruptions. Gradually, the process became a habit. After so many years I have become so used to it that I find it difficult to start working till nightfall. Somehow the adrenaline does not start to flow until then.

Don't you feel sleep-deprived?

I work through the night, starting at dusk and stopping at dawn. The 5 a.m. namaaz is a precious ritual. If I sleep at regular hours there is no way I'd be able to wake up for the morning namaaz so I prefer to wrap up my recording at 5 a.m., offer my prayers and then retire to bed peacefully. I feel satisfied and productive this way. I wake up anytime in the late afternoon, have a leisurely bath, read the papers, eat lunch with the family and spend time with the kids. Come evening and I'm ready to visit my studio again. That's the way my system works and now my staff as well. It's a precious pattern, for this way I'm able to catch both – the sunrise as well as the sunset prayers, and I'm not sure how many people are as fortunate as me.

Rekha on Courtesans

Courtesans in our films live in a surealistic world

Dharma was among your earlier films as a courtesan.

Yes, though at that time I was too young to distinguish between characters and merely followed what the dance director or the director said. All I remember about *Dharma* is a qawwali song sequence. Pran saab adopts me as his daughter to pull me out of the mess but my past keeps haunting me.

Zorabai in *Muqaddar Ka Sikander* was your first memorable role as a courtesan with a heart of gold.

Not many people know that I wasn't a part of the original cast. The film was almost complete when Prakash Mehra decided to cast me as Chandramukhi for his modern-day Devdas. Prakashji was

> Rekha has worked in over 100 films in her four-decade career, of which she played a courtesan in eighteen. *Yatra* was her last role as an ageing courtesan. In *Parineeta* (2005), she did an item number as a club dancer.

very clear about the look of my character. 'No yards and yards of fabric, please,' he warned Bhanu Athaiya, my costume designer, who is revered for her expertise in period films. The mujra outfits called Peshwas are usually in zardozi, brocade or Banarasi but we used chiffon laced with zari borders. Also, instead of the regular churidar worn beneath the dress Bhanu provided me with stretch pants, which were apparent when I take the pheras in the opening song '*Salame ishq meri jaan...*' Traditionally, specific colours are reserved for specific gharanas among courtesans but since the director wanted me to look vibrant we concentrated on bright colours except for the climax, where I wear white.

What are your shooting memories of this film?

My entire shooting for the film was completed in one schedule at Mohan Studios. I had just got back from a long holiday in London and was unprepared for the midsummer heat in Mumbai. On the first day of the shoot, I was given a very lengthy scene at the end of which I had to die in the arms of my co-star. This was my first death scene and I was petrified of performing it with an actor who was a master of death scenes! Still jetlagged, I somehow sailed through the first few days of shooting. Those days there were no air-conditioned studios and all my memories of *Muqaddar Ka Sikander* are associated with a burning summer. The art director had created plastic flooring with an elaborate false ceiling that radiated heat like a furnace when the lights came on. In the olden days, all films were shot in sync-sound except for the outdoor sequences, which were dubbed later. We looked forward to the dubbing sessions. B.R. Theatre had recently launched their luxurious recording theatre with advanced equipment and plush leather seats. I have warm memories of spending many afternoons in the freezing cold and perfecting my lines.

Why do you think *Mukaddar ka Sikander* was such a huge success?

Now when I look back, I feel everything about it was just perfect – the choreography, costumes, language, drama, performances and the message that was imparted. I was speaking Urdu for the first time and writer Kader Khan sportingly supervised my diction. That was the first time I discovered the magic of voice modulation. All these years I had never bothered about voice projection and suddenly, through this film, I discovered myself. The sound recordist could not believe the overnight transformation I underwent. After *Do Anjaane, Ganga Ki Saugand* and *Mr Natwarlal, Muqaddar Ka Sikander* was my fourth superhit with Amitji. In the next few years, we did many films together but somehow for my fans *MKS* always holds a special magic.

Suhaag came close on the heels of *Muqaddar Ka Sikander*, was there pressure to live up to the expectations of '*Salame*...'?

Manmohan Desai had put up a huge kotha set at Roop Tara Studio in Dadar. This is where both the songs '*Athra baras ki*... ' and '*Imtehan hai tera*... ' were shot. Shooting with Manji was always fun because he provided great food and great company. *Suhaag* was a rare experience that offered me an opportunity to perform many dance forms – mujra, bhangra and also a dandiya – all superbly choreographed by dance master Kamal. It was so typical of Manji to target all territories in one shot. Now one understands why he refrained from basing his stories in a specific region. Manji had loved my Santhali look during the picturization of '*Wafa jo na ki*... ' and asked me to wear something similar. It was his idea that I drape a short sari during '*Imtehan hai*... ' and Bhanu Athaiya chose a shocking pink and parrot-green sari matched with a backless blouse. I was terribly overweight and therefore extremely self-conscious but there was no arguing with the director and when the camera rolled I performed the jhatkas-matkas and submitted to the moment. Something must have worked about those movies that people remember them fondly after so many years. In those days we took pride when the director 'Okayed' our shot in one take. Today, actors are more aware of their craft and run to check the monitor after every shot. Our generation relied on the director. The new actors rely on the monitor.

And how did you land up with *Umrao Jaan*?

Subhasini Ali, then the wife of director Muzaffar Ali, convinced my mother to sign me on for *Umrao Jaan*. Subhasini speaks fluent Tamil and that was sufficient for my mother to take an instant liking to her. As long as my mother was active, she decided my assignments. This may sound ridiculous but in my long career I have hardly heard any stories. I don't know the Hindi script and have all these years learned dialogues prompted by an assistant. I accepted the film unaware of the legend of *Umrao Jaan Ada* but one look at Muzaffar and you knew he was an artiste – his clothes, folders, files, home filled with curios and paintings, his sets decorated with exotic chandeliers, in fact the production design of the film was exquisite. The first time he met me he presented me with a Begum Akhtar album packed in a leather folder and said, 'These are the kind of textures I'll be using in my film.' A few days later, he brought me some sketches of costumes. He was very particular that the design and the fabric of the costume must look authentic. Subhasini and I jointly worked on the costumes. Some were created from my mother's old saris, some obtained directly from textiles. Benaras tissues were the fabrics of the nineteenth century and we used them by mixing and matching them with old zari borders.

Was it tough matching steps to mujras choreographed by Kathak experts Gopi Krishna and Kumudini Lakhia?

Well, there was a combination of many choreographers. Those days Gopiji had a very enthusiastic assistant called Venu who attended all our rehearsals but seldom praised our efforts. Every time we looked at Venu for approval, he shook his head in denial. Till the end of the film we longed for him to say something positive but he never did. The first schedule of the film was shot in Lucknow and the entire unit travelled together by train. Muzaffar came to fetch us at the station without any security and it's a miracle how he managed to whisk us out of the crowds. From the station we drove directly to his mother's grave to seek her blessings before the shoot and only later did we go to our hotel.

All this must have been a new experience for you as an actor?

It was the first time for me. The shooting commenced with the '*Inn aankhon ki masti mein…*' mujra. When I arrived on the sets I was surprised to find all the royalty of Lucknow on our sets dressed in beautiful achkans and jewels, all part of the mehfil. Muzaffar had very cleverly invited all his friends and relatives to participate in the shoot, which not only saved on production cost but added to the ambience. We were shooting round-the-clock and there was hardly any free time between shots. The only time I got some respite was when Faroque Shaikh went for his namaaz. I longed for his prayer breaks because that was the only time I could run to my room and fall sleep.

Tell us about your climax *mujra* '*Ye kya jagah hai dosto…*'

It was shot in Malihabad, about a three-hour drive from Lucknow. I was advised to do my make-up beforehand because there would be no facilities at the location. My staff and I travelled in an ambassador car and despite all precautions arrived at the destination layered with dust. It's freezing cold in Uttar Pradesh in winter and I had to shoot the song sequence dressed in very delicate fabric. During the final antara I had to wander to the neighbouring home looking for my separated mother, an important moment in the film. The director wanted me to look forlorn but my teeth were chattering and no amount of glycerin could help because the liquid froze before I could apply it in my eyes. Many years later, when I met Pakistan's Abida Parveen and she told me that every time she watched this song she would become tearful. Actors don't feel emotional while shooting tragic scenes or funny while shooting comedy and fear while shooting horror. At that moment all we are focused on is getting the shot right. In those days all of us hopped from one city to another and literally lived out of our Volkswagens. For me it was yet another day at work but the people on the sets were involved in the story-telling and their reactions were real, and this reflected on screen. I was disconnected while shooting the scene but watching it always makes me sad.

Why is that so?

I think what happens is that while performing the actor takes over the individual but later the actor feels protective about the individual for going through so much heartache to project an emotion. Acting is a complex, intriguing process and emotions are inconsistent and fascinating. People don't believe me when I say this but I have shot Girish Karnad's *Utsav* on autopilot. I have no memories about any of my scenes in this film and yet the human body is a strange thing that makes you go through all the right motions despite the fact that you could be going through your worst crisis. There is no logical explanation for this.

Utsav was adapted from the early century play *Mrichchakatikam*. Had you heard or read about it before saying 'yes' to the role?

Of course not, and what surprises me is that nobody from this so-called art-house cinema community deemed it fit to educate me with relevant literature. Not that I missed it because I was not in the frame of mind to absorb information. All I knew was that Vasantsena was a palace courtesan. What baffles me is that considering this was my first authentic period film why nobody thought it necessary to do a test shoot or a dress rehearsal before the actual shoot. I landed in Manipal on the day of the shoot and was told that since there were no five-star hotels in Manipal the artistes were being put up at people's homes. I was put up with the Pai family in Mangalore. The first day of shoot was Shekhar Suman's song '*Bhor bhaye…*' when Vasantsena appears at his doorstep out of the dark night. The film was shot in night shifts and I have a problem about keeping awake late so I would often fall asleep while waiting for my shot. Our still photographer, Karan Kapoor, has captured many such moments.

It was your first film with Girish Karnad as a director?

Yes, and for some reason he found me very amusing and said I would make a very good comedian provided somebody offered me the right script. The only time he got upset with me during the film was when he discovered that I had trimmed my long tresses without informing him. The script mentioned two specific moments when Vasantsena uncoils her bun and lets her tresses fall down her back. He had no idea about my truancy as long as my hair was tied up in the Ellora bun, but when we began shooting those specific scenes he was devastated to discover that the length of my hair had become short. He felt deprived of his most special moments in the film. I tried my best to compensate this with hair extensions but it was a laborious process and all of us got frustrated!

How much do you identify with the character of Vasantsena?

I don't think of such comparisons. I loved the relationship between Charudutt's wife, Anuradha Patel, and the courtesan. There is a dialogue where the wife says she feels proud that a woman like Vasantsena desires her husband. It's a surrealistic almost idyllic moment, because real life is far more complicated! I'm often asked why film-makers frequently cast me as a courtesan. My answer is I don't know and don't want to analyse it.

How did Mira Nair offer you *Kamasutra* and what was your impression about her?

Much before Mira Nair offered me *Kamasutra* she had wanted me to do *Salaam Bombay*. But I had refused because I was not willing to dress in revealing clothes or do a love-making scene. But Mira left a mark on me. She is razor-sharp, confident and passionate about her craft. She is a visionary and a great story-teller. Her knowledge about film-making and her ability to get what she wants is admirable. *Kamasutra* was shot in Khajuraho and this was my first visit to the quaint village. I fell in love with the quietude and the heritage of the place. It was my first international film where I speak my lines in English. I was self-conscious because I have not had any formal education but Mira was encouraging. On the first day, I arrived on the sets to discover that there was no director in sight. Mira was seated far away, operating from a monitor. This was my first big setback. I was not used to performing without looking at my director, without 'Start sound... Rolling... Action...' A monstrous crane fell over my face and I was asked to rattle off my lines. I froze!

So how did you come to terms with the new technology?

I tried my best and improved over the weeks but I continued to feel inadequate and low in confidence. I had no reason to because the entire unit (actors and technicians) were extremely considerate, particularly Mira, but I was going through a diffident phase and continued to feel insecure. On another level, I felt privileged to have an opportunity to be exposed to such a marvellous experience. It was the most efficient production unit I had worked with in my entire career. They had twenty trucks parked outside the set segregated for catering, make-up, office, equipment, lights and costumes. One truck was reserved for the director and how beautifully Mira had done it up! Covered in Sanganeri paintings and lined with labelled shelves, the ambience resembled a fairyland. The shoot began at the crack of dawn. Everyone was given a wake-up call at 2 a.m. and by 3 we were in our make-up vans getting ready. On the sets everyone was addressed by their character's names. So whereever I went, whatever I did, I was addressed by everybody as Rasa Devi. The assistants carried walkie-talkies so each move of ours was monitored. Zoya Akhtar was one of the assistant directors in *Kamasutra* and she has carried forward the work culture to Hindi films beginning with *Dil Chahta Hai*.

Those who work with her say Mira is magical?

Mira has remarkable managing skills involving both stars and shoots. She treated her actors like royalty. She had arranged for special masseurs at the hotel and offered the best cuisine on the sets. She knew how to live life to the fullest. Her hotel room was a paradise. One has to learn from her how to make a home away from home. There were books, curios, plants, music, photographs, carpets, rugs... Everything you would have in a home. My memories of *Kamasutra* off the sets overshadow those on the sets. I played the love guru, a teacher of erotica, but I'm not sure if I was effective. Today I feel that I may have portrayed her better had I not been as diffident. I spent the entire outdoor shoot crying in my room. I wanted to quit the film after the first few days and even offered to pay for the damages but Mira didn't permit me. She was very positive and kept boosting my morale. She came to me with high expectations and I feel I let her down. I was so miserable I never mustered up the courage to watch *Kamasutra*. I still haven't.

Yatra is your last release.

So far last, because in show business you never say never. Almost a decade after *Kamasutra*, Nana Patekar contacted me to meet director Gautam Ghose and I agreed to do the film for the experience of working with Nana, Ghose and Deepti Naval. My character Lajwanti has many layers and could have been portrayed very differently but I have portrayed her as per the director's interpretation. *Yatra* was shot in Hyderabad at Ramoji Rao Studio and Saroj Khan choreographed my mujra assisted by Birju Maharaj's assistant, who added a different flavour to the dance. Unfortunately, all the efforts could not bring any magic to the film. The experience confirmed one thing, however, that every time I doubted my instinct as an actor I have been proved wrong.

Acknowledgements

I would like to thank all the actors and directors featured in this book for their trust and time.

Winner of the National Award for Best Book on Cinema 2011

Winner of the National Award for Best Book on Cinema 2012

edited by **sandip ray**

deep focus

reflections on cinema

satyajit ray

foreword by **shyam benegal**

COMING SOON